The Presidency and Domestic Policy

"The Presidency and Domestic Policy"

*Comparing Leadership Styles,
FDR to Clinton*

William W. Lammers
and
Michael A. Genovese

CQ PRESS

A Division of Congressional Quarterly Inc.
Washington, D.C.

CQ Press
A Division of Congressional Quarterly Inc.
1414 22nd Street, N.W.
Washington, D.C. 20037

(202) 822-1475; (800) 638-1710

www.cqpress.com

JK 511 .L35 2000

Lammers, William W.

The presidency and domestic
policy

Copyright © 2000 by Congressional Quarterly Inc.

Book design: Dennis Anderson

Cover: Ed Atkeson

Printed and bound in the United States of America

04   03   02   01   00   5   4   3   2   1

Library of Congress Cataloging-in-Publication Data

Lammers, William W.
    The presidency and domestic policy : comparing leadership styles, FDR to Clinton /
William W. Lammers, Michael A. Genovese.
        p.   cm.
    Includes bibliographical references and index.
    ISBN 1-56802-124-0 (paper).—ISBN 1-56802-125-9 (hard)
    1. Presidents—United States—History—20th century.   2. Political leadership—
United States—History—20th century.   3. United States—Politics and government—
1933–1945.   4. United States—Politics and government—1945–1989.   5. United
States—Politics and government—1989–   I. Genovese, Michael A.   II. Title.
JK511.L35 2000
352.2'234'0973—dc21
                                                                      99-088686

To Mary Lammers

WILLIAM W. LAMMERS, eminent presidential scholar, loving husband and father, devoted teacher, good friend, and generous mentor, died on October 7, 1997, of cancer. Shortly before his death, Bill submitted a draft of this book to CQ Press. Two days before he died, he asked me to see his manuscript through to publication. As a former graduate student of Bill's at the University of Southern California who went into presidential studies largely because of his influence, I was honored to fulfill his request. The manuscript itself was in excellent shape; only minor revisions, updates, and changes were necessary. This book, then, is Bill Lammers's. It is, in my opinion, his finest work.

Michael A. Genovese

Contents

List of Tables

Preface

PRESIDENTS OF the United States are fascinating individuals. Each brings to the White House a unique set of personal characteristics, policy preferences, and leadership styles, and, having attained office, each proceeds to govern in a distinct way. Presidents achieve varying degrees of success, leave office with reputations that range from public admiration to disgrace, and, in some instances, profoundly shape domestic policy.

But just how important are the differences among presidents, and just how much have individual presidents shaped policy? It is easy to over-emphasize presidential differences in interpreting the development of domestic policy. For some presidents, imposing constraints—from weak electoral positions to a weak economy—have precluded landmark developments. For others, the limits of a highly institutionalized office have restricted their choices of action. And then there is Congress. According to important new research, the role of Congress in developing and shaping policy has at times been both more extensive and more creative than sometimes imagined.

Any understanding of presidential leadership and the formation of domestic policy thus must begin with a closer look at individual leadership roles and the circumstances that shape opportunities for success. For that reason, the chapters in this book devoted to presidents who have served since 1932 combine an individual perspective with a description of the circumstances in which the president sought to make his mark. In this way, we hope to be sensitive to the unique qualities each president brought to the task of governing while controlling for the level of opportunity each faced when entering office. This perspective allows our final comparisons of the strong performers, consideration of the strategies that have worked, and an assessment of possible future leadership roles.

Acknowledgments

Many people assisted in the completion of this work. The University of Southern California and Loyola Marymount University provided institutional support of great help. The expert research assistance by Pauline Batrikian, Amy Montes, and Astrid Morales proved invaluable. Thanks also are due to typist Monica LaBelle for her excellent work. The peer reviewers, both anonymous and revealed (Nancy Kassop and Robert Spitzer), provided comments that were particularly helpful in revising the manuscript for publication. Finally, Brenda Carter at CQ Press, for her editorial support, and Sabra Bissette Ledent, for her excellent copyediting, deserve major-league kudos. To all of you, many thanks.

The Presidency and Domestic Policy

And people talk about the powers of a President, all the powers that a Chief Executive has, and what he can do. Let me tell you something—from experience! The President may have a great many powers given to him in the Constitution and may have certain powers under certain laws which are given to him by the Congress of the United States; but the principal power that the President has is to bring people in and try to persuade them to do what they ought to do without persuasion. That's what the powers of the President amount to.

—HARRY S. TRUMAN

Strategies for Assessing Presidents

CITIZENS EXPECT their presidents to accomplish great things. They hold these officeholders responsible for the health of the economy, world peace, the overall state of the nation, even the weather (global warming). Yet all occupants of the White House face a series of roadblocks, checks, and balances that inhibit behavior and make governing difficult.[1]

Given their constituents' high expectations and their own limited resources, presidents must develop complex strategies to bridge this expectation–resource gap. If they fail to do so, they run the risk of political failure, voter disapproval, and electoral defeat. Presidents, then, face formidable obstacles, but they are not helpless. A wide range of options and opportunities are available to a politically astute, power-wise leader.

This book attempts to understand the styles and strategies presidents employ in their efforts to govern successfully. In doing so, it examines four dimensions of presidential activity—approaches to advisory processes and decision making, administrative strategies, public leadership, and congressional leadership—in the context of the domestic policy agendas of modern presidents (Franklin Roosevelt to Bill Clinton).[2] It also looks at how different *opportunity levels* (high, moderate, and low) have affected presidential leadership, and how these presidents played the political hands they were dealt.

Level of opportunity is measured by extrinsic factors such as public demand, pro- or antigovernment sentiments, issue ripeness, available resources, competing issues, and the strength of the president's party in Congress. Factors more centered on the presidency itself are the size of a president's election victory, the issues over which the presidential contest was fought, and the president's popularity. Opportunity levels set reasonable expectations—that is, high-opportunity presidents should achieve more than low-opportunity presidents. (Later this chapter more fully develops the idea of "windows of opportunity" by relying on the writings of John Kingdon to help explain how opportunity levels are determined.) What determines whether presidents achieve the political results their opportunity levels permit? *Skill.*

When presidents are divided along opportunity lines, it is easier to determine who the more skillful presidents are and what strategies and tactics they employed to achieve their goals. There is, however, one difficulty with this approach: although indicators of presidential opportunity are available, ultimately the categorization is somewhat subjective.

If level of opportunity establishes a possible range of presidential performances, the leadership style employed by presidents helps determine the interaction and public face they present to the people, Congress, and other political actors. Presidents display tremendous differences in their leadership styles. Some seek to emulate the aggressive style of President Franklin Roosevelt; others choose less assertive approaches. Ronald Reagan, who admired Roosevelt's speaking style and could even mimic his voice, adopted a public style based in part on FDR's. George Bush's lack of action found some of his aides actually making lists of "speeches not given" because of his reluctance to engage in a strong public role. Jimmy Carter often pursued positions he judged to be in the long-run public interest, whether popular or not, whereas Bill Clinton relied heavily on opinion polls in developing policies and shaping his messages.

Leadership styles encompass *strategic choices.* Some presidents have sought to "hit the ground running"; others have been characterized as "hitting the ground stumbling," or even "marching in place."[3] In their public leadership, some presidents have effectively sought to "go public" to build support for legislation.[4] In fact, candidate Bill Clinton's enthusiasm for Theodore Roosevelt's use of the presidency as a "bully pulpit" to elicit public support for his programs led President Bill Clinton to take to the road in a continuation, as it were, of his election campaign. Other presidents have sought less-visible means of achieving their goals. That may explain why top-level negotiations (known as bipartisan summits) between administration leaders and congressional leaders have been used with increasing frequency. In another strategic choice, presidents frequently engage in policy shifts in the third year of their terms to reshape the direction of their administration—and their reelection prospects.

In choosing a leadership style, presidents are influenced by a variety of factors, including their own personalities and prior career experiences. Many presidents rely on their historical favorites for views of how the president should lead. Woodrow Wilson and Franklin Roosevelt are high on this list, but "silent" Calvin Coolidge rates only occasional mention. Some presidents have deliberately chosen a leadership style that contrasts with that of their predecessor. John Kennedy, for example, sought more assertive public leadership than that provided by Dwight Eisenhower. Carter strove to do away with the trappings of the "imperial presidency" and be a "man of the people." Reagan's short answer was to be the mirror image of Carter as he pursued a more optimistic persona and a more focused approach to his first-year agenda. Bush showed an aversion to Reagan's limited attention to detail, and Clinton sought to have a more robust domestic agenda than Bush's. The combination of presidential wishes to be different and the public's tendency to seek leaders who compensate for the problems of their predecessors has contributed to sharp swings in leadership styles from president to president.

The readily observed differences in leadership styles have not produced agreement among political scientists on how much these differences affect public policy.[5] Those who believe individual skill has a limited impact on policy outcomes have emphasized the extent to which presidential actions are shaped by the opportunities produced by power relationships in Congress, economic conditions, and levels of public support for new policy initiatives, among other things. Indeed, as his second term began, Clinton lamented that his time in office thus far had not presented opportunities for achievements comparable to those experienced by presidents who had left large legacies.

In view of the uncertainty surrounding the impact of individual presidents on policy, it is time to take a harder look at the ways in which leadership styles and strategies have actually shaped policy outcomes. After all, far too often passage of major legislation has been attributed to presidential leadership when it actually may have had little influence. During Franklin Roosevelt's years in the White House, for example, he frequently received credit for congressionally driven achievements. Of course, the ideal way to determine presidential influence on policy would be to place different occupants of the Oval Office in the same circumstances and measure the various outcomes. Such a study would reveal, for example, how much more legislation Lyndon Johnson could have achieved than a possible second-term Kennedy administration, or how much more policy impact a president without media relations problems such as those contributing to Clinton's "ten-second honeymoon" might have accomplished in 1993.

While no two presidents serve under identical circumstances, a comparative approach can offer valuable insight into the extent to which leadership can make a difference. Such an approach requires assessing presidents' leadership styles and the strategies they pursued, as well as how well they were able to meet challenges and use opportunities effectively. The differences revealed can then be used to examine the impact of leadership styles on policy. The next section sets the stage for these analyses by describing the key concepts of leadership style, challenges and opportunities, and policy legacies.

Leadership Styles

In 1960 presidential scholar Richard Neustadt published a seminal study of presidential leadership.[6] The wide audience for the ideas he developed in *Presidential Power* included presidents themselves. Moreover, John Kennedy and several of his predecessors sought Neustadt's personal advice in organizing their presidencies. The lasting interest in Neustadt's ideas stems from the perspective he took of looking at presidential leadership from the vantage point of presidents themselves.

Neustadt's analysis was grounded in the view that the creation of Congress and the presidency as separate institutions with shared and overlapping powers usually makes it difficult for presidents to succeed with new policy initiatives. The leadership style prescribed by Neustadt was closely modeled on the one used by Franklin Roosevelt. (As the son of a New Deal official and an avid reader of the memoirs and early biographies of Roosevelt, he was clearly enamored with FDR's leadership style.) It called for presidents to pay careful attention to the manner in which their actions would affect their professional reputation, public prestige, and possible subsequent options. By shrewdly considering those factors in their leadership efforts, presidents would then be better able to bargain effectively within the Washington community. According to Fred Greenstein, the effective president Neustadt envisioned was "a tough political operator." Such presidents were powerful because they cared about and cultivated power, because they were attuned to what it took to have an impact on their political environment, and because they were well informed about that environment.[7]

More recent studies of presidential leadership have built on interpretations of leadership styles that Neustadt instigated. One found that recent presidents have used their public roles to put pressure on Congress rather than rely on their own bargaining roles within the Washington community.[8] Other studies have revealed that presidents display a broader range of leadership styles than the one envisioned by Neustadt with his emphasis on FDR's approach. Greenstein's 1982 reassessment of Eisenhower, for example, paints a portrait of a president who employed a "hidden hand" leadership style. He engaged in few public quarrels on political issues, preferring instead to operate more actively and skillfully behind the scenes. This modus operandi largely escaped the notice of the public (and most political commentators) during his eight years in office.[9]

Other analysts, following up on Greenstein's seminal work, have further explored the broad diversity in leadership styles. Some found that President Carter had a very distinct leadership style as he sought to provide "trusteeship" leadership by promoting measures he judged to be in the long-run public interest—such as a comprehensive energy package—rather than proposals molded to short-run political calculations. In dealing with that orientation, Carter's congressional aides periodically wondered whether they ever would receive an easy issue to promote. Assessments of Reagan's leadership have often explored his "Teflon"-like ability to dodge the negative fallout from some of the controversies that emerged from his administration. Other analyses have focused on his ability to retreat quietly on issues such as tax increases while losing little support from voters who continued to view him as the premier tax cutter. Presidents clearly have been choosing a variety of ways to govern and therefore to lead.[10]

Leadership styles have four specific dimensions: approaches to advisory processes and decision making, administrative strategies, public leadership, and congressional leadership. These dimensions are examined in the sections that follow.

Approaches to Advisory Processes and Decision Making

Presidents recruit and organize their staffs and conduct their decision making in strikingly different ways. They recruit their cabinet and staff with an eye toward coalition building and acquiring the specialized skills and expertise they consider important. Some presidents organize their staffs around strong chiefs of staff (for example, Bush) or limited or even no chief of staff role (such as Carter).

Administrative and management issues loom large in tales of presidential success or failure. Whether Iran-contra or Watergate, nearly all presidential blunders can be traced to managerial problems. While a sound decision-making process does not guarantee a good decision, advisers and managers who ask the right questions, challenge group assumptions, and guarantee a wealth of useful and varied information can certainly make a difference in presidential decision making.[11]

Administrative Strategies

Administrative strategies often have a prominent place in a president's overall leadership style. Some presidents may pursue "good government" administrative issues. President Carter, for example, was intensely committed to civil service reform and President Clinton endeavored, in an effort led by Vice President Al Gore, to "reinvent government." Such strategies may be important over time in shaping the capacity of the federal government to carry out various policies. For short-term political purposes, however, they are not likely to generate significant electoral benefits as voters more often focus on the broad policies rather than the possible increases in administrative efficiencies.

A president's administrative strategies also can affect policies more directly. For example, a president may use executive orders to interpret or carry out provisions of a law; make decisions affecting the budgetary process, including the manner in which appropriated funds are actually spent; and shape administrative and judicial action through the presidential appointments process.

Public Leadership

The public role of the president is an enormously important dimension of presidential leadership. Indeed, the White House actually resembles a public relations firm. During the early years of the Reagan presidency, some one hundred White House staffers were involved in various aspects of listening to and communicating with the public.[12] Strategies are concocted for developing the president's personal popularity, enlisting support for policy initiatives, and devising bully pulpit appeals that seek to modify public attitudes and actions.

Presidents seek personal support for good reasons beyond personal vanity. Popular presidents are likely to gain better press coverage and may find that the nation is more responsive to their public appeals. High popularity also can discourage primary challengers as a president seeks reelection.[13]

Popularity can make a difference as well in dealing with Congress.[14] In 1981, for example, Reagan's popularity was a consideration as the conservative "boll weevil" Democrats from the South began lining up in support of his economic program. Overall, popular presidents have tended to propose broader programs than less-popular presidents.[15] Their success rates may not be higher than those of unpopular presidents, but that may stem from their more ambitious proposals.[16]

Congressional Leadership

John Kennedy, acknowledging the difficulties presidents generally have in their dealings with Congress, commented after he moved into the White House in 1961, "Congress looks a good deal more powerful from up here." Presidential difficulties with Congress are not hard to understand. Members have their own reelection concerns over which presidents usually have little influence. On specific votes, members are likely to be guided by personal beliefs, perceptions of constituency preferences, lobbying by segments of their core constituencies, and campaign fundraising opportunities.

A persistent theme in studies of presidential relationships with Congress has been the difficulties presidents encounter when trying to change the voting positions of representatives and senators.[17] In summarizing the considerable recent research on presidential efforts to shape congressional voting through bargaining, presidential scholar George Edwards III noted, "In most instances, presidents exercise their skills at the margins, not at the core, of coalition building."[18] Matthew Kerbel found, however, that presidents could make a difference if they exercised a measure of flexibility in their personal dealings with members of Congress and established an effective organizational capacity for handling those relationships. Nev-

ertheless, the thrust of his analysis is "the extent to which power is difficult to exercise from the Oval Office." [19] Given existing constraints, Congress watchers are likely to see the more effective presidents appealing for
votes on only a few key issues and at points during committee votes rather
than during floor proceedings.

Presidents generally hold two or three meetings a month with congressional party leaders and key committee chairs to review strategies on
top agenda items and sometimes make a pitch for their programs. President Reagan did just that in a May 1981 meeting on his economic plan, designed to stimulate the stagnating economy. Direct involvement by chiefs
of staff also has become a common aspect of a president's legislative leadership. During Reagan's first term, Chief of Staff James Baker directed a
Legislative Strategy Group that met almost every day in the first half of
1981 to review developments on Capitol Hill and review possible strategies. Sometimes, involvement by a chief of staff becomes a central aspect
of the legislative bargaining and coalition-building processes. In 1990, for
example, Bush chief of staff John Sununu helped to develop a deficit-
reduction package, and in 1994 Clinton chief of staff and former member
of Congress Leon Panetta launched a round-the-clock effort to achieve a
compromise on the stalled crime bill in the House of Representatives. The
selection of a chief of staff who understands Congress has become an important dimension of presidential relationships with that body.[20]

Sometimes the presidential involvement in legislation goes beyond the
monthly meetings with congressional leaders and committee chairs. They
may provide chiefs of staff with lists of legislators they are willing to see
upon request, and on key votes they may contact fence-sitting legislators
by phone or invite those members to the White House for a chat. Despite
his reputation for being uninterested in Congress, President Richard Nixon
actively pursued legislative consultation in 1969, holding over two hundred meetings with one or more members of Congress.[21] And all presidents, most notably Lyndon Johnson who had served in both the House
and the Senate, have worked the phones to push favored legislation.

Presidents can choose from a variety of strategies in attempting to influence legislative outcomes. Although agenda setting is shared with Congress, it can be an important strategy. Tactics for agenda setting include
advocating an issue in an electoral campaign, giving prominent emphasis
to an issue in the annual State of the Union address, making speeches to
groups interested in a particular agenda item, mentioning the item in press
conferences, and symbolically labeling top priorities in the first message

sent to Congress or (with the aid of a legislative supporter) ensuring that the bill addressing a particular issue is the first one passed in a new session of Congress. One of the more unusual instances of agenda setting occurred in the early days of the Clinton administration. The president's selection of First Lady Hillary Rodham Clinton to preside over the development of a major health care program signaled members of Congress as well as key interest groups that health policy would be an important issue in the new administration.

Although Bill Clinton moved quickly in his term to put forth his health care agenda, presidents often have their best chances of influencing legislation if they act at the very beginning of their first year in office—known as the "honeymoon." [22] By moving rapidly, presidents can capitalize on their postelection popularity and act before opposed members of Congress, interest groups, and affected agencies have a chance to mobilize. In the second year Congress often is caught up in reelection concerns which may reduce opportunities for presidential success. After the midterm elections, presidents generally are confronted with additional constraints if their party suffers the usual midterm losses of congressional seats. Since 1932 the party in the White House has lost an average of twenty-three House seats; in 1938, 1942, and 1994 the Democrats lost over fifty House seats. Precisely because of the greater opportunities offered by a fast-start strategy, Paul Light argued that presidents should not seek to develop ideal proposals, but instead should proceed quickly with existing policy ideas and campaign pledges.

Despite the apparent advantages of a fast-start strategy, presidents have varied markedly in the extent to which they have used this approach to congressional relations. Partisan differences have been persistent, with Democratic presidents far more likely to follow in Franklin Roosevelt's footsteps of 1933 and pursue a "First Hundred Days" jump-start on Congress. Surprisingly, however, the record of major legislative enactments reveals that when presidents and Congress work together in the later years in a presidency, that period may be just as productive as the first year. [23] Presidents, then, may not be particularly influential late into their terms, but the process does not necessarily stagnate.

Leadership Styles and the Policy-making Cycle

As noted, presidents can choose from a wide variety of strategies in forming their leadership style (see Table 1–1, which shows some of the strategies

TABLE 1–1 Presidents' Uses of Select Strategies during Their First Terms, 1933–1996

	Press Conferences (monthly average)	Major Domestic Addresses[a] (per year)		Ability to Sustain Popularity (rank)	Vetoes of Major Legislation (per year)
Roosevelt	5.8 (1)	2	(3)		
Truman	3.0 (2.5)	2	(3)	(7)	4.85 (2)
Eisenhower	2.1 (5.5)	1.75	(6)	(2.5)	4.25 (3)
Kennedy	1.9 (7)	1.6	(8.5)	(2.5)	1.38 (6)
Johnson	2.1 (5.5)	1.6	(8.5)	(6)	1.76 (5)
Nixon	0.6 (9.5)	1.75	(6)	(5)	6.68 (1)
Carter	1.2 (8)	1.5	(7)	(4)	4.13 (4)
Reagan	0.5 (9.5)	2	(3)	(1)	
Bush	2.7 (4)	1	(10)		
Clinton	3.0 (2.5)	2.5	(1)		

Sources: Lyn Ragsdale, *Vital Statistics on the Presidency, Washington to Clinton* (Washington, D.C.: CQ Press, 1996,) 167–168; Paul Brace and Barbara Hinckley, *Follow the Leader: Opinion Polls and the Modern Presidents* (New York: Basic Books, 1992), 32; Richard A. Watson, *Presidential Vetoes and Public Policy* (Lawrence: University Press of Kansas, 1993), 42; and Harold W. Stanley and Richard G. Niemi, *Vital Statistics on American Politics*, 4th ed. (Washington, D.C.: CQ Press, 1993), 255–284.

Note: Rank orders are in parentheses.

a. Excludes State of the Union address.

chosen by Presidents Roosevelt through Clinton during their first terms). These choices are made throughout the so-called policy-making cycle, when presidents and their staffs must develop their initial policy proposals, generate public support for the proposals, facilitate legislative passage, and shape policy implementation through administrative action.[24] Other groups may have roles as well in the policy-making cycle—among them, members of Congress, interest group leaders, state government officials, and the media. Any evaluation of presidential performances thus cannot occur without recognition of the roles played by other key players. Nevertheless, the central consideration in evaluating any president's performance is the *strategies* that were pursued and the *skill* with which they were exercised.

Challenges and Opportunities

Some presidents face greater challenges than others in both the international and domestic arenas. Presidents Harry Truman and Richard Nixon began terms as the nation was waging unpopular wars—in Korea in 1952 and in Vietnam in 1968.

Policy challenges often create opportunities because of a widespread desire for action. In 1981 public frustration over slow economic growth and high inflation created widespread sympathy for trying something new—in this instance, Reagan's supply-side tax cuts. Public frustration with existing conditions does not mean, however, that the policies proposed will address voter concerns or that policy makers will be able to build political support for any one specific option. Clinton, for example, found it extremely difficult to convert voter desires for reform of the health care system into support for one specific approach.

A president's opportunities for addressing major policy challenges are shaped by many factors, among them: the public mood, the level of public support, the legislative setting, the availability of promising issues, economic and budgetary considerations, and foreign policy influences. These factors and those that often restrict opportunities for second-term presidents are described in this section, along with the reasons why opportunities may have been declining for more recent presidents.

Public Mood

The public periodically displays a strong desire for government action, heightening presidential opportunities. President Kennedy, who was interested in these cycles, talked with historian and staff aide Arthur Schlesinger Jr. about their underlying patterns.[25] Over time, as problems grow and government action is seen as insufficient public sentiment builds for reform. At such times presidents can claim a mandate for change that often moves Congress to act. The desire for government action occurred in the first fifteen years of the twentieth century to the advantage of Presidents Theodore Roosevelt and Woodrow Wilson and again in the 1930s, the 1960s, and the 1980s. Likewise, presidents serving in between, such as Truman and Eisenhower, did not enjoy comparable desires for action.[26] Nor, for various reasons, including broader public skepticism about the scope and role of government, along with the constraints of budgetary deficits, did a comparable groundswell occur in the 1990s.

Levels of public trust in government also can have an enormous impact on a president's level of opportunity. During the 1960s presidents seeking to establish new programs were dealing with an electorate that, by today's standards, had a far higher degree of trust in the federal government. From the vantage point of the far more cynical 1990s, the 1960s appears to have been a stunningly different period: over 60 percent of the public agreed with the view that one can trust the government in Washington to do the right thing all of the time or most of the time, whereas when Bill Clinton entered the White House in 1993, the portion of the population with a similar view had fallen to only 22 percent.

Public Support

Differences in levels of public support are yet another factor in the opportunities open to presidents (see Table 1–2). Elections can produce several advantages. For example, a large winning margin can give presidents the opportunity to argue that they received a "mandate" for their policies. In addition, a large winning margin may give presidents the opportunity to claim that they pulled legislators into office on their "coattails." Leading students of voting behavior discredit the view that large segments of the electorate produce a mandate by understanding a president's policy goals and voting on that basis.[27] Nevertheless, in 1981 Reagan, who had campaigned hard on his economic program and won by 10 percent, plausibly asserted the existence of a mandate and gained an initial advantage with Congress.

Public support of the president's party also can make a difference. From the 1930s to the 1960s Democratic presidents such as Kennedy, Johnson, and Carter benefited from belonging to a party that enjoyed a considerable advantage in party identification over the Republicans (see Table 1–2). This advantage has largely disappeared in recent years, as party identification figures have become more even and the number of independent identifiers has grown substantially. As a result, party identification is becoming less important in voter choices among presidential candidates. Party strength also may be reflected in the extent to which the party a president defeats becomes discredited in the eyes of the voters. Discredited opposition parties worked to the advantage of Roosevelt in 1933, Johnson in 1965, and Reagan in 1981.[28] A discredited party serves as a weak opposition, thereby allowing the president more political latitude.

The Legislative Setting

The size of the president's party in Congress is one very important indicator of the opportunities available to presidents to shape policy (Table 1–3), but ideological orientations within the party may work against the president. For Democratic presidents, at least until the 1980s, conservative voting tendencies among southern Democrats frequently derailed new

TABLE 1–2 Public Support Dimension of Presidential Opportunity Levels, 1933–1996

	Winning Margin in First-Term Election (percent)	Percentage of Total Vote in First-Term Election	Reelection Two-Candidate Margin of Victory (percent)	Party Identification (percent)			Popularity by Year, First Term (percent)				
				President's Party	Independents	Opposing Party	1	2	3	4	Average
Roosevelt	17.8 (1)	57.4 (2)	+ 24.3				n.a.				55 (5)
Truman	—	—	+ 4.4[a]				84	43	55	36	69 (2)
Eisenhower	10.7 (3)	55.1 (3)	+ 15.4	28	23	47 (7)	68	66	71	73	71 (1)
Kennedy	0.2 (9)	49.7 (7)	—	45	23	30 (3)	76	71	65	75[b]	50 (6)
Johnson	17.3 (2)	61.1 (1)	—	52	23	25 (1)	66	50	44	43	57 (4)
Nixon	0.7 (8)	43.4 (8)	+ 22.2	25	30	45 (8)	63	58	51	58	47 (8)
Carter	2.1 (7)	50.1 (6)	- 9.3	40	37	23 (2)	63	45	38	42	50 (7)
Reagan	9.7 (4)	50.7 (5)	+ 18.2	23	35	41 (6)	58	44	44	56	61 (3)
Bush	7.8 (5)	53.4 (4)	- 5.6	28	36	35 (5)	64	68	71	40	
Clinton	7.0 (6)	43.0 (9)	+ 9.4	36	39	26 (4)					

Sources: Lyn Ragsdale, *Vital Statistics on the Presidency: Washington to Clinton* (Washington, D.C.: CQ Press, 1996), 103–104; and Kevin Phillips, *Arrogant Capital: Washington, Wall Street, and the Frustration of American Politics* (Boston: Little Brown, 1995), 8.

Note: Rank orders are in parentheses.

a. Truman had been elected vice president in 1944.

b. Figure is for Lyndon Johnson, who succeeded to the presidency in November 1963.

TABLE 1–3 Congressional and Budgetary Dimensions of Presidential First-Term Opportunity Levels, 1933–1996

	Size of President's Party in Congress		Level of Surge/ Decline in President's Party		Midterm Election Change in President's Party		Budget Deficit as Percentage of Total Election Year Spending
	House	Senate	House	Senate	House	Senate	
Roosevelt (D)	313D–117R (1)	59D–36R	+90 (1)	+ 9	+ 9 (1)	+10	58.1 (1)
Truman (D)	243D–190R (6)	57D–38R	+24 (4)	− 2	−45 (8)	−12	51.0 (2)
Eisenhower (R)	221R–213D (7)	48R–46D	+22 (5)	+ 1	−18 (6)	− 1	2.2 (9)
Kennedy (D)	262D–175R (4)	64D–36R	−22 (10)	+ 2	− 4 (2)	+ 3	0.3 (10)
Johnson (D)	295D–140R (2)	68D–32R	+37 (2)	+ 1	−47 (9)	− 4	5.0 (8)
Nixon (R)	192R–243D (8.5)	42R–58D	+ 5 (6)	+ 6	−12 (4)	+ 2	14.1 (6)
Carter (D)	292D–143R (3)	61D–38R	+ 1 (7)	+ 0	−15 (5)	− 3	18.2 (4)
Reagan (R)	192R–243D (8.5)	53R–46D	+34 (3)	+12	−26 (7)	+ 1	10.3 (7)
Bush (R)	175R–260D (10)	45R–55D	− 2 (8)	0	− 8 (3)	− 1	14.6 (5)
Clinton (D)	258D–176R (5)	57D–43R	−10 (9)	0	−52 (10)	− 8	21.0 (3)

Sources: Norman J. Ornstein, Thomas E. Mann, and Michael J. Malbin, *Vital Statistics on Congress, 1997–1998* (Washington, D.C.: American Enterprise Institute, 1998), Tables 1–19, 2–3, 2–4; *Statistical Abstract of the United States* (Washington, D.C.: Government Printing Office, select years).

domestic policy initiatives and negated any advantages produced by the size of the party's delegation in Congress.

Although control of Congress by the president's party can be an advantage to the White House on some issues, David Mayhew found that some policy opportunities also may arise when presidents form coalitions with members of a Congress controlled by the opposition party (known as divided government). In 1996, for example, Republicans in Congress and a Democratic president concluded that each had a better chance in the fall elections if Congress enacted and the president signed major legislation than if they had to face voter dissatisfaction with continued stalemate on issues such as welfare reform. Thus, surprisingly, Mayhew's study of the period 1946–1990 revealed that the amount of major legislation passed with divided government was comparable to the results obtained when one party controlled both branches of government.[29]

Related to the strength of a president's party in Congress is the length of the president's coattails on election to office for the first time (see Table 1–3).[30] Newly elected Republican president Ronald Reagan enjoyed an increase of thirty-five seats in the House and a Republican recapture of the Senate by adding twelve new Republican members. By contrast, Democrat John Kennedy's election produced no gain in the Senate and a loss of twenty-one seats in the House. When members of the president's party sense that presidential coattails may have helped to expand the size of their party's vote, greater voting support for the president's policies may be forthcoming.

A president's success in the legislative arena owes something as well to Congress's organizational characteristics and the policy preferences and political skills of those in powerful positions.[31] In the two decades after World War II, southerners' dominance of congressional committees was a major issue. In fact, when Kennedy moved into the Oval Office in 1961, ten of the fifteen top committee chairmen were from the South and in most instances were decidedly conservative. The political skills of party leaders and the Speaker of the House also can make an important difference. For example, Kennedy's opportunities were reduced in early 1962 when the death of House Speaker Sam Rayburn, D-Texas, brought to power John McCormack, D-Mass., a less skillful Speaker.

More recently, in 1994, efforts by the Speaker of the 104th Congress, Newt Gingrich, R-Ga., to capitalize on Republican gains in the 1994 midterm elections and pass the legislative proposals contained in the Republicans' "Contract with America" succeeded for a time in pushing President Clinton's agenda to the sidelines. Yet by 1996 Gingrich's stunning fall in popularity and a widespread public perception that House Republicans had strayed too far to the right moved the ball back into Clinton's court, providing him with considerable opportunity for centrist strategies.

Promising Issues

John Kingdon, who applies the label "windows of opportunity" to promising issues, has identified situations favorable to government action on a given issue.[32] According to Kingdon, a "window of opportunity" exists when three influences converge: recognition that a problem needing a solution exists, the availability of a policy proposal around which support can be built, and the presence of a "political stream" of forces able to instigate change such as a popular president with considerable support in Congress (considered earlier in this chapter).

For problem awareness, Kingdon argues that social and economic conditions that might seem to warrant a high level of attention by presidents, members of Congress, and the press may actually generate little comment. This tendency to overlook problems is most likely to occur when no acceptable solution seems to be available. The deafening silence in the face of mounting budget deficits at points during the 1980s and the postponement until after the 1988 election of any attempt to cap the surging costs of the savings and loan debacle illustrate this tendency.

Economic Conditions and Budget Deficits

Economic conditions and budget deficits also play a key role in shaping a president's level of opportunity. In 1997, for example, the impact of a strong economy was central to Clinton's ability to negotiate a balanced budget proposal with Republicans. As negotiations proceeded, each Congressional Budget Office projection of the amount of money needed to be found in spending cuts, or the amount needed to absorb tax cuts, was lower than the last. This congressional sleight of hand helped each side avoid having to sign off on some of the more painful decisions they had been discussing.

Other impacts of the controversy have been at least as dramatic. A sense that the economy was performing badly helped to create opportunities for promoting new policies in 1933 and 1981. Conversely, in the mid-1960s, a rapidly growing economy helped to create opportunities as Congress actually lowered taxes while also instigating landmark Great Society programs.

Deficits have had an enormous impact on presidential opportunities as well. Periodically, large deficits and the concern they generate have given presidents an opportunity to promote deficit-reduction packages. More frequently, however, deficits have reduced opportunities for presidents to establish new programs. In 1993 Clinton found it necessary to move away from new spending initiatives as he complained that his budget package was beginning to make him look like an "Eisenhower Republican."

Foreign Policy Influences

The demands of foreign policy, especially those involving the deployment of U.S. troops to trouble spots, often have strong yet unpredictable impacts on opportunities for domestic action. The success with which Bush executed the 1990–1991 Persian Gulf War produced a surge in popularity that seemed to give him some additional basis for promoting domestic policy initiatives. Clinton's first term saw quite a different outcome despite his desire to be primarily a domestic president. In October 1993 eighteen American soldiers were killed in Somalia, and in a chilling scene viewed worldwide on television, the body of one was dragged through the streets of Mogadishu, the Somali capital. Suddenly, strategies for effecting the withdrawal of American forces were placed at the top of Clinton's agenda rather than strategies for promoting his health care reforms.

Foreign entanglements, then, may generate public support, but quite frequently they weaken a president's opportunities for domestic policy initiatives. Other important examples include the impact of the Vietnam War on Lyndon Johnson's Great Society programs and Jimmy Carter's involvement in unpopular foreign policy issues, among them the attempt to free U.S. embassy personnel taken hostage in Iran in 1979.

The Second Term

Presidents generally have less opportunity for effective leadership in their second term. Limitations begin with their typical reelection efforts. Sometimes presidents have won landslide victories, but their campaigns revolved around slogans like "Four More Years" or "Reelect the President" rather than efforts to develop support for new initiatives. The departure of staff and cabinet may be a problem as well. A president's key aides, weary after four years of very long hours and tempted by financially lucrative opportunities, may leave the administration. In dealing with Congress, presidents can anticipate a decline in their party's strength in the midterm elections during their sixth year in office. A president's lame duck status is yet another reason a member of Congress would doubt that there are advantages in being "on the president's team." Finally, on occasion presidents have contributed to their own difficulties. Perhaps actions taken in their first term come "home to roost" in the second—the Watergate scandal in the early 1970s, Reagan's Iran-contra scandal in 1986, and Clinton's fund-raising and sexual escapades in 1997–1998 are examples. Or presidents may take politically unwise actions in the flush of victory such as FDR's Supreme Court–packing scheme in 1937.

Declining Opportunities?

Any study of presidential performance over several decades must heed changes in the potential for presidential leadership. Ryan Barilleaux and Richard Rose have argued that presidents are now immersed in a "postmodern" presidency that makes their job more difficult than the one held by their predecessors between about 1933 and 1973.[33] Presidents, they conclude, face political obstacles with fewer resources and greater external demands than ever before. The perspectives of Barilleaux and Rose include several dimensions mentioned in the preceding review of the factors that determine a president's opportunity level. They are: changes in the public's confidence in the federal government, changes in legislative settings, and the impact of federal deficits. Several other factors, however, warrant attention such as the dramatic proliferation of interest groups. In the 1960s the number of consumer, environmental, and civil rights groups grew sharply. The business community, feeling increasingly beleaguered, responded with its own surge of organizational activity, in part through the new opportunity to organize as political action committees. And since the mid-1970s, many new groups have organized for and against the agenda being promoted by the Christian right.

Categorizing and Comparing Presidents

The three modern presidents who enjoyed the greatest opportunities to shape domestic policy were Franklin Roosevelt, Lyndon Johnson, and Ronald Reagan (see Table 1–4). Unlike FDR, whose administration ushered in a dramatic change in party control of government, Johnson represented a continuation of Democratic Party control. Yet he was aided by a tremendous backlog of "unfinished business" in the form of legislative proposals that were moving forward in Congress. Reagan's opportunities were somewhat fewer than those of FDR and LBJ, but he had more than any of the other post-1932 presidents. Presidents with moderate opportunity levels were Harry Truman, Dwight Eisenhower, and John Kennedy. The low-opportunity presidents were Richard Nixon, Jimmy Carter, George Bush, and Bill Clinton.

The rest of this book is devoted to assessing and then comparing the performances of these presidents. It assesses their levels of political opportunity, the scope of the strategies they pursued, and the skill with which the strategies were exercised. The categorization of presidents by opportunity level (high, moderate, and low) allows a fairer comparison of their skills based on their performances within an opportunity level. Is it fair to expect Bush or Nixon or Carter or Clinton to achieve as much as FDR or LBJ? Individual assessments provide a basis for overall comparisons in the final chapter.

Other lines of assessment are important as well. For example, to what extent do leadership styles have policy consequences? Are these styles simply of media interest, or do they have real policy consequences? And to what extent do presidents get what they can out of a given situation?

TABLE 1–4 Influences and Limitations Affecting Presidential Opportunities, 1933–1997

	Helpful Influences	Limitations
ROOSEVELT		
1933–1937	Intense public desire for action	No general solution to economic problems available
	Discredited opponent and party	Conflicts over policy options in specific areas
	Decisive election victory in 1932	Budget deficit over half of total spending in 1932
	High level of popularity	
	Potential for a majority party coalition	
	Large congressional majorities	
	Many promising issues	
1937–1941	Landslide reelection win	Formation of conservative coalition in 1937
		Congressional losses in 1938
		Few promising issues
1941–1945	Strong election win	Wartime issues predominate
TRUMAN		
1945–1949	Majority party president	Not elected—succeeded to the presidency
	Economic growth and budget surpluses	Unflattering comparisons to FDR and low popularity
		Strength of southern Democrats in Congress and a divided coalition
		Low popularity
1949–1953	Surprise election victory	Focus on Korean War
EISENHOWER		
1953–1957	Decisive election victory	Minority party president
	High popularity	Democratic party strength in Congress
		Few promising issues
1957–1961	Decisive election victory	Two recessions and budget deficit problems
	Some new proposals emerging	Midterm election losses
KENNEDY		
1961–1963	Majority party president	Narrow election victory
	High popularity	No surge in congressional elections
	Some promising issues	Southern Democratic strength in Congress
		Chairs of key committees hostile

continued

TABLE 1–4 *(continued)*

	Helpful Influences	Limitations
JOHNSON		
1963–1965	Two "first years"	Decline in popularity
	Activist public mood	Agenda shift to race riots, the Vietnam War, 1966–1968
	High level of trust in government	High midterm loss of House seats
1965–1969	Landslide victory in 1964	
	Majority party president	
	Large congressional majorities, 1965–1966	
	Many very promising issues	
	Strong economy	
NIXON		
1969–1973	Activist era	Minority party president
	Discredited opponent and party	Weak election victory
	Some promising issues	Democratic strength in Congress
	Fairly strong initial popularity	
1973–1974	Landslide election win	Watergate quickly engulfed his presidency
	Still an activist era	
FORD		
1974–1977	None	Not elected—succeeded to the presidency
		Low popularity after the Nixon pardon
		Weak economic performance
CARTER		
1977–1981	Majority party president	Weak election victory
	Large congressional majorities	Divided Democratic Party majorities in Congress
	Some promising issues	Large deficit
		No easy solutions to inflation, unemployment, and the energy crisis

TABLE 1–4 *(continued)*

	Helpful Influences	Limitations
REAGAN		
1981–1985	Public desire for new economic policies	Little public support for major spending cuts
	Decisive victory and an opportunity to declare a mandate	Democratic control of House, 1983–1985
	Discredited opponent and party	
	Republican surge in Congress and control of the Senate	
	Relatively low deficit	
1985–1989	Landslide election win	Distractions of Iran-contra affair
	Sustained popularity	Return of Senate to Democratic control
		Few promising issues
BUSH		
1989–1993	Close to majority party status	Unflattering comparisons to Reagan
	High popularity, first thirty months	Modest election victory
		Democratic majorities in Congress
		Large deficit
		Few promising issues
CLINTON		
1993–1997	Democratic Party strength in Congress, 1993–1994	Weak majority party status
	Some promising issues	Public lack of trust in government
	Moderate but steady economic growth	Low popularity first twenty-four months
		Republican control of Congress, 1995–1996
		Large initial deficit
1997–	Strong economy	Modest reelection win
	Fairly high popularity	Few promising issues

One might find, for example, that a president with moderate opportunities was actually more effective in maximizing his situation than a president with greater opportunities. Could it be that Roosevelt, Johnson, or Reagan were actually underachievers? Any evaluations also must bear in mind the policy goals a president sought and not simply what policies should have been pursued. Some analysts looking at these and other questions have found that several of the modern presidents have had a major impact on the evolution of the presidency and perceptions of presidential leadership.[34]

Finally, policy legacies also warrant consideration. Fortunately, David Mayhew's interpretation of major legislative actions since 1947 provides an important basis for determining presidential legacies. By looking at journalistic assessments at the end of legislative sessions and then the view of policy experts, Mayhew identified over two hundred major enactments and within that group a small number that were especially important and thus could be labeled "landmark"—that is, "both innovative and consequential." [35] While Mayhew's analysis may be a bit subjective, it captures nevertheless a key element in policy change. Yet Mayhew's lists, although of tremendous value, cannot be taken as a direct indication of successful presidential leadership. A number of studies in recent years have shown that congressional influences often have played a big role in the passage of major new legislation.[36] Those reinterpretations frequently point out that many discussions of national policy making, including the many reviews of Roosevelt, have been overly "president-centered."

The chapters that follow examine the actions and strategies adopted by presidents as significant legislation has emerged. Because it is not feasible to discuss all the major first-term policy enactments for each president, only the landmark policy enactments are reviewed.[37] These assessments will reveal the level of presidential leadership exerted on the measures that have done the most to shape domestic policy since 1933. Some major legislative enactments are considered simply because they are especially illustrative of a president's leadership style or the challenges he faced.

The study described in Chapters 2–11 begins with Franklin Roosevelt because he was the first "modern" president and because of the continuing interest in his leadership and the wide range of strategies he employed.[38] Each chapter includes a brief summary of personal characteristics before turning to leadership styles and policy roles.[39]

All discussions of policy focus on domestic issues since they provide especially fertile ground for examining the impact of leadership styles and strategies. As presidents' legacies are largely created during their first four years in office, the analysis is limited to first terms. President Gerald Ford is not included in this study because he occupied the presidency under unique circumstances for a very short time and was fulfilling part of Nixon's second term. The final chapter develops comparative assessments and addresses prospects for future presidential leadership.

Notes

1. Michael A. Genovese, *The Presidential Dilemma: Leadership in the American System* (New York: HarperCollins, 1995), chap. 2.

2. See Shirley Anne Warshaw, *The Domestic Presidency: Policy Making in the White House* (Boston: Allyn and Bacon, 1997); and Paul C. Light, *The President's Agenda: Domestic Policy Choice from Kennedy to Carter* (Baltimore: Johns Hopkins University Press, 1982).

3. James P. Pfiffner, *The Strategic Presidency: Hitting the Ground Running,* 2d ed. (Lawrence: University Press of Kansas, 1996).

4. Samuel Kernell, *Going Public: New Strategies of Presidential Leadership,* 3d ed. (Washington, D.C.: CQ Press, 1997).

5. Robert J. Spitzer, *The Presidency and Public Policy: The Four Arenas of Presidential Power* (University: University of Alabama Press, 1983).

6. Richard E. Neustadt, *Presidential Power* (New York: Wiley, 1960). For an extension of his views, see Richard E. Neustadt, *Presidential Power and the Modern Presidents: The Politics of Leadership from Roosevelt to Reagan* (New York: Free Press, 1990).

7. Fred I. Greenstein, *Leadership in the Modern Presidency* (Cambridge: Harvard University Press, 1988), 312. For a contemporary critique of Neustadt, see Thomas E. Cronin and Michael A. Genovese, *The Paradoxes of the American Presidency* (New York: Oxford University Press, 1998), chap. 4.

8. Kernell, *Going Public.*

9. Fred I. Greenstein, *The Hidden-Hand Presidency: Eisenhower as Leader* (New York: Basic Books, 1982).

10. See Bert A. Rockman, *The Leadership Question: The Presidency and the American System* (New York: Praeger, 1984); and Genovese, *Presidential Dilemma.*

11. See Richard P. Nathan, *The Administrative Presidency* (New York: Wiley, 1983); Robert F. Durant, *The Administrative Presidency Revisited* (Albany: State University of New York Press, 1992); and James P. Pfiffner, ed., *The Managerial Presidency* (College Station: Texas A&M University Press, 1999).

12. William Muir, *The Bully-Pulpit: The Presidential Leadership of Ronald Reagan* (San Francisco: ICS Press, 1992), 21.

13. Richard A. Brody, *Assessing the President: The Media, Elite Opinion, and Public Support* (Stanford: Stanford University Press, 1991).

14. Melissa R. Michaelson, "The Effect of Public Approval on Presidential Power." (Paper prepared for delivery at the 1994 annual meeting of the American Political Science Association, New York, N.Y., September 2–5, 1994).

15. Brody, *Assessing the President.*

16. For a perspective suggesting popularity has only a marginal impact on presidential success, see George C. Edwards III, *At the Margins: Presidential Leadership of Congress* (New Haven: Yale University Press, 1989); and Paul Brace and Barbara Hinckley, *Follow the Leader: Opinion Polls and the Modern Presidents* (New York: Basic Books, 1992).

17. The limitations of presidential skills compared with the impacts of a legislator's party and ideology are stressed in Jon R. Bond and Richard Fleisher, *The President in the Legislative Arena* (Chicago: University of Chicago Press, 1990). For similar case study conclusions, see Matthew R. Kerbel, *Beyond Persuasion: Organizational Efficiency and Presidential Power* (Albany: State University of New York Press, 1991).

18. Edwards, *At the Margins,* chap. 11.

19. Kerbel, *Beyond Persuasion,* 153.

20. Anthony J. Eksterowicz and Glenn P. Hastedt, "Executive/Congressional Liaison in a Post Cold War Era." (Paper delivered at the annual meeting of the Northeast Political Science Association, Newark, N.J., November 1995).

21. John Ehrlichman, *Witness to Power: The Nixon Years* (New York: Simon and Schuster, 1982), 203.

22. See Light, *President's Agenda,* chap. 9; and Pfiffner, *Strategic Presidency,* chap. 1.

23. Charles O. Jones, *The Presidency in a Separated System* (Washington, D.C.: Brookings, 1994), 128.

24. For examples of the policy-making cycle approach, see Steven A. Shull, ed., *Domestic Policy Formation: President–Congress Partisanship* (Westport, Conn.: Greenwood Press, 1983).

25. Arthur M. Schlesinger Jr., *The Cycles of American History* (Boston: Houghton Mifflin, 1986).

26. For an application of changes in the public mood to several aspects of presidential behavior, see Erwin C. Hargrove and Michael Nelson, *Presidents, Politics, and Policy* (Baltimore: Johns Hopkins University Press, 1984), chap. 3.

27. On the inability of presidents to literally create a mandate, see Edwards, *At the Margins,* chap. 8.

28. Stephen Skowronek, *The Politics Presidents Make: Leadership from John Adams to George Bush* (New Haven: Yale University Press, 1993).

29. David R. Mayhew, *Divided We Govern: Party Control, Lawmaking, and Investigations, 1946–1990* (New Haven: Yale University Press, 1991), chap. 7.

30. The importance of surge as an aspect of a president's opportunity level is effectively discussed in Charles O. Jones, "Campaigning to Govern: The Clinton Style," in *The Clinton Presidency: First Appraisal,* ed. Colin Campbell and Bert A. Rockman (Chatham, N.J.: Chatham House, 1995), chap. 1.

31. For a summary of legislative characteristics and their implications for presidential influence during different time periods, see Roger Davidson, "The Presi-

dency and Presidential Time," in *Rivals for Power: Presidential–Congressional Relations*, 2d ed., ed. James A. Thurber (Washington, D.C.: CQ Press, 1996), chap. 2.

32. John Kingdon, *Issues, Agendas, and Alternatives*, 2d ed. (Boston: Little, Brown, 1994).

33. For major statements of this view, see Richard Rose, *The Postmodern President: George Bush Meets the World* (Chatham, N.J.: Chatham House, 1991); and Ryan J. Barilleaux, *The Post-Modern Presidency: The Office after Ronald Reagan* (Westport, Conn.: Greenwood Press, 1988). For a more measured view of this problem, see Michael A. Genovese, *The Presidency in an Age of Limits* (Westport, Conn.: Greenwood Press, 1993).

34. See, for example, Sidney M. Milkis, *The President and the Parties: The Transformation of the American Political System* (New York: Oxford University Press, 1993); and Charles E. Walcott and Karen M. Hult, *Governing the White House: From Hoover through LBJ* (Lawrence: University Press of Kansas, 1995).

35. Mayhew, *Divided We Govern*, 37.

36. For this view, see, in particular, Charles O. Jones, *Congress and the President: Separate but Equal Branches* (Chatham, N.J.: Chatham House, 1995); and Lance LeLoup and Steven A. Shull, *Congress and the Presidency: The Policy Connection* (Belmont, Calif.: Wadsworth Publishing, 1993).

37. These authors identified landmark legislation enacted between 1933 and 1946 and in 1997 using an approach similar to Mayhew's.

38. Numerous sources were used in assessing each president. These included: works by various administration officials, journalists, and academic writers; historical background discussions for each time period; studies of process relationships; case study analyses of particular policy enactments and the policy evolution of several administrations; public opinion polls; interpretations of presidential success votes in *Congressional Quarterly Weekly Report* and *Congressional Quarterly Almanac;* and the *Public Papers of the Presidents*. The Clinton case was augmented by newspaper accounts, limited personal interviews, papers and panel discussions presented at annual meetings of the American Political Science Association, and an examination of the papers of the Task Force on National Health Reform. Archival research was undertaken at the Kennedy, Johnson, Carter, and Reagan presidential libraries and at the Nixon Presidential Materials Project. Materials examined at these libraries included staff aides' papers on domestic policy, legislative liaison, and public liaison, along with oral histories and exit interviews.

39. For a widely read interpretation of how leadership styles are formed, see James David Barber, *The Presidential Character: Predicting Performance in the White House*, 4th ed. (Englewood Cliffs, N.J.: Prentice-Hall, 1992).

The
High-Opportunity
Presidents

No President . . . ever came to greater opportunities amid so great an outpouring of popular trust and hope.

—NEW YORK TIMES, MARCH 3, 1933

2

Franklin D. Roosevelt
Artful Leadership during Hard Times

THE FRANKLIN Roosevelt presidency (1933–1945), regarded as one of the greatest in U.S. history, raises central issues in the study of presidential leadership. Debate continues about Roosevelt's style of leadership, the scope of his power, and his legacy. His policies broke new ground. In fact, the economic regulatory policies enacted during his tenure were largely intact until the 1990s, and the social security system he helped to create mushroomed in the decades after its birth. That legacy was challenged, however, in 1995 when House Republicans sought to fulfill their "Contract with America," which called for reducing the size and role of government. Roosevelt's leadership style, although emulated by some presidents, has had its critics as well. Important questions have emerged about the extent to which FDR dominated Congress, the sources of his rhetorical successes, and how well—as the first of the high-opportunity presidents—he actually used the extraordinary opportunities available to him during his first years in office.

Personal Characteristics

Franklin Delano Roosevelt (1882–1945) was a unique president in one particular way. Thanks to a willing press, only a tiny portion of the public realized that their buoyant, optimistic president was confined to a wheelchair, the result of the paralyzing disease, polio, he contracted at age thirty-nine. In the mid-1990s, that lack of public awareness became an issue as plans for a Roosevelt memorial proceeded with the view that he should be portrayed as the public had perceived him—standing—

31

rather than sitting in a wheelchair. But for many disabled citizens, this decision denied an important lesson: a president confined to a wheelchair
can provide assertive leadership.

Roosevelt was born in 1882 into an upper-class family; the family tree
dated back to English and Dutch ancestors who arrived in New York in
the seventeenth century and quickly became successful entrepreneurs and
prominent citizens. Theodore Roosevelt, whose presidential leadership
(1901–1909) impressed Franklin as a young man, was a distant cousin,
as well as the uncle of Franklin's wife, Eleanor.[1]

Franklin's boyhood was typical for those raised in a prominent New
York family—life on a large family estate, the enjoyment of a summer
home, and European travel. He was schooled until age fourteen by tutors
at Hyde Park, the family estate located on the Hudson River about eighty
miles north of New York City. After spending his high school years at
Groton, an exclusive preparatory school, Franklin attended Harvard
University and Columbia Law School. At Harvard he pursued some demanding courses but showed only moderate interest. Greater energy was
devoted to his role as editor of the *Harvard Crimson,* the university newspaper. He performed satisfactorily while in law school, but again without
keen interest.

Career Path

As a restless young attorney, Franklin told several of his colleagues that
he intended to pursue a career path modeled on that of his cousin
Theodore. Remarkably, his actual career path was virtually identical to
the one he had outlined. He was elected to the New York Senate in 1910
at the age of twenty-nine and three years later entered the Wilson administration as assistant secretary of the navy. He gained important administrative experience during his seven-year tenure in the Department of the
Navy; indeed, his responsibilities surged during World War I. In those
years he had an opportunity to study Wilson's approach to presidential
leadership, how the federal bureaucracy operated, and some of the difficulties a department could have in its relationships with Congress. In 1920
the Democratic Party nominated Roosevelt as its vice-presidential candidate, but he and his running mate, Ohio governor James Cox, went down
to a convincing defeat.

In August 1921 Roosevelt's life changed dramatically just as he was
beginning a return to legal practice. While vacationing at the family sum-

mer home at Campobello Island, located off the coast of New Brunswick, he was stricken with polio, a disease that at the time took the lives of about 25 percent its victims; the rest were left paralyzed. Despite intense rehabilitation, Franklin permanently lost the use of his legs. It was only with great effort, then, as in his "walk" to the lectern at the Democratic Party's 1932 nominating convention, that he could maneuver himself a short distance with the use of a cane and a strong grip on the arm of a son or Secret Service agent. Even these displays were not without risk, however; at the 1936 convention he fell and only his remarkable composure allowed him to proceed with his acceptance address.

After 1921 Roosevelt pursued his hoped-for recovery in the soothing waters of Warm Springs, Georgia, while continuing his keen interest in politics. His wife, Eleanor, who had become highly active in New York politics, encouraged his political interests by inviting prominent guests to engage him in policy issues. In 1928 Roosevelt took a gamble and won. He had debated holding off on a run for the governorship of New York but decided to enter the race anyway and won by only 25,000 votes. As governor of New York from 1929 to 1933, Roosevelt displayed some of the skills he would use later in the White House. To the surprise and dismay of outgoing governor Al Smith, FDR made it clear that he would be his own man, and he avoided using Smith's top aides. His emerging leadership style included frequent press conferences, major radio addresses, efforts to pressure legislators through press releases, and assertive legislative leadership.

Roosevelt, labeled a progressive governor, promoted programs such as tax relief for farmers and cheaper electric power. In 1930, as the depression worsened, he was successful in establishing a limited state old-age pension for those who met a means test. After his reelection by a landslide in 1930, he established a state emergency relief program and an unemployment insurance program. The State Unemployment Relief Act, passed in a special session of the New York legislature in September 1931, gained considerable national attention because New York was the first state to establish such a plan.

Mounting voter frustration with the magnitude of the nation's economic collapse and President Herbert Hoover's sagging popularity sparked interest in the 1932 race for the presidency. The Democratic Party and others had viewed Roosevelt's reelection effort in 1930 as a test of his potential in a presidential race, and his 700,000-vote victory only heightened their interest. But because a two-thirds majority of the party's delegates to the national convention was required to achieve nomination, he succeeded in capturing the top spot only after a tense struggle. As the fourth ballot approached at the Chicago Democratic convention, Roosevelt supporters worried that if he did not receive the necessary votes the convention would turn to a compromise candidate. But after intense behind-the-scenes maneuvering, John Garner, a Texan and Speaker of the House, released his delegates. A rancorous battle still occurred within the Texas delegation, but their votes finally swung to Roosevelt. A similar move by California delegates, in which Joseph P. Kennedy, father of a later president, played a role, gave Roosevelt the necessary margin.[2]

In moving toward the fall election Roosevelt had a tremendous advantage: the nation was seeking relief from its virtual economic collapse. The downward spiral had begun with the crash of the stock market in October 1929. A spree of stock exchange investing had driven the Dow Jones industrial average from 99 in October 1925 to 381 in September 1929. On October 29 the bottom fell out. By July 1932 the Dow Jones average stood at only 41; stocks had lost nearly 80 percent of their value. A rise in unemployment followed, with an ominous surge to 16.5 percent in 1931 and 25 percent in 1932. Adding to the nation's woes, 4,600 banks failed. Given what is now known about voters' tendencies to cast ballots based on economic conditions, FDR's vice presidential running mate, John Garner, probably had an accurate view of the election. In reflecting on the state of the economy and on Hoover's lack of popularity, he told Roosevelt, "All you need to do is stay alive until election day. The people are not going to vote for you. They are going to vote against the depression."[3]

Roosevelt emphasized themes more than specific programs in his election campaign. His reasons? He was running not only against a highly unpopular incumbent, but also as the nominee of a party that included many conservatives actually to the right of Hoover on some issues. Moreover, in some policy areas he was simply unsure of his preferred course of action. The themes themselves varied. In his "Forgotten Man" speech Roosevelt attacked Hoover's "trickle down" approach to economics by stressing that he was going to pursue reform from the bottom up rather than from the top down. In a major speech in San Francisco, Roosevelt also stressed the importance of improved government–business cooperation.

When the final results were in, Roosevelt had trounced Hoover in the popular vote by 57 percent to 40 percent. In an overwhelming electoral college win, he carried all states south and west of Pennsylvania. In the process he forged a coalition that included southern Democrats (a traditional source of strength for the Democratic Party), northern urban Democrats, and farm belt Democrats, who showed stronger-than-usual support.

What Manner of Man?

Roosevelt was a complex man—in fact, more than many people realized. According to biographer Arthur Schlesinger Jr., Roosevelt wore a mask that was difficult to penetrate.[4] Frances Perkins, his longtime associate who served as labor secretary for his entire presidency, concluded in her memoirs that Roosevelt "was the most complicated person I have ever known."[5] Bruce Miroff reached a similar conclusion after reviewing Roosevelt's writings.[6]

In the spring of 1932 newspaper columnist Walter Lippmann wrote that Roosevelt was "a pleasant man who, without any important qualifications for office, would very much like to be president."[7] That observation revealed a frequently expressed concern that Roosevelt did not possess the convictions and assertiveness needed to serve as an effective president during difficult times. Years later historian Garry Wills asserted that Lippmann's assessment of Roosevelt did not recognize the manner in which his confinement to a wheelchair had affected him. Roosevelt did not dramatically change his views on policy issues after his paralysis. What did change markedly was the resolve Roosevelt showed in his commitment to his leadership roles. In drawing a comparison with the less-than-fervent manner in which upper-class Democrat Adlai Stevenson campaigned for the presidency a generation later, Wills suggested that Stevenson was "Roosevelt without his polio attack."[8]

Despite Roosevelt's complexities, some of his qualities do stand out. For example, he had a tremendous desire to be at the center of any activity he was involved in. Even at Warm Springs he thoroughly enjoyed being the leading figure in social activities as others suffering similar disabilities gathered for therapy and recreation. He also enjoyed occupying center stage at activities ranging from the informal White House staff gatherings for cocktails at the end of most workdays to the periodic poker parties with a few of his top associates.

Roosevelt also impressed people with his enthusiasm, optimism, and energy, prompting observations years later that his "radiant self-assurance was perhaps his greatest political asset."[9] No doubt he recognized that his optimism and enthusiasm were major assets in developing a favorable persona. Yet he also was simply being himself. His optimism extended to his new policy experiments, but there he backed his optimism with hard work. In his eagerness to both maintain firm control of his White House and also keep policy experiments moving, he frequently put in fourteen-hour days which rivaled in extensiveness the work habits of most of his successors.[10]

Tremendous self-confidence characterized Roosevelt as well. He did have some qualms on the eve of his inauguration, yet in his first days in office he kept Congress in session even though his domestic program was by no means ready to be presented. Indeed, his self-confidence seemed to have no bounds. He even tended to invite subordinates who were bogged down with an issue to bring it to him for consideration while often commenting on his own "broad shoulders."

Roosevelt impressed many observers with his genuine friendliness and his desire to put visitors at ease. He also was extremely skilled at persuading people to adopt his preferred position. In fact, visitors, including legislators, often would enter the Oval Office with one point of view and leave anxious to promote a different course of action.

But FDR also could be quite devious and display a ruthless political savvy. Schlesinger wrote that he liked to operate by "manipulating uncertainty." And that trait applied to his own staff. Although Roosevelt, like many other presidents, was reluctant to fire people, he was quite willing to ease aides from prominent roles when their usefulness declined. On a daily basis, his coy and often indirect handling of people and issues caused uncertainty and anxiety among those around him. Schlesinger rejected the view, however, that Roosevelt tended to act in a vengeful manner.[11]

In his approach to knowledge, Roosevelt's interests were broad but shallow. He read some histories and biographies but nothing more complex, and, according to some accounts, he did not read books at all while in the White House. He was far more interested in talking to people and reading newspapers than examining lengthy reports. The eminent retired Supreme Court justice Oliver Wendell Holmes perhaps echoed the view held by many Roosevelt scholars when, after visiting Roosevelt, he offered this assessment: "A second-class intellect. But a first-class temperament!"[12]

Policy Views

Anyone searching for Roosevelt's major policy views must keep in mind his background. His parents had been Democrats, but of the conservative

Grover Cleveland variety. His own ties were more to rural Hyde Park than to urban New York City. Reflecting views common in the turn-of-the-century Progressive era, he was at first skeptical of labor unions. He also developed a strong and lasting interest in conservation. And his experiences as governor of New York had added strong interests in regulation of the utility industry and pension assistance for the elderly.

When he took office, Roosevelt had not yet devised any general approaches to reviving the economy. After all, the times were uncertain and the doctrine of "liberalism," as his policies would later be labeled, was still undeveloped. Roosevelt biographer James MacGregor Burns concluded that "probably the most persistent policy interest Roosevelt had was in the conservation of human and natural resources." [13]

Challenges and Opportunities

By March 4, 1933, the day of his inauguration, Roosevelt was experiencing a public demand for action unmatched since Abraham Lincoln's inauguration in 1861 when the nation was facing the imminent threat of southern secession.[14] The day before his inauguration the *New York Times* said, "No President . . . ever came to greater opportunities amid so great an outpouring of popular trust and hope." And humorist Will Rogers added his own earthy two cents: "The whole country is with him just so he does something. If he burned down the Capitol we would cheer and say 'well, at least we got a fire started, anyhow.'" The desire for action had intensified during the four-month interregnum in which Hoover tried awkwardly and unsuccessfully to enlist Roosevelt's endorsement of new policy initiatives. But Roosevelt resisted Hoover's quest for support because of policy differences, uncertainty about some of his own positions, and a political instinct that told him that any entanglement with Hoover's final actions would only reduce his own opportunities for a fresh start once he assumed office.

Four Immediate Challenges

Four immediate challenges faced Roosevelt and the nation as he assumed office.[15] The most urgent problem was one of mounting bank failures. A third of the nation's banks had already closed their doors, causing nine million people to lose their savings and prompting other frantic deposit holders to withdraw their funds to prevent a similar tragedy. Since even the most conservatively run banks did not have cash reserves to handle such a demand, governors in many states had resorted to declaring bank holidays.

The agricultural economy was a second wrenching problem. Farmers, unable to sell their produce at a profit, also were unable to meet their mortgage payments. In some instances, bank officials trying to instigate foreclosure proceedings faced unruly crowds and feared for their lives.

The lack of economic growth and high unemployment constituted a third difficult problem. The economy continued to function far below capacity, and unemployment levels hovered at around 25 percent—or higher in some manufacturing areas such as Detroit and Chicago. Among blacks, unemployment exceeded 50 percent in some parts of the country, and young adults everywhere found it difficult, if not impossible, to find employment. The devastating impact of widespread unemployment was heightened by the extent to which joblessness affected sole family breadwinners and the absence of any broad-based relief programs.

The fourth immediate challenge was one of providing relief for the destitute. Both private and state relief agencies had been overwhelmed by rising costs and had proven inadequate to the task. As a result, an estimated two million of the nation's citizens were homeless in "Hoovervilles."

Fortunately for Roosevelt, few foreign policy challenges appeared on the immediate horizon during his first term to compete with his determination to take action on the domestic front. In fact, he waited until 1934 to address the issue of tariff reduction. When he finally did, he successfully promoted a fundamental reduction in the nation's tariff system via the Reciprocal Trade Act. In the judgment of historian Robert Ferrell, during Roosevelt's first term the American public lived largely apart from the realities of international relations.[16]

Roosevelt possessed both impressive advantages and sobering limitations throughout his first four years in office. Given the now-established patterns of honeymoons with the voters and rallying tendencies during a crisis, he undoubtedly enjoyed soaring popularity during his first months in office. By 1935, however, Roosevelt was confronting the typical third-year slump as his popularity sank to only 50.5 percent.[17]

The president also had to confront the likelihood that enthusiasm for expanded federal economic activity would recede. In 1935 the first national poll conducted by George Gallup vividly portrayed low levels of public support for new programs and increased spending. Despite unemployment levels of over 20 percent, only 9 percent of respondents found the relief and recovery effort too small. Of the rest, 31 percent judged it to be about right and 60 percent termed it too great.[18]

Although Roosevelt had achieved a solid victory (57 percent of the popular vote) in the 1932 election, he realized he headed a party that had displayed a poor record in its efforts to win control of the White House. Only Democrats Grover Cleveland and Woodrow Wilson (in a three-way race) had been elected to the presidency since the Civil War. Moreover, FDR had received a smaller percentage of votes than Republicans Calvin Coolidge in 1924 and Herbert Hoover in 1928. Roosevelt, then, faced the need to build a coalition that was broad enough to prevent the anti-Hoover voters of 1932 from returning to support a Republican candidate in 1936.

When he entered office in 1933, Roosevelt had large majorities (not counting independents) of 313–117 in the House and 59–36 in the Senate. Indeed, an unprecedented 90 Democrats were added to the House. Gains in the midterm election of 1934 drove those numbers up even higher: 322 in the House and 69 in the Senate. Congress was not without problems, however. Large majorities, as in one-party state legislatures, tend to divide into factions that can be unruly.

At first, southerners were quite supportive of FDR's programs because of the desperate poverty in their region. Yet over time the more than one hundred southern Democrats found allies among Republicans who shared some of their underlying suspicions about "too much government." Roosevelt was fortunate in having generally able party leaders, but some potentially hostile southern Democrats were the chairmen of key committees.

In general, though, when Roosevelt moved into the Oval Office the national dynamics were ripe for action. The public not only wanted action to address issues such as unemployment, but also action against the leaders of some of the economic sectors—banking, the stock market, and electric utilities. Proposals for dealing with these problems were available, some developed in the last Congress but stalemated or stopped by a presidential veto. Agricultural assistance, creation of the Tennessee Valley Authority, and regulatory reforms were high on the list. For some problems, the collapse of financial institutions had produced major congressional investigations and in some instances specific proposals that could act as a basis for rapid legislative action in 1933.

Policy ideas were gleaned from an impressive array of sources, even the previous administration. Despite its often-cautious efforts, the Hoover White House had developed some ideas that would emerge as part of Roosevelt's program, most notably the emergency banking legislation enacted at the outset of the "First Hundred Days" session of Congress in 1933. State governments proved to be a fertile ground for policy ideas as well.

Many, in fact, had taken actions the previous decade that could be incorporated into new federal programs. Roosevelt was aware of many of these developments through his own experiences while serving as governor of New York.[19]

Economic Problems and Solutions

Roosevelt may have gathered a wide array of broad approaches to promoting economic recovery, but little agreement existed on any one approach. The depression was worldwide, and its causes were difficult to correct. They ranged from a global system of tariff protection to a decade-long problem in the United States of agricultural overproduction and lack of consumer demand caused by highly uneven patterns of income distribution.[20] In view of this situation, some policy makers promoted nationalization of specific economic sectors such as banks and railroads; others wanted to break up large corporations; and still others wanted to see the government develop a more comprehensive planning role. Many business groups supported the U.S. Chamber of Commerce in its call for price and working condition agreements among producers in major sectors of the economy such as coal, oil production, and manufacturing. Because prices had been declining in general and even more sharply for agricultural commodities, some members of Congress pushed for policies to create inflation.[21]

Thus despite the existence of many proposals for a general solution to the nation's economic problems, none were clearly understood and politically feasible. Relief efforts and structural reforms such as new regulatory provisions could help, but less was known about how to revive an economy mired in high unemployment and underuse of the nation's manufacturing capacity.[22] Different monetary policies targeting the money supply and interest rates might have helped. Yet, as monetary policy analyst Herbert Stein concluded, they were not understood at the time.[23]

Later in FDR's tenure, during World War II, the nation found that massive federal deficits, when combined with price and wage controls to prevent inflation, could provide the "jump-start" that had been advocated by British economist John Maynard Keynes. His writings impressively challenged earlier economic concepts, as he argued that debts could increase aggregate demand in the economy by, first, putting greater purchasing power in the hands of the consumer through lower taxes, and, second, providing demand through cash payments that citizens would spend through direct government purchases of goods and services. His ideas went far beyond those accepted by both Hoover and Roosevelt that spending programs such as highway and dam construction could provide valuable jobs. He envisioned a larger "multiplier" effect that would create additional new jobs.

Use of Keynesian economics faced two formidable barriers, however. First, Keynes's ideas were only beginning to gain circulation as Roosevelt took office. After Keynes published a major *New York Times* article in late 1933 advocating greater deficit spending, a few members of Roosevelt's inner circle began to take him more seriously. In the spring of 1934 Labor Secretary Frances Perkins arranged a meeting between Roosevelt and Keynes, but little came of that effort. "I saw your friend Keynes," Roosevelt later reported to Perkins. "He left a whole rigmarole of figures. He must be a mathematician rather than a political economist." Keynes commented to Perkins on the meeting as well, saying he had "supposed the President was more literate, economically speaking." [24]

The second barrier Keynesian economics faced was Congress itself. Even had the justifications for deficit spending been accepted, Congress, alarmed at the already high deficit spending on relief efforts, was unlikely to favor going further down that path. The deficit in FDR's first term was over half of total spending (see Table 1–3). To anyone for whom a balanced budget was a key policy goal, this dramatically reduced opportunities for new spending. The federal government also was very small, with under 700,000 employees. Consequently, while some government spending could be reduced by cutting specific programs such as veterans' benefits, limited opportunity existed for reducing spending by cutting the pay of federal officials.

Ultimately, Roosevelt was more willing than Hoover to experiment with deficit spending. But the basic constraint remained—the absence of a viable macroeconomic policy to dramatically alter the forces within the United States that had caused the unparalleled economic collapse in the first place.

Voices for Change

The lack of solutions that would produce widespread support was felt even more acutely as Roosevelt's first term progressed. Support for more sweeping government action was emerging from some quarters, however. In California the strong showing in 1934 by Democratic gubernatorial candidate Upton Sinclair, a socialist and prominent author, scared more conservative segments of that state's population and dramatized electoral support for sweeping reform. In Michigan the strident radio broadcasts of the Reverend Charles Coughlin protesting against bankers and an international conspiracy drew audiences estimated at 30–45 million. His shifting positions and volatile personality created difficulties for Roosevelt despite efforts to enlist his support for New Deal programs. The economic frustrations of the elderly also exploded onto the national scene. The effort to organize support for a federally funded social security program was led by Dr. Francis Townsend, an elderly physician living in Long Beach, California, who had grown angry watching senior citizens search for food in garbage cans.

The political strength and agenda of Sen. Huey Long were a force to be reckoned with as well. Nicknamed "the Kingfish," the formerly powerful governor of Louisiana led a movement calling for every American to "be a King." His crowd-pleasing advocacy of redistributive economic policies produced mounting support in 1935, to the point that he represented a significant third-party threat in the 1936 election.

Thus Roosevelt's challenge as his first term progressed was to seize the opportunities created by stronger voices for change without having the large expectations of their followers (and many members of Congress) lead to defeat of the measures that could command majority support. FDR would have to strike a delicate balance between pushing legislation through Congress and getting too far ahead of public opinion. In other words, he had to recognize when to move, when to retreat, when to wait.

The Court

In devising strategies, Roosevelt only had to look as far as the judicial branch of government to see a potential source of hostile action. The makeup of the Supreme Court reflected the Republicans' prior dominance of national politics. From 1933 to 1936 the Court blocked FDR's New Deal legislation by declaring laws unconstitutional, often by a narrow 5–4 vote. Roosevelt's programs were breaking new ground, and the Court was reluctant to give judicial sanction to this new, expanded role for the federal government. In the spring of 1935 the president held a spirited press conference in which he accused the Court of having a "horse and buggy mentality." Then, in a rare concession, he allowed direct use of his language in press accounts of the gathering.

President Roosevelt contributed to his own problems in early 1937 after his reelection landslide. He made a rare political miscalculation in seeking to expand, or "pack," the size of the Supreme Court. Since no vacancies appeared on the Court during his first term, leaving him unable to make an appointment, he proposed that the maximum size of the Court be increased to fifteen and that when a justice reached age seventy he be authorized to appoint an additional justice. The measure was defeated, however, when Republican and southern Democratic members of Congress formed a congressional coalition, the origin perhaps of the conservative coalition that prevailed on many domestic issues well beyond Roosevelt's days in the White House.

Leadership Style

Roosevelt had a very clear leadership orientation: he wanted to be at the center of action in his presidency while exercising strong leadership. He never thought of the possibility of undertaking his responsibilities in any other way. He loved politics, craved the limelight, and was totally comfortable in the vortex of power.

The Advisory Process and Approach to Decision Making

In recruiting his cabinet, FDR paid considerable attention to the traditional issues of geographic region and ideology. The selection of Cordell Hull to fill the position of secretary of state brought a southerner and advocate of lower tariffs to the cabinet. A leading conservative voice was provided by Henry Morgenthau, an FDR neighbor from New York, who served as secretary of the Treasury. Henry Wallace, an agriculture expert from Iowa, filled the important secretary of agriculture post. Labor Secretary Frances Perkins, the first female cabinet member, was initially opposed by labor. She came by way of the Roosevelt administration in New York. Harold Ickes, who had been involved with Progressive era reforms in Chicago, was the often rather cautious head of the Department of the Interior. For his postmaster general, Roosevelt followed common practice and selected Democratic Party leader James Farley. Filling the other cabinet posts were George Dern, secretary of war; Homer Cummings, attorney general; Claude Swanson, secretary of the navy; and Dariel Roper, secretary of commerce.

As in more recent administrations, Roosevelt's cabinet members were influential individually but rarely as a group. The evaluation of cabinet meetings by Harold Ickes echoed more recent experiences as he wrote:

> The cold fact is that on important matters we are seldom called upon for advice. We never discuss exhaustively any policy of Government or question of political strategy. The President makes all of his own decisions and, so far at least as the cabinet is concerned, without taking counsel with a group of advisers. On particular questions he will call into his office persons directly interested. . . . Our cabinet meetings are pleasant affairs, but we only skim the surface of things on routine matters. As a matter of fact, I never think of bringing up even a serious departmental issue at Cabinet meeting, and apparently the other members follow the same policy, at least to a considerable extent.[25]

Staff operations in the Roosevelt White House differed dramatically from the large operations that have become standard in more recent presidencies.[26] It consisted of only a few official positions; key roles were filled by people with formal appointments in various departments. Veteran Roosevelt confidant Louis Howe provided sage political advice. Raymond Moley filled an even broader role. A member of the group of Columbia University professors known as the "brain trust" who advised FDR during the 1932 campaign, he carried out duties that included some staff coordination, speech writing, and lobbying key members of Congress. Moley was known for being taciturn, tough, and intolerant of second-raters. As a result, he provided fodder for Washington jokes. One parodied a well-known hymn: "Moley, Moley, Moley, Lord God Almighty. . . ."[27] His influence eventually waned, however, and he later became a staunch critic of the New Deal.

FDR adviser Thomas Corcoran combined high intellectual ability, keen political skills, and a stamina that allowed him to work days and nights on end without rest. As often happens with top presidential advisers, he went on to become a prominent Washington lawyer and lobbyist known as "Tommy the Cork."

Harry Hopkins, a hard-driving social worker who had headed FDR's relief program in New York, was a key figure in the Roosevelt White House. As a sharp-tongued critic of bureaucratic red tape, Hopkins became famous for getting things done in a hurry. He was such a prominent adviser during World War II that he actually moved into the White House. On some issues, such as the scope of relief efforts, Hopkins was allied with Frances Perkins and First Lady Eleanor Roosevelt, an important domestic policy adviser.

In the wake of her extensive political involvement in the 1920s, the first lady viewed her move to the White House with some trepidation. She was deeply concerned that she would end up being confined to the traditional role of White House hostess. She moved quickly, then, to develop a distinctive niche. During FDR's first term, she promoted relief programs, in particular the National Youth Administration, and often served as "ombudsman" for people having difficulty with a particular domestic program. Mrs. Roosevelt traveled extensively as well, acting as the eyes and ears of the president. In fact, her reports and recommendations based on her travels and meetings with constituents became so extensive that the president periodically tried (without much success) to limit her memos to three a day. Along with relief issues, she was interested in policies that would help blacks. There is no evidence that she modified her husband's views, but the responses to her public actions helped FDR gauge public opinion.[28]

FDR's search for new policy ideas during his first term created a great deal of energy and enthusiasm nationwide. Lawyers, professors, state officials, a diverse cadre of interest group leaders, and some businessmen came to Washington with the hope of pursuing both the personal opportunities the policy search offered and the chance to change public policy at a crucial juncture in the nation's history. The president's strong desire for information was fed by the hundred some advisers who frequented the White House. He controlled their access himself, however, rather than working through a chief of staff. Senior staff characterized him in that role as "dominant, dramatic at times, animated, attentive, and friendly."[29] In his quest for new policy ideas, the president emphasized competition rather than formal processes. At points, more than one group would work on a given proposal. This method produced useful competition among advocates of different views, but it also produced bruised egos and considerable confusion.

Two patterns were apparent in Roosevelt's decision-making process. First, he was intensely concerned with the status of public opinion on various issues. According to Garry Wills, he had a strong desire not to get too far out in front.[30] Second, in making decisions about his legislative program, he engaged in extensive pre-submission consultation, particularly on which issues should go on his "must" list.

Administrative Strategies

Roosevelt's administrative strategies were an integral part of his presidency. He once underscored that importance by asserting, "A cabinet member may get along without much administrative ability, but a President can't."[31] One strategy was the use of competitive appointments to elicit different kinds of information. For example, he appointed both George Peek, a favorite of farmers, and Rexford Tugwell, his left-leaning brain trust confidant, to advise him on agriculture policy. By placing people in competitive situations, Roosevelt hoped to gain more information as they contested for his favor.

His second strategy was to establish new agencies—indeed, a record-setting sixty opened their doors during the first two years in office. According to A. J. Wann, Roosevelt took this step because he: (1) felt the existing departments had enough to do; (2) believed new agencies could give a new program full attention; (3) anticipated it would be easier to terminate a program; (4) hoped to attract talented people to the new agencies; and (5) saw the new agencies as a way to ensure that administrators with sympathies toward him and the Democratic Party would be in charge.[32]

More fundamentally, for Roosevelt administrative action was an essential tool in shaping policy implementation. Thus he often sought broad legislative enactments that would provide considerable administrative discretion. Acting on this broad authorization, the president and his executive departments and agencies could themselves decide how to carry out policy initiatives.

Perhaps Roosevelt's desire to experiment with policies through administrative action rather than tight legislative formulation is best illustrated by his relief and job policies. Several broad bills passed in 1933 provided the basis for shaping a wide variety of programs that included the Civilian Conservation Corps (CCC), the Public Works Administration (PWA), and the Federal Emergency Relief Administration (FERA). The CCC, a Roosevelt favorite, hired young men from urban areas and put them to work on public works projects such as public park expansion, erosion control, and reforestation. By 1942 the CCC had employed more than 3 million young men plus 250,000 veterans and had planted an estimated 75 percent of all the trees that had ever been planted in the country.[33]

The Public Works Administration was headed by Interior Secretary Harold Ickes. The PWA produced carefully designed projects, from new federal dams to several prominent buildings in Washington.

Roosevelt used the broad authority granted him by the 1933 legislation creating the Federal Emergency Relief Administration to experiment with a variety of approaches. In its first year (1933–1934) the program, run by Harry Hopkins, concentrated on getting money to the destitute quickly.

Roosevelt did not like the cost or the notion of a public dole, however, and created the Works Progress Administration (WPA) to quickly push work projects. Some were useful, but others reflected the tension between a desire to spend quickly and the need for carefully designed projects. Critics suggested that the agency's acronym stood for "We Piddle Around." Nevertheless, between 1935 and 1943 WPA construction projects included approximately 650,000 miles of highways, 125,000 public structures, and 125,000 bridges.

Other agencies and programs were created without additional legislation. The National Youth Administration (NYA), established in 1935, provided more than 2 million students with part-time jobs and assisted 2.5 million more who were not in school. In Texas, Lyndon Johnson, fresh from his Washington position as a congressional aide, became at age twenty-seven the youngest NYA director in the country. Another program included a project in which unemployed writers would produce histories of their states.

Roosevelt's administrative approach to relief and government job efforts has drawn various reviews—both favorable and unfavorable. Critics have lamented the lack of coordination, the poorly designed projects, and the inadequate efforts to develop necessary job skills. More sympathetic observers have emphasized the inherent difficulties involved in efforts to balance different objectives in creating government jobs.

Few have denied, however, that administrative adaptation was central to Roosevelt's approach. His administrative style gave him the substantial flexibility he sought and fit quite well his personality and the relatively small-scale operations of the federal government in the 1930s. That being said, confusion did sometimes occur, and his style ultimately intensified questions about the proper division of control between presidents and Congress over administrative agencies.

Public Leadership

Roosevelt's public role was a central component of his leadership efforts. In keeping with both his personality and his recognition that public attitudes were extremely important, he developed an optimistic persona—an obvious strategy for any president trying to lead a country during a difficult economic period. And his speaking skills and buoyant optimism, expressed quite intensely in the opening days of his administration, showed results. In fact, top aide Raymond Moley believed it "was the confidence of the public rather than any specific reforms that led to the recovery which followed." [34]

Roosevelt's "fireside chats" were central to his confidence-building efforts. This public relations device received its name in an unusual way. Offered two choices of radio introductions by Robert Trout of CBS, FDR enthusiastically chose the folksier one: "The President wants to come into your home and sit at your fireside for a little fireside chat." [35] His talks, usually given on Sunday night, sometimes were heard by almost half of the nation's population.

Roosevelt planned his fireside chats carefully. Generally less than a half-hour in length, they emphasized themes rather than specific factual information. Roosevelt also paid careful attention to his delivery, to the point in fact of inserting a false tooth in his mouth to achieve what he believed was a slightly better vocal quality. [36] The careful scheduling of his radio chats to maintain their special nature was a chief concern as well. During his first four years in office, he gave only eight fireside chats. An important indication of the extent to which his talks were used to reassure the public rather than to promote specific legislation was their timing: only four were given while Congress was in session.

FDR's first fireside chat on March 12, 1933 (only eight days after taking office), demonstrated both his skills and his tendency to focus on issues other than support for specific legislation. In that instance, he was not hoping to move a Congress that already had enacted the Emergency Banking Act; his major goal was to restore public confidence in the banks once they reopened. He said in part:

> It needs no prophet to tell you that when the people find that they can get their money—that they can get it when they want it for all legitimate purposes—the phantom of fear will soon be laid. People will again be glad to save their money where it will be safely taken care of and where they can use it conveniently at any time. I can assure you that it is safer to keep your money in a reopened bank than under the mattress. [37]

President Roosevelt also communicated with the public through the nation's newspapers. In fact, he held more press conferences than any of his successors. In contrast to today's large, televised conferences, FDR invited about two dozen reporters into the Oval Office, usually on Tuesdays and Fridays. Members of the press corps were flattered to be in the inner sanctum, where, aides hoped, they would be less apt to notice the president's wheelchair. As the reporters clustered around his desk, Roosevelt, generally quite relaxed, almost always answered questions easily and without hesitation. He seemed to genuinely enjoy the banter, as well as the pursuit of the angles that would make good stories. Enthusiasm for this format was so intense that the reporters actually broke into applause after the first conference. Using this mechanism, the president could promote favorable personal coverage and help steer publicity toward issues he was promoting in Congress.

Despite Roosevelt's skills, he could only shape newspaper coverage to a degree. By late 1934 his unusually lengthy honeymoon with the press corps had begun to fade. Roosevelt frequently asserted that he was opposed by 89 percent of the papers, but a study by Graham White produced a different conclusion. He found strong support for Roosevelt's early New Deal program, along with general and at times bitter, but by no means unqualified, opposition to the president's subsequent domestic programs.[38]

Congressional Leadership

The president spent a lot of time dealing with Congress, sometimes three to four hours on legislative matters in a given day. He worked very closely with party leaders in both houses and utilized other legislators such as Sen. James Byrnes, D-S.C., for vote-counting activities. From the White House Raymond Moley coordinated the administration's considerable legislative lobbying in 1933; by 1935 Thomas Corcoran had become FDR's primary lobbyist.

Of the unusually extensive range of legislative strategies and tactics favored by Roosevelt, the most far-reaching was to hold Congress in session throughout the spring of 1933 after the banking crisis was resolved. This tactic was part of an agenda-setting strategy that included careful attention to a presidential "must" list. Another key strategy consisted of sidestepping conflict over specific policy approaches in those areas in which the president wanted rapid congressional action. This strategy was carried out by introducing bills that had many different components to enhance their congressional support.

Yet another Roosevelt strategy entailed showing considerable flexibility in the coalitions he sought to create. During 1933 and 1934, despite some critics' outcries against his dangerous steps toward collectivism, Roosevelt pursued a centrist coalition strategy without any particular effort to push to the left. His "all class" coalition policies included not only relief and reform measures but also a sharp reduction in veterans' benefits and adoption of the national ethics codes for business favored by the U.S. Chamber of Commerce. In 1935, as he moved somewhat to the left, he spoke of a "tender sadness" as he looked back on his failed hope that "the leaders of finance and big business would learn something." [39] Even taking Roosevelt's third-year shift into account, Arthur Schlesinger characterized Roosevelt's coalitions as centrist, pointing out that "Roosevelt was opposed about as often on the left as on the right." [40]

Other strategies and tactics were aimed directly at members of Congress. For example, the White House would try to force action when a bill appeared to be stalled in committee, woo the support of various committee chairs, harness the parliamentary skills of several members of Congress from the South, encourage individual legislators to develop proposals on their own, and show a frequent willingness to compromise. In part because the many new members in Congress in both 1932 and 1934 were strongly committed to greater federal action, there is little evidence that the White House tried to change a large number of floor votes.

Legislative Enactments

The special session of Congress that extended from March 9 to June 16, 1933, and was known as the "First Hundred Days," produced a sweeping set of legislative responses to the horrendous problems created by the depression (see Table 2–1). Lawmakers passed landmark legislation in each of Roosevelt's first three years in office and again in 1938. One broad area of response was regulation. Economic regulation was used extensively to address the problems in key sectors such as agriculture, labor relations, and banking and stock market operations. Regulations also were introduced to cope with developments in communications stemming from sharp increases in radio use. Relief policies and the development of the landmark Social Security Act of 1935 were a second broad area of response.

Economy Act and Veterans' Benefits

Passage of the Economy Act in 1933 and the fight over veterans' benefits were evidence of Roosevelt's efforts to build an "all class" coalition that included conservative support. The employment- and salary-cutting provisions of the Economy Act, which Roosevelt had advocated in his

TABLE 2–1 Legislative Enactments during FDR's "First Hundred Days," 1933

March 9	Emergency Banking Act
March 10	Reconstruction Finance Corporation (expanded)
March 20	Economy Act
March 22	"Beer" Act
April 5	Civilian Conservation Corps
May 12	Agricultural Adjustment Act
	Emergency Mortgage Act
	Federal Emergency Relief Act
May 18	Tennessee Valley Authority
May 27	Securities Act
June 13	Home Owners Loan Act
June 16	National Industrial Recovery Act
	Railroad Coordination Act
	Banking Act

campaign, gave the president the authority to make major reductions in government employees and salaries. Projected salary cuts were in the 15 percent range, with projected savings of $100 million.

The fight over veterans' benefits began with the inclusion in the Economy Act of a commitment to major reductions. Veterans' benefits were hard to ignore if spending was to be cut because they constituted almost a quarter of the federal budget.[41] Roosevelt gained passage of the bill easily in the House, but he began to face resistance in the Senate. To aid his cause, he forcefully promoted the notion that he was willing to be the "whipping boy" of the veterans' lobby. His early popularity undoubtedly helped him to eventually achieve success with a reluctant Senate.

But Roosevelt's early victory did not end the controversy. A group of veterans gathered in Washington to press their demands, and some observers feared violence or a sad repeat of events in 1932 in which federal troops (acting on orders of Chief of Staff Douglas MacArthur rather than President Hoover) had forced World War I veterans, pressing for full payment of their war bonus certificates, to leave.[42] Roosevelt did not resort to such draconian measures. He sought early relief jobs for this group, and Eleanor Roosevelt visited veterans several times to boost morale. Ultimately the group left quietly. By the end of the special session, however, Congress had begun to worry about the next congressional election and so sought to reduce the size of the initial cuts. Lawmakers were surprised and concerned to learn that some veterans with war disabilities had suffered pension reductions far in excess of 25 percent. Faced with this situation, Congress forced Roosevelt to restore $100 million in cuts. Never-

theless, expenditures on veterans' benefits dropped more than 40 percent
between fiscal 1932 and 1934.

Agricultural Adjustment Act

Roosevelt spent much of 1933, and indeed his entire first term, pursuing
new policies for agriculture. Although modifications were required in the
wake of Supreme Court decisions, the landmark legislation that eventually emerged created an enduring system of assistance for some specific
crops such as wheat and cotton. Once again, the president enlisted multiple legislative strategies.

Despite the widespread desire for action, differences of opinion among
agricultural interests posed major problems for FDR just as they had during Hoover's largely unsuccessful efforts to provide leadership on farm
policy.[43] The advocates of dumping surpluses overseas were vocal. After
all, twice in the 1920s their ideas had been endorsed by Congress only to
fall victim to a presidential veto. Some farmers supported a protective tariff to protect them from lower-priced competition from foreign sources.
Yet another strategy, favored by some leading agricultural economists,
called for giving farmers financial incentives to reduce production in order
to raise prices. This approach had obvious appeal at a time when some
farmers found it economically more worthwhile to slit the throats of their
sheep and burn their crops than pay transportation costs to bring them to
market. Finally, some strategists proposed improving the farmers' plight
by promoting inflation. Higher prices would mean higher profits.

The plan Roosevelt proposed and Congress ultimately adopted called
for a new Agricultural Adjustment Agency (AAA) to pay farmers for taking cropland out of production or reducing their hog production. A processing tax leveled on a wide variety of food processors would finance the
program. While reduced production was central to the legislation, the bill
also allowed experimentation with a wide variety of other approaches, including overseas dumping.

Given the decade-long deadlock on agricultural policy, Roosevelt realized that only by exerting strong leadership would he see an agricultural
bill pass in the special session. The scope of the bill clearly helped to ensure its passage since various groups could see some possibility that their
approach would be used. Despite the alarm expressed by some conservatives about any movement toward deliberate inflation, Roosevelt was able

to mollify the advocates of inflation by accepting a vague amendment (which he never implemented) giving some legislative basis for their preferred approach. His budget director reflected conservative views when he stated in dismay, "Well, this is the end of Western civilization."[44] Another amendment pushed by the president would institute a highly popular program of mortgage relief for farmers.

Roosevelt employed many different tactics to ensure passage of the agriculture bill, beginning by sending key aides out to build a broad base of support among the often factious agriculture interest groups. Fortunately, interest group advocates had grown tired of the lengthy impasse that had prevented previous action and were anxious to find some grounds for compromise. Roosevelt also signaled his choice of George Peek, a favorite of many farmers, rather than the left-leaning Rexford Tugwell, to head the new agency. At a key juncture in the debate, he asked the Senate Agricultural Committee into his office in a successful effort to achieve a prompt reporting of his agriculture bill. When food processors and grain elevator operators began to put up stiff resistance to the new processing tax, Roosevelt and his key aides had to resort to further lobbying. Presidential leadership, in short, translated a general desire to do something about the plight of agriculture into landmark legislation.

Later, however, Supreme Court decisions forced reconsideration of agriculture policies. In the wake of a Court ruling against the Agricultural Adjustment Act in 1936, Roosevelt's aides consulted with agriculture interest groups and devised a modified approach organized around conservation objectives while maintaining the general thrust of financial incentives for reduced production. Because the Court decision had overturned the 1933 processing tax being used to finance the agriculture program, Congress and the White House had to look elsewhere in the budget for annual revenue of approximately $500,000. The new proposal, created in a frenzied effort by the Treasury Department, constituted a bold departure from the manner in which businesses had been taxed. After significant changes by congressional committees, a strong bill emerged which Roosevelt touted in the fall election.

Regulation of Financial Institutions

Efforts to regulate financial institutions produced the one instance of a "rubber stamp" Congress in 1933 but also repeated instances of significant congressional contributions. Passage of the Emergency Banking Act early in the "First Hundred Days" session of Congress found Roosevelt quickly borrowing ideas for legislation from departing Hoover administration officials who agreed to stay on to help draft the new measure. The legislation Roosevelt presented surprised some observers because of its conservative nature. The bill validated the actions the president already had taken, gave him complete control over the movement of gold, penalized hoarding, authorized the issue of new Federal Reserve bank notes, and arranged for the reopening of banks with liquid assets and reorganization of the rest.

Congress greeted this proposal with readiness for immediate action. With the bank holiday already in place, lawmakers knew they must act quickly to maintain public confidence that the banking crisis would be resolved. As a result, the House passed the bill, sight unseen, with a unanimous shout after only thirty-eight minutes of debate. Some senators protested that the legislation would give too much power to the large banks, but the Senate acted quickly nevertheless after limited debate, and the bill passed by a margin of 73–7. The legislation, then, was approved for Roosevelt's signature on the same day it was received on Capitol Hill.

Roosevelt also introduced landmark changes in the banking system, including modifying the role of the Federal Reserve system, prohibiting banks from selling securities, and creating the Federal Deposit Insurance Corporation. Although the president made no significant effort to promote the legislation and strongly opposed a key provision, these measures frequently are listed as one of the accomplishments of the first hundred days of his administration.

Roosevelt had a bigger role in a second landmark banking measure passed in 1935. He had encouraged Marriner Eccles, recently appointed chairman of the Federal Reserve Board, to develop the new banking bill. In the Senate, Carter Glass, D-Va., substantially modified Eccles's proposals. Roosevelt contributed to those negotiations by designating certain provisions "must" legislation. The final provisions substantially expanded the authority of the Federal Reserve Board in its relationships with the regional banks.[45]

The passage of securities industry regulations in 1933 and 1934 was yet another example of the joint efforts of Roosevelt and Congress to achieve fundamental changes in regulatory policy. Reform of the stock and bond sale procedures had been a popular plank in the 1932 Democratic platform, and a highly publicized congressional probe into Wall Street activities was igniting the public's anger and bringing additional attention to the issue. Once again, Roosevelt's regulatory proposal was based on plans solicited from various participants, leading to ruffled feathers. The text of the final bill reflected Benjamin Cohen's extensive knowledge of the British Companies Act. Quite coincidentally, Cohen, a member of FDR's brain trust, and his collaborator, James Landis, were staying in the same hotel as the main target of the congressional investigation, financier J. P. Morgan. The authors of the legislation were relieved that there was no sign of recognition when they occasionally shared an elevator.

When finally passed, the Securities Act of 1933 was an important first step toward transforming the nation's securities markets. It gave the Federal Trade Commission the power to supervise issues of new securities, required each new stock to be accompanied by a statement of relevant financial information, and made company directors liable for misrepresentation.

By 1934 Roosevelt had realized that more changes were needed. On February 9 the president asked Congress for legislation to regulate the New York Stock Exchange. To promote that process, he designed a bill more comprehensive than the one being considered by Congress. This development produced an indignant response from the business community. The president of the exchange proclaimed that it was "a perfect institution."[46] Financiers argued that the legislation would turn Wall Street into a deserted village, and some talked about moving their operations to Canada. Had public opinion polls been available, however, they likely would have shown widespread support for a major policy initiative. Public hostility toward the investment community was fueled in part by the realization that some large investors had employed a method known as "selling short" to profit from a decline in stock prices after an increase in the spring of 1933.

The new legislation, the Securities Exchange Act, created a Securities and Exchange Commission and gave that agency substantial regulatory authority. Key provisions expanded on the 1933 legislation and addressed issues such as the accuracy of information being given to prospective customers, the use of marginal purchases (which had been a major factor contributing to the 1929 stock market crash), and insider trading. Roosevelt selected Joseph P. Kennedy, a major financial contributor to his 1932 campaign and a shrewd operator within the business world, to head the new agency. Some observers viewed the appointment with skepticism; others preferred an agency head who knew the various "tricks of the trade."

Labor Policies

Policies addressing the nation's labor movement and working conditions, like many other policies, did not unfold smoothly. Toward the end of the "First Hundred Days" Roosevelt became alarmed when he learned that serious support had developed in the Senate for a thirty-hour workweek. To counteract this development, the president quickly proposed the National Industrial Recovery Act (NIRA), which was, in most respects, a movement to the right; it allowed the creation of pricing agreements for various sectors of the economy, called for fair competition codes for industry, barred child labor, fixed minimum wages, and recognized the right of collective bargaining by labor. In 1934 Roosevelt successfully opposed new legislation authored by Sen. Robert Wagner, D-N.Y., while also orchestrating passage of a resolution that authorized existing agencies covered by NIRA provisions to take a somewhat larger role during the next year on labor issues.[47]

When the new Congress convened in 1935, policies on labor–management relations became a major issue. In *Schechter Poultry Corporation v. United States* the Supreme Court had ruled that some provisions of the NIRA were unconstitutional.[48] While clearly desiring some protections for labor, Roosevelt nevertheless continued to resist an explicit endorsement of Senator Wagner's bill, known as the National Labor Relations Act. Troublesome issues for him included the explicit ban on company unions and the creation of a three-person National Labor Relations Board (empowered to administer the regulation of labor relations in industries engaged in or affecting interstate commerce) rather than placing the labor program in the Department of Labor. This was one of the relatively few instances in which the president was not in favor of a separate regulatory board.

Roosevelt continued to be coy and indecisive in various meetings with Senator Wagner and top labor leaders as the bill proceeded through committee hearings. At a press conference well after the basic components of the bill had been discussed extensively, he commented that he had "not given it any thought one way or the other."[49] The president seemed to be at least fairly supportive of the legislation, and the activism his New Deal created may have contributed to the moderate rise in unionization between 1933 and 1935. Although Roosevelt ultimately accepted key provisions of the proposed legislation, including the establishment of a separate labor relations board, Lawrence Chamberlain correctly argues that the same newspapers that had reported during the spring the president's wavering on the bill suddenly began giving him far too much credit for this landmark legislation.[50]

In keeping with his long interest in having government itself protect workers, Roosevelt was far more supportive of the federal minimum wage program established by the Fair Labor Standards Act.[51] He had been a proponent of minimum wage provisions in the industry codes negotiated under the NIRA and became an even stronger proponent when the Supreme Court eliminated those provisions in 1935. When specific legislation was submitted to Congress in 1937, Labor Secretary Frances Perkins was a forceful advocate. Nevertheless, considerable legislative maneuvering was required, in part because of some opposition by labor leaders to a measure they believed would undercut their ability to attract members and because of conflicts over questions such as whether to impose a lower minimum wage for the southern states. The legislation finally passed in 1938 called for a minimum wage of twenty-five cents an hour. All increases in the minimum wage since 1938 have been achieved by amending the original legislation.

Relief, Welfare, and Social Security

Attempts to deal with the human suffering caused by the depression generated substantial legislation in Roosevelt's first term. By proposing and achieving the congressional passage of not one but three relief and social welfare measures in 1933, Roosevelt established both the basis for the federal role in citizens' well-being that Hoover had staunchly resisted and the basis for considerable experimentation. Dissatisfaction with the ad hoc nature of many of these programs as early as 1934 produced interest in broader programs in both Congress and the White House. In the face of possible congressional action on aspects of what would become the Social Security Act of 1935, Roosevelt began his own planning process and worked to avoid preemptive congressional action.

The signing of the Social Security Act on August 14, 1935, brought into being a measure that Walter Lippmann described as "the most comprehensive program of reform ever achieved in this country in any administration." [52] Like the NIRA and the AAA, the act contained multiple components. The main ones were: (1) retirement benefits for citizens over the age of sixty-five who contributed to the Social Security fund through payroll deductions; (2) unemployment compensation shared by both the federal and state governments; and (3) means-tested, jointly operated welfare assistance for the needy in the categories of aged (not otherwise covered by the new system), blind, disabled, and dependent mothers and children. The Aid to Families with Dependent Children (AFDC) program built on the programs already adopted by all states except South Carolina and Georgia that extended at least meager aid to widows with children.[53]

Despite the large Democratic majorities in Congress, Roosevelt recognized that passage of a comprehensive social security measure would not be easy because of conflicting pressures. Conservatives were skeptical, and many southerners, politically responsive to economic interests in their states, feared that New Deal measures might disrupt the supply of cheap black labor. Those views would be a particular challenge because the House Ways and Means Committee was packed with southerners and led by a skeptic of many of FDR's programs. Yet other interests wanted a larger package than the president felt the federal government could afford. The concerns of the elderly were not hard to understand. They had been particularly hard-hit by the bank failures and lost savings. Yet to any serious student of government economics, the Townsend Plan, devised by Dr. Francis Townsend, an elderly California physician, was simply unrealistic. It called for the federal government to pay all citizens over age sixty a monthly pension of $200 and to finance the pension fund with a 2 percent tax on business transactions. Critics of the plan pointed out that the tax would be highly regressive and that over half of the nation's national income would go to only 9 percent of the population. Nevertheless, at least ten million people signed petitions supporting the plan. Thus for the president a fundamental challenge was to deter opponents of his proposal from the left and the right from blocking passage of any legislation.

Roosevelt and key aides worked diligently to develop the proposed legislation.[54] In seizing the initiative from Congress in 1934, he established a Committee on Economic Security (CES) chaired by Labor Secretary Frances Perkins. Other key members were Treasury Secretary Henry Morgenthau and relief administrator Harry Hopkins. Committee staff members were drawn, when possible, from states known for their political innovations and experimentation. For example, staffer Edwin Witte had been a key figure in Wisconsin's reform efforts. Significantly, the CES never included in any significant way the leading advocates of universal pensions for the elderly. With an eye toward southern states, Roosevelt also convened an advisory council chaired by a representative of that region.

The CES debated a state role in social security, but that approach was judged to be administratively unfeasible. The states did, however, have a major role in all other programs, including AFDC and unemployment compensation. This role stemmed from a combination of factors, including: a respect, shared by FDR, for the potential of state governments as policy innovators; a recognition that as of 1935 the federal government had a limited capacity for administrating a broad range of welfare programs; and a concern about which kinds of programs would be most likely to withstand a challenge in the Supreme Court.

Because the CES mandate was very broad, the White House considered including health insurance in the social security legislation. During the fall, the committee briefly examined a possible health insurance component, but some leaders of the American Medical Association protested vehemently. Roosevelt reacted to their protest by sending a clear signal to Frances Perkins that he did not want his proposal to include a health insurance component.

Roosevelt had spoken to Perkins quite emphatically about wanting broad social security coverage for the elderly, but he also was deeply concerned about financing mechanisms. He gravitated toward a payroll program modeled on private pensions, in part because the size of the existing deficit produced little enthusiasm for a plan financed from general tax revenues. (He also preferred the pension approach because he felt that its similarity to private pension plans would make his new program easier to sell.) Finally, Roosevelt concluded that use of a separate financing mechanism would deter politicians from tampering with the program in the future. "We put those payroll contributions there so as to give the contributors a legal, moral, and political right to collect their pensions and unemployment benefits," the president explained. "With those taxes in there, no damn politician can ever scrap my social security program." [55] Yet Roosevelt was concerned about future costs, and this led to a last-minute scaling back of the proposal. Roosevelt readily agreed to Morgenthau's proposed changes in the bill he had submitted and stated, "It is almost dishonest to build up an accumulated deficit for the Congress of the United States to meet in 1980. We can't sell the United States short in 1980 any more than in 1935." [56] Morgenthau then testified before the

House Ways and Means Committee and recommended an increase in the initial tax from 0.5 percent to 1 percent and a commitment to building up a large trust fund.

Congress passed Roosevelt's social security measure only after a variety of maneuvers by the White House. For example, Roosevelt fought unsuccessfully to have the bill considered by a single committee. Edwin Witte and Frances Perkins, who represented CES, made strong presentations, but the House committee also heard emotional testimony by advocates of the Townsend Plan.

Other Significant Legislation

Three other landmark measures also were enacted during Roosevelt's years in the White House. In 1934 Congress created the Federal Communications Commission (FCC), which assumed responsibility for regulating the radio broadcasting industry—a role formerly carried out on a modest scale by the Federal Radio Commission. In its lame-duck session before Roosevelt's inaugural in 1933, Congress had tried to expand the Radio Commission's regulatory powers over the nation's rapidly growing radio industry, but Hoover, who appeared to resent changes in the legislation he had developed as secretary of commerce, exercised a "pocket veto" by refusing to sign the legislation at the end of the session.

A second landmark measure was the 1934 National Housing Act. In 1933 Congress had indicated its willingness to act in the housing area by passing provisions to protect both farmers and urban dwellers from foreclosure. It was anxious to act again in 1934. Roosevelt proposed establishing a Federal Housing Agency that would guarantee home mortgages made by savings and loan institutions. In addition, a mandatory system of building inspection would protect purchasers from shoddy construction practices—all too common for moderate-income dwellings. In assessing the scope of the National Housing Act, housing policy expert Joseph L. Arnold pronounced it a landmark enactment.[57] The importance of this legislation was stressed in presidential messages to Congress in 1934. Among rank and file citizens who had witnessed the decline in home ownership and the proliferation of highly unstable home financing arrangements, sentiment for reform was strong. The act also was easy to promote because it would generate employment in the home construction industry as well as direct housing assistance. The real estate lobby, which had opposed some of Roosevelt's policies, also endorsed this legislation.

The third landmark measure was the 1944 G.I. Bill of Rights. This measure provided war veterans with educational assistance, from secondary schooling to college, and housing assistance. This uniquely successful domestic policy both aided veterans and relieved a potential labor surplus by having significant numbers of World War II veterans enter colleges and universities rather than the labor market.

Two other measures passed in Roosevelt's first term—one creating the Tennessee Valley Authority (TVA) and the other increasing taxes—help to underscore the manner in which the president and Congress were contributing to major policy enactments. The establishment of the TVA in 1933 was an important example of the collaboration characteristic of the first hundred days of Roosevelt's term. Shortly before his inauguration, Roosevelt and Sen. George Norris, an Independent Republican from Nebraska and a leading progressive, visited the Muscle Shoals site on the Tennessee River being considered as the location for a major hydroelectric power plant. FDR encouraged Senator Norris to raise his sights and pursue a program larger than the one proposed in his earlier bill vetoed by Hoover. Roosevelt believed the TVA project would fill two needs: it would serve as a "yardstick" for measuring the electric costs being charged by private utilities, and it would provide conservation and regional development in a rather backward area. Encouraged, Norris proceeded to draft a very comprehensive legislative proposal which FDR supported.

In the legislative battle that followed, the private utility industry proposed amendments designed to scale back the project. They fought especially hard for provisions to restrict the use of TVA transmission lines. Senator Norris, however, played a key role in gaining Senate passage. President Roosevelt took a particular interest in the activities of the conference committee that was reconciling the House and Senate versions of the bill. He made it clear that he strongly opposed restrictions on TVA's use of transmission lines. The president's position held and the sweeping TVA proposal became a major new regional policy.

The Revenue Act that Congress passed in August 1935 was an indication of the persistence with which FDR pursued his third-year shift toward the left and the nature of his legislative leadership. The Treasury Department had been developing some changes in the tax laws, but the president indicated in January 1935 that he was not interested, and he did not mention a tax plan in his January State of the Union address.

On June 19, in a surprise tax message to Congress, Roosevelt attacked the revenue system as having "done little to prevent an unjust concentration of wealth and economic power." He went on to endorse "the very sound policy of encouraging a wide distribution on wealth." When the Senate clerk finished reading the speech, only Sen. Huey Long spoke: "Mr. President, before the President's message is referred to the Committee on Finance, I just wish to say, Amen!"[58]

The proposal was popular with the Americans who were followers of Huey Long and others who blamed business leaders and the wealthy for the country's economic plight. The proposal drew outcries, however, from wealthy Americans and corporate officials. Millionaire newspaper publisher William Randolph Hearst directed his editors to call Roosevelt's proposal a "Soak the Successful" tax plan. His newspapers and many others also labeled the legislation "The Wealth Tax of 1935."

Inside Congress, views were mixed. It was quite evident that Sen. Bryon Harrison, D-Miss., chairman of the Senate Finance Committee, was expressing the president's views rather than his own when he advocated the bill. For some members the legislation raised conflicts about its impact on their campaign contributors. Some of the more radical members charged that the proposal was a hoax. Outside Congress, the weather was a factor. It was a typically hot July in Washington, and lawmakers were having to remain in town to consider yet another piece of major legislation.

After his initial proposal, Roosevelt became more cautious. He refused to respond to a letter from Senator Long asking for details about his preferences, and Treasury Secretary Henry Morgenthau was fairly noncommittal in hearings before the tax committees of both houses of Congress. In a conversation with Morgenthau, the president also indicated neither a concern for legislative bargaining nor a genuine reluctance to see the establishment of his proposed inheritance tax. When Morgenthau asked the president whether he really wanted the inheritance tax passed, he responded: "Strictly between the two of us, I do not know. I am on an hourly basis and the situation changes almost momentarily."[59]

The president's bill fared well in the House Ways and Means Committee and moved quite easily to the House floor. The Senate Finance Committee, however, was not ready to accept a major new bill on such short notice, and it voted to remove the inheritance tax provision. Rather than initiating a new tax on short notice, it proposed to increase the existing estate tax. Once the inheritance tax provision had been removed, the legislation moved fairly quickly through the Senate, and the House relented on the inheritance tax issue when the conference committee convened. The final bill provided for major—not landmark—changes in tax policies. Key provisions included: a graduated corporation tax (from 12.5 to 15 percent); a tax on corporate dividends; a significant increase in estate and gift taxes; and an increase in surtax rates on incomes over $500,000.

In abruptly raising the tax issue, Roosevelt had created a major item on the congressional agenda. And he had promoted the bill with an unusually strong appeal for income redistribution rather than deficit reduction. Yet despite cries from the wealthy that Roosevelt was a "traitor to his class," the results were certainly not revolutionary. Some critics viewed the tax bill as a largely symbolic effort; others noted that it did little more than modify the greater regressiveness at the state level stemming from the increased use of sales taxes.

Roosevelt and Congress

President Roosevelt relied heavily on strategies in dealing with Congress. They included getting off to an extraordinarily fast start in 1933, designing legislation that appealed to multiple interests, agenda setting with his "must" list, assembling centralist coalitions in 1933–1934 followed by a shift to the left in 1935, and exerting public leadership in order to sustain general support for his presidency and his legislative initiatives. Interestingly, the Roosevelt White House made few efforts to sell specific legislative measures to the public. And any attempts to persuade individual legislators were reserved more often for committee votes than for final floor votes.

Yet Congress also made immense contributions. In 1933, for example, it moved ahead with the Banking Act despite Roosevelt's reluctance, and he was forced into proposing the National Industrial Recovery Act because of his fears that a thirty-hour workweek bill would pass. Often, issues were pushed by forces Roosevelt sought to corral rather than by his deliberate actions. Some fundamental legislation, including the landmark National Labor Relations Act (also known as the Wagner Act), was enacted without any direct presidential support. Recognizing that Congress's role was sometimes inappropriately characterized as a rubber stamp, historian Alberto Romasco aptly concluded that "the nature of the early New Deal was decisively influenced by the ongoing cooperation, rivalry, and spirit of bargaining and compromise which characterized the relationship between Roosevelt and . . . the 73rd Congress." [60]

According to George Edwards III, the president's predominant role in policy making is that of a facilitator rather than a director of policy change.[61] This view fits the Roosevelt case. In the process of trying new policies, Roosevelt created an environment in his relationships with Congress in which not only his personal staff but also agency heads, legislative specialists in Congress, state officials who had knowledge of specific programs, and interest group leaders both to the right and left of Roosevelt all had important influences in shaping far-reaching changes in domestic policy.

An Assessment

One forceful assessment of the New Deal was Roosevelt's landslide victory in the 1936 election. In gaining reelection, he engineered an enduring "inclusive coalition," brought together through his first-term policy achievements and his public leadership. Farmers were attracted by his administration's efforts to help blacks and agriculture; urban workers were attracted by relief programs and the Wagner Act; and westerners were fans of his conservation measures. The National Youth Administration, established by executive order in 1935 to furnish high school and college students with part-time jobs, appeared to have had an impact on the younger voters. Roosevelt also did very well with Jewish voters, which reflected in part his willingness to appoint Jews to the upper levels of his administration.[62] The strength of that coalition was apparent not only in Roosevelt's 1940 and 1944 election victories, but also in President Harry Truman's ability to achieve his come-from-behind victory in 1948.

A fundamental expansion of economic regulation was at the heart of New Deal domestic policy. Roosevelt may not have always been the dominant figure, but he usually was a significant contributor. In agriculture, the first policy steps were taken amid considerable confusion. Plowed-under crops and the slaughter of young pigs (even though some of the pork was used in relief programs) created a negative public image. Nevertheless, in part with the aid of New Deal policies, the price of both cotton and tobacco almost doubled by 1936 from its lowest level in 1933. More fundamentally, Roosevelt's agriculture policies, beginning with the broad Agricultural Adjustment Act of 1933, became the basis for subsequent price and planting controls. With only moderate adjustments, these policies continued until the 1990s.

The expanded regulation of financial institutions that took effect in the early Roosevelt years produced landmark changes in the banking system, including the establishment of deposit insurance. Americans quickly accepted the regulation of financial institutions and greeted with enthusiasm the regulation and protection of home mortgages which became an extremely popular vehicle for expanding home ownership.

Other regulatory policies also had transforming impacts. Most notably, the establishment of the National Labor Relations Board and the provisions of the Wagner Act led to the rapid unionization of basic industries during the late 1930s and a far stronger labor movement after World War II. Union membership increased from some three million in 1936 to over eight million in 1941 and fourteen million by 1945.

The New Deal social policy producing the longest-lasting legacy was the Social Security Act. Each of its components, with the exception of the controversial Aid for Families with Dependent Children program, was intact well into the 1990s. Unemployment insurance was less controversial. The basic pension program for the elderly, which was substantially modified not only in 1939 but also in later decades, proved to be the most prominent part of the 1935 legislation and one of the New Deal's most popular programs. In this instance, Roosevelt's choice of an insurance model for recipients of Social Security provided the basis for a far broader program than was envisioned at the time by critics who preferred immediate universal pensions. Over the years, Social Security became the one area of social spending in which American policy efforts rivaled those of the more generous social welfare states.

The slow pace of Roosevelt's efforts to assist blacks, especially when faced with the vigilante lynchings of blacks, has raised the possibility of unused opportunities. One key issue in the 1930s was antilynching legislation; about twenty lynchings occurred a year in the early 1930s before falling to about two a year at the end of the decade.[63] The House could muster support for the legislation, but passage by the Senate was hampered by the likelihood of a southern filibuster. In the face of continuing tragedies and some support from religious groups and leaders of the National Association for the Advancement of Colored People (NAACP), Roosevelt agreed in 1934 to meet with NAACP leader Walter White. The president explained to White that "southerners, by reason of the seniority rule in Congress, are chairmen or occupy strategic positions on most of the Senate and House Committees. If I come out for the anti-lynching bill, they will block every bill I ask to keep America from collapsing. I just can't take that risk. . . . Whatever you can get done is okay with me, but I just can't do it."[64] Yet Roosevelt continued to denounce the lynchings, and, finally, after more encouragement he indicated his willingness to sup-

port an antilynching bill provided it did not tie up other reform legislation. But he declined to place an antilynching bill in his category of "must"
legislation, and, in the end, efforts to pass antilynching legislation were
unsuccessful.[65]

Using administrative strategies, the Roosevelt White House apparently did by the late 1930s succeed in reducing discrimination and extending some aid to blacks; disparities between whites and blacks did decline somewhat.[66] For many blacks, however, Roosevelt acted too slowly.
Only reluctantly did he yield finally to pressure to establish a Federal Employment Practices Commission in 1941.

The biggest disappointment for Roosevelt and the nation was the modest extent to which the country's economy improved during the 1930s.
While the economy did grow significantly, the unemployment record was
poor. The gross domestic product increased from $58.3 billion in 1933
to $82.5 billion in 1936 and $100.5 billion in 1940, but the unemployment figures never dropped below 14 percent before World War II, and
the averages for Roosevelt's first and second terms were 22.8 percent and
18 percent.

Given the economic policy options available during the early 1930s,
the president did not miss an obvious opportunity. When the Social Security tax contributed to a major recession in 1937, Roosevelt became
more convinced of the importance of fiscal policy. Nevertheless, because
he showed more interest in such ideas than members of Congress, they
could not be successfully promoted.

Roosevelt often has been criticized for not developing a clear philosophy for his New Deal to guide his policy directions. But, given the tremendous lack of agreement on specific policies among policy advocates and
members of Congress during Roosevelt's first term, the charge of a lack of
direction warrants considerable skepticism. In that setting, efforts to pursue a single course that included strong government action would have
raised profound questions about the degree of influence a president should
be able to assert.

In shaping New Deal policy responses, Roosevelt showed numerous
skills—and some flaws. He sought ideas from a wide variety of sources,
pursued active and ongoing congressional leadership with an impressive
range of strategies, parlayed his fireside chats into an effective communications device, and often molded final policy impacts through the use of
administrative strategies. In his legislative leadership, FDR's level of influence did have its negative consequences as various members of Congress

grew to resent his degree of control. That resentment was particularly strong in 1935 as the president began to change policy directions. One junior senator who spent his first months in office watching Roosevelt engage in that switch and who observed his tactics for ten more years would conclude that a president ought to show more respect for the independence of Congress. The views of that junior senator from Missouri, Harry Truman, would take on considerable importance after he took the oath of office in 1945.

In his decision-making process and administrative strategies, Roosevelt's effort to "manipulate uncertainty," as Arthur Schlesinger used the phrase, also has continued to draw criticism. At points, this strategy created confusion and resentment. For some, Truman's very forthright approach was seen as a welcome change from Roosevelt's sometimes overly elaborate maneuvering. The vast expansion of the federal government in recent decades has rendered this aspect of Roosevelt's leadership style far less feasible for today's presidents.

Ultimately, assessments of Roosevelt's performance often come back to the importance of his public roles. For Garry Wills, Roosevelt's ability to reassure was the real strength of the New Deal.[67] Bruce Miroff more broadly concluded, "Although Roosevelt could not vanquish the Great Depression, his administration relieved the worst of mass distress, while restoring confidence in the power of democracy to meet both the material and moral needs of its citizens."[68]

How well did FDR play the hand dealt him? Overall, very well. He was a high-opportunity/high-achievement president who cast a giant shadow over all who followed him into the White House.

Notes

1. The discussion of Roosevelt's early experiences are drawn in part from Frank Freidel, *Franklin D. Roosevelt: A Rendezvous with Destiny* (Boston: Little, Brown, 1990).

2. James MacGregor Burns, *Roosevelt: The Lion and the Fox* (New York: Harvest/HBJ, 1984).

3. Earl Black and Merle Black, *The Vital South: How Presidents Are Elected* (Cambridge: Harvard University Press, 1992), 90.

4. Arthur M. Schlesinger Jr., *The Age of Roosevelt* (Boston: Houghton Mifflin, 1958), chap. 35.

5. Frances Perkins, *The Roosevelt I Knew* (New York: Viking Press, 1946), 3.

6. Bruce Miroff, *Icons of Democracy: American Leaders as Heroes, Aristocrats, Dissenters, and Democrats* (New York: Basic Books, 1993), 235.

7. Quoted in ibid., 10.

8. Garry Wills, *Certain Trumpets: The Call of Leaders* (New York: Simon and Schuster, 1994), 26.

9. Miroff, *Icons of Democracy*, 236.

10. A. J. Wann, *The President as Chief Administrator* (Washington, D.C.: Public Affairs Press, 1968).

11. Schlesinger, *Age of Roosevelt*, 554.

12. Burns, *Roosevelt*, 157.

13. Ibid., 237.

14. Freidel, *Franklin D. Roosevelt*, 92.

15. William Leuchtenberg, *Franklin D. Roosevelt and the New Deal* (New York: Harper and Row, 1963); and Richard S. Kirkendall, *The United States, 1929–1945: Years of Crisis and Change* (New York: McGraw-Hill, 1974).

16. Robert H. Ferrell, *American Diplomacy: The Twentieth Century* (New York: Norton, 1988), 185.

17. Kenneth S. Davis, *FDR: The New Deal Years, 1933–1937* (New York: Random House, 1995), 571.

18. George Gallup, *Gallup Poll Monthly Report, 1935–1971* (New York: Random House, 1972), 1.

19. Clarke E. Chambers, *Seedtime for Reform: American Social Science and Social Action, 1918–1933* (Minneapolis: University of Minnesota Press, 1963); and Theda Skocpol, *Protecting Soldiers and Mothers: The Political Origins of Social Policy in the U.S.* (Cambridge: Harvard University Press, 1992).

20. For representative discussions, see Robert B. Carson, *What Economists Know: An Economic Policy Primer for the 1990s and Beyond* (New York: St. Martin's Press, 1990), chaps. 3 and 5; and Kirkendall, *United States, 1929–1945.*

21. For a recent review of options that were considered, see Colin Gordon, *New Deals: Business, Labor, and Politics in America, 1920–1935* (New York: Cambridge University Press, 1994), chap. 1.

22. For a review of economic knowledge at the time, see Carson, *What Economists Know*, chap. 3.

23. Herbert Stein, *Presidential Economics: The Making of Economic Policy from Roosevelt to Reagan and Beyond* (Washington, D.C.: American Enterprise Institute, 1988).

24. Carson, *What Economists Know*, 17.

25. Harold L. Ickes, *The Secret Diaries of Harold L. Ickes: The First Thousand Days, 1933–1936* (New York: Simon and Schuster, 1953), 308.

26. This discussion of Roosevelt's staff structure draws in part from Charles E. Walcott and Karen M. Hult, *Governing the White House: From Hoover through LBJ* (Lawrence: University Press of Kansas, 1995).

27. Patrick Anderson, *The Presidents' Men: White House Assistants of Franklin D. Roosevelt, Harry S. Truman, Dwight D. Eisenhower, John F. Kennedy, and Lyndon B. Johnson* (Garden City, N.Y.: Doubleday, 1968), 25.

28. Joan Hoff-Wilson and Marjorie Lightman, eds., *Without Precedent: The Life and Career of Eleanor Roosevelt* (Bloomington: Indiana University Press, 1984).

29. Patricia D. Witherspoon, *Within These Walls: A Study of Communication between Presidents and Their Senior Staff* (New York: Praeger, 1991), 14.

30. Garry Wills, "What Makes a Good Leader," in *Understanding the Presidency,* ed. James P. Pfiffner and Roger H. Davidson (New York: Longman, 1997), 440–444.

31. Wann, *President as Chief Administrator,* 11.

32. Ibid.

33. Otis L. Graham Jr. and Meghan Robinson Wander, eds. *Franklin Roosevelt: His Life and Times, An Encyclopedic View* (New York: G. K. Hall, 1985), 63.

34. Raymond Moley, *After Seven Years* (New York: Harper, 1939).

35. Davis, *FDR,* 60.

36. Betty H. Winfield, *FDR and the News Media* (New York: Columbia University Press, 1994).

37. Halford Ryan, *American Rhetoric from Roosevelt* (Prospect Heights, Ill.: Waveland Press, 1986), 231.

38. Graham J. White, *FDR and the Press* (Chicago: University of Chicago Press, 1979), 91.

39. Ibid., 512.

40. Schlesinger, *Age of Roosevelt,* 555.

41. Ibid., 239.

42. Martin L. Fausold, *The Presidency of Herbert C. Hoover* (Lawrence: University Press of Kansas, 1985), 201–203.

43. On agricultural politics, see Alberto U. Romasco, *The Politics of Recovery: Roosevelt's New Deal* (New York: Oxford University Press, 1983); and Rexford Tugwell, *Roosevelt's Revolution: The First Year—A Personal Perspective* (New York: Macmillan, 1977).

44. Leuchtenberg, *Franklin D. Roosevelt and the New Deal,* 50.

45. Sidney Hyman, *Marriner S. Eccles: Private Entrepreneur and Public Servant* (Stanford, Calif.: Stanford University Graduate School of Business, 1976), 181–189.

46. Leuchtenberg, *Franklin D. Roosevelt and the New Deal,* 90.

47. Lawrence H. Chamberlain, *The President, Congress and Legislation* (New York: AMS Press, 1967), 170.

48. *Schechter Poultry Corporation v. United States,* 295 U.S. 495 (1935).

49. Davis, *FDR,* 528.

50. Chamberlain, *The President,* 175.

51. Willis J. Nordlund, *The Quest for a Living Wage: The History of the Federal Minimum Wage Program* (Westport, Conn.: Greenwood Press, 1997), chap. 3.

52. Quoted in Davis, *FDR,* 523.

53. Walter I. Trattner, *From Poor Law to Welfare State: A History of Social Welfare in America,* 4th ed. (New York: Free Press, 1989), 202.

54. Sources used for this case include J. Altmeyer, *The Formative Years of Social Security* (Madison: University of Wisconsin Press, 1968); Perkins, *The Roosevelt I Knew;* Edwin L. Witte, *The Development of the Social Security Act* (Madison: University of Wisconsin Press, 1963); Henry J. Pratt, *Gray Lobby* (Chicago: University of Chicago Press, 1976); Jill Quadagno, *The Transformation of*

Old Age Security: Class and Politics in the American Welfare State (Chicago: University of Chicago Press, 1988); and John B. Williamson and Fred C. Pampel, *Old-Age Security in Comparative Perspective* (New York: Oxford University Press, 1993).

55. Freidel, *Franklin D. Roosevelt*, 150.

56. Davis, *FDR*, 460.

57. Joseph L. Arnold, "Housing and Resettlement," in Graham and Wander, *Franklin Roosevelt*, 187.

58. This account is drawn in part from John F. Witte, *The Politics and Development of the Federal Income Tax* (Madison: University of Wisconsin Press, 1985).

59. John Morton Blum, *From the Morgenthau Diaries: Years of Crisis, 1928–1938* (Boston: Houghton Mifflin, 1959), 303.

60. Romasco, *Politics of Recovery*, 27.

61. George C. Edwards III, *At the Margins: Presidential Leadership of Congress* (New Haven: Yale University Press, 1989), 223.

62. Election statistics are drawn from William E. Leuchtenberg, "The Presidential Election of 1936," in *History of American Presidential Elections, 1789–1968*, vol. 3, ed. Arthur M. Schlesinger Jr. (New York: McGraw-Hill, 1971).

63. Freidel, *Franklin D. Roosevelt*, 83.

64. Quoted in Davis, *FDR*, 484.

65. Leuchtenberg, *Franklin D. Roosevelt and the New Deal*, 186.

66. Bruce J. Schulman, *From Cotton Belt to Sunbelt: Federal Policy, Economic Development, the Transformation of the South, 1938–1980* (New York: Oxford University Press, 1991).

67. Garry Wills, "What Is a Political Leader?" *Atlantic*, April 1994, 79.

68. Miroff, *Icons of Democracy*, 233.

3

You've got to give it all you can that first year. Doesn't matter
what kind of majority you come in with. You've got just one
year when they treat you right, and before they start
worrying about themselves.

— LYNDON B. JOHNSON

Lyndon B. Johnson

Legislative Leadership
and a Credibility Gap

ON MARCH 31, 1968, Lyndon Johnson (served 1963–1969) stunned a nation weary of the Vietnam War and urban unrest with this nationally televised announcement: "I shall not seek—nor will I accept—the nomination of my party for another term in this great office of all the people." [1] He only went public with his decision after Sen. Eugene McCarthy, D-Minn., made a surprisingly strong showing in the March 1968 New Hampshire primary. Just four years earlier Johnson had been widely praised as a masterful legislative leader and one of the truly great presidents of the twentieth century. In fact, 1964–1965 had produced by far the biggest outpouring of new legislation since FDR's first term. Then things fell apart. Johnson went from high-opportunity/high-achievement president to political villain in a few short years. Lady Bird Johnson pronounced her husband's White House years as "the best of times, the worst of times." Johnson's leadership skills—and his limitations—were an essential part of the story of this eventful period.

Personal Characteristics

The lanky, six-foot five-inch Lyndon Baines Johnson (1908–1973) was a product of both Texas and Washington. He was raised in the Texas hill country west of Austin by a mother with high ambitions for her son and a father with a populist political orientation and a career that included ranching, real estate, state lawmaking, and service in a low-paying state job. After Johnson graduated from a small, unaccredited high school, he spent a year in California and then attended Southwest Texas State Teachers College rather than the more prestigious University of Texas at Austin. In college he was a largely indifferent student, but he spent long hours talking with one of his political science professors. He also enjoyed campus politics, became an influential figure on campus while an aide in the president's office, and observed the state legislature in nearby Austin. Lyndon was a young man in a hurry as well; he graduated in only two and a half years. Before pursuing a life in politics, he became the only president after Herbert Hoover to teach in a secondary school—both in a poor rural school composed largely of Hispanic students and later in Houston. In these early years Johnson was highly active in local politics. He got his start in national politics by gaining a congressional staff position after working on a local campaign.[2]

Career Path

Johnson had more extensive political experience in Washington than any other post-Hoover president. With the exception of the two years he spent as the Texas administrator for President Franklin Roosevelt's National Youth Administration, he held various positions on Capitol Hill from that of a staff aide beginning in late 1931 to Senate majority leader from 1955 to 1961, the year he became vice president. During those years Johnson showed not only intense ambition but also considerable skill in seeking out mentors who could both teach him the art of politics and help him to advance his career. That list included Sam Rayburn, D-Texas, who served as Speaker of the House on and off between 1940 and 1961; Sen. Richard Russell, D-Ga., the acknowledged dean of the southern senators; and to some degree President Roosevelt himself.

Lyndon's earliest days on the Hill found him working long days and nights as he quickly learned the ropes in the office of Rep. Richard Kleberg, D-Texas, and then often ran the place. All the while he was observing Roosevelt's early leadership of Congress with fascination. In 1934 he met and married Claudia "Lady Bird" Taylor, the daughter of a successful Texas farmer and merchant. In 1935, with the help of Sam Rayburn, Johnson was appointed as the nation's youngest state director of Roosevelt's newly created National Youth Administration.

When his local member of Congress died in 1937, Johnson rushed into an aggressive candidacy in which he literally talked himself to exhaustion but won the coveted House seat. LBJ was viewed as a "comer" by Roosevelt, and through the influence of both fellow Texan Rayburn and Roosevelt he gained important committee assignments. Frustrated, however, with the seniority system in the House he sought a Texas Senate seat unsuccessfully in a special election held in 1941. He was luckier in 1948, although he won by a narrow margin, earning him the nickname "Landslide Lyndon." The election results were challenged by his opponent.

In the 1930s LBJ had been a staunch New Dealer on economic issues, but in the 1940s he began to vote more conservatively as both Texas and the nation became less supportive of the New Deal agenda. Among other things, he went along with popular sentiment in Texas and voted for the 1947 Taft-Hartley Labor Act and against federal civil rights actions such as antilynching laws.

Johnson's Senate career reached a new height in 1953 when he became its surprisingly young minority leader; two years later he was selected majority leader. LBJ built that position into one of greater influence and generally has been regarded as one of the modern Senate's most effective party leaders. The techniques he used as majority leader resembled those he used so effectively later as president. For example, he prided himself on an extensive information system that included detailed knowledge of what the Republicans were up to. And from time to time he engineered vote trades by arranging aid for a given senator's state, but he preferred to find ways he could gain the needed vote without asking a senator to thwart strong constituency sentiment. Finally, Johnson built loyalty among junior members with good committee assignments, and he was a master at dealing with legislative procedures.[3]

LBJ's move to the presidency actually began with his belated bid for the party's nomination in 1960. But his efforts to capitalize on his Washington influence were no match for the strong primary performance by Sen. John Kennedy, D-Mass. After Kennedy turned to Johnson to take the second place on the ticket in an effort to shore up his support in the South, LBJ campaigned diligently in the fall election.

As vice president, Johnson was not a part of Kennedy's inner circle nor did Kennedy use Johnson in a major way in dealing with the Senate. He believed it would produce resentment from that chamber. The tragic events in Dallas on November 22, 1963, however, changed everything.

What Manner of Man?

The drive for power that Johnson had displayed throughout his career was both intense and rooted in personal insecurity. He had virtually no hobbies other than politics and the pursuit of business deals that had made him a very wealthy man by the time he became president. His energy seemed boundless, yet at points he drove himself to the point of exhaustion. During his first weeks in the presidency, for example, he seldom slept more than three or four hours a night. His long-standing routine was to begin work about seven, take a nap about four, and then continue working well into the evening. Sixteen- to eighteen-hour days were not uncommon.

Johnson's insecurities often have been traced to early childhood experiences in which his mother, who was a descendent of a fairly prominent Texas family, sought to compensate for her own downward social mobility with her aspirations for Lyndon.[4] Apparently, her high aspirations, coupled with little expression of parental love, shaped both his insecurities and his intense desire to succeed. But whatever the precise causes, Johnson was a man with many resentments. His targets included those with a better education than he had had—including in particular the "Harvard crowd" around Kennedy—and a press corps he felt paid too much attention to his failings. Because of his frequent mood swings, some writers have concluded that he suffered from aspects of a manic-depressive personality.[5]

The president's relationships with other individuals were complex. He thoroughly enjoyed the process of manipulation and often was extremely effective in one-on-one situations as he combined his legendary arm-twisting with carefully reasoned arguments. He also enjoyed occasional vulgarity, as when he would comment to an aide who had just seen a leading senator, "Open your fly. The senator has your pecker in his pocket." Some young aides also were startled when he continued to dictate notes from a toilet seat. And he could be cruel, as when he forced Vice President Hubert Humphrey to shoot a deer on the LBJ Ranch specifically because he knew Humphrey would hate the act. Yet he often seemed to view staff as "family" and could, on occasion, be quite caring when they faced difficulties. Loyal staff aides learned to ignore his tirades, while some, such as Wilbur Cohen, simply concluded that it was interesting to work for a complex person. Top aide Joseph Califano captured his many dimensions when he wrote, "The LBJ I worked with was brave and brutal, compassionate and cruel, incredibly intelligent and infuriatingly insensitive, with a shrewd and uncanny instinct for the jugular of his allies and adversaries. He could be altruistic and petty, caring and crude, generous and petulant, bluntly honest and calculatingly devious—all within the same few minutes."[6]

Johnson possessed a very high degree of native intelligence. Although he had not attended a prestigious college and had little interest in books, his intelligence was apparent as he soaked up knowledge quickly. For example, as vice president he became quite knowledgeable about the technical aspects of space flight, and in his presidential years he grasped the complexities of economic policy from his economic advisers. His intelligence also was evident in his arguments with others. Sen. Harry Byrd Sr., D-Va., for example, observed that he had never won an argument with LBJ.

Policy Views

Johnson, who found political ideologies too inflexible, was not a typical liberal. He seemed to have a love affair with economic growth but had little interest in redistributive policies that would aid the poor by increasing taxes on the wealthy. These ideas came together in 1964 as he promoted his War on Poverty along with a major tax cut. He also viewed labor unions skeptically, taking the view that strikes were too often a waste of resources. His close ties with the business community over the years—and his own investment successes—generated sympathy for its concerns.

LBJ did, however, support many liberal causes. Born into a family that periodically suffered economic difficulties in one of the nation's poorer states, Johnson identified easily with the view that government efforts could help people help themselves, and he showed genuine concern for the impoverished. In one poignant moment during his White House years he actually cried as he viewed the depression era poverty depicted in the movie *The Grapes of Wrath* based on John Steinbeck's novel. Perhaps reflecting his own days as a teacher, he also believed in the importance of education. In Johnson's encompassing view of his new programs, "government could directly or indirectly alleviate any distress."[7] Thus his vision of his "Great Society," while motivated by desires for personal greatness, was rooted in strong beliefs as well.

On racial issues, Johnson changed his views dramatically over the course of his career. In the mid-1950s, as he began thinking of a possible presidential bid, he moved away from a voting record on racial issues that paralleled that of other southern members of Congress. Yet by 1962 he was advocating stronger steps than Kennedy wanted to take, and he increasingly saw civil rights issues in moral terms. In that switch he was influenced partly by personal events—such as when a black staff aide had difficulty finding "colored only" accommodations when driving back to Texas.

In broader terms, Johnson saw his domestic policies as part of a "consensus" in which all major segments of society would receive rewards. In some respects, this view resembled aspects of Roosevelt's "all class" coalition effort during 1933–1934. Johnson's thinking also reflected a concern for the concept of a national community as these policies were to come together. In a way, Johnson saw himself as a benevolent father to the nation.

Challenges and Opportunities

Johnson's White House years found him enjoying both splendid opportunities and daunting challenges. In his first two years LBJ enjoyed a greater opportunity to achieve major domestic policy change than any post-Hoover president except Roosevelt. At the outset, his potential for influence was enhanced by a national sense that the components of Kennedy's domestic program not yet been passed should be enacted in the name of the martyred former president.

Johnson also benefited from having, in effect, two first years in office. In 1964 the first-year honeymoon effect enhanced his personal popularity, and with his landslide election win the same year he was able to argue credibly that he now had a mandate for the domestic programs he had been promoting. In addition, because he had an opportunity (which he capitalized on handsomely) to work on new proposals throughout 1964, he was able to move his program in Congress more quickly in 1965 than a president who had not enjoyed that additional time. In turn, the surge of Democratic strength in Congress not only suggested the existence of a mandate but, in more practical terms, provided a group of new Democratic members of Congress who were in large part strongly committed to the president's expansive policy agenda.

Two other factors also contributed to Johnson's high opportunity level. First, the lengthy list of programs that had been drawing increased support over the preceding five to ten years represented excellent "windows of opportunity" in that there was substantial agreement on the need for action and in some instances substantial agreement on the appropriate policy design.[8] Second, Johnson was aided by the general activism stirring in American society by 1964. Kennedy and Johnson may have helped to intensify those developments, but the forces of activism were growing nevertheless.

The economic forces that Johnson faced in the mid-1960s were the exact opposite of those Roosevelt faced in 1933. Rather than confronting a depression that would cause an apprehensive nation to look to the government for new policies, Johnson assumed office at a time when economic conditions had seldom been better. Economic growth between 1963 and 1966 produced a three-year peacetime growth record—6 percent in both 1965 and 1966.

In contrast to his unique early opportunities, Johnson's last three years in office saw an unprecedented decline. In Congress the Democrats lost forty-seven seats in the 1966 midterm elections (see Table 1–3). But this loss was only one indication of the basic changes in public attitudes that were occurring. One fundamental source of Johnson's eroding opportunities was the dramatic shift in racial conflicts from the southern states to the cities of the North. This shift began with rioting in Harlem in 1964 and burst dramatically into the national spotlight with the Watts riots in Los Angeles in August 1965. More and more whites had come to believe that efforts to address racial problems were moving too rapidly, and new, more militant civil rights leaders had emerged, often overshadowing the leaders with roots in the South such as the Reverend Martin Luther King Jr. Johnson, then, faced a difficult dilemma: the actions proposed to address urban problems could easily be construed as inappropriate efforts to reward rioters. The timing of this shift in the public's attitudes toward racial issues is important because it came while Johnson was still quite popular and before the divisive issue of the Vietnam War began to have a profound impact on the nation's politics.

As for Vietnam, along with the challenge of addressing domestic policy demands, Johnson had to deal with the nation's commitment to that southeast Asian country.[9] The dilemma was acute. On the one hand, clear majorities in Congress, the public, and many foreign policy experts felt it was important that South Vietnam not fall under communist control.[10] Yet Johnson also faced a situation in which conventional air and land forces would prove ineffective in the face of a guerilla movement supported by a regime that was willing to sustain substantial losses. Johnson first hoped to avoid having the issue disrupt his pursuit of Great Society programs by sidestepping debate and carrying out his military buildup in ways that caused as little disruption as possible to American society. He decided not to call up the nation's military reserves, for example, and relied instead on the young men supplied through the draft. Beginning in the spring of 1966, however, dissent to his Vietnam policies mounted and his two uniquely successful years dealing with Congress on domestic policy were followed by a presidency in increasing disarray. In the spring of 1968 the situation climaxed as a majority of citizens for the first time concluded that the U.S. commitment in Vietnam had been a mistake.

Leadership Style

Johnson sought to model his leadership on his friend FDR. He often spoke of Roosevelt as "a second Daddy to me" and "a book to be studied, restudied, and reread." [11] Any president, in LBJ's view, needed to be the central figure in a political system in which Congress was often reactive. Whereas Truman and Eisenhower had concerns about Roosevelt's assertive effort to lead Congress, Johnson strongly believed that decisive leadership was essential and that Roosevelt's performance was the one to emulate—and hopefully surpass. He also strongly subscribed to the view that the president should speak for all individuals and interests.

The Advisory Process and Approach to Decision Making

As an accidental president, Johnson faced the same task Harry Truman had confronted in 1945—cabinet and staff members would have to be changed, but gradually and while maintaining a public perception of continuity between the two presidencies. By virtually all accounts, Johnson handled the initial transition very well with his emphasis on reassurance and continuity.

Inevitably, key personnel did begin to change; some wished to leave and others bowed to Johnson's preferences. In the cabinet, Attorney General Robert Kennedy stayed until mid-1964, when he was replaced by the deputy attorney general, Nicholas Katzenbach. Other key cabinet officials with domestic policy responsibilities included Treasury Secretary Henry Fowler, Secretary of Health, Education and Welfare John Gardner, Secretary of Agriculture Orville Freeman, and Secretary of the Interior Stewart Udall.

The heart of Johnson's advisory process was at the staff level, where he modeled his system in part on FDR's staff operations. [12] At various times several different people fulfilled aspects of the chief of staff role, but Johnson was very much in charge of overall operations. Among other things, he recruited some prominent Texans, such as his own longtime aides Bill Moyers and Henry McPherson, both of whom had served in the Kennedy administration. Moyers served as deputy director of the Peace Corps and McPherson as deputy undersecretary of the army. Moyers, despite his youth, had risen rapidly in Johnson's eyes and was given a prominent role in the early months of the Johnson presidency.

With his staff in place, Johnson launched an unusually broad search for domestic policy ideas.[13] He encouraged Walter Heller, chairman of the Council of Economic Advisers, to expand the process he had instigated for developing proposals dealing with poverty. In July 1964 the president created a system of outside task forces that would seek ideas from a broad range of experts. These groups were to operate in secret and avoid weighing either budgetary concerns or political feasibility as they worked to develop the best possible proposals in each policy area. At the beginning, each task force was made up of about a dozen individuals, some drawn from outside government. About half were chosen for their academic credentials; the other slots were divided among business, labor, and other interest groups. Under Califano's direction, interagency task forces took on new importance as well. Presidential commissions also were established on occasion, such as the Kerner Commission on Civil Disorders in the wake of rioting in Detroit in 1967.

The task forces dealt with virtually every area of policy development in the Johnson administration. In 1964 those areas included agriculture, education, environmental pollution, health, income maintenance, metropolitan and urban problems, and transportation. As a testament to the relentlessness with which Johnson pursued his desires for new legislation, 145 task forces were convened during Johnson's five years in office.

The decision process that emerged was multifaceted. Some of the task forces, especially at the outset, largely refined ideas already debated in Congress. For example, Congress had been looking at the pros and cons of various Medicare proposals since the late 1950s. New ideas also emerged, including for additional health programs and for an innovative urban program known as Model Cities.[14]

Johnson usually paid considerable attention to issues of political feasibility. He phoned committee chairs frequently and read the opinion polls avidly. He also provided ample access for various interest groups of all persuasions as final proposals were being developed. In late 1964 the negotiating process on federal aid to education produced such extensive agreement that congressional passage actually was surprisingly easy. In putting forth new legislation, LBJ often used his back channels with various friends from his lifetime in Washington. Although he usually stressed feasibility, he did on occasion put forward measures that faced an uncertain future. One of the more notable instances was his promotion of legislation addressing housing discrimination in 1966.

Because Johnson was a firm subscriber to the view that his popularity and clout would decline over time, he sought to move new proposals quickly. Moreover, because he believed that "consensus" could be achieved with programs that had some gains for virtually all Americans, he emphasized a broad range of new initiatives.

Johnson's search for ideas and the results that emerged have sometimes been criticized for a lack of new direction; he seemed better able to fine-tune ideas already on the legislative agenda. An analysis by Mark Peterson has provided some confirmation of this view. He found that many of LBJ's proposals already had been considered in Congress and were not highly innovative.[15] Johnson, however, did not come to power under the same conditions enjoyed by Roosevelt or Reagan—that is, as representatives of parties that had been out of power and as candidates oriented toward new approaches. Rather, Johnson was the head of a party that had been struggling to pass its existing agenda.[16]

Administrative Strategies

President Johnson did not consistently engage in administrative issues— he had neither the time nor the interest—yet he did encourage members of his staff such as Joseph Califano to deal with policy implementation issues. The few formal reorganization proposals that did come to light rarely commanded his attention.[17] Although Johnson periodically would reach down into the bureaucracy and become engaged in a highly specific issue, his primary goal was to pass legislation; administrative bottlenecks could be dealt with later. In 1966, for example, he gained passage of a water act even though somewhat similar legislation passed in 1965 had not yet been implemented.

Not surprisingly, LBJ's administrative style created problems. The rapid emergence of new programs for states and urban areas led to considerable confusion, and some felt there was not sufficient follow-through in the implementation of civil rights legislation. In his desire to move rapidly to wage a war on poverty, Johnson also sought to implement a system of community participation, which some critics found unwieldy and ineffective. By the end of the Johnson administration, it had become clear that administrative issues required greater attention.

Public Leadership

Johnson was neither well prepared nor well equipped to deal with public leadership. His years in the Senate had not provided the skills he needed to make effective public addresses. As for the media, he had become accustomed to dealing with the often cooperative Texas press, but parsing with the more adversarial White House press corps would be another thing altogether. He could be highly persuasive in small groups, but his natural speaking style before large audiences included exaggerations and promises more befitting a speech at a local courthouse than a national address. In contrast to Kennedy who was at ease in dealing with television, Johnson continually experimented but frequently was dissatisfied with his results. On television he simply lacked the personal warmth and appeal of a Kennedy or an Eisenhower.

Yet with the aid of skilled speechwriters, and when speaking from the heart on some domestic topics, Johnson could be rather effective. His 1964 State of the Union address was rated better in substance than in style, but it generally received a favorable assessment. A commencement address delivered at the University of Michigan the same year and commonly known as the "Great Society Speech" was one of his more well-received efforts. Written by Richard Goodwin, who was following Johnson's instructions to avoid a laundry list of programs, the final result included lines such as: "We have the opportunity to move not only toward the rich society and the powerful society, but upward to the Great Society." Another oft-quoted line was: "The Great Society . . . demands an end to poverty and racial injustice, to which we are totally committed."[18] His early statements on civil rights also drew generally favorable reviews.

Public speaking became more difficult as Johnson became embroiled in the dual problems of conflict over the Vietnam War and urban unrest. On the problem of urban unrest, he was torn between the desire to express concern for the injustices contributing to it and the desire to avoid the appearance of being unresponsive to the calls for strong measures to prevent further rioting. He often resorted to recitations of economic progress and the scope of new programs, but they did little to stifle the growing concern about the state of the nation.

Johnson's difficulties in relating to the public were intensified by his great difficulty in developing a persona beyond that of a deal-making Washington politician. A letter from former legislative aide and future staffer Henry McPherson to Press Secretary Bill Moyers after Johnson's first press conference points to some of those difficulties. He wrote:

> Obviously he started cold and ended warm. Throughout, however, there showed the public man's guarded apprehension before the press. In such interviews the observer gets the feeling that the entire exercise is meant not to convey information to the people, but to conceal as much as possible from prying newspapermen. Truth and real feelings only get out through the chinks in the wall. As a consequence people come to think of a man as "political" because he never says what he feels or what is apparent to everyone.[19]

But Johnson's approach to the public was handicapped by more than his technique; his tendency toward deception also contributed to his ineffectiveness. Lies about small matters, such as whether any of his relatives died in the Alamo, left many reporters and members of the public wondering whether he was trustworthy on larger issues. And his tendency to make bold claims for his new policies, including labeling his poverty effort a war, often produced skepticism when the policies produced less-than-advertised results. Various statements about Vietnam, starting with his 1964 campaign pledge to avoid American involvement, contributed as well to what many labeled his "credibility gap." For Mary Stuckey, credibility involves "the connection between word and action, a connection that, if broken, cannot be replaced. During Johnson's administration, that connection was visibly and clearly severed for the first time on the presidential level."[20]

The president also found it hard to deal with the media in part because of his desire to manipulate the press. Formal press conferences were held somewhat sporadically and took on a combative quality as Johnson's popularity fell. In one of his more vivid comments, he responded to a reporter, "Why would you ask the leader of the Western world a chicken-shit question like that?"

Difficulties in relating to the public and the press were reflected in his popularity ratings. He was intensely interested in polling results and often would attribute a decline in approval ratings to various policies such as those on civil rights or Vietnam. Yet he also contributed to his own problems with the persona he had created. He could not realistically present himself to a skeptical press as anything other than a Washington insider. Moreover, his poor press relations reduced his chances for positive personal stories.

Congressional Leadership

Legislative leadership was a central dimension of Johnson's view of his presidency. He continued many of the practices he had used as majority leader, including carefully reading the *Congressional Record*, zealously pursuing information, paying careful attention to coalition possibilities, and pushing hard to get a key vote. While vote trades were considered periodically, the president also liked to use his extensive information about issues to push the merits of various proposals.

In the course of his attempts to persuade members of Congress, the president spent more time dealing with committee chairs than with rank and file members. Just as in his Senate days, Johnson went about gaining the support of individual legislators in many different ways—specific trades, or appeals to the public interest, or a carefully developed appeal. The manner in which he carefully built his relationship with Senate Republican minority leader Everett Dirksen of Illinois in a successful effort to enlist his support for the Civil Rights Act of 1964 was simply one of the more widely noted instances in which Johnson's effort to garner votes was based on factors other than a direct bargain for something Dirksen desired.

On occasion Johnson would use public addresses to help spur passage of his legislation, but more often his primary role was playing the "inside game" of dealing with key committee chairs. In rallying public support, he felt more comfortable with efforts to mobilize interest groups and opinion leaders than with public addresses.

Although the White House had no formal office of public liaison, staffers promoted interest group activity heavily. They also called on opinion leaders, including key business figures, to solicit public endorsement of various legislative measures.

Finally, in his legislative strategies Johnson was committed to the importance of a fast start. As he said after he retired, "You've got to give it all you can that first year. Doesn't matter what kind of majority you come in with. You've got just one year when they treat you right, and before they start worrying about themselves."[21] With his fast start he would establish some priorities, such as Medicare in 1965, but he was by no means reluctant to pursue a broad agenda. At the outset of his administration he seemed to think often of Roosevelt's legislative performance in his first two years in office and to pursue legislation with an eye toward rivaling—if not surpassing—FDR's accomplishments.

Legislative Enactments

During Johnson's five years in the White House, the nation witnessed the most extensive outpouring of domestic legislation since Roosevelt's first term. Three landmark bills were enacted in 1964, followed by three more in 1965. Journalists wrote that Johnson had enacted the remaining components of the New Deal agenda in only eighteen months. The pace slowed after 1965, but Congress continued to pass major legislation, including a landmark housing measure in 1968. Johnson's leadership was a key factor in several of these developments.

1964: A Remarkable Beginning

Johnson very definitely hit the ground running in 1964. In 1963, during his first weeks in office, he had provided the nation with the reassurance it needed, followed by a strong State of the Union address in January 1964 calling for swift enactment of stalled measures and a new "War on Poverty." The Eighty-eighth Congress (1963–1965), which had given President Kennedy considerable difficulty, responded to Johnson's leadership and the rising mood of activism in the country not only with three landmark measures but also with several major policies, including one targeting urban mass transit and one targeting the environment—a wilderness act setting up a system of lands free from intrusion. To passage of the War on Poverty program, a substantial tax cut, and the Civil Rights Act of 1964, Johnson applied different styles of presidential leadership.

Economic Opportunity Act. Johnson exhibited his broadest range of influences when he pushed adoption of the Economic Opportunity Act of 1964. This measure was promoted as the president's War on Poverty, but ultimately other efforts within his overall Great Society program would have more central roles in the push to reduce poverty. The initial appropriation for the "war" was $800 million; by 1968–1969 it had risen to $1.7 billion.

The action began on Johnson's first day in the White House. President Kennedy had asked Walter Heller, chairman of the Council of Economic Advisers, to develop a poverty proposal for 1964, but he had given him little specific guidance. Johnson gave Heller strong encouragement with the comment, "That's my kind of program. It will really help people." A frenzied planning process ensued, with various agencies trying to promote their programs among the many ideas being considered. Johnson devoured lengthy proposals at his Texas ranch over the Christmas holidays. Kennedy brother-in-law Sargent Shriver, who had headed JFK's Peace Corps, took over development of the final proposal and later became head of the new Office of Economic Opportunity.

Broadly, the proposal emphasized creating job opportunities and services in poverty areas rather than supporting incomes. One important idea, borrowed from recent experiments by the Ford Foundation, was local participation in the design of needed services. As finally passed, the Economic Opportunity Act called for the establishment of Community Action Programs (CAPS) which would determine the need for a variety of local service programs.

The act included other programs as well. A Job Corps program would relocate youth in residential centers and train them. A volunteer program, known as Volunteers in Service to America (VISTA), was envisioned, along with a legal services program for the poor, neighborhood health centers, and a preschool program called Head Start.

Passage of this legislation was a testament to Johnson's political skills.[22] After encouraging a bold planning process, he highlighted the measure in his State of the Union address, proclaiming "an unconditional war on poverty in America" and referred frequently to the War on Poverty in his daily remarks. He also highlighted submission of his program to Congress in March with a special one-hour television interview carried by all three networks. Finally, virtually all segments of American society received calls and letters in a campaign to develop expressions of support. The administration enlisted not just antipoverty volunteers and minorities, but also prominent educators such as university presidents, heads of various religious organizations such as the National Council of Churches, corporate and labor leaders, and state and local officials. In April, Johnson, sensing a tough fight in Congress, decided to pursue public support more directly by using his first trip as president (to Appalachia) to dramatize the nation's poverty problem. He also called legislators whose support was identified as uncertain. When the bill passed in the House by a larger-than-expected margin of 226–184, veteran observers were amazed. House majority leader Carl Albert, D-Okla., reportedly told the president, "I can't figure out . . . how in the world we ever got this through."

Tax Cut Legislation. Johnson used very different tactics to promote passage of the tax cut President Kennedy had proposed in 1963.[23] Kennedy had called for reductions in every tax bracket with total reductions of $11 billion for individuals and $2.6 billion for corporations. After difficulties and amendments, the measure passed in the House before Kennedy's death, and now Johnson had to ensure its passage by the Senate.

Over lunch with Sen. Harry Byrd, Johnson struck a deal in which Byrd promised rapid action on the legislation and the new president promised to cut the size of the proposed deficit in his new budget to half of the $10 billion originally planned by Kennedy. With his typical delight in secrecy and surprise, LBJ then gave the press the impression that it would be impossible to keep the new budget under $100 billion even as he was hard at work producing a lower figure. He kept his side of the agreement with a proposal that cut Kennedy's proposed deficit by almost $5 billion. Commenting later on his efforts to achieve the reduction, Johnson said, "I worked as hard on that budget as I have ever worked on anything."[24] The size of the proposed tax cut was reduced slightly as well. In so doing, he had sent a message that deficits would be watched closely, thereby garnering support for his tax cut from the more conservative members of Congress. In the end, then, approval of the tax cut came easily, and Johnson was able to sign this landmark measure on February 26, 1964.

Civil Rights Act. The most historic action in 1964 came with passage of a civil rights bill. During the last six months of his life Kennedy had responded to the often violent civil rights demonstrations in Birmingham, Alabama, with new urgency and by submitting a specific legislative proposal that, among other things, sought to end discrimination in public accommodations such as restaurants, hotels, and transportation. Other provisions called for strengthening voters' rights. At the time of his death, Kennedy's measure had been making progress in the House, but it faced an uncertain future.

Johnson took over leadership of the civil rights bill with considerable intensity and a very distinct strategy. Public support for the bill had increased in the wake of Kennedy's assassination, also spurred perhaps by the public activism that seemed to be emerging. In the House, supporters of the bill overcame southern resistance through the committee system, and the Civil Rights Act passed on February 10 by a vote of 290–130. It then faced deliberation in the Senate.

A keen knowledge of the Senate was crucial as Johnson developed his strategies. One key step was to indicate to Sen. Richard Russell, D-Ga., leader of the southern contingent, that he would not accept a significant compromise on the proposed legislation. Sensing that he was better off working behind the scenes, Johnson dealt closely with Sen. Hubert Humphrey (D-Minn.) on legislative strategies. Since the support of Republicans was necessary to break a filibuster, Humphrey was instructed to work closely with the Republican minority leader, Everett Dirksen. Johnson also had several conversations with Dirksen about the issue. As the filibuster began, Humphrey successfully orchestrated an effort by supporters of the legislation to gradually wear down the southern Democrats. Dirksen then brought additional Republicans into the supporters' camp, and the filibuster was broken.

The historic Civil Rights Act of 1964 owed its passage to many factors. Civil rights protests, rather than presidential leadership, had put the issue on the public's front burner by the spring of 1963. Growing public support also was a factor, especially among whites outside the South. President Kennedy's actions beginning in June 1963 and the actions of key legislators such as Senators Humphrey and Dirksen made a significant contribution as well. Finally, President Johnson contributed to the act's passage by refusing to bargain with the southerners and by encouraging the legislative strategies that ultimately produced the necessary Republican votes.

While the measures described here gained congressional passage rather easily, some stalled in 1964, such as the Medicare program of health insurance for the elderly and federal aid to education. President Johnson, however, was not entirely sorry to have Medicare still on the table; it would provide a good campaign issue for the fall election. The election, though, was his for the taking. After his decisive win in 1964 and the addition of thirty-seven Democrats to the House, the scene was set for another highly prolific period of congressional action.

The Eighty-ninth Congress: A Flood of New Legislation

The Eighty-ninth Congress (1965–1967) produced an extraordinary flow of legislation, including three landmark measures in 1965 — Medicare, federal aid to education, and the Voting Rights Act—and a steady pace of major enactments, including an innovative Model Cities program in 1966 and several significant environmental measures. President Johnson did have some failures, however. One was home rule for the District of Columbia; another was a labor-endorsed measure that would have expanded the opportunity for unions to acquire members by eliminating state right-to-work laws. Nevertheless, Johnson enlisted a variety of strategies in promoting an unusually successful legislative agenda.

Medicare. By 1965 the time for enacting health insurance for the elderly had arrived.[25] There was strong public support, and, as noted, Johnson had made Medicare a major issue in the 1964 campaign. The remaining stumbling block appeared to be the resistance of congressional committee chairs. Johnson and the chairman of the House Ways and Means Committee, Wilbur Mills, ultimately became the key figures as Congress debated a broader plan of health coverage than was originally envisioned.

Johnson contributed to the passage of Medicare in several ways. First, he used a combination of the findings of an advisory panel, staff work by Wilbur Cohen, under secretary of health, education, and welfare, and the contributions of Nelson Cruikshank, representing the AFL-CIO, to expand the original legislation. At this juncture, a fateful decision was made: Johnson's planners decided not to incur the wrath of the American Medical Association (AMA) over fee structures; under Medicare, the usual and customary fees could be charged. Second, Johnson gave the bill added importance by touting it in his State of the Union address and then having it symbolically designated the first bill to be considered by both houses of the new Congress. Third, in a classic display of his ability to manipulate an individual legislator, LBJ confronted Senator Byrd's reluctance to report out the bill by inviting him to the White House and, to Byrd's surprise, arranging for television cameras to be present as he left the executive mansion. The startled senator, when asked on camera about the bill, indicated somewhat reluctantly that his committee would report it out. Finally, once the legislation had been passed, Johnson shrewdly promoted the program with a group of AMA leaders, thereby helping to achieve smooth implementation of the new measure.

Federal Aid to Education. Before 1965 federal aid to education (elementary and secondary) had been debated often but never enacted. In

1965, however, both changing conditions and presidential strategies contributed to swift passage. The most important condition that changed was southern resistance to the legislation. Southerners, who had wanted aid for segregated schools, saw their bargaining position crumble with passage of the Civil Rights Act of 1964. In addition, just like in 1933 for agricultural interests, the lobbying groups that had been fighting over the issue for years seemed more willing to compromise.

President Johnson had made the education issue a priority in the fall campaign, and he wanted to act quickly in 1965 before opposition could form to a new proposal.[26] He began by appointing, without announcement, a presidential task force, headed by John Gardner, president of the Carnegie Corporation (and later LBJ's secretary of health, education, and welfare). The task force proved to be one of Johnson's most successful. It met in secret and consulted behind the scenes with key groups such as the monsignors of the Catholic Church, Jewish organizations, southern leaders, and the various education lobbies. Thus through selective intervention without publicity, the executive branch was able to foster a climate of learning and accommodation between the proponents and opponents of general aid to education.[27]

Voting Rights Act. In 1965 pressures for legislation on voting rights mounted when it became apparent that the voting rights provisions contained in the 1964 Civil Rights Act could not be easily implemented in some areas of staunch resistance. The issue was dramatized when the Reverend Martin Luther King Jr. led protests in Selma, Alabama, in March. Like Birmingham two years earlier, Selma was chosen because it was a tough case. Blacks were still being denied the right to vote, and other aspects of segregation were still being practiced despite the provisions of the 1964 Civil Rights Act. Marches and protests brought the expected rough handling and jailings. Johnson federalized the Alabama National Guard to keep order, and television coverage helped intensify nationwide support for additional legislation.

The Johnson administration, which had been considering additional voting rights legislation before the Selma disturbances, now decided to act. The key provision of the new legislation was a trigger mechanism that would use low minority voter registration as a basis for appointing federal voting registrars. Once the bill had been drafted, Johnson met with the leaders of both parties to discuss the next steps. They encouraged the president to make a national address, which he did—but from Capitol

Hill. In that appeal for support he placed the issue in historic terms as he said in part, "I speak tonight for the dignity of man and the destiny of democracy. . . . So it was at Lexington and Concord. So it was a century ago at Appomattox. So it was last week in Selma, Alabama." [28] The public found it one of the most moving and eloquent speeches of his career.[29]

Environmental Measures and Model Cities. Environmental measures also began to emerge. In October 1965, with strong leadership from Sen. Edmund Muskie, D-Maine, Congress set auto emission standards for automobiles. The Johnson administration was more directly involved in passage the same year of the Highway Beautification Act, a cause promoted actively by Lady Bird Johnson.

The Model Cities legislation passed in 1966 had emerged from one of the 1965 task forces.[30] It was developed as a complement to the Community Action Programs Johnson had instigated as part of the War on Poverty and was to be the showpiece of the new Department of Housing and Urban Development. The stated goal of the legislation was to improve the quality of urban life. The main weapon was to be federal block grants that would cover 80 percent of the costs of projects such as low and moderate-income housing, health care, crime prevention, and even recreation. Any city could vie for inclusion in the program, but only 60–70 would be chosen. Interestingly, the Model Cities measure was first labeled a "demonstration" cities program, but, in the wake of urban rioting and demonstrations, its name was changed and it became a more central element in Johnson's urban program.

LBJ found it difficult to promote passage of this legislation in a Congress that was increasingly reflecting voter unease about the direction of his programs. Some opponents of the bill were arguing openly that it simply rewarded those protesters who were burning down the nation's cities. In the face of resistance, industry, labor, civil rights, and religious groups undertook a massive lobbying campaign. Twenty-two top business officials, including Henry Ford II and David Rockefeller, sent telegrams of support. Johnson and several top aides, together with future housing and urban development secretary Robert Weaver (the nation's first black cabinet member), sought legislative support. Administration supporters on key committees were strongly committed to the bill. When the measure finally reached the House floor, Johnson was able to hold together most of his northern Democratic supporters, and the measure passed by a majority of 178–141. Senate passage came more easily, and another Great Society experiment was launched.

The Ninetieth Congress: Johnson Keeps Trying

As the Eighty-ninth Congress became the Ninetieth Congress (1967–1969) Johnson never stopped trying to promote his domestic agenda. During his last two years in office he faced a sharply reduced Democratic majority in the House with the loss of forty-seven seats in the midterm election and growing national frustration over urban rioting and the war in Vietnam (see Table 1–3). Yet task forces kept turning out new proposals, and Johnson kept seeking various opportunities for additional legislative action. Successes, however, became more elusive as the president found his window of opportunity closing. Some environmental and consumer measures were passed, in part because of strong pressure within Congress. And an administration proposal for increases in Social Security benefits also received congressional approval, in part because of the intense efforts by Johnson's veteran legislative strategist, Wilbur Cohen.

The biggest events of the last two years were passage of the Civil Rights Act of 1968 targeting housing discrimination and the belated effort to raise taxes. The open occupancy legislation addressing discrimination in housing sales and apartment rentals was not the first Johnson administration proposal in this area. The Senate had killed a similar proposal in 1966 with a filibuster, and another bill was buried in committee in 1967. A like fate was predicted in 1968 when similar legislation was introduced for a third time. The situation, however, had changed. The tireless advocacy by the NAACP's Clarence Mitchell on the part of the black community helped. Senator Dirksen then switched his position, which was critical to Senate passage. With Dirksen in the aye column for the first time, Democrats were able to garner enough Republican votes to break a filibuster, and the measure passed.

House action occurred in the midst of the widespread urban rioting that followed the April 1968 assassination of Martin Luther King Jr. Sections of the nation's capital erupted in flames. Before King's assassination, supporters had been worried about the bill's prospects. Members of the House, looking at an election in the fall, were highly sensitive to the public opposition. This issue was especially difficult for northern Democrats who represented districts in which some whites were deeply concerned about how the legislation might affect the composition of their neighborhoods. At the same time, the measure had to survive the House Rules Committee, which often had sought to kill civil rights legislation.

After the King assassination Johnson again urged members of the House Judiciary Committee to act on the legislation. With some members concluding that a dramatic step would be helpful and amid strong lobbying by many different groups, the committee reported out the Senate bill intact and it went to the House floor. The full House passed the legislation within twenty-four hours.

Johnson and Congress

It is not easy to determine just how much credit Johnson deserves for the legislative outpouring that occurred during his years in the White House. Some statistical studies of a large group of measures have had little success in isolating a significant influence stemming from presidential skill. Jon Bond and Richard Fleisher, for example, concluded that Johnson won about 5.5 percent more often than might be expected from the nature of the underlying coalition strength in the House, but about 3.2 percent less often in the Senate.[31] Mark Peterson found that Johnson facilitated the large amount of legislation that emerged by not squandering his opportunities.[32]

Favorable circumstances also helped Johnson enormously. His legislative skills would not have produced a comparable outpouring of legislation had he held office in 1961. Yet he made significant contributions to passage of some landmark measures, including his uncompromising stance on the 1964 Civil Rights bill and the very president-centered process that led to enactment of the War on Poverty. Strategies and tactics, in short, can make a difference. Johnson made the most of his opportunities and served as a facilitator during a period of strongly desired action on both ends of Pennsylvania Avenue.

An Assessment

The Johnson years produced fundamental changes in American life. The most far-reaching change was in the position of blacks in American society. The Civil Rights Act of 1964 ended segregation in public facilities such as restaurants and transportation systems, in theory at least, and the Voting Rights Act of 1965 dramatically increased the availability and use of the right to vote. In Selma, Alabama, over 50 percent of blacks were registered to vote four years after the protests had begun, and increases in some areas of Mississippi were even more dramatic. While not producing as dramatic a change, the Open Housing Act of 1968 offered blacks greater home buying opportunities.

Another fundamental change was the expansion of access to health care for the elderly and segments of the poor along with some change in the organization of the health care system. Medicare, by addressing a very real health insurance need for the elderly, proved to be highly popular. It also contributed to the increase in life expectancy Johnson had hoped for in 1965. Unfortunately, the program, which initially paid all "usual and customary fees" coupled with the costs of expanded longevity, became increasingly expensive. Medicaid provided valuable coverage for some of the nation's poor, but it was continually affected by tensions between Washington and the states and problems of administrative complexity.

The federal aid to education program paid out significant funds initially, but the compromise formula used to achieve passage reduced the amount of targeting possible. As funding declined, the federal government once again had a very small role by the 1990s, as both authority and funding responsibilities shifted to the states. The Johnson era environmental policies had some initial impacts, but the Nixon years, when interest in environmental issues soared, produced stronger efforts.

Johnson's economic policy legacies were mixed. At first it appeared that the "golden era of the economist" with its tax cuts had ushered in a new ability to manage economic growth with fiscal policy tools. Growth was indeed substantial, and unemployment was low. But as Johnson attempted to fund both guns (Vietnam) and butter (the Great Society) the burden on the economy caused a downturn in a variety of economic indicators.

Many assessments of Johnson's War on Poverty have concluded that "poverty won." But this is a misleading interpretation of a complex set of relationships. If one looks simply at the portion of the population living below the poverty line, a dramatic improvement occurred—from 20 percent in 1963 to 12 percent in 1968. This decline in the number of poor was the result in part of the tight labor market during those years, which has been variously attributed to the growth created by the tax cut and the additional military spending incurred by the onset of the Vietnam War. The decline in poverty among the elderly can be traced in part to the impact of Medicare beginning in 1966. Later, when Medicare assistance for health costs was combined with the substantial rise in Social Security benefits in the 1970s, the number of poor elderly declined significantly.

The performance of programs specifically included in Johnson's War on Poverty is more debatable. Their potential impact was muted in part by the military spending that prevented Johnson from increasing outlays for his most effective programs in 1966. Ultimately, then, only modest resources were committed to those programs. Food stamps and the earned income tax credit, while not receiving much public attention during Johnson's time in office, assumed higher profiles in later years. In addition, Head Start showed positive results and found lasting interest and support well into the 1990s.

Overall, Johnson's performance in office revealed both impressive talent and glaring weaknesses. On the plus side, Johnson often built coalitions that were, according to one legislative aide, designed to be razor thin to get the most in a legislative package. His intense interest in seizing opportunities was evident not only during the good times of 1964–1965, but also in 1968, when, among conflicts abroad and conflicts at home, he successfully seized the opportunity to pursue open housing legislation. Moreover, Johnson's use of his task forces to generate legislative proposals was, arguably, one of the more successful presidential efforts of that type.

Thus when Johnson's performance is measured in terms of his ability to use his high opportunity level in 1964–1965, he warrants high marks. In terms of getting the most from situations, a recent assessment by former Sen. Eugene McCarthy seems most perceptive. He concluded: "Johnson could get what there was in a situation, but not more." [33]

On the minus side, Johnson played an often inept public role in trying to help the country move beyond his "politics of the best possible coalition." Between his initial staunch espousing of the case for civil rights and his strong speech on voting rights in 1965, he was at points quite effective. But when faced with the difficult issues arising from urban riots, his persona as a legislative bargainer and the sense that he was not entirely trustworthy reduced the measure of effectiveness a president might have had in that situation. A slave to his own frenetic pace and desire to pile policy on policy, Johnson sometimes lost sight of his goal—the improvement of the American community. Passing legislation replaced evaluation of where the country was going and what the implications of his policies might entail. More generally, his continual quantitative emphasis on what his administration had done to increase material goods in American society and his ongoing quest for new government programs simply failed to satisfy a nation that desired both a sense of direction and a measure of reassurance about the direction of its domestic policies and its ability to confront difficult problems.

At the same time, his desire to produce a "happy consensus" around his Great Society was a failure. Rather than acquiring the happy consensus and public admiration he craved, Johnson found himself on the receiving end of criticism from all directions. One indication of his sense of failure was the direction his life took after leaving the presidency. He returned to his Texas ranch and remained almost totally removed from public affairs until his death in 1973.

As a skilled politician, Johnson also must have realized that the rupture in the Democratic Party coalition that accompanied Richard Nixon's 1968 defeat of Hubert Humphrey was widely viewed as a repudiation of his dreams of a Great Society. In the short run, Nixon would be in a position to push for curtailment of many of Johnson's programs. More fundamentally, however, the divisions in a coalition that had triumphed in 1964 raised difficult issues. Could the Democratic Party, especially in the South, continue to sustain white support in the face of new (but not a voting majority) participation by blacks? In turn, could the party bring back those segments of the New Deal coalition such as Catholics and union members who had been frustrated not only with Johnson's Vietnam policies, but also with the urban upheavals the nation had undergone during his years in office?

While these questions could only be answered in time, several conclusions about Johnson's leadership stood out. He was a president who really did care deeply about the programs he was promoting, and he had impressive political skills, which he used to move his legislative agenda. Yet his strategy of seeking to pursue "something for everyone" was a painfully inadequate vision for a nation going through a period of rapid social change.

Notes

1. Lyndon Baines Johnson, *The Vantage Point: Perspectives of the Presidency, 1963–1969* (New York: Holt, Rinehart and Winston, 1971), 429.

2. On Johnson's background, see in particular Robert Dallek, *Lone Star Rising: Lyndon Johnson and His Times, 1908–1960* (New York: Oxford University Press, 1991); and Paul Conklin, *Big Daddy from the Pedernales: Lyndon B. Johnson* (Boston: Twayne Publishers, 1986).

3. Rowland Evans and Robert Novak, *Lyndon Baines Johnson: The Exercise of Power* (New York: New American Library, 1966).

4. James David Barber, *Presidential Character: Predicting Performance in the White House* (Englewood Cliffs, N.J.: Prentice-Hall, 1972); and Doris Kearns Goodwin, *Lyndon Johnson and the American Dream* (New York: Harper and Row, 1976).

5. John R. Bumgarner, *The Health of the Presidents: The 41 United States Presidents through 1993 from a Physician's Pointe of View* (Jefferson, N.C.: McFarland, 1993).

6. Joseph A. Califano, *The Triumph and Tragedy of Lyndon Johnson* (New York: Simon and Schuster, 1991), 10.

7. Conklin, *Big Daddy from the Pedernales,* 193.

8. James L. Sundquist, *Politics and Policy: The Eisenhower, Kennedy, and Johnson Years* (Washington, D.C.: Brookings, 1968).

9. David M. Barrett, *Uncertain Warriors: Lyndon Johnson and His Vietnam Advisers* (Lawrence: University Press of Kansas, 1993), chap. 1.

10. Michael P. Sullivan, *The Vietnam War: A Study in the Making of American Policy* (Lexington: University of Kentucky Press, 1985), 112.

11. Stephen Hess, *Organizing the Presidency,* rev. ed. (Washington, D.C.: Brookings, 1988), 94.

12. Ibid., chap. 7.

13. Charles E. Walcott and Karen M. Hult, *Governing the White House: From Hoover through LBJ* (Lawrence: University Press of Kansas, 1995), 152–153.

14. Emmett S. Redford and Richard T. McCulley, *White House Operations: The Johnson Presidency* (Austin: University of Texas Press, 1986).

15. Mark A. Peterson, *Legislating Together: The White House and Capitol Hill from Eisenhower to Reagan* (Cambridge: Harvard University Press, 1990), 243.

16. This major distinction between Johnson's circumstances and those of Roosevelt and Reagan is drawn from Stephen Skowronek, *The Politics Presidents Make* (Cambridge: Harvard University Press, 1993).

17. Marlan Blissett, "Untangling the Mess: The Administrative Legacy of Lyndon Johnson," in *Lyndon Baines Johnson and the Uses of Power,* ed. Bernard J. Firestone and Robert C. Vogt (Westport, Conn.: Greenwood Press, 1988), chap. 4.

18. Irving Bernstein, *Guns or Butter: The Presidency of Lyndon Johnson* (New York: Oxford University Press, 1996), 132.

19. Letter to Bill Moyers from Henry McPherson, March 19, 1964, special file, public relations, 372, Lyndon Baines Johnson Presidential Library, Austin, Texas.

20. Mary E. Stuckey, *The President as Interpreter-in-Chief* (Chatham, N.J.: Chatham House, 1991), 78.

21. Quoted in Hess, *Organizing the Presidency,* 22.

22. Barbara Kellerman, *The Political Presidency: The Practice of Leadership* (New York: Oxford University Press, 1984), chap. 7.

23. Phillip M. Simpson, "Lyndon B. Johnson and the 1964–1968 Revenue Acts," in Firestone and Vogt, *Lyndon Baines Johnson and the Uses of Power,* chap. 13.

24. Johnson, *Vantage Point,* 36.

25. Sheri I. David, *With Dignity: The Search for Medicare and Medicaid* (Westport, Conn.: Greenwood Press, 1995); and Theodore R. Marmor, *The Politics of Medicare* (New York: Aldine Publishing, 1973).

26. Bernstein, *Guns or Butter,* chap. 7.

27. Michael R. Reople and Lance W. Bardsley, "Strategies for Governance: Domestic Policy Making in the Johnson Administration," in Firestone and Vogt, *Lyndon Baines Johnson and the Uses of Power,* 21.

28. Johnson, *Vantage Point,* 165.

29. Conklin, *Big Daddy from the Pedernales,* 216.

30. Bernstein, *Guns or Butter,* chap. 18.

31. Jon R. Bond and Richard Fleisher, *The President in the Legislative Arena* (Chicago: University of Chicago Press, 1990), 206.

32. Peterson, *Legislating Together,* 244–246.

33. Eugene McCarthy, remarks at a meeting of the Town Hall of Los Angeles, June 14, 1995.

The press is trying to paint me as now trying to undo the
New Deal. I remind them I voted for FDR four times. I'm
trying to undo the "Great Society."

4

—RONALD REAGAN

Ronald Reagan
One Big Year

RONALD REAGAN (served 1981–1989) swept into the White House more committed to changing domestic policy than any president since Lyndon Johnson. The actor-turned-politician was a high-opportunity president with a clear agenda, but the debates continue about how much change he actually accomplished and what kind of leadership style his presidency really embodied. Granted, the landmark economic legislation passed in 1981 was a tribute to Reagan's effective "going public" and fast-start strategies. And many aspects of his media strategies have drawn praise. Even the "Teflon factor"—Reagan's ability to sustain personal support even in the face of adverse developments—has generated considerable interest. But just how much did this high-opportunity president achieve?

Personal Characteristics

Ronald Wilson Reagan (1911–) is the only president since 1932 to have changed his party identification (in his case, from Democrat to Republican). He also is the nation' s oldest president. Eisenhower was seventy when he left the presidency; Reagan celebrated his seventieth birthday during his first weeks in office. And Reagan is the nation's only divorced president.

"Dutch," as he was sometimes known, grew up in small towns in northern Illinois. His father, who suffered from bouts of alcoholism, persistently changed sales jobs. Jack Reagan, an avid Democrat, was pleased at one point to acquire a minor job with one of Roosevelt's New Deal agencies. Ronald attended Eureka College, a nearby small, church-related school. He enjoyed drama, football, and his involvement with student government while completing his economics major with the aid of a "quick study" approach to examinations.

Career Path

Reagan followed an unusual career path to the presidency. After graduating from college in 1932, he went into broadcasting in Des Moines, Iowa, where he reported "live" (working from a teletype delay) baseball games being played three hundred miles away in Chicago. During one game, his rhetorical skills were tested when the teletype of the play-by-play from Chicago was interrupted and he had to fill in the empty time. In 1937 Reagan accompanied the Chicago Cubs on a spring training trip to Los Angeles. There, a studio screen test sparked the beginning of an acting career. On the payroll of Warner Brothers Studio, Reagan often played the "all American boy." In 1940 he also found time to marry Jane Wyman, a well-known actress. Two years later he entered the U.S. Army Air Corps and was assigned to making training films in nearby Culver City, California.[1]

Reagan entered the political arena, in a manner of speaking, after World War II. From 1947 to 1952 he served as president of the Screen Actors Guild, a labor union representing actors. In that turbulent era "Red-baiters" were charging that communists had infiltrated the movie industry, and aggressive hearings by the House Committee on Un-American Activities produced heated controversies among Guild members. He also participated in several Democratic Party electoral campaigns, including that of staunch liberal Helen Gahagan Douglas, who lost the 1950 California Senate race to Richard Nixon. With his acting career on the wane, Reagan divorced in 1948 and four years later married another actress, Nancy Davis. In 1957 the Reagans starred together in their last movie, and he then accepted an offer from General Electric to lecture its employees and host a weekly TV program. In writing his own speeches, and at points in listening to his new arch conservative father-in-law, Reagan began to change his political philosophy. In 1962 he formally switched to the Republican Party, and in 1964 the newfound darling of the conservatives delivered a national televised speech in support of Republican presidential nominee Barry Goldwater. The speech was so well received that Reagan began to realize he might have a career in politics.

In 1966 Reagan used a strong campaign, the advantage of running against an unpopular incumbent seeking a third term, and a growing Republican tide to win election as governor of California. His eight years in office saw the emergence of a distinct leadership style.[2] He encouraged his staff to prepare brief "mini-memos," and he delegated responsibility extensively. He also used public addresses effectively to support his favorite causes and on occasion to gain leverage with the legislature. Despite his rhetoric of limited government, he actually presided over a period of considerable expansion in state government. The conditions surrounding this development were a strong economy, an activist public mood in areas such as the environment, and an assertive state legislature to which Reagan sometimes paid limited attention. And how did Reagan get around his own rhetoric about limited government? He possessed a shrewd ability to go along with various new or larger programs while maintaining the public's perception that he opposed government expansion. Often, people seemed to conclude that he was at least trying to constrain government operations.

After leaving the governor's office, Reagan made an unsuccessful bid for the Republican presidential nomination in 1976. He gave the incumbent president, Republican Gerald Ford, a real scare in the primaries, as he did well especially in the South and with conservatives. In the 1980 race for the Republican presidential nomination Reagan was the best-known conservative in a field that included former House member and Central Intelligence Agency director George Bush, Senators Robert Dole (Kans.) and Howard Baker (Tenn.), and Rep. John Anderson (Ill.). After a strong Bush showing in Iowa, Reagan used a win in New Hampshire to help gain momentum for his nomination victory.

The fall election between Reagan and incumbent Jimmy Carter was closer than Reagan's ten-point margin would suggest. The lead changed hands several times, with the decisive shift occurring in the last days before the election and in the wake of a televised debate in which Reagan seemed able to shake the image some held of a candidate whose extreme views would be dangerous. He was aided as well by the ongoing hostage crisis in Iran, a weak U.S. economy suffering from high levels of both inflation and unemployment, and Carter's lack of popularity.

What Manner of Man?

Ronald Reagan was known for his confidence and optimism for himself and the nation. An avid storyteller, he was very fond of happy endings.

And there was no doubt in his mind that America's story could continue to be one of unbounded success. His optimism was especially evident during the economic difficulties of 1982. Staff aide Peggy Noonan found this trait part of a long-standing desire to cheer people up, possibly stemming from his early experiences in a family with an alcoholic father.[3]

Reagan also possessed a good sense of humor—and an ability to use it effectively. During a 1984 presidential debate with his Democratic challenger, Walter Mondale, he helped diffuse the age issue by commenting that he would not raise the question of Mondale's youth and inexperience. Self-deprecation often came to his rescue as well. In the wake of newspaper stories suggesting that he occasionally dozed off at meetings, he commented, "perhaps we should put a chair in the cabinet room with a sign saying, 'Ronald Reagan Slept Here.'" Reagan's humor often helped to deflect personal criticism and to convey the image of a president who was not overly impressed with himself.

In fact, it was perhaps that modesty that led his colleagues to find him an easy person to like. Secretary of Education Terrel Bell put it quite simply, "It is hard not to like Ronald Reagan."[4] Nevertheless, he had few close relationships. He spoke often and eloquently of "family values" and was devoted to Nancy, but spent little time with his adult children from either of his marriages. As for staff members, a variety of "kiss and tell" (or, for some, "kick and tell") memoirs frequently pointed to a president who was friendly—but only up to a point. Peggy Noonan, for example, found Reagan a very friendly man who had few close friends.[5] And official biographer Edmund Morris found his subject so unfathomable that he felt compelled to resort to creating a fictitious character to explain Reagan in his 1999 book *Dutch: A Memoir of Ronald Reagan.*[6]

While often somewhat distant, Reagan was rarely vindictive. In selecting a chief of staff, for example, he was willing to hire on Texan James Baker even though he had led Bush campaigns against Reagan in both 1976 and in 1980. He also sought to avoid petty or vindictive actions in his relations with legislators.

Reagan's cheerfulness and modesty, however, masked greater ambition than many realized; he had discussed the possibility of running for Congress as early as the 1940s. Journalist and veteran Reagan watcher Lou Cannon concluded that many observers underestimated him because they failed to see beyond a genial demeanor to a hard, self-protective core that contained both a gyroscope for maintaining balance and a compass pointing toward success.[7] According to Cannon, Reagan's political opponents often made this mistake, thereby leaving themselves unsure why they ended up losing.

During his political career Reagan sought and used information in unusual ways. He liked to glean information and insights in person rather than in writing. He also possessed an ability to read audiences, an advantage developed through his long experience as an actor and public speaker. As early as his 1966 race for governor, he seemed to be ahead of the polls in determining which ideas could be promoted most effectively.

Despite his strong emphasis on the uniqueness and goodness of America, Reagan apparently engaged in no sustained study of American history. A former devotee of science fiction, he and Nancy put sufficient credence in astrological interpretations to warrant changes in the president's schedule if the signs were not right. Stories from *Reader's Digest* and the conservative journal *Human Events* would at points shape his thinking more than analytical materials.

Reagan often used the information he had gathered in the stories he enjoyed telling—even if they were not true. For example, he repeatedly referred to a "welfare mother" in Chicago who was ripping off the system even though his secretary of health and human services had declared the case bogus three times. On environmental policy he asserted that there were as many trees in the country as at the time of the American Revolution. (The U.S. Park Service, however, stated that the correct figure was approximately 30 percent.) He also sometimes ignored seemingly obvious conclusions. For example, when his administration called for tax increases on businesses to the sum of almost $100 billion over three years, he persisted in talking about the new policy as a tax reform rather than a tax increase.

Policy Goals

According to Fred Greenstein, "Reagan . . . was startlingly uninformed about and inattentive to the specific content of policy—a president who appears to have been more dependent on his aides for detailing direction than any president since Harding." [8] Major policy plans would be handed to him and often simply accepted without question. But for those issues important to him, such as the best ways to present his economic policy ideas, he was interested in at least a moderate degree of detail.

In fact, tax cuts were a cornerstone of Reagan's policy views. [9] During the course of the 1980 campaign, he advocated "supply-side" economics (later called "Reaganomics") which envisioned tax reduction as a spur to economic growth and ultimately greater tax revenue even though rates were lower. Lower tax rates also were viewed as a strong incentive for people to work more.

Fewer government regulations were a prime Reagan objective as well. His concerns often reflected his opposition to the social regulations of the Great Society more than the industry-specific regulatory policies that characterized the New Deal. With an eye in part toward regulatory issues he wrote in his diary, "The press is trying to paint me as now trying to undo the New Deal. I remind them I voted for FDR four times. I'm trying to undo the 'Great Society.'" [10] Many members of the nation's business community loudly criticized the expansion of government regulation into areas such as environmental and consumer protection, and Reagan was highly sympathetic to that view. In his assessment, fewer regulations would be a major step toward increasing the productivity of the American economy.

Cuts in domestic spending were another Reagan goal, but virtually no specific targets were suggested. Instead, he spoke generally of eliminating "waste, fraud, and abuse," often accompanied by anecdotes from his California experiences. He also spoke on occasion of greater roles for the states rather than the federal government in determining policy. He even mused about the possibility of changing Social Security into a voluntary system, but he realized this was not a feasible policy goal.

Yet another policy goal was increased spending on defense. The president felt strongly that America's military posture had been allowed to deteriorate under Jimmy Carter's leadership. Thus when "deficit hawks" such as Office of Management and Budget Director David Stockman looked for ways to reduce the deficit, Reagan would often point out that funding for the military was a separate category and was "off limits."

Surprisingly, the oft-touted goal of balancing the budget came last on Reagan's policy list. At first, he promised a balanced budget by 1983, but the deficits mounted nevertheless. Even as the administration sought choices among policy goals, Reagan insisted that defense building and tax reductions take priority.

Reagan's ideas were thus a mix. On social issues he opposed abortion and generally endorsed a conservative agenda but with far less emphasis than he reserved for his economic goals. Even so, he advocated tax cuts and spending cuts with less fervor than Republican leaders such as Newt Gingrich would express a decade later. Some conservatives, then, were uncertain about the real level of commitment held by the fun-loving president. While Reagan often was perceived as an ideologue, some observers saw even at the outset of his administration signs of his pragmatism and aspects of a "consensus politician." [11] With that mix, Reagan was determined to set the nation back on the right course to the "American Dream."

Challenges and Opportunities

The economic challenge Reagan faced was formidable. Since 1973 the U.S. economy had been characterized by high levels of unemployment, lower productivity which was contributing to stagnant incomes, and high inflation. With inflation levels over 10 percent in both 1979 and 1980 coupled with another increase in unemployment, Americans sensed that something new had to be tried.

Momentum was the key to Reagan's opportunities at the outset of his administration. According to Joseph White and Aaron Wildavsky, the election did not create a mandate but it did create an opportunity.[12] In a three-way race with low turnout, Reagan had actually received the support of little more than a quarter of the eligible electorate. Nevertheless, his final election surge to a ten percentage point win, along with Republican success in capturing control of the Senate and gains of thirty-four seats in the House, shocked the denizens of Capitol Hill. Democrats were in disarray, and Speaker Thomas "Tip" O'Neill, D-Mass., anxiously proclaimed that he would not use procedural steps to stand in Reagan's way. The president's initial popularity ratings were not especially high, but they were boosted in April in a most unusual way: the March 31 near-fatal attempt on Reagan's life raised his public support by over 10 percent and that high 50 percent figure held for the coming months. Sensing new opportunities, Republican leaders in Congress were anxious to cooperate.

Among the promising issues, tax cut measures were popular with the public and in Congress, and a proposal similar to Reagan's three-year tax cut (described later in this chapter) had made considerable progress in 1978. The Democrats also were interested in some degree of tax reduction. To members of Congress on both sides of the aisle, Reagan made a strong case for his "supply-side" approach to boosting the economy, even though few prominent economists favored the idea. But at least the sense of economic disarray had created a strong desire to give a new approach a chance.

Public support for other Reagan measures varied and tended to drop off after his first year. Both voters and members of Congress were fairly skeptical about the merits of deregulatory policies—after all, environmental regulations often were quite popular. At first, the public also supported an increase in defense spending, but that support declined markedly after 1983. Domestic spending cuts were popular in the abstract, but not for popular programs like Social Security. Unfortunately for Reagan, there were no easy spending reduction targets that could generate the savings he hoped to achieve.

Reagan's second-term opportunities were not especially large. The victory over his Democratic challenger, Walter Mondale, was aided more by a strong economy and Reagan's far greater skill as a campaigner in the age of television than by support for a new agenda. One of Reagan's few strong issues was his advocacy of tax reform. The impact of the Iran-contra controversy on Reagan's popularity (his administration, contrary to stated policies, had carried out a policy of selling arms to Iran and using the profits to aid the contras fighting the oppressive Sandinista government in Nicaragua) and the public's increasing perception of a presidency in disarray further reduced interest in new Reagan policy initiatives. The president did regain some public standing, however, during his last year in office as he moved from a hardened stance toward the Soviet Union, calling it an "evil empire," to a more flexible policy after Soviet reformer Mikhail Gorbachev sought improved relations with the United States.

Leadership Style

Reagan's orientation to presidential leadership was somewhat unusual. Despite abandoning his earlier commitments to most of FDR's domestic policies, he admired Roosevelt's rhetorical skills and, like FDR, placed great emphasis on the importance of reassuring the electorate. At the same time, in his cabinet room he prominently (and symbolically) displayed a portrait of "silent" Calvin Coolidge. In Reagan's view, a president's proper role was that of "preacher"; he was skeptical of a more activist role for the nation's leader.

Much of Reagan's leadership orientation had developed over the course of his career, especially during his years as governor of California. Both Reagan and his advisers also were motivated, however, by a very simple rule: find out what Jimmy Carter did and then do the opposite. Thus the president and his staff cultivated the media at the outset, recruited seasoned Washington figures for several key staff positions, and established a limited, focused first-year agenda.

The Advisory Process and Approach to Decision Making

Reagan's cabinet, which he selected quickly and with limited personal involvement, tilted toward elderly businessmen with establishment ties. It included one woman, Jeane Kirkpatrick, ambassador to the United Nations, and one African American, Samuel Pierce, secretary of housing and urban development. Donald Regan, secretary of the Treasury, brought to his office a background in the securities industry. James Watt, secretary of the interior, was noted for his harsh criticism of many environmental regulations. Two Californians also had prominent positions—Caspar Weinberger served as secretary of defense and William French Smith as attorney general.

The configuration of the top staff positions had a major impact on Reagan's accomplishments. He decided on a "troika"—in which James Baker served as chief of staff, Edwin Meese as special counselor to the president, and Michael Deaver as special assistant to the president for special events. This decision, which came as a surprise to Meese who had served as Reagan's chief of staff during his governorship, was made with the encouragement of longtime Reagan adviser Stuart Spencer and pollster Richard Wirthlin. Meese loved organizational matters, but some Reaganites questioned his ability to actually get things done and worried about the impact of his strong conservative views. Reagan thus asked James Baker to be chief of staff but to share power with Meese and Deaver. Top staff aides in areas such as legislative liaison and press relations reported to Baker; Meese chaired a series of cabinet councils. Through the Office of Planning and Evaluation (OPE) Reagan also instituted an effort to coordinate policy with poll results in order to better link policy efforts to public opinion.

The centrality of Baker's role was much in evidence in 1981 as Reagan's fast start with Congress emerged. Michael Deaver, a longtime Californian who was close to both Reagan and the first lady, was responsible for planning all special events and had a major media role. Interestingly, the public only became aware of the extent to which the Reagan White House was functioning as a troika when the press reported who was coming and going from Reagan's side in the spring of 1981 as he recovered from his bullet wound at George Washington Hospital.[13]

The cabinet process that emerged took on a fair degree of importance. Meese coordinated a group of what was at first seven cabinet councils (later two) composed of four to six department heads who had overlapping policy areas. At their meetings the councils reviewed policy and developed options. During Reagan's first term, more than five hundred such meetings were held, more than half devoted to economic affairs. Adding to their prestige, Reagan often attended.[14] The gatherings produced some important ideas, and cabinet officers were given a sense of involvement, but at points these councils engaged in a rather routine shuffling of proposals. Their importance also was limited by the tendency for final decisions to be made at the staff level. Nevertheless, until abandoned in the second term, they did enhance the contributions of cabinet members to the administration—much more so, in fact, than in most other presidencies.[15]

At the beginning of Reagan's second term he sent James Baker to head the Treasury Department and its former secretary, Donald Regan, replaced Baker as chief of staff. Regan's autocratic leadership style quickly drew wide criticism, and many Washington observers were relieved when Regan was fired after the Iran-contra scandal and replaced by veteran legislator Howard Baker, a Tennessee Republican. Nancy Reagan was a driving force in that shift, as she openly despised Regan and felt he was not doing enough to protect the president's reputation.[16]

Among the domestic advisers, David Stockman, director of the Office of Management and Budget, played an extremely important role in the Reagan administration. Only thirty-four at the time of his recruitment, Stockman had served as a staff aide to Rep. John Anderson, R-Ill., and two terms as a member of Congress from Michigan. (In one of those strange coincidences, while at Harvard Stockman had worked as a babysitter for Daniel Patrick Moynihan, who later, as a Democratic senator from New York, would be an outspoken critic of Reagan's economic ideas.) To the left politically in the 1960s, Stockman had changed his views dramatically by the late 1970s. While a member of Congress, he zealously sought budget cuts. Elsewhere in the administration, Martin Anderson, who early on helped to shape Reagan's economic policy position papers, headed the Office of Policy Development. Another player in Reagan economic policy was Murray Weidenbaum, an economics professor from Washington University with a specialty in regulation and its impact on business. He served as chairman of the president's Council of Economic Advisers for two years. Beginning in 1983, however, the top positions began to change as Anderson and Weidenbaum left, feeling that few new ideas were being pushed. Other domestic positions also began to experience rapid turnover.

Reagan's role in the decision-making process appeared limited. He often presided passively at the larger meetings and then made decisions as

he interacted with a few advisers and responded to formal recommendations. On occasion, he made decisions without thoroughly reviewing his
options. In early 1981, for example, he quickly endorsed a proposal for reducing Social Security benefits for those retiring before age sixty-five.

As his presidency progressed, Reagan sought to establish basic
decision-making guidelines but seldom displayed curiosity about policy
issues and possible new approaches. In 1981 the Reagan administration
made a concerted effort to maintain a short agenda by focusing on taxes
and spending. Other issues, such as social policy and deregulation, were
kept off the front burner, at least in the beginning. After Reagan's troubles
with Social Security in 1981, James Baker strove to avoid any policy moves
that would jeopardize political support on that issue. He accomplished
this feat by checking the political feasibility of an action often and paying
considerable attention to Richard Wirthlin's polling. One result of those
assessments was that few proposals were introduced by the administration for statutory changes in regulatory policies; Reagan and his advisers
had concluded that success in Congress was unlikely. Especially after the
first year, Reagan also displayed a willingness to compromise. As a result,
the "Reaganauts" such as Edwin Meese complained frequently that the
"pragmatists" such as James Baker were exercising too much influence.
Yet an interest in quiet compromise, perhaps even while denying a retreat,
had long been part of Reagan's decision-making style.

In the long run the president's decision-making approach had both its
strengths and its limitations. Colin Campbell concluded in 1986 that the
troika arrangement in the first term successfully brought a range of policy options to the president and seemed to meet his needs quite well.[17]
During the momentum of the first year he was able to energize his administration to produce some 223 proposals—a performance rivaling
that of the generally more action-oriented first-year Democratic administrations.[18] The level of promotion declined markedly, however, after the
first year. While a measure of decline was inevitable, Reagan's staff processes also reflected a chief executive with limited interest in the more
subtle ways in which public policy might be guided to shape a more conservative agenda.

Administrative Strategies

The significance of Reagan's administrative strategies was dramatically
demonstrated in August 1981 as he reacted to a strike by the nation's

designed to complement the visuals of television. His style is best characterized as conversational, even chatty. In keeping with the apparent inti-
macy of the television medium, Reagan spoke to the electorate in a friendly,
informal fashion, reducing the formal distance between himself and his
audience." [25]

Good results did not occur by chance: various strategies were used
carefully. During his earliest days in the White House, Reagan tried to
cultivate members of the Washington press corps. Staff members were encouraged, however, to limit their own availability to the press, especially
on issues of political strategies and where difficult questions might be involved.[26] Press conferences were used infrequently, and a variety of techniques such as gestures to whirling helicopter blades or to his partially
deaf ear were used when Reagan did not want to answer a difficult question. Under the guiding influence of Michael Deaver, the White House developed a "theme for the day" in media coverage. Deaver emphasized not
the technical aspects of stories but the "visuals" and paid careful attention
to such detail as where the president might best stand in different situations. Communications Director David Gergen (whose expertise was later
used for a time by Bill Clinton) also brought considerable skill to his role.
In fact, the president was supported in his public leadership role by a staff
of over one hundred people who helped him to "write, talk, and listen to
the American public." [27]

The administration's emphasis on domestic policy during its first two
years at the expense of attention to some key foreign policy issues was
unique. This focus was especially vexing, however, to Secretary of State
Alexander Haig, who repeatedly lobbied Reagan to devote himself to foreign policy issues. Reagan gave no fewer than five major speeches dealing
with the economy in 1981 and another three in 1982. Speeches on domestic matters then virtually disappeared; none were made during the final
two years of the first term and only three during the entire second term.

Unquestionably, the president's most effective addresses were on economic issues in 1981. He made no other major addresses immediately
prior to major votes on other issues, however, and the effort to promote
a federalism initiative in 1982 proved to be a failure.

The Reagan White House referred frequently to the bully pulpit as the
president sought, through his messages, to expand on his general views of
America and what actions might be appropriate for its citizens. He sought
to promote three broad themes: (1) a free society that rests not on competition between individuals but on the development of voluntary associ-

ations and the art of teaming up; (2) the imperfect quality of human nature; and (3) personal responsibility.[28] Reagan talked more extensively about these and other issues in religious terms than did Carter despite his less-apparent religious commitment. While he did not use moralistic themes more than other presidents, his economic policies were discussed in moralistic terms to an unusual degree.[29] William Muir believes Reagan's use of the bully pulpit had a very significant impact: "To the American public he restored a common sense view of human nature, human goodness, and human society. He renewed public confidence in America's private and public institutions, not the least the American presidency. Furthermore, virtually everywhere on earth he inspired popular appreciation of the free market and liberal democracy." [30]

In fact, of all the presidents Reagan was one of the most skilled in sustaining his personal popularity. Part of the explanation is that his persona combined qualities many citizens found likeable—in other words, it was not the persona of a typical "politician." He also owed his success to the so-called Teflon factor, allowing him to dodge the impact of negative developments in his administration, and his use of the lightning rod strategy in which he would claim convincingly, in a variety of areas, that he was not aware of the specific actions of others in his administration. Richard Ellis has argued, however, that this strategy, which was applied in a limited way, did not isolate him from the unpopularity associated with Secretary of the Interior James Watt. After the first year, criticism of Watt became increasingly coupled with criticism of the president.[31]

Yet another aspect of Reagan's ability to sustain his popularity was his capacity to maintain the public perception that he was a person of strong convictions while actually engaging in a surprising number of compromises and retreats. On tax policy, for example, he was able to maintain his reputation as a tax cutter despite the fact that no fewer than fourteen of the eighteen tax bills he signed actually increased taxes. The manner in which he quietly handled his compromises without being branded as "just another politician" may well have been quite central to his popularity with the public.

Congressional Leadership

In organizing his legislative liaison operations, Reagan recruited an experienced and able group of aides.[32] They included veteran lobbyist Max Friedersdorf and Kenneth Duberstein, who was responsible for the difficult task of mobilizing support for Reagan's 1981 economic package in the House. Chief of Staff James Baker, as head of a Legislative Strategy Group (LSG), also had an extremely important role in congressional relations, especially in 1981. The LSG met almost daily and was responsible for many strategic decisions as well as coordinating both legislative and public support-building efforts.

Reagan was at points quite willing to lobby members of Congress. In 1981 he met no fewer than sixty-nine times with various groups of members. He had considerable confidence in his own persuasive abilities and undertook a direct lobbying role with enthusiasm. That enthusiasm did not cover a wide range of issues, however, and his legislative liaison aides preferred to focus closely on the president's personal agenda. As a result, after 1981 the task of promoting policies in Congress fell increasingly to his legislative liaison staff.

Legislative Enactments

Ronald Reagan began his presidency with a fairly clear and fixed view of his priorities. He was determined to focus attention on economic issues and push for enactment of a select few big-ticket items. This strategy helped him achieve some significant early victories.

1981: The Big Year

Reagan's first year in office produced two important measures. The Economic Recovery Tax Act (ERTA) provided multiple changes in the nation's tax policies, including reduced tax rates on individuals and corporations of 5 percent the first year and 10 percent each of the next two years. In addition, the bill indexed taxes to correct "bracket creep" (when inflation forces taxpayers into higher tax brackets)—in retrospect, an extremely significant development. Other key changes included: a reduction, from 70 percent to 50 percent on investment earnings, in the marginal, or "last dollar earned," tax bracket; tax advantages for business, including more rapid depletion allowances and a "safe harbor" arrangement for leasing tax advantages to other industries; and a reduction in the federal inheritance tax to allow estates of up to $600,000 to be inherited tax-free. On the spending side, the Omnibus Budget Reconciliation Act of 1981 (OBRA 81) reduced existing spending levels by approximately $37 billion and projected future (partly unspecified) cuts for a three-year total of

$130.6 billion. In the first year, cuts focused primarily on programs providing assistance for the working poor and on federal grants to the states.

Reagan contributed to his year of success with multiple strategies and considerable energy.[33] At several key points he successfully went public to place pressure on reluctant members of Congress. His first foray occurred when he addressed a joint session of Congress a month after the assassination attempt. He was welcomed warmly with hand waving and many outbursts of applause. He then attacked the Democratic proposals as the "old way." The president closed with an effective appeal to the public to support his plans and a pledge: "loyalty to only one special interest—the People."

A second dramatic effort occurred two days before the House vote on Reagan's tax cut bill because the administration still lacked the votes needed to pass it. After a persuasive appeal, the president urged Americans to contact their senators and representatives and tell them this was "an unequaled opportunity to help return America to prosperity and make government again the servant of the people." Speaker O'Neill described the speech as "devastating." In view of the swift and overwhelming public response, Democrats became reluctant to oppose the legislation and resistance crumbled.[34]

As noted, Reagan's big year began with his key decision to focus on a limited agenda. Unlike Carter who had put forth a large agenda in 1977, Reagan would avoid potentially divisive social issues during his first months in office. To buy time, however, he used a major address in March to stress his commitment to conservative values while also emphasizing the importance of judicial appointments. He would change regulatory policies, he hinted, through administrative strategies rather than efforts to pass new legislation. To an unusual degree Reagan was successful in 1981 in focusing legislative attention on his preferred economic issues.

Once in office, Reagan adopted a fast-start strategy and began immediately to create his proposals. David Stockman worked around the clock seeking budget cuts, and some cabinet members were barely able to locate their desks before being lobbied to accept the cuts Stockman was proposing. Many reductions were quickly approved in an elaborate committee process. Nevertheless, Stockman faced immense problems as he contemplated the need for future spending cuts. To help achieve speed and to reduce likely congressional resistance, he decided to simply earmark some $75 billion for "unspecified" future cuts.

Developing the tax cut proposal was a difficult process in part because of the uncertainty about economic assumptions. The fundamental problem was that Reagan was proposing to simultaneously wring inflation out of the economy and provide the framework for strong economic growth. Unfortunately, for anyone setting monetary policy these goals are contradictory; fighting inflation and promoting growth require, respectively, restrictive and expansionary money supply policies. The pressure on policy makers to agree on some kind of economic projection was intense. In the compromise that ensued, a "rosy scenario" was adopted to reduce the pressure for difficult decisions. This step postponed a resolution of positions on monetary policy while also imposing relatively little "pain" for Congress and the public to absorb.

In dealing with Congress, Reagan strategists correctly reasoned that they would have a stronger chance of achieving their tax cut if that body first enacted spending cuts to demonstrate its discipline. The White House and Congress also took advantage of the "reconciliation" process for establishing budgetary guidelines. Democrats as well as Republicans had promoted use of this process, first established in the Budget and Impoundment Act of 1974, as a step toward producing a more rational allocation of spending priorities. Reagan himself had used the process earlier in the year and to his considerable advantage as members of Congress were asked, before committee hearings were held, to support his overall budget outline, with general spending targets in various program areas.

In seeking votes, Reagan dealt with individual members extensively and persuasively. In the House he especially targeted the Boll Weevil Democrats, a group of southern Democrats who were sympathetic to many of his objectives. The president, in most instances, adopted a soft sell. After all, he was in a relatively strong position because both he and his plan were highly popular in most of the Boll Weevils' districts. In other instances, the White House undertook classic deal making for votes.

Reagan strategists had intended passage of the Omnibus Budget Reconciliation Act of 1981 and its spending cuts to justify the tax cut portion of the president's package. Some policy makers, however, were skeptical of the scope and nature of the spending cuts, which avoided controversial and large growth areas such as Social Security and Medicare. Even some Republicans privately raised their eyebrows, and some voices of the business community such as the *Wall Street Journal* expressed their concern as well.

In the face of such skepticism, the tax cuts proved to be as difficult to pass as the spending cuts. The legislation itself was plagued by several ma-

jor, legislatively spawned changes and intense bidding wars for supporters, lured by modifications of tax reductions to aid specific interests. The
Republican efforts to gain support proved difficult not just because of
Democratic resistance but also because many Republicans worried that
passage of the bill might lead to fulfillment of a long-standing fear—increasingly large federal deficits.

In the Senate, Reagan sought and received help from several legislative
leaders for passage of his tax reduction package. He had met with Senate
majority leader Howard Baker several times before inauguration day, and
Baker continued to work with both Reagan and his Legislative Strategy
Group in the days leading up to the votes on the tax cut legislation. Privately, Baker had misgivings about the economic package and publicly referred to the plan as a "river boat gamble," but generally he worked quite
effectively in garnering Republican support. The chairmen of two Senate
committees also had influential roles. Pete Domenici, R-N.M., the new
chairman of the Budget Committee, played a key role in his willingness to
go along with the popular new president. Even more important, Sen. Robert Dole, R-Kans., new chairman of the Senate Finance Committee, helped
to broker the extensive changes that were being proposed by lobbyists
and their legislative advocates.

The tax bill that finally emerged from the Senate was considerably different from the one Reagan had proposed. The president and his aides
clearly supported two of the changes, which they had been reluctant to
propose because of likely political attacks. The first, the introduction of
tax indexing (as of 1985), was successfully promoted by Sen. Lester Arm-
strong, R-Colo. This change, passed easily, contributed significantly to
the large deficits in Reagan's second term. The second change, introduced
by Senator Dole and again privately applauded by Reagan, was the reduction, from 70 percent to 50 percent, in the tax on investment income
in the top marginal tax brackets.

The changes viewed with greater concern were the tax advantages in-
serted for businesses. David Stockman quickly labeled the amended legislation a "Christmas Tree" bill. Lobbyists had seen a grand opportunity
for inserting some of their favorites into the larger bill and had pushed
with considerable skill. The costs of these measures alarmed Stockman,
who told journalist William Greider that he and others "did not really
know what all those numbers added up to."[35]

By July David Stockman had become so alarmed that he and Baker
aide Dick Darman privately debated the merits of quietly maneuvering to

get the tax measure in the Senate defeated by refusing to make some of the necessary last-minute deals. They decided, however, to avoid sabotage and hope that the problems in the president's taxing and spending policies would be corrected at a later date. As the bargaining continued, enough votes were gathered for passage of the bill by the Republican-controlled Senate.

The tax cut legislation also met obstacles in the House. The Democrats, recognizing that some form of tax cut would pass in 1981, tried to craft an alternative to Reagan's proposals. They sought to reduce taxes less, especially in the top income brackets. At the same time, however, they were quite willing to engage in a variety of bargaining efforts that gave advantages to various business groups. The focal point for this effort was the House Ways and Means Committee, newly chaired by Daniel Rostenkowski, D-Ill.

Adopting the same strategy he had used for passage of the spending cuts, Reagan pried enough southern Democrats away from their party to gain passage of his proposal. His "inside" efforts included a weekend stay at Camp David for fifteen wavering Democratic members of Congress. In the wake of the orchestrated "stroking" with direct presidential attention, twelve of the fifteen ultimately voted for Reagan's tax cuts. Then, in a more dramatic "outside" gesture, he went public two days before the vote in a highly effective manner.

Reagan dominated Congress in achieving passage of his economic policies. His triumphant signing of the new legislation in August 1981, however, constituted the high-water mark in terms of both influence and support for his economic policies. During his August vacation, a sharp drop in the stock market was attributed to investors' nervousness about deficits and the likelihood of inflation. In response, Reagan strategists devised a modest plan for further spending reductions and some tax changes. The president was sufficiently concerned to undertake another address to the nation. In this instance, however, members of Congress had little enthusiasm for reentering difficult policy areas and approved only $4 billion of the $13 billion in reductions Reagan had requested.

Policy Responses: 1982–1989

After a successful first year when Reagan "hit the ground running" and achieved several key legislative victories, relations between the president and Congress began to sour. Power began to shift to Congress as Senate Republicans and, on occasion, Reagan critics grabbed control of the agenda. Reagan's second term was marked by passage of a landmark tax bill and continuing budgetary conflicts with a headstrong legislature. At points, the president's large requests for defense increases were labeled "DOA"—dead on arrival—when his budgets were delivered to Congress.

Responses to the Recession.   In the economic downturn that began to overtake the country in late 1981 through 1982, unemployment surged close to almost 10 percent. The government was clearly taming inflation, but economic uncertainty was widespread. In this context several important measures emerged from Congress. One key enactment was the Joint Training Partnership Act (JTPA); another was a bill calling for new transportation spending, largely to provide jobs. Passage of JTPA came only after considerable lobbying by the Reagan administration. The president had been highly critical of the Comprehensive Employment Training Act (CETA) passed during the Carter administration because of its cost and partial use of public sector jobs. He was anxious, then, to end CETA and establish a new program. The proposed JTPA relied more heavily on the private sector. On Capitol Hill successful compromises emerged with the efforts of an unlikely pair of senators—Republican Dan Quayle of Indiana and Democrat Edward Kennedy of Massachusetts.

Reforming the Federal Tax System.   The debate surrounding the passage of tax cuts in 1981 was only the first of many tax policy debates held during the Reagan years. In 1982 Congress, worried about the mounting deficits, passed the Tax Equity and Fiscal Responsibility Act (TEFRA). The combination of Reagan's cuts and loss of tax revenue as the nation slid into a recession produced unprecedented peacetime projections of red ink. The 1982 deficit was projected to be over $100 billion and future figures far larger. Senate Finance Committee chairman Robert Dole, who was caustically critical of Reagan's supply-side approach to the economy, provided the primary leadership. Some provisions of the act addressed what were widely perceived to be the excessive favors granted to businesses in the 1981 legislation. The heart of the measure, however, was a tax increase—$98 billion over three years. The bill reduced the 1981 tax cut by about a quarter; most of the restored revenue was to come out of corporate taxes. In his January 1981 State of the Union address Reagan had loudly condemned the view that budgets could be brought into balance by increasing taxes. Thus key aides, knowing that he would not accept a tax increase, sold the new legislation to Reagan by stressing its tax reform nature, not its tax-raising elements.

A second deficit-reduction package containing tax increases was passed in 1984. It called for some $13 billion in spending cuts and another $50 billion in new taxes. Sometimes described as a hodge-podge, the bill had no central goal other than to find politically feasible ways of reducing the deficit. Once again, Reagan quietly added his signature to a tax increase.

Two years later, after much debate, the Tax Reform Act of 1986 emerged from Congress.[36] This bill was based on a simple principle: achieve lower tax rates across the board by eliminating many of the loopholes or special deductions being used by taxpayers. The measure was intended to be "revenue neutral" rather than a tax increase or decrease. Moreover, fewer deductions for marginal economic activities such as "hobby farms" and unnecessary real estate projects might lead to more efficient allocation of economic resources.

The Reagan administration and members of Congress contributed extensively to the emergence of this legislation. Reagan, who liked the emphasis on simplicity, asked Treasury Secretary Donald Regan to develop the initial proposal. And early on, several members of Congress, including Sen. Bill Bradley, D-N.J., strongly advocated passage of such a scheme. Regan's proposal, however, did not garner strong support when it was made public in the fall of 1984. President Reagan then contributed to his own problems when he stated (incorrectly) prior to even an initial briefing that no individual or corporation would suffer a tax increase. The Treasury Department, by now led by James Baker, was asked to develop a new proposal.

Reagan unveiled his new tax reform proposal in May 1985 amid considerable fanfare. He began with a presidential address and then went on the road, emphasizing the bill's populist themes and touting the tax cut it would provide for average Americans. One of his favorite lines was: "There is one group of losers in our tax plan, those individuals and corporations who do not pay their fair share. . . . These abuses cannot be tolerated. . . . The free ride is over."[37] Reagan clearly enjoyed being a strong promoter.

Despite the public's enthusiasm for reform, actual passage of the legislation was bumpy. The House Ways and Means Committee found it far easier to talk about reducing special deductions than to actually make those decisions. As they began modifying the initial proposal, loopholes began to creep back in, leaving less room for reducing rates without reducing tax revenues. The Senate Finance Committee, chaired by Robert Packwood, R-Ore., then acted to rescue the driving principle by requiring that proposals that cost revenue be matched by other increases. The development of the final bill was still an arduous task, but these committee actions were instrumental in achieving a remarkably broad tax reform bill.

Social Security and Medicare. Social Security and Medicare, difficult policy issues for Reagan, underwent considerable change during his years in office. At the outset of his tenure Reagan stumbled with a poorly thought-out proposal for reducing benefits for retirees between the ages of sixty-two and sixty-five. The proposal, which called for immediate reductions in benefits, even for those on the verge of retiring with the anticipation of a larger benefit, emerged as David Stockman (who later found the idea flawed) struggled to find spending cuts in early 1981. Chief of Staff James Baker was surprised and concerned when Reagan accepted the proposal without calling for additional review and tried without success to distance Reagan from it.

The response to the idea on Capitol Hill was dismay. In less than a week the Senate passed by a 98–0 vote a resolution calling for the president to abandon his proposal. Reagan, deciding not to fight Congress, signified his "surrender" with a brief note saying he was not wedded to any one approach to Social Security reform. Nevertheless, the administration later tried to achieve budgetary savings by reducing the minimum Social Security benefit—a minimum designed to assist those who otherwise would receive very low benefits because of the low wages they had received. But the political opposition formed quickly, and the proposal was defeated. Congress also learned from the incident. Some committees (supported by some Republicans) had been moving toward gradually increasing the age of eligibility for Social Security from sixty-five to sixty-eight as well as reducing the cost of living adjustments (COLAs). These notions, however, were abandoned.

The next strategy to come forward for handling Social Security was top-level negotiation.[38] As the impacts of inflation (forcing higher cost of living increases) and a weak economy (reducing Social Security tax collections) intensified, the pressure for action to preserve the system's finances intensified as well. In response, the president formed a bipartisan commission to review Social Security reform and release its recommendations after the 1982 midterm elections. Composed of fifteen appointees by Reagan, Speaker Tip O'Neill, and Senate majority leader Howard Baker and headed by economist Alan Greenspan, the commission included views that ranged from ardent calls for no reductions by Claude Pepper, D-Fla., the "dean" of congressional advocates for the elderly, to calls for significant reductions by representatives of the White House viewpoint.

The result was a stalemate. In late November observers feared that the Social Security Administration (SSA) would have to halt some of its monthly benefit payments as of July 1983 unless an agreement could be reached. David Stockman briefed the president on the stalemate in the commission and then asked two specific questions. First, would he accept the basic outlines of a compromise that had produced partial commission agreement, and second, would he agree to have the White House initiate secret negotiations with the commission? Reagan, the pragmatist, decided that this was the best he could get out of the situation and answered yes to both questions.

The resulting "gang of nine" operated in secret while the commission continued to provide a "front" for their operations. The group included White House and congressional officials who could speak for the two principals—Reagan and O'Neill—and excluded officials with the most polarizing positions. The White House was represented by OMB Director David Stockman; Chief of Staff James Baker; Richard Darman, deputy assistant to the president; and Kenneth Duberstein. The legislative delegation was composed of Senate Finance Committee chairman Robert Dole, Sen. Daniel Patrick Moynihan, and House Ways and Means Committee chairman Daniel Rostenkowski. Robert Ball, longtime head of the Social Security Administration, and commission chairman Alan Greenspan rounded out the group.

After initial difficulties and periodic checking with Reagan and O'Neill, the gang of nine was able to reach a compromise agreement. But the process was delicate. Both Reagan and O'Neill had to sign off as supporting the proposal before it could go back to the full commission and become public. The support of the congressional leaders of each party—to ensure passage of the bill—was needed as well. Neither Reagan nor O'Neill was pleased with aspects of the agreement, but under the pressure of time they agreed to it. Once that tense moment had passed, a party-like atmosphere engulfed Blair House, the site of the negotiations.

Despite the pressure of time and the efforts by party leaders to sell the compromise as "shared pain," final congressional passage was not easy. The committee chairs were generally cooperative, but last-minute lobbying and different preferences in the House and Senate produced considerable nervousness until the conference committee reached a final compromise. Once again taxes were increased—when combined with the Medicare portion of the tax—from 6.7 percent to 7.51 percent in 1989. In more direct terms, some 36 million retirees would lose an average of $120 from COLA delays (as well as suffer a cumulative long-range impact); some 110 million workers would pay an extra $200 in taxes by 1987; and retirees reaching age sixty-five in 2002 would see the age of eligibility gradually increased to age sixty-seven. As for the winners and losers in this compromise, O'Neill received more of what he wanted than Reagan, but the president could take comfort in knowing that he had ensured that the nation's Social Security checks would be delivered on time in July.

Social Security issues cropped up again in 1985 amid Republican efforts in the Senate to develop a significant deficit-reduction package.[39] With the help of California's Republican senator Pete Wilson who arrived on a hospital gurney, Senator Dole was able to achieve a 49–48 vote in favor of eliminating that year's cost of living adjustment. House Republicans were less enthusiastic, however, and a group of sixty-seven wrote their Senate colleagues suggesting that they change their position. Reagan then made a deal with Tip O'Neill that enraged Dole and Senate Budget Committee chairman Peter Domenici, R-N.M., because they had thought the president was supportive of their efforts and now felt they had encouraged their colleagues in a difficult vote for no good reason. Thus the last effort to deal with Social Security in the Reagan years ended as the president agreed to oppose a COLA delay in exchange for O'Neill's support of a slight increase in defense spending.

Regulatory Policy Changes. On balance, the Reagan administration pursued a surprisingly limited deregulation agenda, and the changes in regulatory policy that were enacted reflected Reagan's policy interests. Among other things, he pursued modification of savings and loan association regulations, the regulatory process for cable television, and agricultural regulations. But the president did not contribute extensively to the public debate on these issues, and they apparently were not high presidential priorities. Nevertheless, in varying degrees the administration did speak its piece as the proposals made their way through the legislative process.

The 1982 Garn–St. Germain legislation modifying regulations for savings and loan institutions represented a major step beyond the regulations issued in 1980. The driving force behind this act was the difficult situation confronting the savings and loan industry. In a period of high inflation, these institutions could not pay sufficient interest to attract savers and thereby generate the capital needed to continue to provide home mortgage loans. In response to this situation, Congress relaxed the rules governing the kinds of loans that could be made and the level of interest rates that could be paid. The Reagan administration was supportive of the measure, but the savings and loan industry also had strong backers in Congress, including Democrats such as Rep. Fernand St. Germain of Rhode Island who in 1980 had helped to shepherd the initial reform bill through Congress. Unfortunately, the new bill would soon worsen an already difficult situation.

Civil Rights. Ronald Reagan had a long history of opposing affirmative action, civil rights legislation, and efforts to use the federal government to promote equality in the workplace. His views were based in part on his conservative philosophy which called for a reduced role for the federal government in dealing with domestic issues, but they also stemmed from his inability to recognize racial and sexual discrimination as serious problems. Reagan's faith in individual initiatives and hard work made it difficult for him to recognize the existence and impact of discrimination, and he saw many of the programs of the 1960s and 1970s as big government intruding into the lives of citizens and business. Reagan thus played only a limited role in the passage of civil rights legislation. When the Voting Rights Act came up for renewal in 1981, the White House firmly opposed the provision stipulating that one could use statistical results rather than prove intent in obtaining judgments that voting rights had been infringed. Attorney General William French Smith testified forcefully against the provision, but Congress rejected the administration's position. In the Senate, Jesse Helms, R-N.C., tried to filibuster, but the administration did not encourage this step because the sixty votes needed to vote cloture and limit the debate appeared at hand.

In the debate over making Martin Luther King Jr.'s birthday a national holiday, opponents of the measure pointed to the costs incurred in losing a federal workday. The Reagan administration appeared to be supportive of that view, but President Reagan decided against a veto of this legislation, stating somewhat grudgingly that he would go along with the measure because some people saw in it a lot of "symbolic importance."

Federalism Initiatives. One of Reagan's goals was to transfer power from the federal to the state governments, and he had modest success with his efforts to change federal-state relations. His most concerted attempt occurred in 1982 when he proposed that Washington and the states swap functions—for example, the states would accept total responsibility for Aid to Families with Dependent Children (AFDC) and the federal government would take over Medicaid. Reagan tried to sell the program to the public and even visited several state legislatures. Governors welcomed the greater discretion in some programs, but they were concerned about the possible long-term loss of funds. The legislation died in 1982.

In 1981 the administration tried, with partial success, to cut several programs, including AFDC and Medicaid. On Medicaid in particular, Reagan ran into strong and effective legislative resistance led in the House by Henry Waxman, D-Calif. Overall, Reagan succeeded in further slowing the rate of growth in federal spending for federal-state programs; funding had peaked in 1978 and actual reductions occurred in 1982 and 1987. Whether intended or not, one important consequence was that the states, in view of the strong economy between 1983 and 1988, began to raise taxes. As a result, the portion of state and local budgets coming from federal grants-in-aid declined from 25.8 percent in 1980 to 18.2 percent in 1987.[40]

Reagan and Congress

Reagan demonstrated a range of skills in promoting passage of his economic program in 1981. He focused his agenda, displayed unusual skill in his public appeals, worked hard to gain the votes of individual members of Congress, and showed a willingness to stand firm when others might have decided to compromise. Without such an effort, there would have been a tax cut in 1981 but not one nearly as large. Congress also played an important role, including making key changes in the original proposal that Reagan had been reluctant to request. Moreover, its legislative leaders had offered considerable help in the various bargaining processes.

A more distant view, however, of Reagan's performance over his eight-year tenure reveals that it was not particularly strong. While the ingredients for increased legislative success may have been on hand, his success in 1981 was more the result of short-term calculations rather than a significant lasting realignment of views.[41] Mark Peterson found Reagan's legislative presidency after 1981 hard to distinguish from those of his predecessors.[42] After 1981 Reagan pursued a limited legislative agenda amid the policy initiatives emerging from Congress during his second term.

An Assessment

The promise of a "Reagan Revolution" sets a formidable standard by which to judge an administration. A better perspective is simply to consider the scope of Reagan's legacy in shaping government programs and economic performance along with his impact on the presidency itself.[43]

During his years in the White House, Reagan clearly limited the potential expansion of the federal government's domestic activities. His rhetorical appeals contributed to this containment, but after 1981 the mounting federal deficit and the nation's soaring trade deficit—from $24.2 billion in 1980 to $152.7 billion in 1986—became other, ever-increasing constraints as even liberals in Congress abandoned advocacy of expensive new programs such as national health care. The Reagan administration also sharply curtailed the pace of new regulations and reduced some regulations already in place in specific areas. Similarly, the rates of increase in federal grants-in-aid slowed, and the states began to show somewhat greater independence.

Yet some expansion did take place. The number of federal employees actually increased by more than 8 percent between 1980 and 1988. While taxes were cut in 1981, the government later sought additional revenue through both the tax code and the Social Security system. As a result, the portion of the nation's gross domestic product (GDP) being absorbed by the federal government declined only marginally—from 19 percent in 1980 to 18.4 percent in 1988.

A more significant legacy is found in the mix of spending for government programs. Spending on defense rose from $133 billion in 1980 to $290 billion in 1988, or from 22 percent to 27 percent of the federal budget and from 4.9 percent to 5.9 percent of GDP. Within domestic categories, the expenditures held down were largely in the area of discretionary spending. Spending on entitlement programs such as Social Security and Medicare grew considerably, in part as a result of the legislation enacted in 1983.

Scholars and others continue to debate the strength of Reagan's economic performance. One clear area of improvement was the sharp decrease in the inflation rate—from 13 percent at the beginning of the Reagan administration to 4 percent in 1983. It remained low as well in the years that followed. Reagan's main role was to stand behind the Federal Reserve Board as chairman Paul Volcker pursued tight money policies to wring inflation out of the economy. Other presidents might have pushed for new spending to fight unemployment rather than take on the inflation fight so quickly. Along with his perseverance and Volcker's policies, Reagan was aided by a sharp drop in energy costs and a change in the inflation index itself that removed the cost of homes from annual inflation calculations.

Job creation efforts and growth appear to have been fairly good for the best years of 1983–1988, but more lackluster if the steep recession of 1982 is included. Growth averaged 2.4 percent in Reagan's first term and 3.3 percent in his second. By contrast, Carter's average was 3.1 percent, and the results under Reagan were well below growth levels achieved in the 1960s and 1990s. While some new jobs were created, the problem of stagnant hourly wages continued without significant improvement. Unemployment levels also remained stubbornly high—an average of 7.5 percent over Reagan's eight years in office and 6.5 percent for the second term. More positively, after the early recession the recession-free period was unusually long.[44]

The sources of economic growth in the 1980s are often attributed to the ultimate impact of Reagan's policies—not the original plan. While Reagan had hoped to achieve additional savings and investment through tax policies, the result was actually a worse performance than in the 1970s. Two forces were behind this outcome. First, the nation's savings rate and thus available funds for firms to invest declined from the 1970s, and, second, the need to finance an ever-larger federal debt drew money away from potential private sector investment. Although the productivity increases from any increased investment are difficult to measure, no significant rise in productivity was evident for the 1980s. Deficits, while not planned, were nevertheless seen widely as providing exactly the kind of stimulus to the economy advocated by supporters of Keynesian views. The phrase "back door Keynesian" sometimes was used to express that interpretation.

The impacts of Reagan's tax policies continue to be debated. Supporters of supply-side economics argue that the amount of tax revenue collected suggests that taxes could have been cut with less of an impact on revenues than was usually envisioned. A more common view is that tax increases after 1981 had a primary impact on sustaining revenue flows. Still others point out that Reagan's tax policies were a source of increased income inequality. The more affluent segments of the population clearly gained a larger portion of the national income throughout the 1980s. For example, between 1977 and 1988 the top 10 percent of the nation's families by income enjoyed a 16.5 percent increase in income, while the lowest 10 percent experienced a decline of 14.8 percent. Figures for the very rich showed the greatest change. The incomes of the top 5 percent increased by 23.4 percent, and those of the top 1 percent increased by 50 percent.[45]

Many factors other than Reagan's tax policies, however, contributed to the increase in income inequality. One important influence was the growth of households with two high incomes. As a result, before-tax income inequities also increased. As for the tax rates themselves, the Congressional Budget Office estimated that between 1981 and 1990 the effective tax rate for the bottom fifth of the nation's families moved from 8.3 to 8.9 percent, while the rate for the highest fifth of the population dropped from 27.4 to 25.5 percent.[46]

The Reagan legacy also includes an unprecedented increase in the federal debt. Sen. Patrick Moynihan believes that was actually the intent of the tax cutters in 1981 as they sought to build a wall around future federal spending. Administration supporters, such as Edwin Meese, deny that viewpoint and may well point correctly to the initial enthusiasm surrounding the power of tax cuts to stimulate economic growth and additional revenue.[47] Nevertheless, the result was to indeed create a wall around potential spending. The national debt increased threefold—from $700 billion in 1980 to over $2 trillion as Reagan left office. During his presidency, the United States went from being the world's largest creditor nation to the world's largest debtor nation. Partial defenders of Reagan's economic performance, such as Michael Boskin, head of President George Bush's Council of Economic Advisers, have pointed out that because of the economic growth during the Reagan years the deficit was less troublesome as a percentage of the gross domestic product than might otherwise have been the case.[48] Detractors have viewed the accumulated debt as a more pressing problem. In particular, the large interest costs incurred, sometimes exceeding 15 percent, complicated later efforts to balance the budget.

Reagan, then, clearly did not lead a revolution, but he did leave his imprint on domestic policy. By using his various roles more forcefully, he might have achieved greater policy change and he might have done more to promote specific new policy techniques. Yet he faced a basic constraint: the public simply did not share his desire for a more dramatic change in the scope of domestic programs. It had been simple to agree with the view that government should eliminate "waste, fraud, and abuse" or cut taxes, but this agreement did not translate into support for cutting back popular programs such as Medicare and environmental protection.

Finally, Reagan left a legacy in presidential leadership. His ability to reassure the public was important during the difficult period in which inflation was weakening the economy, and he showed that the bully pulpit could be used effectively to encourage some private sector activity. Perhaps most ironically, by handling the media aspects of his role effectively and revealing unusual skill in quietly compromising on a variety of issues, he also showed that a pragmatic ideologue who was not enthusiastic about the role of government could make the task of presidential leadership seem more manageable than many had imagined when he took the reins of government from Carter.

But did Reagan's achievements meet the high opportunity level he encountered on entering office? Apart from his first-year successes, he did not achieve what might have been expected of a high-opportunity president. In this sense, he proved the least effective of the three high-opportunity chief executives.

Notes

1. Garry Wills, *Reagan's America: Innocents at Home* (Garden City, N.Y.: Doubleday, 1985); and Lou Cannon, *President Reagan: A Role of a Lifetime* (New York: Simon and Schuster, 1991).

2. Gary G. Hamilton and Nicole W. Biggart, *Governor Reagan, Governor Brown: A Sociology of Executive Power* (New York: Columbia University Press, 1984).

3. Peggy Noonan, *What I Saw at the Revolution: A Political Life of Ronald Reagan* (New York: Random House, 1990), 154.

4. Terrel H. Bell, *The Thirteenth Man: A Reagan Cabinet Memoir* (New York: Free Press, 1988), 32.

5. Noonan, *What I Saw at the Revolution.*

6. Edmund Morris, *Dutch: A Memoir of Ronald Reagan* (New York: Random House, 1999).

7. Cannon, *President Reagan,* 217.

8. Fred I. Greenstein, "Ronald Reagan—Another Hidden-Hand Ike," *P.S.: Political Science and Politics* (March 1990): 7.

9. Ronald Reagan, *An American Life: The Autobiography* (New York: Simon and Schuster, 1990); and Martin Anderson, *Revolution: The Reagan Legacy* (Stanford, Calif.: Hoover Institute Press, 1990).

10. Reagan, *An American Life,* 316.

11. David Stockman, *The Triumph of Politics: How the Reagan Revolution Failed* (New York: Harper and Row, 1986), 9.

12. Joseph White and Aaron Wildavsky, *The Deficit and the Public Interest: The Search for Responsible Budgeting in the 1980s* (Berkeley: University of California Press, 1989), 67.

13. Cannon, *President Reagan,* 70–72.

14. Stephen Hess, *Organizing the Presidency,* rev. ed. (Washington, D.C.: Brookings, 1988), 161.

15. Shirley Anne Warshaw, *Powersharing: White House–Cabinet Relations in the Modern Presidency* (Albany: State University of New York Press, 1996), 155–156.

16. Jane Mayer and Doyle McManus, *Landslide: The Unmaking of a President, 1984–1988* (Boston: Houghton Mifflin, 1988), 361–364.

17. Colin Campbell, *Managing the Presidency: Carter, Reagan, and the Search for Executive Harmony* (Pittsburgh: University of Pittsburgh Press, 1986), 99.

18. Mark A. Peterson, *Legislating Together: The White House and Capitol Hill from Eisenhower to Reagan* (Cambridge: Harvard University Press, 1990), 260.

19. Kenneth O'Reilly, *Nixon's Piano: Presidents and Racial Politics from Washington to Clinton* (New York: Free Press, 1995), chap. 9.

20. Robert R. Detlefsen, *Civil Rights under Reagan* (San Francisco: ICS Press, 1991), 4.

21. Barbara H. Craig and David M. O'Brien, *Abortion and American Politics* (Chatham, N.J.: Chatham House, 1993), 173.

22. William K. Muir Jr., *The Bully Pulpit: The Presidential Leadership of Ronald Reagan* (San Francisco: ICS Press, 1992).

23. Richard A. Harris and Sidney M. Milkis, *The Politics of Regulatory Change: A Tale of Two Agencies* (New York: Oxford University Press, 1996), 100.

24. Peter J. Boettke, "The Reagan Regulatory Regime: Reality vs. Rhetoric," in *The Economic Legacy of the Reagan Years: Euphoria or Chaos?* ed. Anandi P. Sahu and Ronald L. Tracy (Westport, Conn.: Greenwood Publishing, 1991).

25. Mary E. Stuckey, *The President as Interpreter-in-Chief* (Chatham, N.J.: Chatham House, 1991), 115.

26. Mark Hertsgaard, *On Bended Knee: The Press and the Reagan Presidency* (New York: Farrar, Straus, Giroux, 1988).

27. Muir, *Bully Pulpit*, 21.

28. Ibid., 2.

29. Barbara Hinckley, *The Symbolic Presidency: How Presidents Portray Themselves* (New York: Routledge, 1990), 75.

30. Muir, *Bully Pulpit*, 189.

31. Richard J. Ellis, *Presidential Lightning Rods: The Politics of Blame Avoidance* (Lawrence: University of Kansas Press, 1994), chap. 3.

32. Stephen J. Wayne, "Congressional Liaison in the Reagan White House: A Preliminary Assessment of the First Year," in *President and Congress: Assessing Reagan's First Year,* ed. Norman J. Ornstein (Washington, D.C.: American Enterprise Institute, 1982), 44–66.

33. See especially, Anderson, *Revolution*; Samuel Kernell, *Going Public: New Strategies of Presidential Leadership,* 3d ed. (Washington, D.C.: CQ Press, 1997); Stockman, *Triumph of Politics*; Darrell M. West, *Congress and Economic Policymaking* (Pittsburgh: University of Pittsburgh Press, 1987); and White and Wildavsky, *Deficit and the Public Interest.* At the Ronald Reagan Presidential Library the personal files of David Gergen, O. M. Oglseby, and Murray Weidenbaum were examined, as well as an exit interview by Kenneth Duberstein.

34. Kernell, *Going Public,* 150.

35. William Greider, "The Education of David Stockman," *Atlantic Monthly,* December 1981.

36. Timothy J. Conlan, Margaret T. Wrightson, and David R. Beam, *Taxing*

Choices: The Politics of Tax Reform (Washington, D.C.: CQ Press, 1990); and Jeffrey H. Birnbaum and Alan S. Murray, *Showdown at Gucci Gulch* (New York: Random House, 1987).

37. Conlan et al., *Taxing Choices,* 80.

38. Paul C. Light, *Artful Work: The Politics of Social Security Reform* (New York: Random House, 1985); and White and Wildavsky, *Deficit and the Public Interest,* chap. 14.

39. George Hager and Eric Pianin, *Mirage: Why Neither Democrats Nor Republicans Can Balance the Budget, End the Deficit, and Satisfy the Public* (New York: Random House, 1997), 140–143.

40. David Mervin, *The Presidency and Ronald Reagan* (New York: Longman, 1990), 110.

41. West, *Congress and Economic Policymaking,* 80.

42. Peterson, *Legislating Together,* 266.

43. John L. Palmer and Isabel V. Sawhill, eds., *The Reagan Experiment: An Examination of Economic and Social Policies under the Reagan Administration* (Washington, D.C.: Urban Institute Press, 1982); Larry Berman, ed., *Looking Back on the Reagan Presidency* (Baltimore: Johns Hopkins University Press, 1990); Joseph Hogan, ed., *The Reagan Years: The Record in Presidential Leadership* (New York: St. Martin's Press, 1990); and B. B. Kymlicka and Jean V. Matthews, *The Reagan Revolution?* (Chicago: Dorsey Press, 1988).

44. *Budget of the United States Government, FY 1998, Historical Tables* (Washington, D.C.: Government Printing Office, 1997).

45. Kevin P. Phillips, *The Politics of Rich and Poor: Wealth and the American Electorate in the Reagan Aftermath* (New York: Random House, 1990), 17.

46. Robert D. Reischauer, *Setting National Priorities: Budget Choices for the Next Century* (Washington, D.C.: Brookings, 1996), 20.

47. Edwin Meese III, *With Reagan: The Inside Story* (Washington, D.C.: Regnery Gateway, 1992), 158.

48. Michael J. Boskin, *Reagan and the Economy: The Successes, Failures and Unfinished Agenda* (San Francisco: ICS Press, 1987), chap. 9.

The Moderate-Opportunity Presidents

*[Truman] saw the purpose of American politics as the
creation of opportunity for the common man, whom he
envisaged in various ways: blue collar workers who wanted
a job without having to buy a union card or pay off a labor
leader in advance, a small businessman struggling against
monopolistic practices (whether by corporate bigness or by
labor unions), a member of a white ethnic minority or a
black struggling against discrimination . . . The business of
representative government was to see that everyone had
a fair deal.*

5

—HISTORIAN ALONZO HAMBY

Harry S. Truman

A Broker with Beliefs

ON APRIL 12, 1945, Vice President Harry Truman walked to the special
Capitol Hill basement office used by House Speaker Sam Rayburn for an
after-hours conversation and a glass of bourbon with some of his friends
in Congress. On arrival, he was told that Stephen Early, President
Franklin Roosevelt's press secretary, wanted him to call the White House.
Early's strained voice and instructions for coming to the White House
warned the vice president that all was not well. In fact, ashen-faced, Truman proclaimed, "Jesus Christ and General Jackson," as he put down the
phone. Not many minutes later he entered the White House where First
Lady Eleanor Roosevelt awaited him. As she put her arm on his shoulder,
she told him the bad news: "Harry, the President is dead." For a moment
the vice president was unable to speak. Then he said, "Is there anything I
can do for you?" Eleanor replied, "Is there anything we can do for you,
for you are the one in trouble now."[1]

In the midst of a world war an uncertain nation wondered what kind of leadership would be provided by a president who had been regarded by many only a decade earlier as a senator of little stature and the product of a political machine. Yet despite some low points in public support, Harry Truman (served 1945–1953) generally managed to land on his feet and govern quite effectively. His come-from-behind election win in 1948 stunned the nation.

Personal Characteristics

Harry S. Truman (1884–1972) was born in Lamar, Missouri, the oldest of the three children of Martha and John Truman, a mule trader. Harry's parents wanted to give him a middle name in honor of one of his grandfathers, but, unable to decide which one, they settled on simply a middle initial—"S"—which stands for nothing.

After graduating from high school in Independence, Missouri, Harry, unable to afford college, took a series of jobs in nearby Kansas City that included railroad timekeeper and bank clerk. At age twenty-two he took over management of his grandmother's six-hundred-acre farm and became a self-described "dirt farmer." After returning in 1919 from distinguished military service in France during World War I, Harry opened a haberdashery store in Kansas City with a war buddy. It failed, however, in the wake of a recession that decimated sales for select men's wear.

Career Path

Truman's political career in Missouri began with his election as a county judge in 1922, aided by Kansas City political boss Tom Pendergast. Such judgeships were administrative—not judicial—so Truman controlled hundreds of patronage jobs and many public works projects. From his judgeship, Truman picked up valuable political experience, which later he put to good use. He served as judge for ten of the next twelve years before gaining election to the Senate in 1934. In 1940 he retained his seat against a strong challenger despite the pall cast by sponsor Tom Pendergast's conviction for tax evasion. During his second term, Truman gained considerable experience and exposure to the nation's defense effort as he headed the Senate Committee to Investigate the National Defense Program, which took a hard look at wartime contracts.

In 1944 his selection as the Democratic vice presidential candidate came amid intense political maneuvering. Roosevelt felt that Henry Wallace, his current vice president, was too liberal to warrant renomination. Truman, however, seemed to be a plausible candidate—he apparently appealed to different segments of the party, and he had gained considerable visibility from his Senate committee investigations. After a long delay, Truman was offered—perhaps not too graciously—the second spot on the ticket by FDR at the Democratic convention in Chicago. Roosevelt said through an intermediary, "You tell him that if he wants to break up the Democratic Party in the middle of a war, that's his responsibility." The feisty Missourian responded, "Well, if that is the situation I'll have to say yes, but why the hell didn't he tell me in the first place." [2]

Truman's career path left little room to accumulate experience in foreign policy, and FDR contributed to his vice president's foreign policy gap by unwisely excluding Truman from strategic wartime deliberations. Harry came into office with other valuable experience, however. According to Harold Gosnell, Truman profited from the skills he had developed earlier in his career while acting as a broker among different groups. In Kansas City, as a county administrator allied with the Pendergast machine, he had had to balance the claims made by various ethnic groups as well as by a significant black population. His brokering skills were especially evident later, in 1940, when he needed to build a coalition of diverse segments such as urban ethnic groups, blacks, small town residents, and farmers. [3] Truman also entered the White House with extensive knowledge of different occupational roles, of the country from his wide travels with his Senate committee, and of American history from his voracious appetite for books.

What Manner of Man?

Truman possessed several traits that boded well for a president cast into difficult circumstances. One was his diligence and capacity for hard work. As a youngster he had read a set of encyclopedias from A to Z. In the Senate he studied night after night going over railroad financial reports as part of his committee responsibilities. As president he often was seen lugging six- to eight-inch stacks of folders into the family quarters of the White House (and later Blair House where the Truman family lived for four years while the White House was undergoing renovation) for his evening reading. His habit of rising early originated in his younger days on the farm, and he stuck to that schedule throughout his years in politics. He also kept himself in good physical condition by walking.

Truman was one of the more knowledgeable presidents about American political history. Although he was largely self-taught and tended toward some uncritically accepted popular views, his studies had included an analysis of the leadership approaches and performances of each of his predecessors in the White House. When Truman set out to gather knowledge, he tended to dig into the specifics of issues but limit his examination of theoretical considerations. He knew a lot about the federal budget, for example, but made no pretext of having studied economics.

As for other qualities, historian Donald R. McCoy found the president to be "an honest man who abhorred having any one kicked around."[4] Former House Speaker John Garner, D-Texas, who knew Truman from his days in Congress, remarked as the Missourian assumed the presidency that he was "honest and patriotic and has a head full of horse sense. Besides, he has guts."[5] Indeed, when his business venture failed he resisted the bankruptcy route taken by his partner and struggled for more than a decade to fully repay his debts. And, despite being the product of a political machine and facing financial pressures from past debts, Truman did little to seek personal profit. According to historian Alonzo Hamby, "he took care to see that his hands were clean. Perhaps now and again his position gave him a bit of leverage into business deals, but he never took payoffs and never handled political money."[6]

More recent scholarship on Truman has pointed to some limitations that may have been glossed over in the more flattering portraits.[7] For example, historian Robert Ferrell found Truman more calculating in his political rise than earlier studies had suggested.[8] And Hamby has argued that Truman suffered from a sense of inferiority. "Inwardly, he cultivated a belief that half the world was against him or letting him down, while the other half was conducting a smear campaign against him and his family. He simmered over slights, real or imagined, from others, and occasionally broke off relationships on flimsy grounds."[9] At first, he was somewhat overwhelmed by his presidential responsibilities. Yet, given the magnitude of issues he inherited, even the most highly confident officeholder would have been at least somewhat awed by the job. In his first weeks in office, Truman's emphatic confessions of concern about his inadequacy for the presidency did produce some advice from his friends: tone down the self-doubts.

Years ago Americans were fond of pointing out that Roosevelt proved that a rich man could be president, Truman proved that anybody could be president, and Eisenhower proved that they did not need a president.

preferred to leave low-paying government jobs, and others he could not trust, and so the cabinet and staff changed quite quickly.[19]

Truman proceeded along traditional lines with his staff organization and recruitment. His key aides for daily operations included Matthew Connelly, appointments secretary; Donald Dawson, coordinator of patronage; George Elsey, speechwriter and legislative analyst; and Press Secretary Charles Ross. Charles Murphy drafted bills and prepared Truman's September 1945 long message to Congress, and David Niles was responsible for minority groups. He never appointed a chief of staff, but his special counsel to the president, Clark Clifford, wore many hats, and John Steelman, in some respects, filled a role that resembled that of chief of staff later in Truman's presidency.[20]

Truman's advisory processes often produced lively debates over policy options. The leading proponent of the more liberal positions was Clark Clifford. A lawyer and native of St. Louis, Clifford had left his legal practice to take a series of Washington positions, and Truman found him to be a lucky inheritance. Described by journalist Patrick Anderson as both "smooth as silk and tough as nails," Clifford occupied the large office next to Truman's and got along very well with the president.[21]

Administrative Strategies

Administrative strategies were a central dimension of Truman's domestic policy leadership. He was especially interested in "good government" issues in the wake of the rapid expansion of government agencies begun with the New Deal and the war effort. The Republicans in Congress, basking in the large gains in the midterm election and anticipating the end of the Truman presidency in 1949, had a similar interest. Thus in 1947 the Republican-controlled Congress established the Commission on the Organization of the Executive Branch of the Government to help a new president (Republican, they were sure) cope with the problems of executive branch organization. Truman, pledging his full cooperation, appointed former president Herbert Hoover to head the new commission. To the Republicans' dismay, however, Truman was the president to benefit from the commission's findings after he narrowly defeated the Republican presidential nominee in the election of 1948. Indeed, he was pleased with the nineteen extensive reports produced by 1949 because he believed the commission had acted in a nonpartisan manner. In part because of Truman's strong public endorsement, all of the Hoover Commission's recommendations were later signed into law.[22]

Early in his tenure, Truman, confronted with labor disputes, faced demands for strong administrative strategies with more direct policy implications. The nation's labor unions had grown considerably—to the point that they had 14.8 million members, or a third of the labor force. Once the unions were freed from the wartime agreement not to strike, a wave of labor disputes spread throughout major sectors of the economy. By 1946 some 116 million man-hours had been lost because of strikes. Union leaders argued with some justification that they had made heavy sacrifices during the war when compared with farmers and various professionals.[23]

The first major labor dispute was sparked by the railroad workers. Despite the fact that some of the leaders now threatening to strike had been enthusiastic supporters of the Democratic ticket in 1944, Truman took a strong stand against the threat of labor strikes. Indeed, at an Oval Office meeting with labor leaders, he admonished them, saying, "If you think I'm going to sit here and let you tie up this whole country, you're crazy as hell." They had just forty-eight hours to reach a settlement, he reminded them, and if one was not reached he would take over the railroads in the name of the government.[24] When no agreement emerged, he called his cabinet into session but only to explain—over the strong objections of Attorney General Thomas Clark and some other cabinet members—that he was going to request legislation drafting railroad workers into the military. Later, in the middle of a speech to Congress promising that step, the president received word from Clark Clifford through the clerk of the House that the dispute had been resolved. Reacting to that good news, Truman happily proclaimed, "Gentlemen, the strike has been settled, on terms proposed by the President." Given the scope of the authority he was requesting, many observers were relieved when his proposal was then defeated.

The prospect of a strike by the nation's coal miners created a second major conflict. Once again Truman challenged the union leadership—this time, John L. Lewis, the shrewd but sometimes overly flamboyant champion of the miners union. Clark Clifford advocated taking a tough stance, reasoning in part that Truman would find it politically expedient to oppose an unpopular union leader. Nevertheless, in his overall responses to labor strikes Truman showed a willingness to use administrative actions to defend what he saw as the larger public interest. In one of the more significant setbacks of his presidency, however, Truman's 1952 seizure of the nation's steel mills during the Korean War in response to an industry-wide labor strike was overturned by the Supreme Court.[25]

Ultimately, the most important area in which Truman applied his administrative strategies was civil rights, where the same forces that had prevented Senate passage of measures like the antilynching bill in the 1930s persisted. Truman's early prejudices about race had given way to a more enlightened view, and he became, in some ways, a champion of civil rights at a time when it was potentially dangerous to do so.

Before taking administrative action in this area, Truman sought other lines of influence such as advocating civil rights measures in major addresses. In a January 3, 1946, radio speech, he went public and criticized the "small handful of Congressmen" in the House Rules Committee who had prevented a vote on a permanent Federal Employment Practices Commission (FEPC) which would have continued the operation established by FDR in 1941.[26] In the face of the expected Senate filibuster, Truman briefly reiterated his support, but he could not change the outcome. Efforts to provide temporary funding also failed. Despite organized protests led by the National Association for the Advancement of Colored People (NAACP), the fate of the FEPC had been decisively determined. Truman did continue some limited protections against employment discrimination, but his fact-finding authority did not include an enforcement function.

Truman finally turned to administrative action on civil rights issues with the creation in December 1946 of the Presidential Commission on Civil Rights (PCCR). His action was prompted by his disgust with several gruesome incidents in the South—among other things, a black veteran was beaten and then blinded after being pulled off a bus, and two blacks were killed in a Tennessee jail. The distinguished members of the PCCR were given the substantial time and broad mandate they would need to prepare a report that, Truman hoped, would provide additional momentum on civil rights issues.[27]

A year later the PCCR issued its lengthy and sweeping report, *To Secure These Rights*. Although the commission's findings dealt with problems confronting many different minority groups, blacks were the main focus of the report's thirty-four major recommendations on voting rights, personal security, the need for a Fair Employment Practices Committee, laws prohibiting housing discrimination, school desegregation in Washington, D.C., and other issues. The report received widespread public attention. The Truman White House mailed out 25,000 copies, publisher Simon and Schuster sold some 36,000 copies for a dollar apiece, and the report was summarized by many newspapers, religious organizations, and interest groups. William White, the executive secretary of the NAACP, praised the report for having "stirred America's conscience." [28]

Truman then used the PCCR report to prompt additional action. In February 1948 he sent a message to Congress calling for a broad range of civil rights protections. Major recommendations included the establishment of a permanent Federal Employment Practices Commission as well as the passage of measures designed to eliminate southern practices preventing blacks from registering and voting and to end discrimination in interstate rail, bus, and airplane travel. But for legislative leaders and Truman himself the handwriting was on the wall: while some legislation might pass the House, a Senate filibuster could not be defeated and the civil rights bills would not pass.

Determined to make progress on this front anyway, Truman turned once again to administrative action. By executive order he established a Fair Employment Board within the Civil Service Commission to address job discrimination. A more dramatic step, however, was his July 26 executive order requiring the nation's military leaders to undertake steps to desegregate the armed forces.

Political calculations clearly influenced Truman's actions. He had not included the PCCR recommendation for desegregation of the armed services in his February 1948 message to Congress, and he was still uncertain of what he would do as late as May 11.[29] He was concerned in part about a significant drop in his Gallup poll support. The announcement of his executive order on July 26 came at a time in which he supported a softer civil rights plank than Hubert Humphrey, then the young mayor of Minneapolis, was advocating for the Democratic Party platform. Truman was obviously hoping to keep the South from bolting the Democratic Party. Yet, while acting as a broker among competing interests, he also was manifesting aspects of personal beliefs in his administrative strategies.

Public Leadership

In his public role, Truman was handicapped by his persona—that of a staunchly partisan, sometimes overly blunt president. At one press conference, for example, he responded to an inquiry about why he had granted an exclusive interview to *New York Times* journalist Arthur Krock by saying, "I'll give interviews to anyone I damn please." On another occasion he told a female reporter to go and read the law in question. When she said she had, he replied, "No, you haven't." [30] Clark Clifford recognized Truman's image problems and in his reelection memo recommended (to no avail) that Truman be seen more often with famous people such as scientists.[31] It is perhaps then not surprising that one study found Truman to be the least successful president in maintaining his popularity.[32]

Truman's approach to press conferences differed markedly from Roosevelt's careful use of the device to help steer newspaper coverage toward the issues and interpretations that fit his legislative strategies. At times, Truman's forthright responses drew favorable responses because of their candor. But at other times he stumbled because of his bluntness and in general did not offer specific policy objectives.

As for his public speaking, Truman's rhetorical skills were invariably compared with those of FDR, placing him at a disadvantage. Clark Clifford assessed Truman's speaking style: "He generally reads poorly from written texts, his head down, words coming forth in what the press liked to call a drone."[33] He tended to emphasize a careful collection of facts in his speeches but had little interest in developing a more effective rhetorical style. In his early days in the White House, Truman was reluctant to make public addresses; he had his lengthy September 1945 State of the Union-type address read by the clerks in Congress. Later, however, he shed that reluctance and even exceeded the average number of major presidential addresses (see Table 1–1). Moreover, Truman was the first president to deliver an entire address solely on the subject of civil rights. In a speech made before a Washington audience of ten thousand members and supporters of the NAACP, he harshly criticized racial discrimination as he proclaimed, "One immediate task is to remove the last remnants of the barriers which stand between millions of our citizens and their birthright. . . . We cannot wait another decade or another generation to remedy these evils."[34]

Congressional Leadership

Most of the president's senior professional staff dealt to some degree with Congress, typically hashing out policy and serving as a representative of the president. For example, Clark Clifford worked on a variety of policy issues, while John Steelman handled individual cases pertaining to public works and federal grants to particular districts.[35] Truman held meetings with Democratic legislative leaders on a regular basis, and he established "back door" access for not only Speaker Sam Rayburn but also many members of Congress through the use of short morning appointments.

As noted, Truman favored placing a large number of issues on the congressional agenda through messages and speeches. Whether the issues were acted on or not, Truman felt presidents were obligated to present a broad agenda. This view was especially evident in his September 1945 message to Congress. In 1948 he similarly outlined a broad agenda in his State of the Union address and in a message to Congress on civil rights issues as he sought in part to highlight differences between his positions and those of the Republican congressional majorities.

Truman also pursued strategies beyond efforts at agenda setting. He engaged in some bargaining, but sometimes with a reluctance that could be traced to his belief in the importance of congressional independence. That belief, however, did not prevent him from becoming involved on occasion in the organization of Congress. For example, he encouraged Sam Rayburn to seek the minority party leadership position in the House after he lost the Speakership because of Democratic losses in the 1946 midterm elections. On several occasions, Truman sought to mobilize public support on specific legislation; on other occasions, he tried to prompt action on measures that had become stalled in committee.

And then there was his strong veto strategy: he vetoed several labor and tax bills, as well as a price decontrol measure. Some of his vetoes were overridden—a reflection of both Republican strength in Congress after the 1946 elections, as well as his willingness to stand firm in the face of likely defeat. During 1947–1948, posturing for the 1948 presidential campaign rather than the passage of legislation was often his primary objective.

Legislative Enactments

Congress faced enormously important and complicated issues during Truman's years in office. At first the agenda was largely set by the need to end the war and convert to a peacetime economy. Economic planning, elimination of wage and price controls, labor–management relations, and tax policy changes were paramount. Yet Truman also sought to shape the congressional agenda and to promote aspects of his Fair Deal, which built on aspects of FDR's New Deal agenda, largely dormant since 1937. One indication of the scope of his agenda was found in his September 1945 message to Congress calling broadly for measures such as increased unemployment compensation, tax reform, crop insurance for farmers, national health insurance, construction of the St. Lawrence Seaway, federal aid for housing, and an increase in the minimum wage.[36] Republicans reacted with surprise and anger at the scope of the program being pushed by an unelected chief executive, using phrases such as "more bureaus and more billions." Although Truman often was unable to mobilize support, his leadership efforts helped to shape various domestic policy responses.

Economic Planning and Price Controls

Truman entered office in the midst of an ongoing struggle over economic policy that eventually would produce the landmark Employment Act of 1946. A conflict about power, the struggle pitted liberal supporters of strong government roles in the economy against Republican and business interests, who longed for a return to their position of power and prestige in postwar America. Elaborate arguments about Keynesian economics and the use of tax policies and deficit spending to achieve economic goals often bypassed key aspects of the underlying conflict.

Although Truman contributed to passage of the Employment Act, it largely owed its life to interest group politics in Congress. The initial legislation was developed through extensive committee deliberations begun in 1944. The interest group response was intense, with labor unions energetically supporting the legislation and prominent business groups such as the U.S. Chamber of Commerce, the National Association of Manufacturers, and the American Farm Bureau expressing their equally vocal opposition. Legislators bargained intently, and even had a "battle of the thesauruses" as conservatives objected to the Keynesian implications of the original "Full Employment Act" designation. Truman contributed to passage of the act by instructing his legislative lieutenants to ensure that it received priority, exerting pressure at a key point to get the legislation out of committee, offering a modest amount of ongoing public commentary, and making a radio address in November 1945 that sought, with apparently little impact, to rally public support when the legislation appeared to be stalled in committee.

The act established a three-person Council of Economic Advisers (CEA) within the Executive Office of the President and called for some responsiveness to economic conditions. The CEA would provide information on the economy, evaluate federal economic policies, and submit an annual report. In addition, Congress established its own Joint Committee on the Economic Report to evaluate information supplied by the CEA and to initiate legislation based on the council's recommendations. Labor leaders and liberal supporters were disappointed by the extensive concessions legislators made to the more conservative members of Congress, who dropped the reference to "full employment" along with provisions providing a broad justification for government action. On the plus side, however, the CEA, after a slow start, proved to be a major presidential resource in pursuing more active fiscal policies.

The question of how to end wartime-induced price controls presented Truman with enormous difficulties because ending such controls was far more difficult than establishing them.[37] Americans had gone along with controls during World War II, and the country had achieved an admirable record of controlling inflation; prices had increased only 30 percent. By contrast, during World War I, when no controls had been imposed, prices had doubled rapidly. Once World War II ended, however, public enthusiasm for controls fell off sharply, and rationing was quickly eliminated.[38]

Congress was of little help to Truman in his dilemma—Republicans smelled an excellent election issue. When Republican Senate leader Robert Taft of Ohio was asked what might be done, he responded rather cryptically that people should "eat less."[39] Truman's efforts to control prices and reduce inflation were repeatedly rebuffed by the Republican-controlled Congress. The failure of Congress to respond to Truman's overtures led the president to denounce the "do-nothing" Congress, and the whole episode became a major campaign issue in Truman's surprising 1948 election victory.

Taft-Hartley Act

Although President Truman and Congress disagreed on labor union organizing rights, they did agree in 1945 on legislation tackling the problem of racketeering in unions.[40] This came as Truman successfully vetoed an initiative sponsored by Sen. Robert Taft that would have restricted unions' rights.

Regulatory policies for unions then became a highly emotional issue in the wake of the shrill 1946 campaign. Unions were roundly condemned as corrupt and charged frequently with being under communist control and at the root of the surge of inflation and the extensive work stoppages. In this context, Truman introduced his own legislative proposals, and no fewer than seventeen bills were dropped into the hopper.[41]

Senator Taft became the predominant player in Congress with the 1947 emergence of the Taft-Hartley Act, a management-supported bill seeking to reverse some of the gains won by unions. It made certain union practices such as a closed shop (only union members) illegal and authorized the president to obtain a court order blocking for up to eight days any strike that imperiled the "national health or safety." The act also increased the size of the National Labor Relations Board (NLRB) from three to five and established the Office of the General Counsel to determine whether to act on a complaint. Despite labor's opposition to many of his views, Taft was a firm believer in the right of labor to strike and to bargain collectively with management. As a result, some of his fights were with legislators who wanted a more restrictive bill than he preferred. But Taft and his colleagues prevailed in the end, thanks in part to a clever political ploy perpetuated early in the legislative battle in which few efforts were made to soften an extremely harsh House bill. That development allowed Taft and some of his supporters to argue that they were promoting a more moderate version in the Senate, which labor strongly opposed but business interests strongly supported.

Once the bill was delivered to him on June 7, Truman had to decide whether or not to sign it. Views were mixed. The White House received over half a million messages from the American public—most of which urged a veto. Overall, however, public opinion was more divided, with 46 percent preferring presidential acquiescence and 38 percent supporting a veto.[42] Union officials and many members vociferously denounced the Taft-Hartley Act. A survey of Democratic Party workers revealed that even in the pro-business, conservative South the vast majority recommended a veto.

Unlike many other Americans, the president's cabinet strongly supported a presidential bill-signing ceremony. Proponents of a signature argued that a veto would in any event be overridden (a widely shared view) and that, while not perfect, this legislation spoke to Truman's concern about the arrogant use of power by some union leaders. The most influential advocate of a veto was Clark Clifford. He argued that this legislation was inconsistent with what the president had proposed in January and pointed out that a veto would put Truman on the side of most working Americans. Along with the advantages of siding with workers on this issue, Truman the politician recognized that any difficulties with the legislation would be laid largely at the feet of the Republican-controlled Congress.

Taking his own counsel, the president submitted a lengthy, harshly written veto message to Congress. He argued that the Taft-Hartley Act

would produce more government intervention, encourage distrust in labor–management relations, and prove to be unworkable for the NLRB.
He followed his veto message with a national radio address in which he
reiterated the goals of his January proposals and argued that the bill was
bad for labor, bad for management, and bad for the country. Later that
evening, Senator Taft also made a radio address in which he charged that
Truman had grossly misrepresented the bill. After the shouting was over,
Congress, as expected, voted by large margins to override Truman's veto.

Tax Policies

The stakes in new tax policy during the Truman years were high. In the
face of the rapid decline in tax revenues after World War II, Republicans
believed a significant reduction in taxes was necessary. Truman also supported a tax cut but more modest in size. In this instance Congress was
more willing to go along with Truman's proposals, as the enacted reduction was close to his original proposal. This legislation was widely viewed
as a short-term measure, however; both the White House and Congress
realized that broader changes would be considered later. As soon as the
1946 midterm election results became known, Harold Knutson, R-Minn.,
presented a tax-reduction bill designed to cut off much of the government's income and compel it to retrench. The Republicans also wanted a
large tax cut to ward off any efforts by Truman to promote new government programs. Rep. Albert Gore, D-Tenn., led his party's fight in the
House as he claimed that this proposal was "right out of the Andrew Mel-
lon primer on special privilege." [43] The bill was changed in an effort to reduce the portions of the tax cut being directed toward those with high incomes, but Truman vetoed the measure in 1947, calling it "the wrong tax
at the wrong time."

Housing Policy

Although Truman set his sights on housing policy almost immediately
upon entering the White House, his first proposals in 1945 drew only a
limited response; Congress was more interested in addressing the pressing
and popular issue of housing assistance for veterans. Indeed, the lack of
an adequate supply of housing was forcing some veterans to go from door
to door in search of a room to rent. Congress responded with the Veterans' Emergency Housing Act of 1946. It provided for price ceilings on new

homes for veterans and assistance to producers of building materials for veterans' housing.

Landmark housing legislation emerged in 1949 as Truman successfully pushed forward a measure providing for both public housing and urban renewal projects for older urban areas. The president had promoted the issue during the 1948 campaign and then submitted a proposal to Congress in early 1949. He also promoted this policy in his public addresses. Despite strong resistance from the real estate lobby, the initiative remained largely intact as it made its way through Congress.

Health Policy and Social Security

Truman's efforts to deal with the New Deal agenda in the areas of health and Social Security produced mixed results. In 1946 Congress quickly rejected his call for national health insurance. Instead, it took more limited action, passing the Hill-Burton Act which launched a program for much-needed hospital construction. Unlike other aspects of Truman's health proposals, the final version of this measure was supported by the American Medical Association (AMA). But to satisfy the AMA, the bill's drafters had to maximize state and local control while giving the federal government little opportunity for modifying decisions made at that level.[44]

Truman made his most aggressive effort to establish national health insurance in the wake of his 1948 campaign when he promoted the issue with gusto. Although initial public opinion polls showed majorities in support, he quickly ran into difficulty. His majorities in Congress were modest, and he faced the continued resistance of southern Democrats. In the battle for public opinion, the AMA viewed his proposal as a life-or-death struggle and spent the unprecedented sum of $1.5 million in a public relations blizzard that claimed Truman's plan would impose the judgments of politicians over those of doctors. Then, in a turn of events not unlike that faced by President Bill Clinton a generation later, a sharp drop in public support eroded what chance he had for a broad new program.

Changes in Social Security proved far easier to achieve. Truman turned to Social Security reform in his second term, as pressures began mounting for expanding a system that had remained the same for over a decade. The Social Security Administration and recipients of its benefits led the campaign for change more forcefully than the Truman administration, but the president was a strong supporter. These efforts were aided by the public's fondness for Social Security, the most popular of the New Deal programs. By the time Congress finished enacting Social Security reforms in 1950, benefits had been expanded by some 77 percent and many more Americans found themselves eligible for Social Security.

Truman and Congress

On the grand scale of things, Harry Truman did not have much success with Congress on domestic issues. Although he was not overly anxious to engage in bargaining tactics, his lack of success stemmed largely from the strength of the same conservative coalition of Republicans and southern Democrats that had largely ended Roosevelt's reform efforts in 1937. But Truman was able to pursue a few strategies with some success, especially vetoes and veto threats. Agenda setting may not have motivated Congress to act, but it did help to perpetuate stalled New Deal issues. Truman also sensed correctly that he could promote his agenda while also portraying the Republicans as extremists after they seized control of Congress in the 1946 elections. In short, Truman was more effective in keeping Democratic issues alive and blunting Republican initiatives through the use of defensive strategies than in leading the charge toward new initiatives.

An Assessment

Perhaps the most dramatic assessment of Truman's skills—and the underlying strength of the Roosevelt coalition—was given by the voters in the 1948 presidential election. Defying all odds, as well as the early polling results and the unanimous thumbs-down prediction by the top fifty political pundits, Truman managed a narrow victory.[45] He had succeeded in following through with his strategy of maintaining the Roosevelt coalition. That strategy consisted of skillfully contrasting Republican positions with his own through veto strategies with Congress and strong public statements. When crowds cried, "Give 'em hell, Harry," there was no doubt who " 'em" was. Following through on his intense desire to preserve New Deal programs from assault by his opponent in 1948, Republican Thomas Dewey, Truman campaigned with fervor as he wound his way through the vote-rich and pivotal midwestern states on a whistle-stop tour. In retrospect, then, Truman was aided by having a majority coalition of party identifiers, even though his party was divided between northern liberals and southern conservatives on many issues ranging from civil rights to national health insurance. An economy on the mend also undoubtedly helped his cause.

Progress on the civil rights front was Truman's most important domestic legacy—most notably his 1948 actions to desegregate the nation's armed services. That process took several years to implement but went surprisingly well and provided important new opportunities for blacks. A half-century later the military often was regarded as the nation's most successfully integrated institution. Supreme Court Justice Thurgood Marshall, who, as a lawyer, once represented the NAACP, observed that Truman, in promoting civil rights, "took over and told the southern bloc where to go."[46] Whatever the case, Truman clearly acted as a broker in making some of his civil rights decisions as he sought to minimize the loss of southern support. Yet he also seems to have changed his views. Longtime aide George Elsey strongly rejected the view that Truman acted out of political expediency: "I don't think there was anything phony at all. It wasn't a sham, it wasn't a pretense, it wasn't a lot of hot air just for political purposes." Ronald Sylvia concluded similarly based on his comparative study of presidents: "Truman reacted to events based on his personal belief in fairness and equity."[47]

Although Truman was less directly responsible for them, two important economic policy legacies also emerged. The landmark Taft-Hartley Act was a central legacy of Truman's first term. This legislation was strongly opposed by some union leaders, and those on the political left within the labor movement also regretted that this law reduced the potential for a broad, class-based labor movement. Nevertheless, unions did well in their organizational efforts during the 1950s. Passage of the Employment Act in 1946 with its creation of the Council of Economic Advisers was not used as a basis for bold fiscal policy steps by either Truman or Eisenhower. By the 1960s, however, the council and its underlying rationale for assertive federal action was serving Presidents Kennedy and Johnson quite effectively in their economic policy proposals.[48]

As a moderate-opportunity president, Truman occupied the presidency during a very difficult time and often shaped policy by successfully opposing aspects of legislation being promoted by the conservative coalition. He was aided in his efforts by his distinctive leadership style. Although all presidents seek to balance good policy and good politics in various ways, Truman's performance, more than those of his predecessors, included a stronger emphasis on the effort to "do the right thing."

Notes

1. David McCullough, *Truman* (New York: Simon and Schuster, 1992), 341–342. For other sources on Truman's background, see especially Robert H. Ferrell, *Harry S. Truman: A Life* (Columbia: University of Missouri Press, 1994); and Alonzo L. Hamby, "The Mind and Character of Harry S. Truman," in *The Truman Presidency,* ed. Michael J. Lacey (New York: Cambridge University Press, 1989).

2. McCullough, *Truman,* 38.

3. Harold F. Gosnell, *Truman's Crises: A Political Biography of Harry S. Truman* (Westport, Conn.: Greenwood Press, 1980), 259.

4. Donald R. McCoy, *The Presidency of Harry S. Truman* (Lawrence: University of Kansas Press, 1984), 16.

5. Robert J. Donovan, *Conflict and Crisis: The Presidency of Harry S. Truman, 1945–1948* (New York: Norton, 1977), 7.

6. Hamby, "The Mind and Character of Harry S. Truman," 29.

7. See Ferrell, *Harry S. Truman;* and ibid.

8. Ferrell, *Harry S. Truman,* 162–171.

9. Hamby, "The Mind and Character of Harry S. Truman," 37.

10. Gosnell, *Truman's Crises,* 175.

11. Hamby, "The Mind and Character of Harry S. Truman," 36.

12. Ferrell, *Harry S. Truman.* For representative discussions of this issue, also see Gosnell, *Truman's Crises,* 275–276; McCullough, *Truman,* 588–592; William C. Berman, *The Politics of Civil Rights in the Truman Administration* (Columbus: Ohio State University Press, 1970), chap. 1; and Kenneth O'Reilly, *Nixon's Piano: Presidents and Racial Politics from Washington to Clinton* (New York: Free Press, 1995), 145–164.

13. Ferrell, *Harry S. Truman,* 193.

14. Donovan, *Conflict and Crisis,* 31.

15. George Gallup, *The Gallup Poll, 1935–1971,* Vol. 1 (New York: Random House, 1972), 523.

16. Susan M. Hartmann, *Truman and the 80th Congress* (Columbia: University of Missouri Press, 1971), 3.

17. It is now uncertain just how long top foreign policy experts felt the war would continue without the use of the atomic bomb. The possibility that the war would end quickly was nevertheless not a part of domestic planning activities at the time of Roosevelt's death. For a recent review of this issue, see Robert Jay Litton and Greg Mitchell, *Hiroshima in America: Fifty Years of Denial* (New York: Putnam's Sons, 1995).

18. Robert J. Donovan, *Tumultuous Years: The Presidency of Harry S. Truman, 1949–1953* (New York: Norton, 1982), 127.

19. Gosnell, *Truman's Crises,* 234.

20. Charles E. Walcott and Karen M. Hult, *Governing the White House: From Hoover through LBJ* (Lawrence: University of Kansas Press, 1995), 149.

21. Patrick Anderson, *The Presidents' Men: White House Assistants of Franklin D. Roosevelt, Harry S. Truman, Dwight D. Eisenhower, John F. Kennedy,*

and Lyndon B. Johnson (Garden City, N.Y.: Doubleday, 1968), 113. Also see Clark M. Clifford, *Counsel to the President: A Memoir* (New York: Random House, 1991); and Douglas Frantz and David McKean, *Friends in High Places: The Rise and Fall of Clark Clifford* (Boston: Little, Brown, 1995).

22. According to Peri E. Arnold, the Hoover Commission was a uniquely broad and successful effort. Peri E. Arnold, *Making the Managerial Presidency: Comprehensive Reorganization Planning, 1905–1980* (Princeton: Princeton University Press, 1986), 154.

23. McCullough, *Truman.*

24. Cabell Phillips, *The Truman Presidency: The History of a Triumphant Recession* (New York: Macmillan, 1966), 114–115.

25. *Youngstown Sheet and Tube Co. v. Sawyer,* 343 U.S. 579 (1952).

26. Phillips, *Truman Presidency,* 31.

27. Barton J. Bernstein, "The Ambiguous Legacy: The Truman Administration and Civil Rights," in *Politics and Policies of the Truman Administration,* ed. Barton J. Bernstein (Chicago: Quadrangle Books, 1970), 281.

28. Donald R. McCoy and Richard T. Ruetten, *Quest and Response: Minority Rights and the Truman Administration* (Lawrence: University of Kansas Press, 1973), 100.

29. Ruth P. Morgan, *The President and Civil Rights: Policy-Making by Executive Order* (New York: St. Martin's Press, 1970), 18.

30. Carolyn Smith, *Presidential Press Conferences: A Critical Approach* (New York: Praeger, 1990). Also see Elmer E. Cornwell Jr., *Presidential Leadership of Public Opinion* (Bloomington: Indiana University Press, 1966), 164–165.

31. McCullough, *Truman,* 556.

32. Paul Brace and Barbara Hinckley, *Follow the Leader: Opinion Polls and the Modern Presidents* (New York: Basic Books, 1992), 32–35.

33. Halford R. Ryan, *Harry S. Truman: Presidential Rhetoric* (Westport, Conn.: Greenwood Press, 1993), 8.

34. Berman, *Politics of Civil Rights in the Truman Administration,* 62.

35. Walcott and Hult, *Governing the White House,* 35.

36. McCullough, *Truman,* 468.

37. Problems with postwar economies are effectively reviewed in Hugh Rockoff, *Drastic Measures: A History of Wage and Price Controls in the United States* (New York: Cambridge University Press, 1984).

38. Robert H. Ferrell, *Harry S. Truman and the Modern Presidency* (Boston: Little, Brown, 1983), 87–88.

39. McCullough, *Truman,* 520.

40. James T. Patterson, *Mr. Republican: A Biography of Robert A. Taft* (Boston: Houghton Mifflin, 1972), 305–306.

41. The legislative history of the Taft-Hartley Act is extensively reviewed in R. Alton Lee, *Truman and Taft-Hartley: A Question of Mandate* (Lexington: University of Kentucky Press, 1966).

42. Ibid., 93.

43. John F. Witte, *The Politics and Development of the Income Tax* (Madison: University of Wisconsin Press, 1985), 132.

44. Paul Starr, *The Social Transformation of American Medicine* (New York: Basic Books, 1982), 350.

45. McCullough, *Truman,* 710.

46. Carl T. Rowan, *Dream Makers, Dream Breakers: The World of Justice Thurgood Marshall* (Boston: Little, Brown, 1993), 415.

47. Ronald D. Sylvia, "Presidential Decision Making and Leadership in the Civil Rights Era," *Presidential Studies Quarterly* 25 (1995): 398.

48. John P. Frendreis and Raymond Tatalovich, *The Modern Presidency and Economic Policy* (Itasca, Ill.: F. E. Peacock, 1994), chap. 10.

*I'll tell you what leadership is. It's persuasion, and
conciliation, and education, and patience. It's long, slow,
and tough work.*

     —DWIGHT D. EISENHOWER

6

Dwight D. Eisenhower
A Skilled Centrist

IN 1952 a nation frustrated with a stalemated war in Korea turned to a
highly esteemed former military leader. Dwight Eisenhower (served 1953–
1961), affectionately called "Ike," proved to be a popular president who
easily won reelection in 1956. His critics, however, often painted him as
lazy and ineffectual. After he had recovered from his September 1955
heart attack, some even enjoyed suggesting a broader role for his chief of
staff as they asked, "Now what do we do if Sherman Adams gets sick and
Eisenhower has to be president?" In 1960 presidential scholar Richard
Neustadt expressed his own doubts about Eisenhower's leadership skills
in his classic study *Presidential Power,* thereby echoing the already widespread skepticism.[1] When staffers such as speechwriter Arthur Larson depicted a president who was politically astute and deeply involved in the
direction of his administration, they were expressing a minority view.

More recent analyses have been far more complimentary. In 1967, in
the middle of the Vietnam War, liberal journalist Murray Kempton cast
a look back at the Eisenhower White House and concluded, "He was the
great tortoise upon whose back the world sat for eight years. We laughed
at him; we talked wistfully about moving; and all the while we never knew
the cunning beneath the shell."[2] Fred Greenstein's 1982 portrayal of a
president who defended the dignity of the office while working actively
behind the scenes as a "hidden hand" president was followed by other,
more favorable works.[3] In view of these wide-ranging assessments, perhaps

yet another look at Eisenhower's leadership style will reveal whether his achievements matched his moderate opportunities.

Personal Characteristics

Dwight David Eisenhower (1890–1969), like nineteenth-century presidents Zachary Taylor and Ulysses S. Grant, became president by virtue of his status as a war hero. But he was the only president with a lengthy military career to serve in the twentieth century. Although his election in 1952 led many pundits to wonder publicly whether he had sufficient experience for the job, his career path included a surprisingly diverse set of relationships. Indeed, historian Stephen Ambrose challenged the conventional wisdom when he concluded that "Eisenhower knew Washington and its modus operandi at least as well as any of his predecessors, and far better than most." [4]

Ike grew up in Abilene, Kansas, the third of seven sons. His father worked as a mechanic for a creamery operated by the River Brethren, a branch of the American Mennonite sect to which the Eisenhowers belonged. After graduating from high school and putting a brother through college for one year, Ike sought an appointment to West Point—a move made not only out of career interest but also out of financial necessity. At West Point, Ike displayed considerable athletic talent until a knee injury ended his football career. In 1915 he graduated in the top half of a class that produced, remarkably, fifty-nine generals. [5]

After graduation Ike was sent by the army to San Antonio, Texas, where he met Marie "Mamie" Doud, the daughter of a wealthy Denver meat packer. They married in 1916 and had two sons, one of whom died of scarlet fever. Ike's other son, John Sheldon Eisenhower, was the father of David Eisenhower who married the daughter of Ike's vice president, Richard Nixon.

Career Path

Eisenhower's military career was rich in experiences. During World War I he commanded a tank training center, earning along the way the Distinguished Service Medal and a promotion to captain. Just before the end of the war he was sent to the Panama Canal Zone. Ike showed a keen interest in staff relationships from the outset and in 1926 graduated first in his class at the army's elite command and general staff school. While stationed in Washington in the early 1930s and serving as aide to the army chief of staff, Gen. Douglas MacArthur, Eisenhower testified before congressional committees on the army's budget, among his many other duties. His Washington years also gave him an opportunity to observe closely the Roosevelt presidency, with the help of his brother Milton, a high-ranking official in the Department of Agriculture. From Washington Eisenhower accompanied MacArthur to the Philippines, where his activities included speechwriting and observing a general with zealous interests in self-promotion.

With the advent of World War II, Eisenhower's career skyrocketed and he eventually became a national hero—a phenomenon that stemmed not only from his military achievements but also from his public relations skills. His public acclaim grew as he ultimately became commander of the Supreme Headquarters, Allied Expeditionary Force, with the responsibility for planning and coordinating the 1944 Normandy invasion. In that role he often was praised for his ability to mold diverse personalities into an effective organization.

After the war Eisenhower served for three years as the army chief of staff, two years as president of Columbia University, and then as commander of the North Atlantic Treaty Organization (NATO). In the spring of 1952 he resigned the NATO post to pursue the Republican Party's presidential nomination.

Despite Eisenhower's widespread popularity, the contest for the Republican nomination was actually very close. Ohio senator Robert Taft had the support of many party loyalists and the intense support of those who wanted U.S. foreign policy to take on a more isolationist hue. Eisenhower also was handicapped by his late entry into the race. The first convention vote in Chicago found him nine votes short of a majority. But then Minnesota senator Edward Thye announced that his state would switch nineteen votes from favorite son Harold Stassen to Eisenhower.[6] The die was cast.

In the fall campaign Eisenhower was aided by his likeable personality and his foreign policy themes.[7] Republican stalwarts, and even a large number of Democratic Party identifiers, proudly wore his campaign button proclaiming "I like Ike." His foreign policy stance produced considerable support as well. Voters were frustrated over the endless war in Korea and hoped that Eisenhower, who had promised to go to Korea if elected, would be able to end the conflict. Interestingly, Eisenhower drew little support from his charges of corruption and cronyism in the Truman White House.

Domestic issues took a back seat in Eisenhower's campaign. He was far more familiar with and interested in foreign policy, and he recognized that he was the candidate of a party with sharp divisions between those wanting to largely maintain existing programs and arch conservatives who sought a major assault on New Deal programs. The bottom line: there was little basis for claiming any mandates on domestic policy.

What Manner of Man?

Although at first Eisenhower was not really sure he wanted to be president, he was quite confident that he would succeed in the office once he decided to make that commitment. In his eyes, he was simply the best man to make important decisions, and he thought himself a better judge of people than many of those who considered themselves to be politicians. He, of course, did not count himself among the politicians.

Eisenhower was known for his idealism and optimism, but his aides sometimes wished for a bit more cynicism. That, however, was not Eisenhower's nature. Chief of Staff Sherman Adams, who had observed that nature firsthand, gave an account: "In a determination to reach a difficult but desired objective, the idealistic and optimistic Eisenhower would reveal a faith in the higher motives of mankind that astonished the more cynical members of his cabinet." [8]

When Eisenhower did display his temper, it sometimes was more for effect than a real outburst. For the most part, he was upbeat and prone to calling on uplifting aphorisms such as "Long faces do not win battles." In fact, some observers found Eisenhower's optimism and frequent smile reminiscent of FDR's generally sunny disposition.

Indeed, in his dealings with others Eisenhower tended to go against the stereotypes of military leaders—he was surprisingly mild. During his military days, for example, one of his subordinates had to report the loss of a document containing top-secret information. He wrote in his diary, "Had to tell Ike today, though I hated like poison having to add to his worries." He then reported that Eisenhower had been considerably upset, but "he was so considerate I could have wept." [9] As president, Eisenhower worked assiduously to establish cordial, productive relationships, even with his former opponent Robert Taft. When Taft died unexpectedly in 1953, Ike felt he had lost a real friend. Overall, he viewed his relationships with others as educational efforts and seemed to make surprisingly few enemies.

As for Eisenhower's intellectual capabilities, some observers guessed him to be intelligent but untutored. National Security Council official Robert Bowie found that the president had considerable talent for pulling together people with diverse views or cutting through diverse arguments to get at the heart of an issue. Others recognized his effective cognitive style (explicit reasoning about means and ends) which allowed him to consider both the long-term and short-term consequences of an action and perceive issues and phenomena as part of more comprehensive patterns.[10]

Yet Eisenhower was not very assertive in his search for new, substantive domestic policies, and he seemed to lack originality in his evaluation of ideas. He seldom read serious books, and in choosing guests for social events such as his stag dinners at the White House he generally preferred the company of successful businessmen. He almost never associated with academicians, yet he had served briefly as president of Columbia University.

Policy Views

Although Eisenhower was personally quite conservative in his policy views, he felt the Republican Party had to move to the "middle of the road" to compete effectively with the Democrats. He had been raised as a Republican, had remained one throughout his military career, and as of 1952 regarded any expansion of Democratic domestic policy as harmful to the nation. The view that he was a moderate was fostered in part by Democratic Party efforts to recruit him as their nominee in 1948.

Of the few policy goals stated in the 1952 campaign, a central one was: reduce spending and achieve a balanced budget. He also vowed not to cut popular programs, especially Social Security.[11] As for agricultural policies, he promised to continue price support programs at least through 1954. Other campaign positions included amending the Taft-Hartley Act, providing supplementary aid to health care and education, promoting a tax cut, and taking a position on the tidelands controversy that was favorable to the economic interests of coastal states such as Texas, which were seeking affirmation of their long-recognized titles to the oil-rich lands beneath their offshore waters.

Although he rarely demonstrated a clear ideological bent in public, the private Eisenhower was fairly conservative politically.[12] Among other things, he argued that the Tennessee Valley Authority was an example of "creeping socialism" and a flawed policy because it asked taxpayers in other regions to help finance inexpensive public power that would be used to attract industry from their own states. But on some issues, such as housing assistance and Social Security, Eisenhower saw an appropriate role for the government.

On civil rights and race, Eisenhower's stance was said to be a combination of "sympathy, understanding, and empathy with paternalism and some racist notions." [13] Several years after the 1954 Supreme Court decision overturning the concept of "separate but equal" for the nation's schools,[14] Eisenhower confided to aide Arthur Larson, "I personally think the decision was wrong." [15] According to staff aide and journalist John Emmett Hughes, the president at one point indicated that in his view the Supreme Court decision had set back race relations in the South by fifteen years. For Eisenhower, the route toward desegregation would be best achieved not by decisions and laws but by changes in attitudes.

Once in office, Eisenhower proceeded with a fairly definite set of policy goals. One analysis of his legislative programs for 1953 and 1954 concluded that he set out to balance the budget, lower taxes, encourage private enterprise, and reduce the scope of federal activity.[16] He also was strongly committed to fighting inflation, but expressed less concern about unemployment. According to journalist Robert Donovan, Eisenhower's primary goals were to modify and modernize New Deal programs that had demonstrated their worth by their successful longevity.[17]

Challenges and Opportunities

During his eight years in office Eisenhower had many opportunities to act on his preference for dealing with foreign rather than domestic issues. He began by putting the stalled Korean peace talks back on track; an armistice ending the Korean War was signed in July 1953. In the spring of 1954 he finessed U.S. action in North Vietnam in the face of the looming defeat of the French by Vietnamese nationalists. The United States did, however, make commitments to the government in South Vietnam that gradually would expand.

On the home front, Eisenhower faced a related foreign policy challenge in the form of Sen. Joseph McCarthy's intensifying charges that communist infiltration of the federal government had contributed to the 1949 communist victory in China and a weakening of the overall U.S. position. Eisenhower was reluctant to take on McCarthy directly, but he did make some mild, behind-the-scenes efforts to strengthen opposition to the senator's actions. He was afraid a public battle with McCarthy might divide the Republican Party and focus too much attention on an issue the president wanted to ignore. "I will not," Eisenhower said to his brother Milton, "get into a pissing contest with that skunk." [18] Later, McCarthy's strident attack on the military turned public opinion against him—that and the question posed to him at a dramatic congressional hearing, "Have you no decency, sir?" He was censored by the Senate in 1954.

In 1956, his reelection year, Eisenhower faced tough foreign policy decisions in two new hot spots: Egypt and Hungary. In the conflict over Egyptian efforts to regain control of the Suez Canal from the British, Eisenhower protested the attack by England, France, and Israel against Egypt. The British eventually lost control of the canal. The 1956 uprising against the Soviet-controlled communist government of Hungary sparked a debate over American involvement in the crisis. The administration ultimately backed away from direct support of the insurgents.

A domestic policy challenge also emerged during Eisenhower's years in office. After delaying action on school desegregation in 1953, a unanimous Supreme Court ruled on May 17, 1954, that "in the field of public education, the doctrine of 'separate but equal' has no place." [19] The Court also instructed the attorneys in the case to return to the Court in a year to argue the issue of remedies to segregation. Based on those arguments, the Court ruled in 1955 that desegregation plans must proceed with "all deliberate speed." [20] With that, the battle was joined—segregationists versus the civil rights movement. The struggle would last for years, with the Eisenhower administration in the fray in the early days.

When Eisenhower entered office in 1953, several factors seemed to be operating in his favor. His victory margin of almost 11 percent over his opponent, Illinois governor Adlai Stevenson, was the third largest since 1932. His first-year popularity average of 68 percent also ranked third, and his four-year average of 69 percent was surpassed only by President John Kennedy during his three years in office (see Table 1–2).

Nevertheless, Eisenhower faced several constraints. The campaign had produced few new issues, and short of a major dismantling of New Deal programs there did not seem to be many promising new ideas. Eisenhower also faced budget difficulties, and an awkward situation in Congress. The 1952 election had produced a moderate Republican gain in House seats (twenty-two), giving Eisenhower an eight-vote margin. He had only a two-vote margin in the Senate. Yet the Republicans were divided on key issues between the "old guard," often from the midwest and west, and those desiring accommodation with New Deal programs.[21] In the midterm elections of 1954 Eisenhower tried to help his party gain additional seats, but it lost control of the House (see Table 1–3).

Eisenhower's reelection to office in 1956 was more a reaffirmation of his strong emphasis on foreign policy and his personal popularity than evidence of support for new initiatives. The successful launch in 1957 of a Soviet space vehicle called *Sputnik* produced outcries for new educational and research efforts, but congressional support for such initiatives was less clear. Finally, Eisenhower's determination to balance the budget each year (indeed, he produced surpluses for three of his eight years in office) served to further limit his options despite the growing popularity of issues such as health insurance and federal aid to education.

Leadership Style

Eisenhower came to the presidency with definite ideas about how a president should lead. Despite his personal popularity, he firmly resisted the "cult of personality" style that his old boss Gen. Douglas MacArthur had displayed in 1951 upon his return to the United States after being abruptly dismissed from his post by President Harry Truman. "Our public life can have no solid base in wishful reliance on a hero, or savior," asserted Ike.[22] Instead, he saw leadership as a process, and often commented that it was surprising how much a person could accomplish if not concerned with gaining credit for his or her actions.

He also adhered to a traditional view sometimes associated with the nineteenth-century Whig Party. He told aide Arthur Larson, for example, that he did not believe presidents should go around crusading for good causes that were not assigned to them by the Constitution—that is, presidents enjoyed all the powers formally bestowed by the Constitution and did not need any more.[23] As for a president's relationship with Congress, Eisenhower preferred a partnership between the two branches. He was quick to criticize FDR's assertive efforts to provide congressional leadership and, especially in 1953, was unusually reluctant to assume a strong role. Given Ike's less ambitious view of the office, anyone evaluating his success must look at Eisenhower's own policy goals, not the FDR standard.

Eisenhower perhaps gave voice to his leadership style when he responded to a question by staff aide and journalist Emmett Hughes. "I'll tell you what leadership is," said Ike. "It's persuasion, and conciliation, and education, and patience. It's long, slow, and tough work." His definition of leadership also was often stated as "deciding what needs to be done and then getting others to do it." [24] It is only left to be said that despite Richard Neustadt's negative portrayal of Eisenhower in *Presidential Power*, Ike's view of leadership was completely in keeping with Neustadt's: effective presidential influence requires skillful persuasive abilities.

The Advisory Process and Approach to Decision Making

Eisenhower's cabinet was quickly characterized by the press as "eight millionaires and a plumber." Gen. Lucius Clay, chairman of the board of Continental Can Company, and Herbert Brownell, a New York attorney who had played a key role in drafting Eisenhower for the Republican nomination and in the 1952 campaign, helped the president select his cabinet. Of those chosen, no one was an old friend, many were strangers, and only Brownell, who became attorney general, and Postmaster General Arthur Summerfield had been active in his election campaign.

Eisenhower's cabinet operations were in some ways unique.[25] A formal agenda for each meeting was prepared by Chief of Staff Sherman Adams, and cabinet members were given background papers (neatly punched for their cabinet meeting binders) to be read before each meeting. The meetings themselves, generally held on Friday morning, typically lasted for three hours. In an effort to achieve some kind of follow-up and follow-through, Eisenhower hired a cabinet secretary. He was the first president to do so.

A few cabinet members figured prominently in domestic policy matters both in cabinet meetings and in their individual advisory roles. George Humphrey, an Ohio businessman and secretary of the Treasury, spoke extensively and with a generally conservative voice on issues such as the need to balance the budget. Agriculture secretary Ezra Taft Benson from Utah, a devout Mormon and the only Taft supporter in the cabinet, was a strong advocate of steps that would reduce the government's role in the nation's farm economy. Oveta Culp Hobby, a Texan who had switched to the Republican Party in 1952, became the first secretary of the new Department of Health, Education and Welfare and contributed a conservative view on most issues. More liberal views were often expressed by Attorney General Brownell. Vice President Richard Nixon tended to look at how Congress might react to a particular policy. One observer of those meetings noted how persistently he pressed to have policies examined in terms of the electoral response they might evoke rather than their merits.[26]

Despite the unusually formal cabinet meeting process, these sessions did not often produce decisions—and when they did it was Eisenhower who "made the final call." Frequently, however, he would defer his decision. Eisenhower liked to use cabinet meetings to help instill a sense of teamwork among his cabinet members. He also believed that cabinet discussions and his statements could help fulfill his objective of having his administration speak with one voice.

When asked whether or not a president should have a chief of staff, Eisenhower drew on his military experiences for his response: "Why should I be my own Sergeant Major?"[27] He selected Sherman Adams to fill that role. Adams, a former member of Congress who had worked on Eisenhower's campaign while serving as governor of New Hampshire, monitored activities both in the domestic departments and agencies and in Congress for the president. In dealing with members of Congress, he was famous (some would say infamous) for his quick, gruff telephone style. Two other staff members with important domestic policy roles were Bryce Harlow, an Oklahoman with considerable experience on Capitol Hill, and Gen. Wilton Persons, whose experience included lobbying Congress for Pentagon programs. Among other things, Harlow provided primary final authorship of Eisenhower's legislative program in 1954. Persons headed the Office of Legislative Liaison for a time and made periodic contributions to domestic policy decisions.[28]

Eisenhower tended to focus his personal involvement in domestic affairs on economic policy and budgetary issues. On economic policy matters, he was briefed weekly by Council of Economic Advisers head Arthur Burns and his assistant for economic policy, Gabriel Hague. According to cabinet records and the memoirs of cabinet members, the president reviewed economic policy options extensively, particularly during the recession of 1954.[29] On budgetary matters, Eisenhower sat down with Bureau of the Budget director Joseph Dodge to review his options, particularly in the fall of 1953 when he was trying to reduce the budgets of many programs. One of the top officials in the Bureau of the Budget found Eisenhower "more budget minded" than any executive he had ever known.[30]

Eisenhower also sought information through periodic meetings with business leaders, labor leaders, and others holding a variety of policy views. As noted, the president granted business leaders extensive access, both in Oval Office meetings and through social contact. He met with labor leaders on occasion as well, as he sought areas of agreement and opportunities for each person to gain a clearer understanding of the other's likely next steps. On civil rights issues, however, he was reluctant to meet with anyone holding strong positions on either side, and his 1955 selection of the first black to serve on the White House staff did not increase access for civil rights advocates.[31]

Perhaps the most interesting advisory role was that assumed by Eisenhower's youngest brother, Milton. His brother's career aspirations had taken him at a young age to Washington, where he served as the top public information officer in the Department of Agriculture in the 1930s. During Eisenhower's presidency, Milton was in nearby Baltimore serving as president of Johns Hopkins University. The closeness of their relationship has been compared to that manifested later between brothers John and Robert Kennedy. As Milton later described that role, he did not see himself as one who should urge specific actions. Rather, he could ask helpful questions in a relationship in which the president knew that he did not have his own agenda.[32] On some issues, Milton outlined possibilities for more liberal positions.

In weighing some policy decisions, Eisenhower sought the "middle of the road" and "progressive, forward looking policies"—both keys to the success of the Republican Party.[33] He often spoke of the need to create "Modern Republicanism" and asserted that "the Republican party must be known as a progressive organization or it will sink." His underlying concern was that permanent dominance by the Democrats was not healthy for American politics and would likely produce too many "wild-eyed, pinkish, programs."[34]

In his decision-making role, Eisenhower looked at himself as something of a national steward. For example, he pointed out the national security implications of the proposed St. Lawrence Seaway and the federal interstate highway program—two projects he supported. He also looked for ways in which private economic activity (such as private development of atomic energy as a source of electric power) could strengthen expanded government programs. Yet his fiscal conservatism, coupled with his desire to pursue a variety of policies, often produced small program initiatives. In fact, Democrats in Congress sometimes described his mostly modest proposals as "sending not just a boy, but an infant to do a man's work."

While Eisenhower and the people around him such as Chief of Staff Sherman Adams obviously viewed many issues in terms of their political implications, he sought to avoid direct trades and vote calculations. In fact, aide Arthur Larson wrote that "if you wanted to get thrown out of the office, say, 'Look, Mr. President, this is going to cost you votes in West

Virginia.'"[35] Ike would, however, sometimes pause and ask how the decision he was about to make would be viewed by an average citizen out in Denison, Kansas. The White House also tested the political waters more directly. Eisenhower, like some of his successors (John Kennedy, Lyndon Johnson, and Gerald Ford), consulted with Congress before submitting his legislative proposals.[36]

Eisenhower's decision-making process for domestic policy was thus one that fit his particular concerns. He was interested in budgetary issues and gave them considerable attention, but he was less interested in developing major new proposals. His decision-making process was geared toward careful review and a preference for cautious policy steps.

Administrative Strategies

Eisenhower took a distinctly positive approach to the "good government" aspects of administrative reform. To Herbert Hoover's regret, however, this did not include creating another Hoover Commission. In fact, Hoover found Ike's approach a sign of weakness, but political scientist Peri Arnold found it an indication of Eisenhower's confidence in his ability to use his political skills in other ways.[37]

In his administrative responses to desegregation issues, Eisenhower acted decisively where the federal law was clear. In 1954 he took steps to end segregation of the public school system in the nation's capital when the Supreme Court established the legal basis for doing so.[38] He also took the final steps toward complete desegregation of the nation's military forces. When Rep. Adam Clayton Powell, D-N.Y., challenged his assertion that segregation of the military was complete, Eisenhower responded to his criticism with action that Powell later hailed publicly.[39] In 1957, in the face of open resistance to desegregation of Central High School in Little Rock, Arkansas, Eisenhower committed federal troops to keeping order and ensuring that the enrollment of black students would proceed in an orderly fashion.

The president was more cautious about administrative roles involving new federal commitments. For example, he did not recommend legislation providing for a Federal Employment Practices Commission, although he did make some effort to enforce compliance with nondiscrimination provisions by private firms contracting with the government. In his statements before the Supreme Court on school desegregation, Attorney General Herbert Brownell had hoped to follow the precedent of Truman's Justice Department in taking a clear position in support of desegregation. But when he sought Eisenhower's support, the president remained cautious. If the Court asked him a direct question, Eisenhower instructed, Brownell should state that he personally believed that segregation was unconstitutional.[40]

Eisenhower's administrative actions in the area of race relations were based on some political considerations; he hoped to increase Republican support in the South and had good working relationships with many Southern Democrats in Congress. His own skepticism about the effectiveness of government action on race relations was evident as well. Yet in his search for the middle road on race relations he made fewer partisan and more civil rights–friendly appointments to the judiciary in the South than several of his successors.[41]

Public Leadership

Eisenhower's lengthy experience with public relations and his view of the president's proper role were much in evidence in his approaches to public leadership. For example, he sought to defend the dignity of the presidency by avoiding any personal conflict with Sen. Joseph McCarthy. He also sought to present the persona of a president who was not simply "another politician."

Eisenhower's personal popularity was impressive; as noted, he is tied with Kennedy (behind Reagan's leading performance) in sustaining popularity despite adverse influences such as recessions. His popularity also translated into favorable press coverage—at least at the outset of his administration. In October 1953, ten months into his administration, one reporter commented that his readers were not yet ready for critical interpretations of the president.[42]

Several strategies contributed to Eisenhower's success. For one thing, he chose veteran reporter James Hagerty as his press secretary and drew on his considerable skills. Hagerty adroitly handled the news media, including in the aftermath of Eisenhower's heart attack in September 1955. He also sat in periodically on policy discussions, a further indication of the importance of his role in the Eisenhower White House.

President Eisenhower's interest in public relations prompted him to agree to televise press conferences in 1955—but delayed telecasts, not the live ones Kennedy began in 1961. Eisenhower carefully prepared for the conferences with the help of Hagerty, and he was the first president to allow reporters to use direct quotes from the event. While Eisenhower and Hagerty were pleased that they could generally anticipate about 90 percent of the questions, the president also employed a strategy of occasionally either "playing dumb" or giving rambling answers to avoid a specific answer that might have unwanted consequences. In fact, often he would respond to Hagerty's suggestion that he not answer a question by saying, "Oh, leave it to me, Jim, I'll confuse them."[43] In some situations, then, Eisenhower was willing to pay the price of appearing incapable of giving crisp, clear answers. He gained flexibility that way.

The president also was fond of the "lightning rod" strategy—that is, he would try to avoid taking the "political heat" for an unpopular policy or blunder by distancing himself from the problem and swinging criticism toward an aide or cabinet member. Agriculture secretary Ezra Taft Benson, who frequently took hotly disputed policy positions, proved useful in deflecting criticism from the president, and the blunt statements by Vice President Richard Nixon cast him in the role of Eisenhower's "hatchet man." And then there was Chief of Staff Sherman Adams, the man the conservative old guard in Congress could easily hate, and sometimes fall guy Herbert Brownell, Eisenhower's attorney general.[44]

Along with his press conferences, Eisenhower devoted considerable energy to his speeches, even going so far to periodically seek coaching from Hollywood celebrity Robert Montgomery. The actor advised Eisenhower's aides on media strategies as well.

Eisenhower, then, was extensively and effectively involved in public relations efforts—a presidential sideline that tended to escape press attention.[45] He even passed on tips to others. As aide Bryce Harlow told it, while visiting New Jersey in 1958 to endorse a local candidate, Eisenhower told the luckless fellow over dinner, "Jim, I've been watching you. You've got to change the way you're going about this thing—you're too wooden. Tomorrow, in the parade, I want you to move your lips, I want you to be talking to the crowd, wave your arms and talk to them, look at them and move your lips; you don't actually have to be saying anything, just look like you're talking, look like you're genuinely interested in them."[46]

In speaking publicly, Eisenhower steadfastly refused to use negative appeals. Mary Stuckey claims Eisenhower was well aware of the potence of negative appeals but preferred to use positive themes. That approach fit his personal preferences and his desire to defend the dignity of the presidency, but it also allowed him to reinforce the notion that he was above the political fray. Vice President Nixon, however, preferred his own playbook. But his heavy use of political attacks drew widespread criticism that carried some fallout for Eisenhower himself.[47]

On some issues, Eisenhower was reluctant to speak out at all. Most notably, he made virtually no use of the bully pulpit to encourage efforts toward desegregation. At his first press conference after the Supreme Court's 1954 school desegregation decision, he was asked the question he doubtlessly anticipated: Do you have any advice to give to the South on how to react? "Not in the slightest," Eisenhower replied. "The Supreme Court has spoken and I am sworn to uphold the constitutional process in the country; and I will obey."[48] Eisenhower's subsequent remarks were confined to a recitation of the degree to which desegregation was occurring and the number of desegregation statutes that had been overturned in lower courts.

In choosing a less public, or hidden hand, brand of leadership, Eisenhower limited his use of the bully pulpit aspects of the presidency, thereby consciously choosing a less-expansive public leadership role. Eisenhower did not have General MacArthur's facility for theatrical pyrotechnics or Adlai Stevenson's gift of lyrical prose, but he was "a shrewd rhetorical strategist and tactician." Moreover, he profited from his ability to focus on middle-of-the-road policies yet generally stay above the fray of partisan battles. Eisenhower also had a unique ability to capitalize on his reputation, obvious sincerity, and a winning smile, while not appearing slick or superficial.[49] But would this style work in the current age in which candidates seek to communicate with thirty-second sound bites and overly scripted performances? Not likely.

Congressional Leadership

Although Eisenhower was known for his modest domestic policy initiatives (in fact, he introduced no major legislation his first year in office), he is credited with creating the first office of legislative liaison in the White House, with the task of promoting presidential policies on Capitol Hill. He also held weekly meetings with legislative leaders, attended periodically by members of the cabinet who would explain major legislative proposals. At these meetings participants would take a look at the timing of various legislative activities for the next week. In some instances, Eisenhower modified his positions on the basis of those discussions. The most unique of these meetings was a three-day session held in December 1953 to go over the president's major legislative agenda for 1954 and to consider the best strategy for minimizing congressional overload.

In dealing with legislative leaders Eisenhower found that he worked surprisingly well with Robert Taft, the Republican majority leader in the Senate. Taft died, however, in July 1953. The leadership efforts of his successor, William Knowland, R-Calif., as first majority leader and then minority leader, did not please Eisenhower—at all. On the House side, he was generally happy with the performance of the Republican majority leader, Charles Halleck of Indiana (served 1953–1954) and included him in the leadership breakfasts even when Joseph Martin, R-Mass., took over the top Republican position after the Republicans lost control of the House in 1954.[50] There were obvious partisan differences when Democrats and fellow Texans Sam Rayburn in the House and Lyndon Johnson in the Senate assumed the top leadership positions in 1955. But Eisenhower sought to achieve good working relations by periodically inviting Rayburn and Johnson to drop by the family quarters of the White House for a cocktail and some casual conversation. Eisenhower was pleased with the professionalism not only of Rayburn and Johnson, but also of some key southerners such as Sen. Walter George, D-Ga.

Particularly in his first year in office, Eisenhower was reluctant to push legislators very hard, but he was willing to listen to their concerns at considerable length. In 1953 he invited every member of Congress to group dinners or luncheons at the White House simply for the purpose of listening; in other settings, he relied simply on gentle persuasion. Also in the first year he was in contact with his party's legislative leaders on a daily basis. Senator Taft was welcome to visit any time, and the president instructed Sherman Adams that any member of Congress who wanted to see him should be granted that access. In meetings with legislators, Eisenhower sometimes went beyond his "patient education" approach to legislative relations. Although he personally disliked patronage, both he and Sherman Adams did stoop to using it on some occasions. In 1953, for example, in the major fight over postponement of a tax cut Eisenhower made it clear that patronage decisions would be influenced by the degree of support given to his positions.

Legislative Enactments

The Eisenhower years saw the passage of only a moderate amount of new legislation. The first year was especially slow, in part because of what the press saw as a very limited presidential agenda—statehood for Hawaii, restoration of the oil-rich tidelands regions to the states, and modification of the Taft-Hartley Act. Perhaps the most noteworthy occurrence during the first few months was Eisenhower's reluctance to promote his own agenda even on an issue like tidelands oil. Eisenhower had his greatest legislative impact in 1954, and his second term produced a landmark civil rights enactment but often stalemates on newer issues.

Taxation and the Budget

Taxation and budgetary issues were high on the list of Eisenhower's legislative concerns. During his 1953 State of the Union address, Ike was greeted with noisy Republican opposition when he made balancing the budget his top priority and relegated a tax cut to a lowly fifth-place mention. "Reductions in taxes will be justified only as we show we can succeed in bringing the budget under control," Eisenhower told his clearly underwhelmed audience.[51]

In taking his position against a tax cut, the president was staring at a projected deficit for fiscal 1954 of approximately $9.4 billion, which was well over 10 percent of total projected spending. Furthermore, Eisenhower felt that some of Truman's defense spending commitments had been grossly underfunded. His budget difficulties were significantly improved, however, by the end of the Korean War.

The president was able to make substantial headway in reducing the deficit by making cuts of approximately $4 billion, and one of his main contributions was to hold down defense spending in the midst of cold war hysteria—an accomplishment perhaps only someone with Ike's spotless military record could have done. When he told legislative leaders that there could be no tax decrease in 1953, Taft loudly protested that the Republicans were committed to a tax reduction. Eisenhower, however, would not be deterred, and he proceeded in 1953 to steer legislators and others away from a tax reduction until budget cuts could be achieved. Taxes were reduced slightly, but Eisenhower used a successful television appeal to help retain an excise tax scheduled to expire January 1, 1954. Although the fight left some congressional Republicans wounded, Eisenhower's diplomacy prevented any bitterness, and his key opponent complimented him on "a good fight" in a cordial letter.

With his budget cuts in place, Eisenhower was able to set his sights on a longer-term tax cut in 1954, enacted in the Omnibus Tax Act. The proposed tax legislation reduced taxes for both individuals and corporations. Individual changes included more medical deductions, changes in the calculation of dependency for children who worked, and a child care tax deduction for working women. Corporations were aided by a liberalization of depreciation allowances, but the general corporate rate remained the same.

The Eisenhower administration played a prominent role in passage of the Omnibus Tax Act. A *New York Times* reporter characterized the White House staff operations as "the smoothest working machine Capitol Hill has seen in years." [52] When the Democrats proposed a larger dependency deduction than he had requested, Eisenhower went on television opposing the change and the $2.5 billion in lost revenue it represented. As part of the selling effort, Secretary of the Treasury Humphrey invited all but three senators to lunch in order to explain the details of the program. In the end, Eisenhower was able to maintain strong Republican support and the bill he had called the cornerstone of his administration emerged from conference committee closely resembling his initial recommendations. This situation again represented shared policy making, but with a strong presidential role.

Atomic Energy Act

Passage of the Atomic Energy Act in 1954, calling for the development of nuclear energy for civilian purposes, reflected both Eisenhower's commitment to the private sector and his style of legislative leadership. Efforts to develop new atomic energy legislation had received considerable attention in the Atomic Energy Commission (AEC) under President Truman, and the Eisenhower administration was moving rather slowly toward promoting additional action. After repeated urging by the Joint Congressional Committee on Atomic Energy (JCCAE), the AEC prepared a preliminary draft of the legislation which the JCCAE used in 1953, but a bill cleared by the White House was not available until 1954.

In early 1954 Eisenhower proposed another bill that included both international and domestic components. The international component, with its provisions for greater international cooperation, was the least controversial. The importance of that aspect of the proposed new legislation was dramatized by an important presidential address, entitled "Atoms for Peace," delivered in December 1953 at the United Nations. President Eisenhower, spurred by the Soviet Union's detonation of its first nuclear device, starkly depicted the horror of modern warfare but also pointed out how such a destructive power could be harnessed for productive civilian purposes. On the domestic side, proponents of public and private nuclear power development generated substantial conflict. Senate deliberations on the bill were slowed in part by a filibuster by legislators wanting a greater commitment to public power, but in both the House and the Senate Eisenhower was able to muster substantial Republican support. When the version of the bill reported out of the conference committee finally arrived at the White House, however, an old worry cropped up: the Budget Bureau feared that the new legislation would, over time, be too costly to the government.

Interstate Highway System

Establishment of the interstate highway system was quite possibly the most important domestic policy action of the Eisenhower administration. Like many members of the American military, Ike had found Germany's autobahn system, initiated by Adolf Hitler in the 1930s, impressive. Highway construction also was viewed as a priority because both the White House and Congress recognized that the tremendous increase in automobile use in the years after World War II required a large-scale federal effort to provide the needed roads.

Eisenhower provided important support for the new system, but ultimately found he had to compromise with Congress on the funding mechanism. He began promoting the idea by forming an Advisory Committee on a National Highway Program and then used an interesting strategy: he had Vice President Nixon gain some favorable publicity by presenting the plan at the July 1954 meeting of the Governors' Conference in New York. On February 22, 1955, Eisenhower sent Congress a message calling for a $101 billion, ten-year program that would include $31 billion in federal assistance to the states. Legislators agreed that a major program was needed but disagreed on the financing mechanism. Democratic leaders preferred greater use of gasoline taxes and some other direct taxes over Eisenhower's financing mechanism which called for the sale of $20 billion in bonds. At the beginning of the 1956 session of Congress the president renewed his support of the legislation and indicated he would not resist the taxing mechanisms preferred by many Democrats. The result was strong bipartisan support for the bill, which Eisenhower signed in June.[53]

Social Security

Even though he was personally uncertain about the Social Security program, Eisenhower followed up on action taken in 1950 to expand its coverage and benefits. At the outset of the Eisenhower administration some members of Congress wanted to see an expanded program, but the U.S. Chamber of Commerce and conservatives such as Sen. Carl Curtis, R-Neb., proposed redesigning the system so that all senior citizens would be immediately eligible and reducing reliance on the "contributory principle" that had been at the heart of Franklin Roosevelt's original proposal. The immediate inclusion of all elderly as recipients would, conservatives believed, reveal the program's total cost and thus would provide a basis for generating political support for reductions in benefits.

Faced with this controversy, the Eisenhower administration, possessing limited expertise on Social Security, was uncertain about the best course of action. In 1954 the Social Security Administration drafted a major defense of the contributory principle that was publicly circulated by Eisenhower aide Arthur Larson. After reviewing the options, which included fundamental changes, the Eisenhower administration chose to avoid a major political battle and in the end recommended "more of the same" to Congress.

Thus later in 1954 Congress extended eligibility for Social Security to some 10.5 million persons, increased monthly benefits, and enacted several significant reforms. Given the popularity of Social Security among both the general public and many members of Congress, the primary role of the Eisenhower administration had been one of providing greater legitimacy for the original design of the Social Security system rather than trying to influence the outcome of the final vote.

In 1956 Congress passed a second major change in the Social Security system—some coverage of the disabled—despite some opposition from the Eisenhower administration. The Social Security Administration, Democratic leaders in Congress, and organized labor supported the change. Senate majority leader Lyndon Johnson was responsible for lining up a winning coalition. Because several key votes were close, Johnson, to achieve passage of the bill, had to enlist Republican support even in the face of opposition from the Eisenhower administration. House passage came more easily.[54]

Civil Rights

The path of civil rights legislation encountered a major barrier in 1956, but became smoother in 1957 when Congress passed a landmark measure. Yet another civil rights measure passed in 1960, in part because of the resurgence of racial violence. In 1956, believing the Supreme Court had addressed school desegregation issues, Eisenhower encouraged Attorney General Brownell to prepare legislation dealing with voting rights. Brownell, who persistently advocated a larger federal role in civil rights, eagerly developed a legislative proposal calling for federal district courts to ensure citizens' access to the polls and for a bipartisan commission to look into instances of discrimination against blacks. These recommendations were far short of the measures hoped for by the growing civil rights movement, but they did alarm defenders of the status quo in the South. Meanwhile, on another front, 103 members of Congress from the southern states (except Lyndon Johnson and a few others) were supporting legislative action seeking to overturn the 1954 *Brown v. Board of Education* decision.

In these turbulent times, then, the voting rights legislation was defeated. Some in the Eisenhower administration blamed the Democrats, including Majority Leader Lyndon Johnson, for not taking a more supportive role. Others argued that the administration's actions suggested an ambivalence toward the proposal. After all, the president had not played a public role in gathering support for the bill. The conclusion reached by Elmo Richardson seemed to fairly assess this situation: "In retrospect, neither party seemed overly anxious to take up the controversial issue in an election year." [55]

The 1957 legislative session produced a very different result. Eisenhower resubmitted his 1956 legislation, with provisions to ensure voting rights as the main component. Passage occurred fairly easily in the House, but the Senate once again posed formidable obstacles. Lyndon Johnson reasoned that the best way to get the measure through was to accede to southerners' demands for a jury trial in cases involving voting rights violations. Eisenhower was reluctant to agree to the demand, but he did not have the votes. Some civil rights groups also were opposed to the jury trial provision but ultimately urged Eisenhower to sign the final bill. The Civil Rights Act of 1957 was the first since the end of Reconstruction. It established a framework for a judicial approach to voting rights violations and established a fact-finding commission.

The Civil Rights Act of 1960 stemmed from growing realization that the earlier legislation was not working effectively and a concern with racial violence that now included terrorist bombings of black schools and churches. The key component of the Eisenhower administration proposal that became law called for the appointment of federal court referees to investigate situations in which discrimination was preventing blacks from

vorite target. There he sought to prevent expansion rather than to achieve a retrenchment. "No one has worked harder than I have to stop the expansion of TVA," Eisenhower boasted.[60]

Along the way, he managed to legitimate policies he inherited from the New Deal presidents. Economist John Witte found that Eisenhower's actions in 1954, legitimizing the programs he had inherited, coupled with his decision not to pursue additional tax reform while in the White House, further legitimated the tax system that had been broadened during World War II to finance the nation's military efforts.[61] Similarly, Eisenhower's decision to support expansion of Social Security in 1954 helped to ensure the longevity of one of the New Deal's most popular programs.

The absence of a broader civil rights legacy continues to generate debate. Attorney General Brownell believed Eisenhower was trying to prevent national polarization over the issue and seek a middle way.[62] On this issue, the critics have been quite harsh. Historian Stephen Ambrose has argued that Ike passed up a major leadership opportunity by not speaking out and offering no encouragement to those seeking steps toward peaceful desegregation. At the same time he allowed opponents to assert that the president was on their side. It is hard to say whether the difficult task of seeking public support through use of the bully pulpit on a highly divisive issue would have produced a different result. Yet one fact is clear: the president who touted the importance of attitudes and the "feelings in one's heart" to modifying race relations chose not to participate in efforts to change those attitudes.

Thus on racial issues and in some other areas Eisenhower may not have entirely maximized his opportunities. He was clearly more interested in foreign policy and rather reluctant to take on new issues. Had he, like French general Charles DeGaulle, assumed a more heroic leadership style, he may have gained some additional policy leverage. The price, however, could have been a less-deliberative policy process.

Whatever the case, viewed in his own terms, Eisenhower could claim considerable success. His middle-of-the-road policies did not turn the Republicans into a majority party, but they did often corral what he saw as excesses in more liberal proposals. He also was able to leave office untainted by a far-reaching scandal such as Watergate (Nixon) or Iran-contra (Reagan). Finally, although the critics were increasingly characterizing the government as stalemated by the end of his second term, he headed toward retirement feeling vindicated that his rather traditional view of the president's role had produced sustained public support.

Notes

1. Richard E. Neustadt, *Presidential Power* (New York: Wiley, 1960).

2. Arthur Larson, *Eisenhower: The President Nobody Knew* (New York: Scribner's, 1968), 200.

3. Fred I. Greenstein, *The Hidden Hand Presidency: Eisenhower as Leader* (New York: Basic Books, 1982).

4. Stephen E. Ambrose, *Eisenhower: The President* (New York: Simon and Schuster, 1985), 18.

5. Robert F. Burk, *Dwight D. Eisenhower: Hero and Politician* (Boston: Twayne, 1986), 21; Greenstein, *Hidden Hand Presidency;* Elmo Richardson, *The Presidency of Dwight D. Eisenhower* (Lawrence: Regents Press of Kansas, 1979).

6. Herbert Brownell, *Advising Ike: The Memoirs of Attorney General Herbert Brownell* (Lawrence: University of Kansas Press, 1993), chap. 5.

7. On the importance of foreign policy issues and Eisenhower's popularity, see Angus Campbell et al., *The American Voter* (New York: Wiley, 1960).

8. Sherman Adams, *Firsthand Report: The Story of the Eisenhower Administration* (Westport, Conn.: Greenwood Press, 1961), 7.

9. Martin J. Medhurst, *Dwight D. Eisenhower: Strategic Communicator* (Westport, Conn.: Greenwood Press, 1993), 8.

10. See John Burke and Fred I. Greenstein (with Larry Berman and Richard Innerman), *How Presidents Test Reality: Decisions on Vietnam, 1954 and 1965* (New York: Russell Sage Foundation, 1989), 66.

11. Michael G. Krukones, *Promises and Performances: Presidential Campaigns as Policy Predictors* (New York: University Press of America, 1984), 76; Barton J. Bernstein, "The Election of 1952," in *History of American Presidential Elections, 1789–1968,* ed. Arthur M. Schlesinger Jr. (New York: McGraw-Hill, 1971), 3215–3266.

12. In fact, Eisenhower was described by a former speechwriter as being "closer to Hoover than the New Dealers." William Bragg Ewald Jr., *Eisenhower the President: Crucial Days, 1951–1960* (Englewood Cliffs, N.J.: Prentice-Hall, 1981), 42.

13. Michael S. Mayer, "Eisenhower and Race," in *Dwight D. Eisenhower: Soldier, President, Statesman,* ed. Joan P. Krieg (Westport, Conn.: Greenwood Press, 1987), 39.

14. *Brown v. Board of Education of Topeka,* 347 U.S. 483 (1954).

15. Larson, *Eisenhower,* 124.

16. Gary W. Reichard, *The Reaffirmation of Republicanism: Eisenhower and the Eighty-Third Congress* (Knoxville: University of Tennessee Press, 1975), 230.

17. Robert J. Donovan, *Eisenhower: The Inside Story* (New York: Harper, 1956), 229.

18. Quoted in Stephen E. Ambrose, "The Eisenhower Revival," in *Rethinking the Presidency,* ed. Thomas E. Cronin (Boston: Little, Brown, 1982), 107.

19. *Brown v. Board of Education of Topeka,* 347 U.S. 483 (1954). Also see Carl T. Rowan, *Dream Makers, Dream Breakers: The World of Thurgood Marshall* (Boston: Little, Brown, 1993), 217.

20. *Brown v. Board of Education of Topeka,* 349 U.S. 294 (1955).

21. Reichard, *Reaffirmation of Republicanism,* chaps. 1–2.

22. Marcus Childs, *Eisenhower: Captive Hero* (New York: Harcourt Brace, 1958), 12. MacArthur was dismissed for defying Truman's wish to avoid expanding the Korean conflict.

23. Larson, *Eisenhower,* 54.

24. Ibid., 15.

25. On Eisenhower's use of his cabinet, see in particular James P. Pfiffner, *The Strategic Presidency: Hitting the Ground Running,* 2d ed. (Lawrence: University Press of Kansas, 1996); and Stephen Hess, *Organizing the Presidency,* rev. ed. (Washington, D.C.: Brookings, 1988).

26. Ewald, *Eisenhower the President,* 177.

27. Ambrose, *Eisenhower,* 52.

28. Charles E. Walcott and Karen M. Hult, *Governing the White House: From Hoover through LBJ* (Lawrence: University Press of Kansas, 1995), 38–43.

29. Donovan, *Eisenhower,* 209–229.

30. Ewald, *Eisenhower the President,* 64.

31. Richardson, *Presidency of Dwight D. Eisenhower,* 110.

32. Milton S. Eisenhower, "Portrait of a Brother," in *The Eisenhower Presidency: Eleven Intimate Perspectives of Dwight D. Eisenhower,* ed. Kenneth W. Thompson (New York: University Press of America, 1984), 5. For more extensive insights on that unique role, see Milton S. Eisenhower, *The President Is Calling* (Garden City, N.Y.: Doubleday, 1974).

33. Donovan, *Eisenhower,* 151.

34. Robert H. Ferrell, ed. *The Eisenhower Diaries* (New York: Norton, 1981), 288.

35. Larson, *Eisenhower.*

36. Eric L. Davis, "Congressional Liaison: The People and the Institution," in *Both Ends of the Avenue: The Presidency, the Executive Branch, and Congress in the 1980s,* ed. Anthony King (Washington, D.C.: American Enterprise Institute, 1983), 59–84.

37. Peri E. Arnold, *Making the Managerial Presidency: Comprehensive Reorganization Planning, 1905–1980* (Princeton: Princeton University Press, 1986), 202.

38. *Bolling v. Sharpe,* 347 U.S. 483 (1954).

39. Peter Lyon, *Eisenhower: Portrait of a Hero* (Boston: Little, Brown, 1974), 558.

40. Brownell, *Advising Ike,* 193.

41. Michael Mayer, "Eisenhower and the Southern Federal Judiciary: The Soboloff Nomination," in *Reexamining the Eisenhower Presidency,* ed. Shirley Anne Warshaw (Westport, Conn.: Greenwood Press, 1993), 57–75.

42. Lyon, *Eisenhower: Portrait of a Hero,* 483.

43. Eisenhower, "Portrait of a Brother," 9.

44. Richard J. Ellis, *Presidential Lightning Rods: The Politics of Blame Avoidance* (Lawrence: University of Kansas Press, 1994).

45. Craig Allen, *Eisenhower and the Mass Media: Peace, Prosperity, and Prime-time TV* (Chapel Hill: University of North Carolina Press, 1996).

46. Bryce Harlow, "The Complete Politician," in Thompson, *Eisenhower Presidency,* 152.

47. Mary E. Stuckey, *The President as Interpreter-in-Chief* (Chatham, N.J.: Chatham House Publishers, Inc., 1991), 54–55.

48. Ambrose, *Eisenhower,* 190.

49. Bernard K. Duffy, foreword to Medhurst, *Dwight D. Eisenhower,* xi.

50. Henry Z. Scheele, "President Dwight D. Eisenhower and the U.S. House Leader Charles A. Halleck: An Examination of an Executive–Legislative Relationship," *Presidential Studies Quarterly* 23 (spring 1993): 289.

51. Reichard, *Reaffirmation of Republicanism,* 98.

52. Ibid., 112.

53. Robert L. Branyan and Lawrence H. Larsen, *The Eisenhower Administration: 1953–1961* (New York: Random House, 1971), 537–562.

54. Martha Derthick, *Policymaking for Social Security* (Washington, D.C.: Brookings, 1979), 304.

55. Richardson, *Presidency of Dwight D. Eisenhower,* 112.

56. Mark A. Peterson, *Legislating Together: The White House and Capitol Hill from Eisenhower to Reagan* (Cambridge: Harvard University Press, 1990), 235.

57. Dwight D. Eisenhower, *Mandate for Change* (Garden City, N.Y.: Doubleday, 1963), 303.

58. "Presidential Success History," *Congressional Quarterly Weekly Report,* December 21, 1996, 3428.

59. Richard A. Watson, *Presidential Vetoes and Public Policy* (Lawrence: University Press of Kansas, 1993). Also see: Robert J. Spitzer, *The Presidential Veto: Touchstone of the American Presidency* (Albany: State University of New York Press, 1988).

60. Richardson, *Presidency of Dwight D. Eisenhower,* 50.

61. John F. Witte, *The Politics and Development of the Federal Income Tax* (Madison: University of Wisconsin Press, 1985), 144.

62. On the question of political motivations and the 1956 election, coverage of his speeches showed a measure of change. See Earl Black and Merle Black, *The Vital South: How Presidents Are Elected* (Cambridge: Harvard University Press, 1992), 180.

[John Kennedy] might have achieved greatness, but he never had a chance.

—ATTORNEY GENERAL NICHOLAS KATZENBACH

7

John F. Kennedy
A Quest for Heroic Leadership

JOHN KENNEDY (served 1961–1963) very narrowly won election in 1960 with a campaign proclaiming the need to "get the country moving again." In foreign affairs he asserted the importance of increased defense spending and a staunch anticommunist posture. Domestically, he stressed the importance of economic growth and endorsed a lengthy list of initiatives. To achieve those goals, he promised "decisive and vigorous" presidential leadership. His promise, however, was short-lived. In November 1963 his term was cut short by an assassin's bullet. Thus, while historians and others can never take full measure of the Kennedy presidency, they can still ask how well did this moderate-opportunity president perform in his short time in office?

Public evaluations of the Kennedy presidency have been strikingly high. For example, one major study in 1983 placed Kennedy at the top of the former presidents the public would like to see in office again. Kennedy was chosen by 30 percent of the respondents, outdistancing Franklin Roosevelt by 10 percent of the respondents.[1] Kennedy's high evaluations stemmed in part from factors unrelated to the merits of his performance. Some respondents were nostalgic for a period in which it seemed that pressing social and economic problems could be successfully addressed. Kennedy's adroit handling of the media, which helped to generate high levels of personal popularity, also contributed to a widespread sense of martyrdom after his assassination.

Members of the Kennedy administration and some presidential scholars have praised Kennedy's leadership as well. They frequently portray a president with outstanding rhetorical skills and a unique ability to digest information quickly from staff aides and documents. Growth in office also is a common theme. Many see Kennedy as a young president who matured in the presidency to become an increasingly effective promoter of civil rights legislation and a major tax cut by 1963.[2] Kennedy's handling of the 1962 Cuban missile crisis also has received high praise.

Other evaluations of the Kennedy presidency have been sharply critical. Some critics contend that Kennedy cultivated popularity by keeping the spotlight on his young, attractive "First Family" while displaying reluctance to work for his domestic agenda.[3] In his dealings with Congress, other critics say, Kennedy was overly deferential. His efforts to build close ties with business interests and his early reluctance to address civil rights issues have drawn criticism as well. In fact, some critics have likened Kennedy's leadership to a rocking chair: it moved a lot but never seemed to get anywhere.

Personal Characteristics

John Fitzgerald Kennedy (1917–1963) inherited his political ambition from his intensely ambitious father. Although a graduate of Harvard University, Joseph Kennedy, who raised his large family in the Boston area, keenly resented the attitudes of many wealthy Protestant patricians toward Irish Catholics and sought to "show them" through financial and political success. And he did. He made a fortune in various business enterprises, including the purchase of undervalued businesses, a Scotch distributorship, and movie industry investments. He also found time for government service. In the Roosevelt administration he served as head of the new Securities and Exchange Commission and as U.S. ambassador to England. By 1960 his estate was worth an estimated $250 million and he was priming one of his nine children, John, for a run for the presidency.

After graduating from a Connecticut preparatory school and spending some time at the London School of Economics and Princeton University (he was forced to withdraw because of illness), John entered Harvard University in 1936 and studied economics and political science. He graduated with honors in 1940. His senior thesis, "Why England Slept," examined British appeasement of fascism before World War II.

Kennedy served in the navy during the war. On August 2, 1943, his PT (patrol torpedo) boat was rammed and sunk by a Japanese destroyer. He led the eleven survivors on a four-hour swim to a nearby island, towing an injured crew member by a life preserver strap. Kennedy and his crew were rescued after friendly natives took a message carved on a coconut to nearby Allied personnel. After the ordeal Kennedy returned to the States where he was hospitalized for malaria. In 1944 he underwent back surgery and was discharged the next year.

In 1951 JFK, then an eligible bachelor and U.S. senator, met the intelligent and attractive Jacqueline Lee Bouvier at a Washington dinner party, and they were married two years later after an off-and-on romance. The young first lady—she was only thirty-one when John became president in 1961—made the White House a center for culture and the arts and became something of a fashion trend-setter in her own right.

Career Path

John Kennedy's political career began with election to the House of Representatives from a lower-income Boston district in 1946. That large freshman class included Richard Nixon, and they became casual friends. Six years later Kennedy successfully challenged Massachusetts Republican Henry Cabot Lodge for his Senate seat and won despite Dwight Eisenhower's strength at the top of the ticket. In 1956 Kennedy sought the second place on a Democratic presidential ticket headed by former Illinois governor Adlai Stevenson, but lost to Sen. Estes Kefauver of Tennessee after a hard-fought convention contest and a well-received convention speech. His defeat ultimately worked to his advantage, however, in that he at once gained greater national attention and avoided the stigma of defeat in the 1956 campaign.

His plans for a presidential bid in 1960 were several years in the making, but not actually announced until January 2, 1960. He decided to show his electability through primary victories, and he won in several important states. One key win was in the largely Protestant state of West Virginia where he profited in part from a huge campaign financing advantage over another Democratic contender, Sen. Hubert Humphrey of Minnesota. The outcome when the Democratic National Convention convened in Los Angeles that summer was still somewhat uncertain, but Kennedy prevailed on the first ballot. Lyndon Johnson, who had belatedly entered the race, was selected as his vice presidential nominee in an effort to help carry the South.

Kennedy's narrow victory (by only 114,000 votes) over Richard Nixon in the fall election can be attributed to many factors. For example, he profited from winning the first presidential debate. And when civil rights leader Martin Luther King Jr. was jailed in Georgia on a driver's license infraction, he decided to call King's wife to offer personally his sympathy and support. That expression, which Nixon had considered and rejected, helped with black voters. He also was aided by a higher than usual degree of Catholic support in the North for the Democratic ticket. Conversely, Nixon succeeded in attracting Democratic white Protestant voters who were reluctant to have a Catholic in the White House—a factor that helped to explain JFK's very narrow margin of victory. Kennedy had followed the polls and had believed he would win by a clear margin. His delight in having won thus was tempered by the closeness of his victory.[4]

What Manner of Man?

According to historian James Giglio, "No president in the twentieth century combined [Kennedy's] rhetoric, wit, charm, youth, and Hollywood appearance."[5] His disarming use of his self-deprecating sense of humor was often on display as well. In early 1960 JFK's opening statement at a Gridiron Club gathering of Washington's leading journalists revealed his skill at diffusing potential criticism with humor. At a time when the scope of his father's financial and personal assistance was drawing skeptical questioning from some quarters, Kennedy began his speech by stating that he had just received a telegram from his father saying: DON'T BUY A SINGLE VOTE MORE THAN NECESSARY. I'LL BE DAMNED IF I'M GOING TO PAY FOR A LANDSLIDE.[6]

More broadly, Kennedy was extremely effective in handling public relations. In fact, he once commented that he thought he might be best suited for a career in real estate sales after his presidency.[7] Running through all his public relations endeavors was his father's influence—and some of these endeavors were stained with charges of deception.[8] The most disputed aspect of JFK's early efforts to "look presidential" came with publication of his book *Profiles in Courage,* which celebrated senators who stuck to their principles and resisted short-run constituency preferences in the face of controversial issues. When journalist Drew Pearson charged that Kennedy had not really authored the Pulitzer Prize-winning book, both JFK and his father were able to gain ABC's retraction (it had aired Pearson's charges) and therefore successfully produce a public perception of authorship that was at some variance with the actual facts.[9] Yet as a credit to his skills, Kennedy was able to change his public image—from that of a scrawny, somewhat introverted young member of the House of Representatives to the attractive, charismatic figure whose presidency evoked images of Camelot.

Kennedy's level of intelligence, as measured in 1930 by an Otis intelligence test, was an above average but far from brilliant 119.[10] He had read extensively in his younger years and continued that practice as president. In 1963, for example, JFK was impressed by Michael Harrington's descriptions of poverty in the United States in his widely read book *The Other America.*

In his dealings with other people, Kennedy was said to be efficient at extracting information and getting to the core of problems. When gathering information, he was skilled at drawing out the ideas of different aides without engaging in open political warfare. But when conflicts did erupt, he often resorted to his own personal charm to smooth them out and to establish improved relationships—such as with former first lady Eleanor Roosevelt after he gained the presidential nomination. More broadly, he was able to cajole, persuade, soothe, and inspire others in ways that made him in the best sense a manipulator of people.[11]

Other frequently noted traits were his high degree of competitiveness and his willingness to take some calculated risks. Some observers described him as being "half Harvard and half Irish"—with at least the Irish side willing to contest elections very tenaciously. His willingness to take risks did not cover all endeavors, however. In 1961, for example, he proceeded cautiously with Congress. He tended to take more risks, though, when in a policy struggle his reputation was on the line. Although Kennedy displayed little vindictiveness, he was willing to engage in forceful combat. Perhaps that trait accounted for his angry, heavy-handed response in 1962 when the steel companies sought price increases at a time when the president was trying to keep inflation in check.

His willingness to take calculated risks also extended to his personal life. After his death it came to light that aspects of Kennedy's personal behavior were fundamentally at odds with the image of the happy family life at the White House he sought to convey and his desire to be a moral leader. Much like his father, he pursued sexual relationships with a wide variety of women, including movie star Marilyn Monroe, would-be starlet Judith Campbell, staff members, and even strangers.[12] Kennedy's trysts entailed obvious risks such as press commentary and blackmail.

Finally, for all his youth, Kennedy suffered from several serious medical ailments—even more than was recognized before his death.[13] He was afflicted with Addison's disease (caused by a hormonal deficiency) and suffered from chronic back problems that frequently required the use of crutches. In fact, some of his medical problems were so severe that he received the last rites on no fewer than four occasions, including twice during delicate back surgery in 1955. Given his multiple health problems, his brother Robert may well have not exaggerated when he noted that JFK lived half of his days on earth in intense pain.[14]

Perhaps his close brushes with death accounted for Kennedy's sense of fatalism which surfaced from time to time. His favorite poem was "I Have a Rendezvous with Death" by Alan Seeger.[15] More poignantly, in viewing the platform from which he was scheduled to speak in Dallas on that ill-fated day of November 22, 1963, he turned to aide Kenneth O'Donnell and remarked, "Look at that platform. With all these buildings around it, the Secret Service couldn't stop someone who really wanted to get you."[16]

Policy Views

In his approach to domestic policy, Kennedy firmly believed that problems could be solved—but with pragmatism rather than conventional ideologies. During his days in the House and Senate he had supported a wide variety of liberal measures such as increases in Social Security and low-income housing assistance, but in part because of their popularity with his constituents. According to journalist Richard Reeves, "He was not a liberal moralist—he did not call himself any kind of liberal—but rather a managerial politician."[17] In a similar vein, political scientist Lewis Paper concluded, "No one would ever mistake John Kennedy for a radical who would always stand on principle."[18]

Overall, then, four perspectives guided Kennedy's domestic policy choices. First, he keenly desired good government–business relations as an avenue toward improved economic growth. Second, he was more interested in pragmatic solutions to the nation's problems than typical liberal responses. Third, in his early approach to civil rights, he generally preferred caution. And, fourth, when he perceived that someone was challenging his leadership role, he was willing to act boldly.

Although Kennedy advocated no overall economic policy during his presidential campaign such as adoption of a Keynesian tax-cutting approach, he repeatedly asserted the need to improve the nation's rate of economic growth—primarily because the nation did not seem to be keeping up with the Soviet Union. More broadly, in his domestic agenda, which he called the "New Frontier," he endorsed many traditionally Democratic measures such as medical care for the elderly, increases in Social Security, additional commitments to housing programs, aid to depressed areas, assistance for the poor, aid to education, and reform of agriculture policies.

On racial issues Kennedy's views were not shaped by direct exposure to the problems. Because of his sheltered family life and lack of interest, he had had virtually no meaningful contact with blacks or other groups suffering during the depression. Similarly, his years in Washington produced little direct involvement with the problems facing blacks. In his eyes, at least at first, desegregation was rational but not necessarily a moral issue, and civil rights protests were simply domestic problems that had to be managed.[19]

Challenges and Opportunities

President Kennedy's foreign policy challenges consumed much of his time in 1961 and, indeed, throughout his presidency. During his first year in office, he confronted a difficult relationship with Soviet leader Nikita Khrushchev, tension over Berlin, and problems in both Vietnam and Laos. His decision in April 1961 to tacitly support an invasion of Cuba by 1,400 Cuban exiles intent on overthrowing the communist government of Cuban leader Fidel Castro proved to be an unmitigated disaster. He quickly accepted full responsibility for the aborted Bay of Pigs invasion and his popularity actually rose, but his decision-making skills were widely questioned by key players in the nation's capital. A year later Cuba was once again the scene of a foreign policy crisis—this time, the so-called Cuban missile crisis. In October 1962, faced with U-2 photographs showing the Soviets in the process of establishing offensive missile capabilities in Cuba, Kennedy conducted a thirteen-day decision-making process that eventually led to a blockade of Soviet vessels trying to enter Cuban waters. In response, Khrushchev backed down and the Soviet missiles were removed. Although Kennedy successfully promoted an atomic weapons test ban treaty during his third year in office, at the time of his death he was facing yet another overseas problem: renewed uncertainty about his Vietnam policies in the wake of the assassination of South Vietnamese leader Ngo Dinh Diem.

Kennedy's opportunities, then, were not very promising for a president seeking to "get the country moving again" and reenergize a sluggish economy. A few factors, however, were operating in his favor. Although his popularity declined in 1963, he had enjoyed high popularity throughout his first two years and his three-year average of 71 percent was the highest among the post-Hoover presidents (see Table 1–2). Since his popularity was not clearly tied to his domestic agenda, however, it was a somewhat uncertain resource.

Another advantage welcomed by the young president was the large number of proposals developed in Congress during Eisenhower's second term that had not gained the support needed for passage or, in some cases, the support needed to override an Eisenhower veto. This list included: Medicare for the elderly, which JFK had personally promoted during his last two years in the Senate; federal aid to education; aid to depressed areas; and several environmental measures, including ones taking aim at water pollution.[20]

Although many of these proposals were favored by a majority of citizens, Kennedy confronted several obstacles in the legislative arena that limited his opportunities. For one thing, in dealing with Congress Kennedy could not claim a mandate from having stressed a few strong themes in his campaign or from having achieved a decisive victory. Indeed, because both Kennedy and many in the Congress had expected a clear victory, the narrowness of his win reduced his potential leverage on Capitol Hill. Moreover, the Democrats lost twenty-one seats in the House—the worst outcome produced by any incoming president—leaving Kennedy with no sense of momentum as well as less partisan support in Congress.

For Kennedy's top legislative liaison aide, Lawrence O'Brien, the size of the likely coalition in Congress took the form of a basic math problem. The figures he often cited for the House were: northern and western Democrats 157, southern Democrats 106, Republicans 174, for a potential conservative coalition vote of 280 that left Democratic leaders unable to gather the 219 votes needed for passage of legislation.[21] In the midterm elections in 1962 Kennedy took off on a whirlwind nineteen thousand miles of campaigning, and the Democrats lost only five seats in the House and gained four seats in the Senate. The conservative southern Democrats continued to toss in the occasional political monkey wrench, however, leaving JFK stymied in pushing forward his legislative initiatives.

At the outset, Kennedy also endured bumpy relations with some congressional leaders. In the Senate Mike Mansfield, D-Mont., Vice President Lyndon Johnson's successor as majority leader, proved to be well liked on both sides of the aisle, but he lacked Johnson's assertiveness. In the House, Speaker Sam Rayburn's declining health and death in the fall of 1961 elevated John McCormack, D-Mass., into that key position. Mansfield, however, possessed only modest skills and a personal dislike of John Kennedy stemming from earlier political conflicts. The committee chairmen in both houses also posed difficulties for the Kennedy administration. Mostly elderly and often conservative, they viewed Kennedy with a high degree of skepticism. The important chairmen, who were on average more than thirty years his senior, remembered JFK only as a young and not very influential senator. Committee control also was a problem. In the Senate southerners controlled ten of the sixteen committees, including Finance and Judiciary; in the House they controlled twelve of twenty committees, including the all-important Rules and Ways and Means Committees. Kennedy thus faced tough committee fights on key issues such as civil rights, federal aid to education, and Medicare.

Economic conditions proved to be another dicey factor in Kennedy's level of opportunity. The economy slumped in early 1961, as unemployment rose to 7.7 percent. Congress, then, was more receptive to measures such as aid to depressed areas than might otherwise have been the case. By 1963, with its lower inflation levels, the president was indicating his willingness to experiment with deficit spending, but the improvement in the economy also made the case for a deficit to avoid recession and stimulate long-term growth, a proposition more difficult to promote in Congress.

Meanwhile, the public mood was another ingredient in the mix of opportunities and challenges. The president found the public's high level of trust in government to be a positive resource, but he was less certain about whether the public really wanted to participate in a period of renewed government activism. Kennedy was familiar with the theory of cycles espoused by aide Arthur Schlesinger Jr., and he hoped that his presidency would coincide with a new cycle of activism. But, despite his inaugural pleas for action, some pundits believed the election produced little indication that the public supported assertive action in the nation's cold war struggle with the Soviet Union.

Leadership Style

Kennedy entered the presidency with a heroic view of presidential leadership.[22] Based on his study of political leadership, he identified, for example, with the role played by Prime Minister Winston Churchill who dramatically rallied British public opinion during World War II. Through family discussions led by his father, he also was thoroughly grounded in key dimensions of Franklin Roosevelt's leadership style.[23] Kennedy may have disagreed with some aspects of FDR's foreign policies, "but he admired Roosevelt's ability to articulate the latent idealism of America, and he greatly envied Roosevelt's capacity to dominate a sprawling government. . . ."[24]

The Advisory Process and Approach
to Decision Making

In keeping with his leadership orientation, President Kennedy sought
White House staff and cabinet members with different backgrounds. For
example, from his Senate staff and election campaigns he selected people
whose political judgment he trusted—among them, Theodore Sorensen
and Richard Goodwin from his Senate staff and former campaign aides
Lawrence O'Brien and Kenneth O'Donnell. Perhaps reflecting his interest
in a problem-solving approach to public policy, Kennedy recruited from
academia prominent Boston scholar Arthur Schlesinger Jr. as a general
aide and Harvard dean McGeorge Bundy as national security adviser. By
selecting some more conservative advisers—such as Bundy as well as investment banker Douglas Dillon as Treasury secretary and former Ford
Motor Company president Robert McNamara as defense secretary—
Kennedy hoped to broaden his political base in the wake of his narrow
election victory.

Sorensen, whose role at points resembled that of chief of staff, and
deputy Mike Feldman helped to shape Kennedy's domestic policy initiatives with the help of an extensive network of presidential task forces
established during Kennedy's first year in office. Other architects of the
president's domestic policy were Walter Heller, an economist from the University of Minnesota who was appointed chairman of the Council of Economic Advisers, and Bureau of the Budget Director David Bell, a former
Truman staffer who taught economics at Harvard. As part of a group
known as the "Quadriad," they often worked closely with Treasury Secretary Dillon and William McChesney Martin, chairman of the Federal
Reserve Board. In a move underscoring his cautious approach to the traditional Democratic liberal agenda on economic policy, Kennedy did not
assign the staunchly liberal economist John Kenneth Galbraith an influential domestic policy role. Instead, Galbraith served as the president's ambassador to India.

The assessments of Kennedy's band of recruits were mixed. Long before some fell under intense criticism for their roles in the deepening war
in Vietnam in the mid-1960s, they often were called the "best and bright-
est." JFK's effort to gather various policy ideas from the nation's universities was particularly welcomed by segments of the nation's academic community. Washington insider Clark Clifford, however, viewed
the Kennedy recruits as "the cockiest crowd I'd ever seen at the White
House." [25]

Administrative Strategies

Kennedy's administrative strategies included modest efforts at "good government" reform and one dramatic use of administrative action for policy purposes. His disinterest in the federal bureaucracy stemmed primarily from his belief that it acted too slowly and had too few new policy ideas. His frustration with the bureaucracy, however, did not motivate him to press for structural reforms.[26]

President Kennedy employed a variety of administrative strategies to achieve his goals. In his use of executive orders, his first action was to direct Agriculture Secretary Orville Freeman to make more food available to the needy in some states such as West Virginia. Later, he displayed an interest in demonstrating the success of pilot programs by concentrating resources from many different sources in one specific location. Yet conversely, as noted earlier, he was slow to act on civil rights matters. In 1962 Kennedy's response to an announced price increase by U.S. Steel revealed that presidents can, when they wish, act decisively through administrative channels—and it revealed Kennedy's willingness to use those channels. The whole episode, which some likened in importance to the 1962 Cuban missile crisis,[27] began when the Kennedy administration pursued a policy called "jawboning"—that is, encouraging businesses to adopt only modest price increases while encouraging labor to limit its demands for wage increases. Following that policy, Secretary of Labor Arthur Goldberg had pressured his former employer, the United Steelworkers of America, to accept a wage increase of 2.5 percent which was well within the Kennedy administration's guidelines. But on April 10, 1962, U.S. Steel president Roger Blough called on Kennedy at the White House and presented him with a memorandum calling for a price increase of $6 a ton, and he cited cost pressures for the 3.5 percent increase, which exceeded the administration's guidelines. Blough and Kennedy argued briefly about whether U.S. Steel had specifically agreed to the earlier guidelines, and Blough departed. That same day, in a step that many observers saw as illegal collusion on prices, seven other steel companies announced a similar price increase.

Kennedy, sensing a threat to his administration, acted forcefully and resolutely. Arthur Goldberg responded immediately to his call and, on hearing of U.S. Steel's actions, offered to resign. But Kennedy rejected his offer and proceeded to draft a statement to the press citing how other Americans had heeded his call for sacrifice—including those who had gone to Vietnam—and making it clear that he wanted the price increases rescinded. At his press conference Kennedy described the steel companies' actions as "a wholly unjustifiable and irresponsible defiance of the public interest." He then added, "Some time ago I asked each American to consider what he would do for this country and I asked the steel companies. In the last twenty-four hours we had their answer." [28]

Determined that nothing would hamper his ability to continue with his anti-inflation strategy, Kennedy proceeded to throw the full power of the federal government into his effort to obtain a reversal by the steel companies. Steel executives were subpoenaed to appear at a grand jury investigation; the Federal Bureau of Investigation called on reporters in the middle of the night—a measure that may have been instigated by the attorney general; and the Federal Trade Commission and congressional committees were encouraged to investigate. The administration also applied economic leverage by promising to steer new contracts to any firm that did not go along with the general steel price increase.

Then, just seventy-two hours after it began, the conflict ended. A small steel company decided to rescind the price increase and all the other companies quickly followed suit. Kennedy was able to attribute his success to his efforts to marshal the public's support as well as his use of his administrative powers. Although he tried to quiet the furor it produced, his widely reported remark "My father always told me that all businessmen were sons-of-bitches, but I never believed it till now" produced derisive "S.O.B." signs and bumper stickers lamenting, "I miss Ike—hell, I even miss Harry." In the coming months, however, the president made a more concerted effort to woo business support through various tax packages.

Until 1963, administrative action also constituted Kennedy's primary approach to civil rights issues. In 1961 he concentrated on appointing blacks to top government posts, but his choice of nominees drew mixed reviews. Civil rights leaders, for example, found fault with his continuing tendency to show deference to southern leaders in Congress by appointing federal judges to the Fifth Circuit Court of Appeals (which covered the southern states) southerners would not find threatening.

Housing desegregation policies were another area in which reliance on administrative strategies proved difficult. Fearing conflict with southerners in Congress and resistance to actual implementation, Kennedy avoided issuing the executive order on housing he had promised to sign "with the stroke of a pen" during the 1960 campaign. In their frustration over his delay, civil rights supporters mailed him pens at the White House. As the midterm elections approached, the president decided to delay his order once more until voters had cast their ballots. When it was finally signed on Thanksgiving Eve 1962, the executive order dealing with housing segregation disappointed civil rights leaders. The order's provisions were not retroactive and applied only to a limited number of federal housing loans. As a result, they covered only 17 percent of the nation's housing stock. In 1963 the head of the Civil Rights Division of the Justice Department, Burke Marshall, noted that the housing order had "not been very meaningful." [29]

When efforts by blacks in 1962 and early 1963 to desegregate public facilities such as universities drew angry responses from whites, Kennedy had to call in federal troops. Several governors also decided to employ National Guard troops to prevent specific instances of desegregation, thereby ratcheting up the resistance and tension.

Public Leadership

In his public role, President Kennedy was known for his idealistic, motivating rhetoric. In his widely acclaimed inaugural address he proclaimed: "Let the word go forth . . . to friend and foe alike, that the torch has been passed to a new generation, born in this century, tempered by war, disciplined by a hard and bitter peace, proud of our ancient heritage . . . [We] shall pay any price, bear any burden, meet any hardship . . . to assure the survival and the success of liberty. . . ."

The president also was known for circumventing his own press secretary in his contacts with the press, which included considerable courting. But that courtship had its limits. Reporters who wrote less-than-flattering accounts of the president found themselves distanced from personal contact with him. The result was generally quite favorable press coverage of the Kennedy White House.

In his efforts to create a winning persona, the president was stunningly successful. His pleasant speaking style featured a Harvard accent, clipped voice, and expressive right hand. He also enlisted the help of his glamorous wife, Jackie, and showed off his two young children. But, perhaps most important, he sought to modify the image of a brash young man on the make and to avoid being perceived as overly partisan.

Press conferences were a key component of Kennedy's public relations and support-building strategies. Unlike Eisenhower who used a taped delay for his press conferences, Kennedy appeared live—the first president to do so. The large audiences his press conferences attracted were taken with his witty responses and his willingness to respond at length on pol-

cation question a hard one to address.[35] Moreover, he faced a set of antag-onistic interest groups that had fought the issue to a standstill. Kennedy's response was to continue to oppose aid for parochial schools—a stand he had taken during the campaign—while expressing concern privately about constitutional issues. His legislative proposal closely paralleled a bill the Senate passed in 1960 providing aid for school construction and teachers' salaries. But the White House made no specific reference to leveraging this aid to force additional desegregation, and on Capitol Hill a conflict was temporarily avoided when Adam Clayton Powell, D-N.Y., a promi-nent African American in the House, agreed to refrain from raising the is-sue until there was a more favorable climate for civil rights.

Kennedy used several strategies in his effort to resolve various conflicts over his proposal. Although he gave no major address on the topic, he ad-vocated his position in several televised news conferences. In the face of vehement opposition to his proposed bill from Catholic Church leaders, Kennedy signaled a willingness to support an amendment that would pro-vide some construction funding for parochial schools. In the end, he set-tled for modest gains in this controversial area.

Employment-related Policies and the Environment

Despite his early losses on key issues, Kennedy was able to use a fast-start strategy to address the problems of unemployment and stagnant wages in 1961. Enactment of the Area Redevelopment Act in June 1961 marked the conclusion of a struggle that had begun in the late 1950s as Congress sought to address the economic problems of depressed areas, including coal mining communities. The legislation that Congress passed provided for funding of commercial and industrial development, technical assis-tance in community planning, and the retraining of unemployed workers.

Changes in minimum wage provisions proved to be more controver-sial, spurring some liberals to heap criticism on Kennedy. The Democratic Party platform had included an increase to $1.25 an hour, and Kennedy also promoted the measure in his February 13, 1961, message to Congress. In Congress legislators wrangled over the extent of coverage as well as the size of the increase from the existing $1.00 an hour. Sen. Paul Douglas, D-Ill., a prominent economist who had written on this subject, promoted expansion, while business groups such as the Chamber of Commerce and spokesmen for small businesses once again argued against a major ex-pansion. The president's original bill called for extending the minimum wage to 4.3 million workers, but Congress exempted more than 700,000 employees—mainly those working for laundries and small interstate businesses.

Environmental concerns had emerged in Congress in the late 1950s, but legislators had made few tangible commitments. By 1963 support for federal action had expanded enough to allow passage of the Clean Air Act which focused on automobile emissions and to a lesser extent on municipal sewage. California led the way in promoting the legislation because automobile pollution had become a problem there, especially in the rapidly growing Los Angeles area. Groups representing other larger cities also supported some congressional action. Kennedy threw his hat in the ring as well; he advocated conservation measures and the importance of a clean environment and committed some federal funding to these efforts.

Social Security, Welfare, and Health

Although it faced a deadlock over Medicare, the Kennedy administration pursued changes in Social Security and welfare policy. Congress further expanded Social Security benefits in 1962. Kennedy, specialists in Congress, and advocates within the Social Security Administration promoted a proposal that would give men the same rights to partial benefits at age sixty-two that women had received in 1956. Kennedy included these reforms in his February 13 message to Congress outlining his program for economic growth and recovery. The proposal was further aided by Social Security Administration analyses indicating that the expansion could be absorbed without additional Social Security taxes. Congress applauded this cheerful news by passing the reforms easily.

In 1961 Congress also followed the president's lead by providing assistance to the children of unemployed parents. Legislators' favorable response to welfare reform proposals stemmed in part from a study conducted by an ad hoc committee headed by Abraham Ribicoff, secretary of health, education, and welfare, and a nationally publicized crackdown on "welfare chiseling" in Newburgh, New York. Kennedy's initial proposal to Congress focused on the rehabilitation of welfare recipients through community work programs. In presenting his proposal to Congress he stressed that public welfare must be "more than a salvage operation" and asked legislators to raise federal funding of state programs from 50 percent to 75 percent.

The new program attracted the support of the National Social Welfare Assembly and many Democratic members of Congress. Republicans opposed to the reforms did not fault the philosophy behind the program but argued that federal involvement should not be expanded. The Republican motion to recommit nevertheless lost by a vote of 233–155 on a near party line vote, and Senate passage came easily once a proposal for health care for the elderly was defeated. HEW Assistant Secretary Wilbur Cohen, who had worked hard on this issue, noted that one of the surprising dynamics surrounding passage of the legislation was the relative lack of conflict.[36]

Tax Policies

Kennedy's efforts to pass tax legislation began in 1961 under the leadership of Douglas Dillon, secretary of the Treasury, and Harvard law professor Stanley Surrey who was serving as assistant secretary and had chaired Kennedy's task force on tax reform. As the recession worsened in Kennedy's first weeks in office, the planning effort turned from a single comprehensive reform bill to a two-stage strategy in which a quick stimulus bill would be passed in 1961 followed by a major reform measure in 1962 or 1963. The president's initial proposal in April 1961 focused primarily on business's use of tax incentives to expand and modernize plants and equipment.[37]

As the debate unfolded, many business interests expressed uncertainty about the merits of Kennedy's proposals. Despite the attractiveness of several provisions granting tax reductions in exchange for investment, some businesses remained skeptical of Kennedy, and conflicts emerged among business interests over the distribution of favorable provisions. Kennedy spoke privately of his disappointment with the reactions of business, but was restrained in his public responses and criticized only the actions of the savings and loan industry. Although early opposition prevented quick action on the tax incentive package, it was finally enacted in 1962. During an often highly partisan process, Republicans at points opposed aspects of the investment tax credit. Numerous changes were made in the legislation at the committee stage in each house, and the Kennedy administration responded to various political pressures by, among other things, revising depreciation provisions for the textile industry.

Kennedy also pursued public support for the tax reform legislation. He promoted the measure in press conferences and used a scheduled June 11, 1962, commencement appearance at Yale University to deliver a major address that stressed the importance of fiscal policies in achieving more rapid economic growth. The reaction to the speech was mixed, and some concluded that it was difficult to analyze economic issues in a commencement speech. Leading liberal economist John Kenneth Galbraith argued that a deficit produced by government programs placing purchasing power in the hands of middle- and lower-income groups would do more to stimulate the economy than tax or budget cuts. Nevertheless, many supporters of Keynesian views on tax policy inside the president's administration were delighted with his strong stand. With some interests looking toward a larger battle in the coming year, the level of resistance declined for the 1962 reforms and Kennedy signed them into law in October.

In January 1963 Kennedy submitted a tax cut package to Congress. Under the tutelage of Walter Heller, Kennedy had become increasingly confident in his own analysis and saw tax cuts as a broader vehicle toward growth than the kinds of programs being operated by the new Area Redevelopment Administration. The administration consulted many business and some labor groups to gain an understanding of provisions likely to draw the greatest support.[38] Treasury Secretary Dillon succeeded in promoting some changes as the detailed proposal was created. The final result was a tax proposal that represented two important "firsts." Kennedy was the first president to promote a tax cut when the government was operating with a deficit and the first to promote a tax cut when the economy was performing well.

The program Kennedy submitted to Congress in January 1963 called for tax reductions in all brackets, a reduction in the corporate tax rate from 52 percent to 47 percent, and special tax breaks for small businesses. The total package called for reducing taxes by $13.6 billion with $11 billion going to individuals and $2.6 billion to corporations. Because it was anticipated that the 1962 reforms would add $3.4 billion in revenue, this package represented in the end a reduction of $10.2 billion. In designing his proposed reductions and a variety of other specific recommendations, Kennedy paid careful attention to measures that would cut the capital gains tax, expand policies related to child care, change deductions for charitable giving, and alter the tax treatment of the elderly. With an eye toward maximizing the likelihood of congressional support, the president, in projecting the resulting deficit, was careful to stay below Eisenhower's largest recession-driven deficit of $12.4 billion.[39]

Despite the administration's efforts to design a politically attractive measure, the House Ways and Means Committee introduced extensive changes. Virtually unanimous Republican opposition in the House was offset by strong support from southern Democrats as Ways and Means chairman Wilbur Mills succeeded in reporting out a bill that could pass on the floor. In an effort to increase public pressure on members of the House, Kennedy undertook both radio and television appeals that reviewed the benefits of the tax cut to individual families but placed the greater emphasis on how the bill would lead to long-term economic growth and prevent a recession in the short term.

The Senate Finance Committee also held extensive hearings over a three-month period. Floor opposition was led by liberals, who unsuccessfully attacked the bill on equity grounds in areas such as capital gains, dividend levels, and exemption levels. The final bill passed easily with bipartisan support and moved to the conference committee. In accepting changes as his bill moved through Congress, Kennedy was quite willing to compromise and see reforms eliminated as a necessary price for gaining passage of the tax cuts he felt would stimulate the economy. When it finally passed in January 1964, the bill became the first landmark enactment of the Johnson administration.[40]

Housing Policy

Kennedy did not succeed in his effort to make the Federal Housing Administration (FHA) into a cabinet-level Department of Urban Affairs; he confronted opposition from rural interests who did not want to see urban interests gain an advantage. Some of those interests also opposed his intention to appoint Robert Weaver, the head of the FHA, as the first black cabinet secretary.

His major housing proposal, however, was successful because, unlike the proposed Department of Urban Affairs, it enjoyed southern and bipartisan support and the support of a variety of interest groups, pleased that it promised to distribute a wide variety of benefits.[41] (Democrats, in fact, were relieved that they no longer had to contend with Eisenhower's threatened veto as they sought to promote alternative approaches to housing policy.) In further expanding on the omnibus measure's wide appeal, the Kennedy administration added "sweeteners" as the bill was being debated in committee to help generate greater support from southern Democrats and other members of Congress from rural areas. Along with providing a community facility loan program that was popular among southern Democrats and members of Congress from rural areas, the final bill broadened and extended programs such as urban renewal, public housing, and housing for the elderly and college students, as well as offered a new middle-income housing program and funding for mass transportation facilities and open spaces in the cities.

Civil Rights

In 1963 Kennedy abandoned his mild administrative strategies for dealing with civil rights issues and changed direction.[42] Events were transforming the civil rights movement and white attitudes outside the South. In trying to desegregate public facilities in Birmingham, Alabama, movement leader Martin Luther King Jr. was pursuing a conscious strategy of taking on the toughest case in the hope of forcing decisive action. The protest campaign included sit-ins at department stores, street marches, and pray-ins. When King was jailed for a brief time, he wrote his famous "Letter from the Birmingham Jail" which made an eloquent defense of civil disobedience and nonviolent protest.

In dealing with the demonstrators, Birmingham Police Chief Eugene "Bull" Connor provided the nation with gripping, repugnant television footage of lunging police dogs and police using high-pressure fire hoses on small children and aggressively brandishing their nightsticks. As a result, the national sentiment swung further toward an end to segregation and community leaders of all stripes called on the Kennedy administration to find ways to achieve desegregation while also eliminating violent confrontations.

In the face of this crisis, the prospect of even more racial violence, and this challenge to his ability to provide strong, heroic leadership, Kennedy was jolted into reassessing his cautious approach and pursuing a more resolute course on civil rights. He proposed additional civil rights legislation, and, in an address to the nation on June 11, 1963, he became the first president to specifically condemn segregation on moral grounds. In that address he stated:

> We are confronted primarily with a moral issue. It is as old as the scriptures and is as clear as the American Constitution. . . . We face therefore, a moral crisis as a country and as a people. It cannot be met by repressive police action. It cannot be left to increased demonstrations in the streets. It cannot be quieted by token moves or talk. It is a time to act in Congress, in your State and local legislative body and, above all, in our daily lives.[43]

After this address, extensive action emanated from the top levels of the Kennedy administration. At the White House Kennedy himself met with a wide array of opinion leaders, and his brother, Attorney General Robert Kennedy, maintained close contact with leading civil rights leaders. Both brothers were initially apprehensive about King's plans for a march on Washington, but they decided in the face of a strong commitment by civil rights leaders that the best strategy was to ensure it would be peaceful. That strategy proved to be successful, when on August 28, 1963, some 300,000 men and women, black and white, participated in a peaceful and dignified gathering at the base of the Lincoln Memorial.

As for its civil rights legislation, the administration promoted it widely and consulted extensively with Congress, both before and after the bill was submitted. According to Burke Marshall, Kennedy was even willing to defer his tax cut proposal if that was required to gain passage of the civil rights bill.[44] By the time of Kennedy's death, this legislation had made substantial headway on Capitol Hill.

Kennedy and Congress

Overall, Kennedy succeeded only to a moderate degree with Congress; he was able to promote some new legislation, but he did not see passage of his landmark bills. His inability to achieve landmark legislation was not especially surprising, however, since presidents without large opportunity levels have had very little success. On some measures of moderate importance before Congress, a stronger bargaining role might have produced different results. On the minimum wage, for example, Lewis Paper concluded that Kennedy may have conceded coverage for laundry workers too soon.[45]

It is not clear whether Kennedy's oft-mentioned desire to remain cautious during his first term and more aggressive after achieving a larger electoral victory in 1964 was simply a rationalization for being cautious. Yet the failures experienced by Presidents Jimmy Carter and Bill Clinton in taking on sweeping first-year domestic agendas suggest that there was some merit in Kennedy's more cautious strategy of trying to avoid highly embarrassing defeats. In assessing the possibilities of that strategy, Wilbur Cohen, who served as an adviser in both the Kennedy and Johnson administrations, concluded that if Kennedy had lived to experience an election victory comparable to Johnson's, about 90 percent of the legislation passed between 1965 and 1968 (LBJ's Great Society) would have been enacted.[46]

An Assessment

Because John Kennedy died in office, his performance as president is not easy to evaluate. Enough is known, however, to address several of the issues raised at the beginning of this chapter.[47]

Policy Legacy

Kennedy's civil rights record is destined to remain the central component of his domestic policy legacy. Although he was highly cautious during his first two years in office, there was little opportunity for passing a new civil rights bill in 1961. Civil rights aide Harris Wofford had hoped for a stronger administrative role, but he did not fault the absence of a legislative initiative.[48] Beginning in the spring of 1963, however, Kennedy submitted a landmark proposal and pursued a broad range of legislative strategies. He also employed forceful rhetoric and held numerous meetings with various opinion leaders and civil rights advocates.

Kennedy also had a role in advancing interest in the use of fiscal policy to stimulate the economy, helping to achieve some major domestic enactments, and pushing legislation that would gain passage after his death. His successors in office continued to promote fiscal policy into the 1970s when challenges to his approach arose. Kennedy's major domestic policy enactments included welfare and Social Security reform, several changes in regulatory policy, and the Area Redevelopment Act. Although JFK did not succeed on many major initiatives, he was able in some instances to make some progress that provided momentum for the Johnson administration.

Performance

Kennedy's efforts to provide heroic leadership allowed him to blend that aspect of his persona into a highly effective public relations effort. In his call for new action, he successfully motivated large numbers of college age students to pursue careers in the public sector.[49] And, despite his initial desire to avoid civil rights issues, his lofty rhetoric may have had an impact on the civil rights movement. In fact, Robert Moses, who served as director of the Mississippi Council of Federated Organizations, believed that a new generation of African Americans seemed to respond to the question of what they could do for their country in ways that Kennedy had not specifically intended.[50] Although he had not tried to educate the public on civil rights issues, his public address on June 11, 1963, did forcefully frame this domestic issue in moral terms.

As for his use of his presidency as a bully pulpit, critics abound. And his record on major voluntary domestic policy addresses speaks for itself; his rate is lower than that of any other president. Moreover, some critics find that his emphasis on dramatic rhetoric risked overreaction such as his statements during the steel price increase controversy.

Was Kennedy then an underachiever? Some harder bargaining might have helped, yet it seems doubtful that he could have accomplished a lot more in this situation with a different leadership style. Left-leaning author and poverty program promoter Michael Harrington concluded that Kennedy did relatively well given his circumstances and his political values.[51] Taking into account his successes with smaller programs as landmark efforts failed, Mark Peterson found that "there was more to Kennedy's legislative performance than symbols."[52] And a voice from inside the Kennedy administration, Attorney General Nicholas Katzenbach, surmised that Kennedy "might have achieved greatness, but he never had a chance." Other observers, however, were not so optimistic. The situation in Vietnam and the possibility of public scandals arising from his personal behavior may have waylaid a promising future. Nevertheless, Kennedy's record reveals that overinflated initial adulation followed by highly critical revisionism made it too easy to obscure a respectable—if not outstanding—performance.

Notes

1. Larry Berman, *The New American Presidency* (Boston: Little, Brown, 1987), 236.

2. The highly favorable interpretations of the Kennedy presidency include: James David Barber, *Presidential Character: Predicting Performance in the White House,* 4th ed. (Englewood Cliffs, N.J.: Prentice-Hall, 1992); and Theodore Sorensen, *Kennedy* (New York: Harper and Row, 1965).

3. See in particular Garry Wills, *The Kennedy Imprisonment: A Mediation on Power* (Boston: Little, Brown, 1982); and Bruce Miroff, *Pragmatic Illusions: The Presidential Politics of John F. Kennedy* (New York: David McKay, 1976).

4. Herbert B. Asher, *Presidential Elections and American Politics: Voters, Candidates, and Campaigns since 1952,* 3d ed. (Homewood, Ill.: Dorsey Press, 1984), 122–125.

5. James N. Giglio, *The Presidency of John F. Kennedy* (Lawrence: University of Kansas Press, 1991), 1.

6. James Reston, *Deadline: A Memoir* (New York: Random House, 1991), 288.

7. Ralph G. Martin, *A Hero for Our Time: An Intimate Story of the Kennedy Years* (New York: Macmillan, 1993), 564.

8. See Wills, *Kennedy Imprisonment;* and John Blair and Clay Blair, *The Search for JFK* (New York: Berkeley Publishing, 1975).

9. Historian Herbert Parmet, after reviewing materials at the John F. Kennedy

Library, concluded that while an ailing Kennedy had sponsored and shaped the work, the research and drafts had been done by several people, particularly Professor Jules Davids of Georgetown University and Senate staffer Theodore Sorenson. Giglio, *Presidency of John F. Kennedy*, 11.

10. Thomas E. Cronin, "John F. Kennedy: President and Politician," in *John F. Kennedy: The Promise Revisited*, ed. Paul Harper and Joan P. Krieg (Westport, Conn.: Greenwood Press, 1988), 4.

11. Patricia Dennis Witherspoon, *Within These Walls: A Study of Communication between Presidents and Their Senior Staffs* (New York: Praeger, 1991), 42.

12. Giglio, *Presidency of John F. Kennedy*, 148–149. For a discussion of Joseph P. Kennedy's personal behavior, see in particular Wills, *Kennedy Imprisonment*.

13. This discussion is drawn from John R. Bumgarner, *The Health of the Presidents: The 41 United States Presidents through 1993 from a Physician's Point of View* (Jefferson, N.C.: McFarland, 1994), 234–249.

14. Martin, *A Hero for Our Time*, 97. The discussion of Kennedy's background also draws from Wills, *Kennedy Imprisonment*.

15. Martin, *A Hero for Our Time*, 537.

16. Richard Reeves, *President Kennedy: Profile of Power* (New York: Simon and Schuster, 1993), 661.

17. Ibid., 480.

18. Lewis J. Paper, *John F. Kennedy: The Promise and the Performance* (New York: Crown, 1975).

19. Harris Wofford, *Of Kennedy and Kings: Making Sense of the Sixties* (New York: Farrar, Straus, Giroux, 1980), 128.

20. James L. Sundquist, *Politics and Policy: The Eisenhower, Kennedy, and Johnson Years* (Washington, D.C.: Brookings, 1968).

21. Memo from Lawrence O'Brien to Theodore Sorenson, February 9, 1961, Sorenson papers, Box 49, Legislative Affairs, February 1–14, 1961, John F. Kennedy Library, Boston.

22. This concept and interpretation draws from Bruce Miroff, *Icons of Democracy: American Leaders as Heroes, Aristocrats, Dissenters, and Democrats* (New York: Basic Books, 1993), chap. 8.

23. At the outset of his administration, JFK showed a knowledge of Neustadt's recommended techniques as he asked Neustadt and Clark Clifford to prepare recommendations for the organization of his presidency and key strategies. He did not want them to work together, however, so he would gain the value of two different reports. Neustadt subsequently served as ambassador to Great Britain and periodically suggested overall strategies to Kennedy.

24. Arthur M. Schlesinger Jr., *A Thousand Days: John F. Kennedy in the White House* (Boston: Houghton Mifflin, 1965), 120.

25. Martin, *Hero for Our Time*, 300.

26. Charles E. Walcott and Karen M. Hult, *Governing the White House: From Hoover through LBJ* (Lawrence: University of Kansas Press, 1995), 111.

27. This discussion draws from Giglio, *Presidency of John F. Kennedy*, 129–133; and James F. Heath, *John F. Kennedy and the Business Community* (Chicago: University of Chicago Press, 1969), 68–73.

28. Quoted in Arthur M. Schlesinger Jr., *A Thousand Days: John F. Kennedy in the White House* (Boston: Houghton Mifflin, 1965).

29. Giglio, *Presidency of John F. Kennedy,* 172.

30. Sorensen, *Kennedy,* 329.

31. As one indication of at least a measure of interest in actual impact, Kennedy asked Sorenson at the end of 1961 to provide a list of what he had asked the citizens themselves to do. The list produced some fifteen items.

32. Mary E. Stuckey, *The President as Interpreter-in-Chief* (Chatham, N.J.: Chatham House, 1991), 63.

33. Ibid., 223.

34. Paul C. Light, *The President's Agenda: Domestic Policy Choice for Kennedy and Carter* (Baltimore: Johns Hopkins University Press, 1981), 70. Somewhat less emphasis on Medicare as a goal is suggested in Alan Shank, *Presidential Policy Leadership: Kennedy and Social Welfare* (Lanham, Md.: University Press of America, 1980), 93.

35. On this issue, see Barbara Kellerman, *The Political Presidency: The Practice of Leadership from Kennedy through Reagan* (New York: Oxford University Press, 1986), chap. 4; and Hugh D. Graham, *The Uncertain Trumpet: Federal Education Policy in the Kennedy and Johnson Years* (Chapel Hill: University of North Carolina Press, 1984).

36. Edward D. Berkowitz, *Mr. Social Security: The Life of Wilbur J. Cohen* (Lawrence: University Press of Kansas, 1995), 150–151.

37. John F. Witte, *The Politics and Development of the Federal Income Tax* (Madison: University of Wisconsin Press, 1985), 155.

38. Records kept by Theodore Sorensen indicate consultation with all of the peak business groups and more than twenty more specific groups. Despite JFK's rancorous dealings with Roger Blough in April, he was surveyed, along with more than a dozen prominent business figures. Many individuals had specific suggestions but generally showed considerable support. George Meany, speaking for the AFL-CIO, stressed tax cuts for lower-income brackets. Memo, "Private Groups and Individuals in Favor of a Tax Cut," Sorenson papers, Box 59, Legislative Affairs, 1961–1964, John F. Kennedy Library.

39. Witte, *Politics and Development of the Federal Income Tax,* 158.

40. Support for the view that this legislation was destined to pass can be found in Giglio, *Presidency of John F. Kennedy,* 139.

41. Shank, *Presidential Policy Leadership,* 66.

42. The lengthy literature on Kennedy's civil rights actions now includes an increasing number of sources that have used not only interviews but also extensive archival research. Carl M. Bauer strongly emphasizes Kennedy's commitments and influence in his book *John F. Kennedy and The Second Reconstruction* (New York: Columbia University Press, 1977). Two important recent interpretations are contained in Hugh Davis Graham, *Civil Rights and the Presidency: Race and Gender in American Politics, 1960–1972* (New York: Oxford University Press, 1992); and Mark Sloan, *Calculating Visions* (New Brunswick, N.J.: Rutgers University Press, 1992). Helpful recent interpretations also can be found in Irving Bernstein, *Promises Kept: John F. Kennedy's New Frontier* (New York: Oxford University Press, 1991); and Giglio, *Presidency of John F. Kennedy.*

43. *Public Papers of the Presidents of the United States: John F. Kennedy, 1963* (Washington, D.C.: Government Printing Office), 468, 469.

44. Burke Marshall, "Congress, Communication, and Civil Rights," in *The Kennedy Presidency: Seventeen Intimate Perspectives of John F. Kennedy,* ed. Kenneth W. Thompson (New York: University Press of America, 1985), 71.

45. Paper, *John F. Kennedy, 275.*

46. While the record of second-term presidents has not been encouraging, there are indications in the records of some second-term governors such as Nelson Rockefeller of New York that changing circumstances—such as a surge of public sector activism—can produce more productive second-term performances.

47. For a review of several issues raised in this discussion, see Thomas Brown, *JFK: History of an Image* (Bloomington: Indiana University Press, 1988), chap. 5.

48. Wofford, *Of Kennedys and Kings.*

49. David S. Broder, *Changing of the Guard: Power and Leadership in America* (New York: Simon and Schuster, 1980).

50. Gerald Strober and Deborah Strober, *"Let Us Begin Anew": An Oral History of the Kennedy Presidency* (New York: HarperCollins, 1993), 272–273.

51. Michael Harrington, *The Other America: Poverty in the United States* (New York: Collier Books, 1997).

52. Mark A. Peterson, *Legislating Together: The White House and Capitol Hill: From Eisenhower to Reagan* (Cambridge: Harvard University Press, 1990), 241.

The
Low-Opportunity
Presidents

8

I gave them a sword.

—RICHARD NIXON TO TELEVISION
INTERVIEWER DAVID FROST

Richard Nixon

An Activist with an Enemies List

THE ADMINISTRATION of President Richard Nixon (served 1969–1974) imploded in 1974 when the president's role in the imbroglio known as the Watergate scandal became known. Nixon resigned in disgrace on August 9, 1974. Yet two decades later his reputation as a foreign policy analyst found him engaged in extensive conversations with President Bill Clinton over U.S. policies toward Russia. By then, new perspectives also were emerging on Nixon's domestic policy leadership. In her reassessment of the former president, historian Joan Hoff Wilson wrote that Nixon accomplished far more than many people thought: "During his first term in office, Nixon acted as an agent of change in five areas of domestic reform: welfare, civil rights, economic policy, environmental policy, and reorganization of the federal bureaucracy." [1] Has Nixon, the first of the low-opportunity presidents, been overlooked and underrated as a domestic policy president?

Personal Characteristics

The early years were not easy for Richard Milhous Nixon (1913–1994). His mother, a Quaker who grew up in Whittier, California, had married "below her position in life." Her husband, Frank Nixon, possessed only a sixth-grade education, and, before moving to California, he had worked as a streetcar conductor in Ohio. Frank was known to be "volatile, unpredictable, and explosive" and a "tyrant who intimidated his children." [2] Even his son Richard admitted, "I tried to follow my mother's example

217

of not crossing him when he was in a black mood."[3] The death of two of Richard's brothers only added to the emotional stress. The family struggled economically, and Richard was pressed into working at his father's grocery store at an early age.

The family's limited finances prevented Richard from attending the eastern schools that had accepted his applications, so he attended Whittier College in California and, later, Duke University Law School in North Carolina. He was a good student and did well in debate tournaments, dabbled some in school politics, and impressed his teammates with his determination—but not ability—as a member of the school football team. At Duke he lived very frugally—in fact, he resided for a time in an abandoned shack. He was a determined student and would later refer to his use of his "iron butt" to graduate third in his class.

When his dreams of a job with a prominent eastern law firm did not materialize, Richard returned to Whittier, California, to practice law. His involvement in a local drama group led to a romance and later marriage to Thelma Catherine "Pat" Ryan, a high school typing teacher. During World War II Nixon worked briefly for the key price control agency in Washington and then served as an officer in the navy. While stationed in the Pacific he was known among his peers as an excellent poker player. After the war he joined many other veterans in the pursuit of political office.

Career Path

In his first step toward the White House, Nixon successfully challenged five-term House incumbent Jeremiah "Jerry" Voorhis of California and joined the surge of Republican victors in the 1946 House elections. Voorhis had become somewhat more liberal than his district, and Nixon blurred endorsements by two different groups within the left-leaning Congress of Industrial Organizations (CIO) to portray the incumbent as the favorite of communist sympathizers. In Washington Nixon burst onto the national spotlight when he supported the claims of journalist Whittaker Chambers that Alger Hiss, a former State Department official and prominent member of the eastern establishment, had associated with communists during the 1930s. The evidence Chambers uncovered and Nixon highlighted led to Hiss's conviction on perjury, but his guilt has long been debated. In a 1950 Senate bid, Nixon successfully challenged Helen Gahagan Douglas, a movie actress turned politician. Her "crime," according to Nixon, was the number of times she had voted with a known communist in the House.

Nixon was chosen by Republican Dwight Eisenhower as his vice-presidential nominee in 1952 to add youth to the ticket, provide regional balance, and please the conservative wing of the party. But after it was revealed that Nixon had received personal financial support from a group of wealthy California businessmen, Eisenhower debated removing him from the ticket. In a melodramatic televised address on September 23 viewed by sixty million people, Nixon denied any wrongdoing and claimed that he and his family lived simple lives. He only admitted receiving a dog, which his children had named Checkers, as a gift and insisted he would not give it back. The "Checkers Speech" drew a strong public response, and the flood of telegrams to Eisenhower's campaign saved Nixon's position on the ticket.

As vice president, Richard Nixon stood by during Eisenhower's illnesses and had few responsibilities. He did enjoy traveling and in 1959 captured the spotlight when he engaged in a spontaneous "kitchen debate" with Soviet leader Nikita Khrushchev in Moscow over the merits of capitalism and communism. Eisenhower was uneasy about retaining Nixon in 1956, but, because he had few alternatives, he decided to leave him on the ticket.

The early 1960s saw Nixon apparently end his career in politics only to reemerge victorious in 1968. In 1960 he narrowly lost the presidency to John Kennedy. Then, in 1962, he challenged the incumbent governor of California, Edmund "Pat" Brown, for his office and lost. Afterward he announced his retirement from politics with the now-famous line "You won't have Nixon to kick around anymore." A move to New York and a new law practice with the Mudge Rose law firm produced a good income, but in the wake of Republican Barry Goldwater's crushing defeat in 1964 he quietly cultivated party support for his comeback. His chance finally came in 1968 when Republicans, looking for someone to take the top spot, turned to a known figure who seemed to have a chance of winning in the midst of continuing social unrest. With his more restrained demeanor, some Republicans suggested there was a "New Nixon." In the general election campaign he promised to enforce law and order and to carry out a plan to end the war in Vietnam, but he did not have a lengthy domestic agenda.

What Manner of Man?

Elliot Richardson, the attorney general in the Nixon administration who resigned rather than fire the Watergate special prosecutor, once commented on his former boss's strategic intelligence:

> He is a realist whose realism . . . is infused with cynicism. This tough-minded outlook is a contributor to the range of his perspective on unfolding events, and it is permanently associated with his thinking. He takes the long view, and that capacity helps to explain the fact that he is perhaps the leading strategist we have had in the White House since World War II. He constantly thought about how to adapt the policies of the United States so as to accommodate our more long-term national interests.[4]

Nixon also was an introvert who suffered from low self-esteem. He even described himself "an introvert in an extrovert's profession."[5] The magnitude of Nixon's loner tendencies was evident in his Oval Office relationships; he sometimes spent more time with chief of staff H. R. "Bob" Haldeman than Haldeman would have preferred and spent considerable time alone. Haldeman at one point recruited a staff member to be the president's "designated friend," but when the real reason for his selection became apparent, Nixon would have nothing to do with him and he soon departed.

On an even more negative note, Nixon often expressed intense hostility and hatred toward individuals and institutions. He did on occasion reveal a generous side, yet more generally he appeared cynical, suspicious, and mean-spirited. Targets of his hostility included liberals, the eastern establishment, the Kennedys, academics, and the press. His final words to staff members as he resigned showed that he recognized the problems his attitudes could create: "Always remember, others may hate you—but those who hate you don't win unless you hate them, and then you destroy yourself."[6]

Despite his frequent hostilities toward others, Nixon also displayed a desire to avoid personal conflict. In fact, he preferred to hand over difficult tasks such as firing people to Bob Haldeman. Nixon aide John Ehrlichman expressed a similar view (and a defense of his own role) when he stated, "We've got the reputation of . . . building a wall around the President. The fact is that he was down under the desk saying, 'I don't want to see those fellows' and we were trying to pull him out."[7]

Nixon was known as well for his propensity to stretch the truth and for the cavalier manner in which he stated complete falsehoods. Some of his truth-stretching was of limited significance, such as his incorrect claim that his wife, Pat, was born on St. Patrick's Day (which she was not) or that (in addressing a French audience) that he had majored in French in college. Other falsehoods had more substantial political purposes, however, such as his incorrect statement in his Checkers Speech that the fund for his personal use had not been kept secret.

Once he was in the White House, Nixon's most fateful use of falsehoods was his insistence that he knew nothing about a White House cover-up of the administration's involvement in a break-in on June 17, 1972, at Democratic National Headquarters in the Watergate hotel/office complex in Washington. In fact, the president had been involved in the cover-up efforts since at least June 23, 1972—over two years before his tapes would tell the true story to the public. According to presidential biographer Fawn Brodie, Nixon enjoyed lying and considered it an important ability. She says he told a friend long before Watergate: "You don't know how to lie. If you can't lie, you'll never get anywhere." [8]

Policy Views

Nixon presented himself within the Republican Party as a moderate, and that in some respects is where he stood. Bryce Harlow, who served as a senior aide to both Eisenhower and Nixon, found Eisenhower more conservative than Nixon.[9] In his views of the use of government, Nixon certainly was no Lyndon Johnson, but he had a greater interest in putting government to work for the people than any of the other three Republican presidents serving since 1933.

The 1968 campaign provided some clues about Nixon's policy positions. On civil rights he departed from a record of general support for civil rights measures earlier in his career by denouncing "forced busing" as a tool for school desegregation and endorsing the "freedom of choice" plans strongly preferred by white southerners. A hard line on "law and order" also emerged as a major theme, but with few specific proposals. Revenue sharing, which later became a major policy initiative, also got some attention. Yet on questions such as welfare reform Nixon said little while actually denouncing the direction of reform he would propose in 1969. Environmental issues, which forcefully emerged during his first term, got little attention from any of the presidential candidates. And they presented few specific economic ideas. Ultimately, the strongest theme of Nixon's 1968 campaign and a recurring aspect of his views was his desire to end the war in Vietnam and, at home, to represent the interests of middle-class whites against what he believed were the failed social policies of liberals and Washington elites.

Challenges and Opportunities

Nixon entered the presidency facing a difficult, challenging situation in several respects, but it did hold some opportunities. Elected with only 43 percent of the vote, he was the first new president in 120 years to face a Congress in which the opposing party controlled both houses. The Republicans clearly also were the minority party in the electorate. Nixon's popularity levels were only a modest 63 percent on average the first year but, of the ten presidents reviewed here, he ranked fourth in popularity for his first term (see Table 1–2). Although he inherited a one-year budget surplus (in the wake of the 1968 tax increase) from his predecessor, Lyndon Johnson, he also faced strong inflationary pressures and intense budget pressures stemming from a combination of continued spending on the Vietnam War and pressures for additional domestic outlays.

Nixon also assumed office with the nation bitterly divided—perhaps more so than since the Civil War. Urban unrest was contributing to the tension, but uncertainty about the Vietnam War was the central factor. Majorities were now indicating that the Vietnam War had been a mistake, but no consensus existed on how the nation should end it. Nixon knew that his time for ending the war was limited, but he gambled he would be able to orchestrate a set of policies he called "peace with honor." Toward that end, he shifted toward less American troop involvement and increased bombing. He did not, however, push hard for an immediate end to the war. This strategy worked for a time, but antiwar demonstrations were picking up across the country, including a major protest on October 15, 1969. Another massive student demonstration was held the following spring to protest the limited American invasion of Cambodia on April 30, 1970, and the subsequent fatal shooting of four student demonstrators by the Ohio National Guard at Kent State University. Growing war protests and the June 1971 publication of the top-secret, war-related document known as the *Pentagon Papers* in the *New York Times* and *Washington Post* produced intense resentment in the White House. These events led to administrative efforts to carry out campaign intelligence activities that became part of the Watergate scandal.

In waging his 1972 election campaign, Nixon suggested peace was at hand, and an agreement was reached in January 1973. The peace deal was reached when Nixon dropped his demand that the withdrawal of American troops be accompanied by the simultaneous and concurrent withdrawal of North Vietnamese troops from South Vietnam. According to historians Joan Hoff Wilson, Arthur Schlesinger Jr., and others, that agreement could have been achieved in 1969.[10] There would have been some political repercussions at home—in 1969, 30 percent of the electorate favored escalation—yet a majority felt the war had been a mistake, and those favoring withdrawal exceeded 50 percent during part of 1970 and well over 60 percent during 1971 and 1972.[11]

Overseas, Nixon had more than just Vietnam on his foreign policy agenda. By means of highly secret negotiations, he was able to open U.S. relationships with China and made a state visit in 1972. Nixon had signaled his interest in such a development several years earlier and was able to use his credentials as a long-standing anticommunist to good advantage in these maneuvers. In American relationships with the Soviet Union, Nixon promoted a policy known as "détente"—the use of agreements and treaties to lessen tensions between nations. He successfully negotiated an agreement on antiballistic missiles and undertook talks aimed at achieving understandings on both countries' levels of future involvement in regional conflicts as well as the changing role of the United States in the international arena. Nixon was motivated to pursue détente by the pressures in Congress for reduced defense spending. Indeed, détente seemed to be the right road toward bringing down future military spending as the nation moved into what was called an Age of Limits.[12]

On the domestic front, the most important policy advantage was an activist public and Congress. Lots of policy proposals were "in the pipeline," and interest groups were pushing for enactment. The environmental movement came into full blossom in 1970 with the first Earth Day, and many interests such as consumer protection continued from the Johnson era. Nixon also sensed an opportunity to constrain less-popular aspects of the Great Society. Issues he had campaigned on, such as resistance to school busing, had significant poll support among whites. He found his prospects for developing new responses restricted, however, by a variety of court decisions and significant resistance in Congress. Thus Nixon was not in an easy position, but he found he could build coalitions on specific issues in Congress while also increasing likely electoral support. Perhaps most centrally, considerable credit would go to a president able to meet the challenge of the slogan that appeared on a supporter's sign at the end of the campaign—"Bring Us Together."

Later, at the end of his first term, it seemed that Nixon had met some of his challenges and might well enjoy new opportunities. Several of his strategies had worked well. His success with China helped his standing with the public, and shortly after the election his administration had reached an agreement with South Vietnam. The agreement was viewed skeptically by the American public, but there was little support for a sustained military effort.[13] In terms of building a coalition, he gained support in the South, especially in the border states as part of his southern strategy and appeals to "middle Americans." The strong economy he had helped to engineer with expansionary fiscal policy combined with wage and price controls aided his reelection chances and would create problems later, but in the short run was performing quite well. Congress was still in an activist mood, and he had some second-term agenda items, including a major cabinet restructuring. Less helpfully, his resounding reelection was over a weak opponent, Democratic senator George McGovern, and he had done little to pull new Republicans into Congress. Then, in April 1973, his presidency began to look increasingly fragile; top aides were being asked to resign and the nation had become focused on a series of abuses labeled Watergate.[14]

Leadership Style

Richard Nixon admired the leadership shown by Presidents Theodore Roosevelt and Woodrow Wilson. While clearly more interested in fulfilling a statesman's role and dealing with foreign policy rather than domestic matters, he also believed that a stable domestic policy base was a requisite for an effective foreign policy. He stated in his *Memoirs* that he was determined to be an activist president in domestic affairs, and at his first cabinet meeting he spurred its members to action, stating that "we do not want the record written that we were too cautious."[15] On occasion, he sought a place in history with bold proposals, such as his 1969 advocacy of sweeping welfare reforms. HEW Secretary and longtime friend Robert Finch, recognizing Nixon's desire, told his deputy John Veneman, "You watch that man. He's going to surprise people. He wants to be remembered in history, and, as a student of Theodore and Franklin Roosevelt, he knows that only presidents who come up with progressive social programs are likely to make a name." [16] In designing his welfare proposal, Nixon also liked to remind his staff it was Benjamin Disraeli, the conservative nineteenth-century British prime minister, who carried out reforms often advocated by liberals.

The Advisory Process and Approach
to Decision Making

In forming his cabinet, Nixon recruited a group of white males who drew little praise for their leadership or managerial skills.[17] He had tried to recruit Whitney Young, an African American and head of the Urban League, as secretary of housing and urban affairs but was unsuccessful.[18] In the end Nixon surrounded himself with several former Republican governors, among others, and came to regret several of his appointments. Quite unlike Eisenhower and in contrast to his own campaign statements, Nixon thought cabinet-level deliberations were largely a waste of time.[19] After all, why should the secretary of housing and urban affairs have to listen to a discussion of the situation in Cambodia? As for individual contributions, several of the cabinet heads in the domestic policy areas had a very limited impact. Former Alaska governor Walter Hickel proved to be a particular irritation to Nixon as secretary of the interior and was fired after just under two years in office.

Several members of the cabinet did have significant domestic policy roles, however. Secretary of Labor George Shultz (later secretary of state in the Reagan administration) had an instrumental role in civil rights issues. And HEW Secretary Robert Finch and Attorney General John Mitchell tackled many school desegregation issues. Finch, a Californian who was very close to Nixon, struggled in his position, in part because his own somewhat liberal views and pressures from within HEW put him at odds with Nixon and several top aides. John Mitchell, who had strongly advocated building support for Nixon in the South, presented a conservative outlook on most policy issues. After joining the Nixon cabinet as secretary of the Treasury in late 1970, former Texas governor John Connally made such a strong impression on Nixon that the president briefly considered Connally as a vice-presidential nominee. Connally was instrumental in Nixon's decision to adopt wage and price controls in 1971.

The Nixon White House had a very strong chief of staff, campaign aide and public relations specialist Bob Haldeman. As Watergate unfolded, Haldeman was roundly criticized by the press for his authoritarian, heavy-handed approach to his job. Nevertheless, Stephen Ambrose found he had the qualities one would like in a chief of staff. He was credited with being intelligent, hardworking, efficient, ruthless, loyal, and tough enough to stand the pressures of a difficult job.[20]

During his first year in office, Nixon's domestic advisory process evolved significantly. At the outset, he was influenced by Daniel Patrick Moynihan, a former official in the Johnson administration and an "anti-bureaucratic" liberal, whom Nixon found far more interesting and engaging in his presentations and conversations than many of the other aides. Pitted against Moynihan was economist Arthur Burns. Leonard Garment, a former law partner of Nixon's in New York, worked on minority issues, while Harry Dent, a South Carolinian with strong ties to Republican senator Strom Thurmond, brought a southern perspective to many policy issues.

The emergence of John Ehrlichman as chief domestic adviser came in the wake of an intense fight over welfare policy in the first half of 1969. Promoters of a major change called a Family Assistance Plan (FAP) included Moynihan, Shultz, and several figures from HEW. Arthur Burns was adamantly opposed to the idea. After that fight, Ehrlichman's role grew, Burns moved to the Federal Reserve Board, and Moynihan saw his influence decline. He resigned in late 1970. The move to elevate Ehrlichman came on Haldeman's recommendation. Nixon then formally created a Domestic Council and placed a large staff under Ehrlichman's direction. Ehrlichman, who saw himself as a centrist, periodically came under fire from some of the more conservative members of the Nixon staff, such as speechwriter Pat Buchanan, as well as from those with more liberal views.[21]

Nixon's greater interest in foreign policy than domestic issues was a preference that found its way to all corners of his presidency. Indeed, he once stated that a president is needed for foreign policy but, in domestic affairs, the cabinet can run the country.[22] Perhaps that is why the fight for the Family Assistance Plan is discussed in his *Memoirs,* but neither environmental issues nor revenue sharing is even mentioned. Ehrlichman found that Nixon believed in making decisions on issues that were potent politically such as abortion, race, aid to parochial schools, labor legislation, drugs, crime, welfare, and taxes. Other decisions—on the environment, health (except cancer research), campus unrest, hunger, transportation, consumer protection, youth, housing and revenue sharing—he delegated to others. In assessing Nixon's level of involvement in late 1970, Bob Haldeman was concerned that the president was not more involved in domestic issues, but he concluded that it would probably take a crisis to get him involved and this was not likely to occur.[23]

In view of Nixon's propensity to delegate much of the domestic decision-making process, an obvious question arises: How well did the men and women acting in his behalf actually function? Based on a survey-based evaluation of the Domestic Council, John Kessel gave that organization quite high marks. It prepared well-documented analyses for the president's contemplation and generally was aware of and responsive to policy concerns in the country.[24] As for Nixon's staff overall, John Greene concluded that "this was a remarkable group of advisers, quite simply the most powerful and efficient presidential staff of the postwar era."[25] A less-flattering review portrayed the staff as suffering from a "strong tendency toward heavy-handedness."[26]

In his decision-making process, Nixon read the polls avidly and was keenly interested in issues of political feasibility. And because his party was in a minority position in Congress, he strove to build a coalition that included southerners, urban Catholics, and Democratic identifiers feeling alienated from the social policies of the Democratic Party. He also sought to co-opt issues being advocated by Democratic leaders in Congress such as his potential rival in 1972, Sen. Edmund Muskie, D-Maine. In keeping with his admonition to his cabinet not to be too cautious, he too was willing to take bold steps.

Administrative Strategies

In its first term, the Nixon administration changed government structures (and contemplated changing more), pursued civil rights goals, and established economic controls in 1971. Indeed, administrative strategies were an unusually important part of Nixon's leadership approach, largely because of the difficulties he faced in dealing with Congress, his desire to produce grand schemes in reorienting the federal government, and his wish to orchestrate a decisive election win in 1972. But in his endeavors, the president did not count the bureaucracy among his friends. As Nixon commented to Bob Haldeman in 1971, "96% of the bureaucracy are against us, they're bastards who are here to screw us."[27]

Nixon attempted to bypass Congress and employ an "administrative strategy" for leadership.[28] By using appointments carefully, exerting regulatory rule making creatively, and expanding the scope of administrative authority, Nixon hoped to govern semi-independently of Congress. This intriguing effort failed, but it did establish the model that Ronald Reagan would later implement with greater success.

Turning first to reorganizational efforts, Nixon appointed a commission, headed by business executive Arthur L. Ash, to reorganize (and rename) the Bureau of the Budget. In its reincarnation, it became the Office of Management and Budget. According to John Greene, this was the most significant domestic reform of the Nixon administration—and one that was accomplished by means of a well-developed lobbying effort on Capitol Hill.[29] Had Watergate not intervened, Nixon also would have pursued a major reorganizational effort aimed at collapsing the existing cabinet structure into fewer "super-cabinet" structures headed by lieutenants highly loyal to him.[30]

Nixon also attempted to transform the Office of Economic Opportunity (OEO), created in 1964 to coordinate the War on Poverty, but he was less successful. He had been critical of OEO during the 1968 campaign, and once in office he hoped to "spin off" programs to other departments. Some observers felt that was a worthwhile step in the face of administrative difficulties at OEO, while others argued that the real intent was to kill the program most opposed by many Republicans—legal services for the poor. Nixon responded by persuading Donald Rumsfeld, a Republican member of Congress from Illinois, to head OEO and moved to extend OEO for two years. Rumsfeld carried out a number of constructive reforms, but Nixon persisted in his opposition by vetoing two bills that would have extended OEO's mandate beyond the two years. Ultimately, Nixon was prevented from substantially dismantling OEO by a court order.[31]

Nixon tackled social policy issues, including crime and civil rights, not only through administrative actions but also through the judiciary appointment process. In 1969 Nixon bowed to conservatives' criticism of the Warren Court for being too activist and reinterpreting the Constitution by nominating Warren Burger as the new chief justice. Burger nicely fit Nixon's criteria for justices who would be "tough on crime."[32] Nixon's efforts to appoint a southerner to the Court failed on both counts. Clement Haynesworth, nominated in May 1969 to replace Justice Abe Fortas, was a competent judge but concerns about his financial and other improprieties led to his rejection by a 55–45 vote. The submission of Nixon's second nominee, G. Harrold Carswell of Florida, was quickly perceived by all but the most loyal Nixon defenders as a mistake. Carswell had a record of supporting racial segregation, as well as one of the highest decision reversal rates of any sitting judge. Senate Republicans were irate about the submission of such an exceedingly mediocre nominee, and his nomination too was defeated, 51–45. Nixon turned away from his southern strategy with his other appointments. In April 1970 he nominated Minnesota judge Harry Blackmun to the Court, and in October 1971 sent the names of Lewis Powell Jr. of Virginia and William Rehnquist of Arizona to the Senate.

Like other presidents who had sought to shape the Supreme Court through judicial nominations, Nixon received some surprises. In particular, Harry Blackmum would write the famous *Roe v. Wade* abortion rights decision in 1973. Significantly, all of Nixon's nominees (except William Rehnquist because of his earlier position in the Justice Department) voted against President Nixon in the 1974 ruling that required him to release portions of his Watergate tapes, including the "smoking gun" tape of June 23, 1972, that established his involvement in the Watergate cover-up.

Nixon also applied his administrative strategies to civil rights issues. In the Civil Rights Division of the Department of Health, Education, and Welfare (HEW), five school desegregation cases were pending, holdovers from the Johnson administration. The Civil Rights Division was headed by Leon Panetta, a young, then-Republican attorney, appointed by HEW Secretary Robert Finch. Nixon proceeded with a series of steps seeking to reduce federal desegregation efforts. First, he and others leaned on Finch to move away from the Johnson administration's strategy of cutting off federal funds to segregated school districts as an enforcement technique and toward a policy (preferred by John Mitchell) of proceeding more cautiously and more slowly through the courts. Mitchell believed this strategy had the likely advantage of targeting hostile views toward the courts rather than toward an agency of the Nixon administration. Second, Nixon and his aides made it very clear that anyone working in the Nixon administration should do nothing that was not absolutely required by law. In the context of this policy, Leon Panetta was fired in early February 1970 for pursuing desegregation too aggressively. Third, in August 1969 Nixon had federal lawyers push for Supreme Court agreement to a delay in HEW-approved school desegregation plans for thirty-three school districts in Mississippi.[33] The Supreme Court, headed by Nixon's newly appointed chief justice, Warren Burger, unanimously rejected the appeal.

When Court decisions eliminated opportunities for delay, President Nixon decided to quietly pursue a plan in which local groups of black and white leaders would help design plans for school desegregation in the South. Vice President Spiro Agnew (to his dislike) was named head of a steering committee for the plan, but much of the actual planning was done by the originator of the concept, Labor Secretary George Shultz. He believed that the South had to accept single (desegregated) school systems and that the best way to go about it was to minimize adversarial relationships as much as possible while working with local leaders and offering enough federal funds to help certain districts expedite the task.[34]

Nixon later complimented Shultz on doing "one hell of a job." Interestingly, he understated his own role. By March 1970, he was quoted as saying on various occasions, "You're not going to solve this race problem for a hundred years, . . . not in our time. Desegregation, though, that has to happen now." [35] In March he delivered a ten thousand-word speech calling for desegregation of all southern schools; he had resisted a different speech because he felt it would be too emotional. In support of the system of local committees, he attended a committee meeting in New Orleans and arranged for committee members to visit the White House. The results were impressive. In 1968, 68 percent of black children in the South attended all-black schools, but by 1972 that figure had fallen to only 8 percent.[36] In his efforts to gain financial support for those efforts, however, Nixon received only a fraction of his request from Congress; some legislators feared the money would not be used to assist in the desegregation of southern schools.

While Nixon was able to achieve surprisingly peaceful desegregation in the South, the question of what policies to pursue where school integration could not be accomplished without busing produced ongoing disputes. Nixon consistently spoke out against "forced busing." Thus when efforts to restrict busing emerged in Congress, he supported those initiatives and also raised the possibility of a constitutional amendment banning busing. Ultimately, the issue was left to the courts. In a 1971 decision, the Supreme Court approved some busing across jurisdictional lines.[37] In 1974, however, the Court (which included four Nixon appointees) ruled against busing plans between cities and suburbs.

In 1969, in an unexpected move, the Nixon administration introduced its "Philadelphia Plan" to push for affirmative action in the construction industry. George Shultz was an important proponent of the plan, and Nixon seemed to be interested in it, in part because of his belief that jobs were an important factor in improving race relations. He also realized that, politically, it would pit organized labor against civil rights leaders. When the construction unions sought a congressional ban of the plan, the Nixon administration was able to sidetrack the effort. Ultimately, the Philadelphia Plan was adopted in fifty-five cities across the country.

Administrative strategies also were applied to economic issues. In 1971 the inflation rate was edging upward despite Nixon's cautious attempts to use a reduction in the budget deficits (beginning in 1970) as a policy tool for checking inflation. While an inflation figure of 4 percent would actually have been welcomed at many points later in the decade, this figure was viewed with considerable alarm in 1970. It was in this context, then, that Congress, despite Nixon's expressed declaration of disinterest, granted him in 1971 the authority to engage in wage and price controls with the expectation that his refusal to use them would become an issue in the 1972 presidential campaign.

In the summer of 1971 Nixon adopted a position that seemed to defy his long criticism of government bureaucracies. On August 15 he announced in a major national address that he was using his congressional authority to establish wage and price controls. As often happens, at the beginning of controls the public response was quite positive. Business investors also were enthusiastic; the Dow Jones industrial average jumped thirty-two points, a big hike in those days.

Nixon's bold policies have produced a variety of evaluations. At the Hofstra University Symposium on Richard Nixon held in 1987, economist Herbert Stein took issue with the suggestion that Nixon's steps represented a strong effort to manipulate the business cycle for reelection purposes and argued instead that the situation confronting the president in the summer of 1971 warranted a bold step.[38] In terms of the comparative assessment of politics and the business cycle developed by Edward Tufte, Nixon's policies were an effort to increase his reelection chances.[39]

On the environmental front, in response to public and congressional desires for action Nixon created the Council on Environmental Quality by executive order in 1969, and he was given high marks when he nominated veteran environmentalist Russell Train to head it. Also during his first term, when Congress responded to environmental initiatives with appropriations Nixon judged to be beyond what could be effectively spent in a given year, he took steps to slow action. In 1971 he took his most controversial step; he impounded as much as 50 percent of the total spending appropriated by Congress for a water bill. Finally, in 1972 Nixon went along with Congress, though somewhat reluctantly, in establishing the Environmental Protection Agency (EPA).

In short, Nixon was one of the more active presidents in his use of administrative strategies, and they often helped him to achieve his policy goals. Unfortunately, one of his strategies took him down a dark path—toward the abuses that became known as Watergate.

Public Leadership

Public roles in the Nixon White House were shaped by two tenaciously held views. Nixon had an intense desire to draw public attention to favorable developments and seemed to believe that any policy problem could be solved by good public relations. Yet he also viewed the press as hostile and slanted toward liberal criticism of himself and his programs. As a result, he constantly sought ways to "get our story out" in what he perceived to be a highly hostile environment.

Despite his dislike of the press, Nixon actually had some success in shaping press coverage. In both elections he was endorsed more often than his Democratic opponent. And although the *Washington Post* began to cover the Watergate story prior to the 1972 election, many observers were surprised at the limited coverage of the break-in. It was only after the 1972 election that the press really focused on Watergate.

Press conferences played only a very small role in Nixon's public leadership. The few he had were oriented toward foreign policy, and he made virtually no attempt to use them to help shape support for his domestic programs. As his first term progressed, press conferences were held less often—only about once every two months (see Table 1–1).

Major national addresses and secondary speaking roles were a more important part of Nixon's strategies. Although he had difficulties with television because of his halting style of speaking, some of his addresses were effective. Early in his presidency he was able to generate support for his administration—at least for a while—by categorizing war protesters as an unpatriotic minority. In October 1969 he defended a continued commitment in Vietnam and praised the "silent majority" against the critics of the war. He achieved his greatest success, however, in generating support for his welfare reform initiative; the public by a three-to-one margin felt his welfare plan was a good idea. In other speeches he focused on: a veto of a HEW appropriation and the postal strike (1970); the economy (1971, twice); and busing (1972). In his secondary speeches throughout his first term Nixon talked extensively about crime, law enforcement, school desegregation, and, to a lesser degree, environmental issues.

Vice President Spiro Agnew also was a quite visible—and vocal— part of the administration's public face. Agnew's angry denunciation of liberals, the media, "unpatriotic war protesters who need to grow up," and "pointy-headed intellectuals" became a part of Nixon's "us vs. them" approach to politics. At points, however, Nixon had some misgivings about Agnew's rhetoric and used Bryce Harlow to rein in some of his speeches. Nevertheless, the overall rhetorical thrust of the Nixon administration was one of cultural confrontation and divisiveness. It appealed to patriotic "Middle Americans" while often denouncing those dissenting from administration policies.

In its extensive public liaison efforts, the administration frequently emphasized reelection politics rather than building support for specific legislation. According to Lyn Nofziger, who served in public liaison capacities for both Nixon and Reagan, the Nixon White House was much more substantially oriented toward public liaison activities than the Reagan one because Nixon aides knew they could not depend on a strong presidential role to "carry the day."[40] One major exception to that perspective, however, was a concerted effort to build support for revenue sharing using the efforts of several governors, including Nelson Rockefeller. Under the direction of Charles Colson, the White House Office of Public Liaison, between late 1969 and the end of Nixon's first term, undertook some support-building activity—especially labor and urban ethnic voters—geared toward reelection concerns.

Nixon's support-building efforts produced some success; he ranked fifth in his ability to sustain personal support (see Table 1-1). He was not able, however, to fully mobilize presidential resources behind specific domestic policy measures.

Congressional Leadership

Nixon recruited several Washington veterans for his legislative liaison efforts. His top aide was initially Bryce Harlow, a veteran of the Eisenhower administration who was instrumental in some of the Nixon administration's early coalition-building efforts. Harlow's relationship with Halde-man and Ehrlichman deteriorated, however, and he resigned.[41] He was followed by William Timmons, former aide to Rep. William Brock III, R-Tenn., and then Clark MacGregor, a former Republican member of Congress from Minnesota.

In allocating his time to congressional leadership, particularly during the first two years in office, Nixon did make at least a moderate effort. Internal staff figures for the years 1969–1972 reveal the following yearly pattern: hours with GOP leadership meetings—24, 16, 13, 15; hours with senators—125, 121, 94, and 23; hours with representatives—87, 115, 69, and 30; and phone conversations with members—204, 140, 180, and 61.[42] The falloff in time spent—quite common in a president's first term—reflected Nixon's frustrations with Congress after his party fared poorly in the 1970 midterm elections. While these figures appear to be rather low compared with those for other presidents, Nixon did not ignore personal relationships with members of Congress to a unique degree.

Assessments of Nixon's success in dealing with members of Congress have generally stressed his limited skills. Despite his earlier service there, Capitol Hill was still rather foreign to him, and he had difficulties in particular in relating to the Senate. Despite his often gruff, "in-your-face" demeanor, he also found it hard to ask legislators for their votes. Recognizing that tendency, legislative liaison aide William Timmons at one point added a note at the bottom of Nixon's talking points for a meeting with a member of Congress, "ASK HIM FOR HIS VOTE."[43]

Nixon employed several legislative strategies, including agenda setting with bold initiatives, as he sought influence in a difficult situation. For example, in his 1970 State of the Union address he laid out an especially strong environmental program. But his chief strategy, according to legislative aide Harlow, was to assume the role of centrist. To gain legislative victories he began by starting with the Republican core and then trying to coax into the fold Democrats from various factions depending on the nature of the issue. House passage of the Family Assistance Plan in 1970, for example, relied on a coalition of Republicans and liberal Democrats. Conversely, to slow school desegregation plans, he attempted to build a coalition of Republicans and conservative Democrats.[44] In fact, Nixon often found some of his best working relationships with southern Democrats.[45] After 1970, however, he adopted a strategy of increasingly going against Congress. As he told Bob Haldeman in a staff meeting at Key Biscayne on November 7, 1970, "Agreed, we don't work with Congress, we go against them." [46]

In the same vein, vetoes were an important aspect of Nixon's legislative strategies, and he used the threat of a veto quite often as a bargaining tool. He also was not afraid to use them: among the presidents (other than Ford) who served between 1933 and 1980, Nixon ranks first in the frequency with which he vetoed significant legislation—an average of 6.7 vetoes of major legislation per year (see Table 1–1).[47]

Legislative Enactments

During Nixon's first term in the White House, the number of major domestic enactments, as defined by David Mayhew (see Chapter 1), equaled 85 percent of those passed during Johnson's full term in office. The action was limited in 1969, reflecting in part Nixon's sparse first-year agenda and the bruising fights over Supreme Court nominees; the largest number of bills were enacted in 1970. Although Nixon exercised little presidential leadership during his abbreviated second term, some additional major legislation was enacted.

Tax Reform

Tax reform remained on the front burner during Nixon's time in office. In 1969 Congress enacted the most sweeping tax reform bill since 1913—a bill that had its origins in the Johnson administration, specifically Treasury Secretary Joseph Barr. He had warned of the prospects of a "taxpayers revolt," spurred on by increased public awareness of tax inequities.[48] The public's belief that a significant number of millionaires were paying no personal income taxes only contributed to its indignation. The Nixon administration submitted proposals and got some of them approved, but the Democratic controlled Congress drastically changed those proposals and added many of its own. Senate minority leader Hugh Scott, R-Pa., was rather pointed in telling the White House staff that they should listen because specialists in Congress knew more about taxes than they did.[49] President Nixon was largely silent before the public on this issue, but he did use a veto threat, and he sought the aid of Republican legislators at a breakfast meeting at the White House. Ultimately, however,

Nixon had to accept tax reforms he did not prefer because Congress was holding hostage an extension in the surtax on incomes that he wanted for the additional revenue it would contribute to the 1970 budget. In assessing the overall effort, John Witte concluded that the tax reform measure was "basically a congressional tax bill." [50]

Nixon played a more active role in tax policy in 1971 as he proposed a tax cut of approximately $25 billion, including an investment tax credit. This effort to stimulate the economy was part of his mid-August establishment of wage and price controls. On another front, Nixon and the Republicans lost a highly partisan battle in which the Democrats, concerned about their inability to compete with the Republicans in fund raising, established a check-off system on tax returns that allowed citizens to donate money to cover the costs of presidential elections. Nixon did manage to defeat some other issues, however, through veto threats.

Crime Legislation

President Nixon, by making law and order a theme of his 1968 campaign, helped to spark the interest of both Congress and the public in law enforcement issues. Thus by the time they proposed new crime legislation, both Congress and President Nixon appeared to be responding to a major concern of average Americans. In the end, three major bills were enacted. The Organized Crime Control Act of 1970 was a comprehensive effort to address organized crime, including the creation of a witness protection program. The second measure, the Omnibus Crime Control Act of 1970, provided a wide variety of crime control provisions, including mandatory sentencing provisions. And the third, a narcotics control program, established several new drug control programs.

General Revenue Sharing

The general revenue sharing legislation enacted in 1972 was the Nixon administration's most significant domestic policy accomplishment. This strategy, which entailed having the federal government return some tax dollars to state and local governments for use as they saw fit, appealed to Nixon for several reasons. In part, it would reduce the dependency on categorical grants, which had grown considerably in the Johnson presidency and were regarded in many quarters as overly cumbersome. At the same time, general revenue sharing was a means of providing additional aid to the suburbs and small towns, which fit nicely into Nixon's reelection concerns.

In creating his revenue sharing proposals Nixon was drawing on the periodic interest legislators and presidents had been showing in this strategy since the 1950s, when it came to the attention of Eisenhower and some Republican members of Congress. A decade later Walter Heller, chairman of the Council of Economic Advisers, showed interest in the plan while serving in the Kennedy administration. In the early days of the Nixon administration, Robert Nathan in the Bureau of the Budget was an important promotor.[51]

As Nixon began to plan his "new American revolution," as he called it in his January 1971 State of the Union address, he was persuaded by John Ehrlichman and others to pursue a more comprehensive revenue sharing approach. That approach called for making approximately $5 billion available to the states in a multiyear plan and for a special revenue sharing plan that would include $11 billion (but with $10 billion coming from other grant-in-aid programs).

Once the plan was launched, the Nixon administration pursued public support for it by unleashing a mobilization effort, headed by Gov. Nelson Rockefeller of New York, that surpassed the effort made for any other single piece of legislation. Indeed, according to one analyst, it was largely through Rockefeller's efforts that revenue sharing passed.[52] The administration also undertook an extensive legislative liaison effort to mobilize support in Congress and to decide on strategy as various alternative proposals emerged.

In the end, then, Nixon largely prevailed; the program finally agreed on included about $5 billion in new revenues and a total of $16 billion over the 1973–1975 period.

Welfare, Social Security, and Health

Welfare, Social Security, and health care were highly salient legislative issues during Nixon's years in office. Interest in welfare reform heightened dramatically in August 1969 when Nixon unveiled a landmark proposal known as the Family Assistance Plan (FAP). FAP would have abolished Aid to Families with Dependent Children (AFDC) and Medicaid and replaced them with a guaranteed annual income of $1,600 for a family of four. In an attempt to provide work incentives, the plan also would offer health benefits to families with incomes considerably above that level.

While radical in scope, this measure actually built on ideas initially advocated by conservative economist Milton Friedman and others as a less-cumbersome and less-bureaucratic form of assistance.

Nixon had several motivations in seeking broad welfare reform. Rapidly climbing welfare costs for AFDC were causing alarm in many quarters, and Nixon felt that, with his bold proposal, he might be able to gain credit for an historic change. Some observers sensed as well that Nixon's desire to aid the "deserving poor" had roots in his own childhood experiences. Key aides, including former Johnson official Daniel Patrick Moynihan, also exerted strong pressure on the president. Other motivations suggested were the president's desire to answer critics who had concluded by March 1969 that he had little in the way of a domestic program, his desire to take a step to please some who opposed his civil rights policies, and his sense that an opportunity was at hand to promote a plan that would lessen the role of federal officials and social workers.[53]

Nixon may have been sincere in his objectives, but he showed uncertainty about the merits of his own plan. The measure was introduced with a presidential address and gained public support by a three-to-one margin. To the surprise of many, the bill also garnered the support of House Ways and Means chairman Wilbur Mills and was passed by a vote of 243–155 in the House. Yet rather than being gratified, Nixon decided Mills had not modified the bill so that Nixon would have to face the conflicts (and costs) his plan would produce. "The Democrats did this to trap us with an unworkable plan," he told Bob Haldeman. By the summer of 1970 Nixon had decided the plan should go nowhere. As Bob Haldeman put in his notes: "About Family Assistance Plan, wants to be sure it's killed by Democrats, and that we make a big play for it, but don't let it pass, can't afford it."[54] Nevertheless, he reintroduced the measure in 1971, and staff analyses by John Ehrlichman suggested that options other than a quiet defeat were being assessed.

The Senate proved to be the deathbed of FAP as Sen. Russell Long, D-La., who regarded its defeat as one of his major legislative triumphs, staunchly resisted a proposal he felt would reduce incentives for work. Nixon continued to seek compromises, but was unable to build the necessary centrist coalition. Conservatives argued that his expensive proposal would unwisely expand the welfare rolls, while liberals such as Sen. Abraham Ribicoff, D-Conn., called for a virtual doubling of the guaranteed income to $3,000.

Other welfare policy changes that did take place during Nixon's first term were an expanded food stamp program and a major new federal commitment known as Supplementary Security Income (SSI). Nixon played a role in expanding the food stamp program when in May 1970 he requested a $1 billion a year increase. The Senate and House then fought over the size of some of the provisions and finally passed a somewhat larger measure. The measure establishing the SSI program was passed in 1972, in a last-minute compromise. The program provided a floor income (initially $140 a month for individuals living alone and $190 a month for couples) for the aged, blind, and disabled. Senator Long was the leading advocate, but Nixon was willing to support this more limited program.

Action on Social Security was even more extensive, with increases passed in 1969, 1971, and 1972. The generous increase in 1972, coupled with indexing, set the stage for funding problems as early as 1977. In each instance, Nixon's proposed figures were lower than the figure Congress adopted. As for indexing for annual cost of living adjustments (COLAs), Nixon had expressed an interest as early as 1969 as a way to eliminate what Republicans perceived to be a pattern of Democrats promoting increases in election years.[55] The actual decision-making process surrounding the 1972 legislation reflected electoral politics, with Nixon and potential nominees for the Democratic presidential ticket (including for a time Wilbur Mills) anxious to cultivate the support of senior citizens.[56] Although he contributed little to actual passage of the 1972 Social Security legislation, Nixon eagerly included references to the benefit increase he had signed in the mailings of the October benefits payments.

Nixon and Congress also displayed considerable interest in health policy. In a February 1971 message to the American people, Nixon sought to respond to liberal calls for a system of national health insurance by promoting the concept of prepaid health plans. These plans, formerly opposed by conservatives, were now labeled health maintenance organizations (HMOs). His proposals also included a call for private mandates to support public spending that resembled in form (but not scope) President Bill Clinton's proposal in 1993. No progress was made on expanded coverage, however, and, in the face of strong resistance by the American Medical Association, Nixon reduced his level of support for HMOs. Meanwhile, while Democratic senator Edward Kennedy of Massachusetts was trying to broaden the scope of HMO development, Nixon was trying to reduce the funding levels being proposed in Congress. Thus legislation was stalemated during Nixon's first term. Later, however, in 1973, a measure encompassing many of Kennedy's desires for a broad program but with funding levels closer to Nixon's preferences was passed.

On a second major health enactment, Nixon succeeded in helping to promote expansion of the federal government's cancer research effort. Nixon proposed the legislation and promoted it publicly to a moderate degree. In this instance, the primary debate in Congress was over the manner in which the additional research would be organized. After elaborate compromises, the National Cancer Institute was created in 1971. Just as for welfare, support could be built for some action but not the broader initial proposals.

Environmental and Consumer Protection Policies

A dramatic surge in environmental protection legislation and to some extent consumer protection and health policies occurred during Nixon's first term. Congress enacted the National Environmental Protection Act in 1969 and made sweeping changes in 1970 that included a major expansion of the effort to achieve clean air. The same year Congress passed a clean water act and then a second water pollution control act in 1972. The year 1970 also saw the establishment of the Occupational Safety and Health Administration within the Department of Labor. Other legislation passed in Nixon's first term tackled pesticide control; increased the funds spent on cancer research and provided for an expanded organizational structure; banned cigarette advertising; and established the Consumer Product Safety Commission. President Nixon clearly was not a significant voice in the sudden emergence of environmental issues in Washington. After all, neither he nor Democratic rival Hubert Humphrey had paid any significant attention to environmental issues in the 1968 campaign. But the environmental movement had been growing as a grassroots phenomenon in many of the states, and problems such as a major oil spill off the coast of Santa Barbara, California, at the outset of the Nixon administration eventually triggered government interest. More generally, many kinds of environmental problems were emerging in the wake of the rapid economic growth the country had been experiencing in the 1960s.

The task facing the Nixon administration was one of relating to this emerging interest while not accepting measures seen as extreme. Nixon also was determined that his potential rival in the 1972 election, Sen. Edmund Muskie, who had specialized in water pollution issues, not gain too much credit from passage of remedial legislation. Toward that end, Muskie, although a major contributor to the development of new water pollution control legislation in 1970, was not invited to the president's bill-signing ceremony. Then after a very active year on environmental issues in 1970, Nixon seemed to lose interest. "The environment is not an issue that's worth a damn to us," he told aide Bob Haldeman.[57] He went on to suggest that he feared the left was using the issue to destroy the system of government and that he was playing into its hands.

When the administration did express an interest in the environment, it was based on budgetary and economic performance issues. At some points, it was clearly interested in shaping legislation that would be less costly and would create less-stringent regulations on business. In fact, when it came to choosing between environmental protection and jobs, Nixon usually opted for protecting jobs. Thus in 1972 he vetoed legislation that would in his eyes have opened the budget far too wide for projects that would be difficult to develop and manage without resorting to a greatly expanded bureaucracy.

A close look at legislative action on major environmental policies during Nixon's first four years reveals several different patterns. In the area of pesticide controls, the Nixon administration's actions were pivotal to congressional adoption of new controls. According to Christopher Bosso, "Nixon's active intervention on the environment (based upon whatever motives) derailed the pesticides subgovernment and paved the way to substantial policy change."[58] In many other instances, the Nixon administration often sought to reduce the controls imposed on business by new legislation. On the Clean Air Act Amendments of 1970, for example, the administration supported some aspects of that sweeping legislation but unsuccessfully fought against amendments that would force the automobile industry to develop technologies that would reduce some polluting auto emissions by 90 percent.

The Nixon administration had only limited involvement in consumer safety legislation, and Nixon himself played only a minor public role in each of the consumer enactments. Interestingly, the Nixon administration took no stand on the legislation banning cigarette advertising on television. On legislation establishing the Consumer Product Safety Commission in 1972, it unsuccessfully supported industry's preference that enforcement action be housed in the Department of Health and Human Services (the commission is an independent federal agency).

Civil Rights

During Nixon's first term, Congress extended the Voting Rights Act of 1965 and strengthened the enforcement provisions for the Equal Employment Opportunities Commission. On the extension of the Voting Rights Act, Nixon indicated his interest in softening some of its provisions and Attorney General John Mitchell presented a critical evaluation, but the president did not speak out publicly in opposition. Congress ultimately prevailed, and the legislation was extended basically intact.

The legislation expanding the enforcement powers of the Equal Employment Opportunity Commission was the culmination of a seven-year drive. The bill became the subject of a filibuster in the Senate, and two cloture votes failed. The legislation finally passed, however.

Nixon and Congress

According to a study by Mark Peterson, Nixon's relationship with Congress had many dimensions.[59] Despite his minority status, the president was more antagonistic than conciliatory toward legislators right from the outset and at times seemed unwilling to compromise. Yet he was willing to push hard for some of his bold programs, and in Peterson's study he did relatively well in gaining support for the large policy measures he submitted to Congress.

Relationships between Nixon and Congress thus showed the potential for substantial congressional influence in the shaping of domestic policy when the times were ripe for action and there were many policy ideas being promoted. At the same time, Nixon promoted some issues successfully, sought to define centrist positions in a number of areas, and displayed an interest in policy changes, which also contributed to an unusually extensive outpouring of legislation. Although he had to accept liberal reforms passed by Congress, Nixon consistently attempted to moderate or reduce congressional efforts while not openly going against congressional or public opinion.

Watergate and the Ford Interregnum

The abuse of power in the Nixon administration will forever be somewhat mislabeled "Watergate."[60] That label was drawn from the burglary attempt at the headquarters of the Democratic National Committee on June 17, 1972. There is general agreement that Nixon did not know in advance of the break-in and considerable disagreement even a quarter-century later about the actual motivation for it.

But the abuse of power in the Nixon administration cannot be confined to events occurring at a hotel/condominium/office complex a few blocks from the White House, however fascinating.[61] The Nixon administration also engaged in illegal surveillance activities, which were not as unprecedented as believed at the time.[62] In the process, "as a wartime president, Nixon and his aides trampled again and again on the civil rights of antiwar protesters and other groups and individuals critical of the government."[63] One extreme case was the September 1971 break-in at a psychiatrist's office in Beverly Hills, California, so the intruders could examine the records of war protestor Daniel Ellsberg. This break-in, like other activities, was carried out by a group known as the "Plumbers" because of their desire to plug leaks.

Another abuse of power was the administration's "enemies list"— prominent journalists, intellectuals, business and labor leaders, and others, who might be targeted for harassment through tax audits, prosecution, and other government actions. The administration also used the Internal Revenue Service to harass political opponents. At a May 1971 meeting attended by Nixon, plans were made to disrupt the campaigns of the strongest potential Democratic challengers. One of those disruptions was a fake letter written by Nixon campaign operatives, attacking Edmund Muskie's wife. In an effort to defend his wife's honor, Muskie gave a very emotional, impromptu speech. Reactions to the episode led to Muskie's withdrawal from the race.

Nixon's final Watergate-related abuse—and the easiest for the public to understand—was his orchestration of a cover-up that included, among other things, the payment of hush money to the Watergate burglars from funds kept in the White House. In October 1973 Nixon set the impeachment process in motion when he fired two attorneys general who would not dismiss the special prosecutor looking into the whole sordid affair. He also resisted turning over his tapes of White House conversations to congressional committees and failed in his attempt to arrange for the release of a sanitized version. The release of those tapes, which showed his involvement in the cover-up since June 23, 1972, led to bipartisan support for impeachment by the House of Representatives and his resignation as a Senate conviction became increasingly certain.

Nixon's abuse of power was not confined to the Watergate scandal, however. He also conducted a secret incursion of neutral Cambodia during the Vietnam War. Nixon believed that the B-52 bombing raids he ordered for Cambodia would disrupt supply lines and eliminate enemy safe havens. Then, on April 30, 1970, Nixon went on television to report that American troops had entered Cambodia. Significantly, the House drew up an article of impeachment based on the president's actions in Cambodia, but it was voted down in the House Judiciary Committee which realized this could become a difficult issue within Congress. Nixon had kept double books to avoid an accurate reporting to Congress, but he had in fact notified a few members of Congress of his actions.

The forces that may have led to the abuses in the Nixon presidency have been examined from many different angles, including Nixon's paranoia, his personal disregard for the law, the staff system he created, the difficult circumstances he faced, and the manner in which Nixon and his key aides responded to the release of the *Pentagon Papers* in 1971. Although the president had approved plans for "dirty tricks" against Democratic candidates prior to 1971 and some other abuses had emerged, there does appear to be considerable merit in the position taken by key aide and political operative Charles Colson that "the pivotal point was the release of the Pentagon Papers."[64]

With Nixon's resignation in 1974, Vice President Gerald Ford succeeded to the presidency. The former longtime House member and House minority leader had replaced Vice President Spiro Agnew in October 1973 after Agnew had pleaded no contest to one count of income tax evasion, paid a $10,000 fine, and agreed to resign as vice president. (The real issue, however, was charges of corrupt practices during his years as governor of Maryland.) Attorney General Elliott Richardson, aware of Nixon's uncertain future, arranged for the speedy negotiation of a plea bargain so that an untainted vice president would be in place should Nixon have to resign.

Ford faced enormous difficulties as president and compounded his problems by pardoning Nixon shortly after assuming office. His efforts to "put our national nightmare behind us" could be defended on some grounds, but the pardon fueled a drop in Ford's popularity from which he never recovered. The 1974 midterm election saw the Republicans lose fifty-two seats in the House and their ranks of party members shrink to only 144. The fairly promising pre-Watergate domestic agenda, which included health care reform, was dead. Efforts to end wage and price controls contributed to inflationary pressures, and the rising high unemployment figures jeopardized any fruitful policy making. In foreign policy, the fall of Saigon to the North Vietnamese in April 1975 was a sad ending to virtually two decades of American involvement in Southeast Asia. It was not surprising, then, when Ford, in early 1976, was confronted with a tough nomination challenge from fellow Republican Ronald Reagan.

Given his perseverance and the skills he displayed in areas such as staff relationships, Ford might well have been a solid performer had he held the presidency under normal circumstances. As history unfolded, however, even a rather effective fall campaign and Democrat Jimmy Carter's limitations as a candidate would not allow him to overcome the difficulties he confronted as Nixon's successor.

An Assessment

Nixon and his presidency, claims historian Arthur Schlesinger Jr., will be debated "until the end of time." But Nixon did leave a substantial domestic legacy, despite the tempestuous times in which he served.

As one would expect from a Republican president facing an activist Congress controlled by Democrats, Nixon seldom designed, promoted, and sold to Congress specific policy measures. His activism on some issues energized Congress, however, and in his efforts to constrain what he saw as Democratic excesses he also helped to shape the domestic legacy that emerged. Environmental policy constitutes an important example of these forces. More programs of lasting duration were created by the Nixon administration than by any of those that followed. For example, the Environmental Protection Agency was established, and fundamental legislation directed toward air and water pollution also was passed in Nixon's first term. These measures, along with some that followed, have led to significant improvements in the quality of the nation's air and water.

Nixon's interest in the structure of the federal government also led to significant changes. The new Office of Management and Budget with its broader role than that of its predecessor, the Bureau of the Budget, helped Nixon and future presidents better address management issues. Although his general revenue sharing scheme would not survive budget cuts by Reagan, that legislation provided for a time new flexibility in federal–state relations. Nixon also saw the establishment of Amtrak and the creation of the U.S. Postal Service as an independent agency.

The president had a moderate impact as well on the expansion of welfare and Social Security that occurred on his watch. Congress approved the indexing of Social Security for inflation. On welfare reform it enacted only a small portion of what the president had proposed, but he was the one who had talked initially of federal support of a minimum income— a notion that Congress had balked at and then enacted a much smaller program. By contrast, increases in Social Security benefits were the result of a bidding war among presidential aspirants, with several members of Congress calling for the higher figures.

Nixon also contributed to changes—some good, some bad, as civil rights leaders saw it—in civil rights policies. In dealing with the nation's schools, he reflected majority white opinion in opposing broad programs such as metropolitan-wide busing. He also expressed little support for some of the innovations that were beginning to emerge such as magnet schools. On a more positive note, his ability to work with southern leaders was impressive in 1970. Moreover, he established the first affirmative action program with his Philadelphia Plan.

A less-positive Nixon legacy was the buildup of inflationary pressures that became increasingly troublesome throughout the 1970s. In fighting inflation, Nixon put into effect wage and price controls along with expansionary fiscal and monetary policies as part of his 1972 reelection bid. A change was warranted at that time, yet Nixon himself saw the problems down the road: "The August 15, 1971, decision to impose [wage and price controls] was politically necessary and immensely popular in the short run. But in the long run I believe that it was wrong. The piper must always be paid, and there was an unquestionably high price for tampering with the orthodox economic mechanisms." [65]

Viewed in a broader perspective, Nixon's domestic performance suffers in one fundamental respect; he tended more to create divisions than to lessen them. Granted, presidents can do only so much to change the nation's climate of opinion, but underlying Nixon's rhetoric was a divisive "us versus them" tone. Since most of this rhetoric was directed toward protestors of the war in Vietnam, another cost of that war is apparent. [66]

This being said, Nixon was able to maintain in early 1973 that some of his goals had been met. He could rightly claim credit for some domestic policy changes, including a slowing of school desegregation efforts. Overseas, he had pursued innovative foreign policies with both China and the Soviet Union. The Paris peace accord, while less than he wanted, had provided an end to American involvement in Vietnam. In addition, the

1972 election had given him his coveted reelection—and by a margin that exceeded Eisenhower's. In overall terms, then, Nixon did reasonably well in achieving his domestic policy goals, especially for a low-opportunity president.

Yet Watergate cannot be ignored in any assessment of the Nixon presidency. It had many consequences which may have been overstated because so many other things were changing at the same time. Sociologist Michael Schudson concluded, "Watergate is for the general public one of the most important political events of the past half century, although not nearly as important as the Vietnam War and somewhat less important than the transformation and tumult of political culture in the 1960s." [67]

At a minimum, Watergate contributed to innumerable changes—almost all of them negative—in the presidency and American politics (not to mention today's unfortunate tendency to label any scandal as "xxxgate"). Among other things, the public has grown more cynical and less trusting of government, the level of political discourse has become harsher, the hunt for scandals pervades politics, investigative journalists and special prosecutors have thrived, and in Congress a combination of younger, more ideologically driven members and the legacy of Watergate has produced reforms that have enhanced opportunities for a congressional role in shaping domestic policy—sometimes at the expense of presidential influence. Arguably, some of the increased voter skepticism has been an appropriate antidote to the high voter confidence in government that pollsters found in the 1960s. Nevertheless, Nixon's resignation in disgrace provided a very poor beginning for a difficult economic and social period for the nation.[68]

Notes

1. Joan Hoff Wilson, *Nixon Reconsidered* (New York: Basic Books, 1994), 17.
2. Michael A. Genovese, *The Nixon Presidency: Power and Politics in Turbulent Times* (Westport, Conn.: Greenwood Press, 1990), 10.
3. Richard M. Nixon, *The Memoirs of Richard Nixon* (New York: Grossett and Dunlop, 1978), 16.
4. Elliot L. Richardson, "Capacity for Greatness," in *Richard M. Nixon: Politician, President, and Administrator,* ed. Leon Friedman and William F. Levantrosser (Westport, Conn.: Greenwood Press, 1991), 3–4.
5. Tom Wicker, *One of Us: Richard Nixon and the American Dream* (New York: Random House, 1991), 24.

6. Bob Woodward and Carl Bernstein, *The Final Days* (New York: Simon and Schuster, 1976), 455.

7. Wicker, *One of Us,* 389.

8. Fawn Brodie, *Richard Nixon: The Shaping of His Character* (New York: Norton, 1981), 25.

9. Wicker, *One of Us,* 410.

10. Wilson, *Nixon Reconsidered,* chap. 4; and Arthur M. Schlesinger Jr., "Discussant," in *Watergate and Afterward: The Legacy of Richard M. Nixon,* ed. Leon Friedman and William F. Levantrosser (Westport, Conn.: Greenwood Press, 1992), 326.

11. Michael P. Sullivan, *The Vietnam War: A Study in the Making of American Policy* (Lexington: University of Kentucky Press, 1985), 112.

12. Michael A. Genovese, *The Presidency in an Age of Limits* (Westport, Conn.: Greenwood Press, 1993).

13. Richard A. Melanson, *Reconstructing Consensus: American Foreign Policy since the Vietnam War* (New York: St. Martin's Press, 1991), 54.

14. Michael A. Genovese, *The Watergate Crisis* (Westport, Conn.: Greenwood Press, 1999).

15. Nixon, *Memoirs;* and Wicker, *One of Us,* 412.

16. A. James Reichley, *Conservatives in an Age of Change* (Washington, D.C.: Brookings, 1981), 58.

17. Rowland Evans Jr. and Robert D. Novak, *Nixon in the White House: The Frustration of Power* (New York: Random House, 1971), 51.

18. Stephen E. Ambrose, *Nixon: The Triumph of a Politician, 1962–1972* (New York: Simon and Schuster, 1989), 236.

19. Wilson, *Nixon Reconsidered,* 53.

20. Ambrose, *Nixon,* 228.

21. John Ehrlichman, *Witness to Power: The Nixon Years* (New York: Simon and Schuster, 1982), 212.

22. Ibid., 207.

23. H. R. Haldeman, *The Haldeman Diaries: Inside the Nixon White House* (New York: Putnam's Sons, 1994), 214.

24. John H. Kessel, *The Domestic Presidency: Decision-Making in the White House* (North Scituate, Mass.: Duxbury Press, 1975), 123.

25. John R. Greene, *The Limits of Power: The Nixon and Ford Administrations* (Bloomington: Indiana University Press, 1992), 27.

26. Richard P. Nathan, *The Plot That Failed: Nixon and the Administrative Presidency* (New York: Wiley, 1975), 3.

27. Haldeman, *Haldeman Diaries,* 6.

28. Nathan, *Plot That Failed;* and Richard P. Nathan, *The Administrative Presidency* (New York: Wiley, 1983).

29. Greene, *Limits of Power,* 54.

30. Nathan, *Plot That Failed,* chap. 1.

31. Wilson, *Nixon Reconsidered,* 63.

32. Ambrose, *Nixon,* 201.

33. Hugh David Graham, *The Civil Rights Era: Origins and Development of National Policy, 1960–1972* (New York: Oxford University Press, 1990), 319.

34. Herbert S. Parmet, *Richard Nixon and His America* (Boston: Little, Brown, 1990), 603.

35. Ibid., 604.

36. Wilson, *Nixon Reconsidered*, 90.

37. *Swann v. Charlotte-Mecklenburg Board of Education,* 402 U.S. 1 (1971).

38. Herbert Stein, "Discussant comments" in Friedman and Levantrosser, *Richard M. Nixon,* 249–254.

39. Edward R. Tufte, *Political Control of the Economy* (Princeton: Princeton University Press, 1978).

40. Franklin C. Nofziger, *Nofziger* (Washington, D.C.: Regnery Gateway, 1992).

41. Evans and Novak, *Nixon in the White House,* 103–110.

42. Ehrlichman, *Witness to Power,* 202–203.

43. Reichley, *Conservatives in an Age of Change,* 87.

44. Ibid., chap. 5.

45. Ambrose, *Nixon,* 406.

46. Haldeman, *Haldeman Diaries,* 208.

47. Richard A. Watson, *Presidential Vetoes and Public Policy* (Lawrence: University of Kansas Press, 1993), 42. Also see Robert J. Spitzer, *The Presidential Veto* (New York: State University of New York Press, 1988).

48. *Congressional Quarterly Almanac 1969* (Washington, D.C.: Congressional Quarterly, 1970), 589.

49. Ibid., 107.

50. John F. Witte, *The Politics and Development of the Federal Income Tax* (Madison: University of Wisconsin Press, 1985), 176.

51. Paul R. Dommel, *The Politics of Revenue Sharing* (Bloomington: Indiana University Press, 1974).

52. Greene, *Limits of Power,* 62.

53. See in particular Reichley, *Conservatives in an Age of Change,* 143.

54. Haldeman, *Haldeman Diaries,* 32, 181.

55. Martha Derthick, *Policymaking for Social Security* (Washington, D.C.: Brookings, 1979), 346.

56. William W. Lammers, *Public Policy and the Aging* (Washington, D.C.: CQ Press, 1984).

57. Haldeman, *Haldeman Diaries,* 246.

58. Christopher J. Bosso, *Pesticides and Politics: The Life Cycle of a Public Issue* (Pittsburgh: University of Pittsburgh Press, 1987), 262.

59. Mark A. Peterson, *Legislating Together: The White House and Capitol Hill from Eisenhower to Reagan* (Cambridge: Harvard University Press, 1990), 247–251.

60. Genovese, *The Watergate Crisis.*

61. Stanley I. Kutler, *The Wars of Watergate* (New York: Knopf, 1990); and

Fred Emery, *Watergate: The Corruption of American Politics and the Fall of Richard Nixon* (New York: Touchstone, 1995).

62. Michael Schudson, *Watergate in American Memory* (New York: Basic Books, 1992), 35.

63. Wilson, *Nixon Reconsidered,* 278.

64. Genovese, *Nixon Presidency,* 130.

65. Nixon, *Memoirs,* 521.

66. Wilson, *Nixon Reconsidered,* 113.

67. Schudson, *Watergate in American Memory,* 13.

68. Genovese, *Watergate Crisis.*

Had our final congressional-leadership breakfast. There was a different tone today—one of a degree of relief that the Democrats will not be responsible for all the problems in the future.

9

—JIMMY CARTER, DIARY ENTRY, DECEMBER 2, 1980

Jimmy Carter

An Outsider's Pursuit of "Trustee" Leadership

IN THE post-Watergate era, Jimmy Carter (served 1977–1981) assumed office seeking to end the ceremonial trappings and power abuses of the "imperial presidency" while promising the nation a presidency "as good as its people." Yet despite his promises of positive new directions, his four years in the White House were a continuing struggle. In 1981 Carter reflected sadly on an election he had lost by ten percentage points, thereby relinquishing control of the White House to Ronald Reagan, the most conservative Republican president since the 1920s.

Carter had sought to govern differently. He liked to pursue policies he viewed to be in the long-term public interest, and he placed less emphasis on bargaining with Congress. His approach also featured a zealous pursuit of administrative efficiencies and a desire to have direct, town meeting-style communication with the public. Did this low-opportunity president turn his trustee leadership into success on the domestic front?

Personal Characteristics

James Earl Carter Jr. (1924–) was the first president to have been born and raised in the Deep South since Woodrow Wilson. He also was the most devoutly religious president serving since 1932. Had he been raised in comparable family circumstances outside of the one-party South, he might well have emerged as a Republican.[1]

Jimmy was the son of a prominent peanut farmer and processor in tiny Plains, Georgia. After high school, he left south Georgia to attend college and graduated from the U.S. Naval Academy in Annapolis, Maryland, in 1946. The young officer carried out many assignments during his brief naval career, including engineering officer on a nuclear submarine. After the death of his father in 1953, he abruptly left the navy and returned to Plains to run the family business.

On one of his trips home from the Naval Academy, young Jimmy met seventeen-year-old Rosalynn Smith, who also had grown up in Plains. The oldest of four children whose father had died when they were young, Rosalynn worked as a cleaning girl in a beauty salon to meet the family's expenses. Jimmy and Rosalynn married when she was only eighteen.

Career Path

Jimmy Carter had less experience in significant administrative and elective positions than any other post-1932 president. After serving on the Sumner County, Georgia, school board and in the state legislature for four years, he ran unsuccessfully for governor in 1966 and successfully in 1970. Restricted by the state's constitution to a single term, he left office in 1974 after pushing for reorganization of the state government and budgeting reforms and making progress in the appointments of blacks. His relationship with the factionally divided legislature was stormy, however, and it is unlikely he would have been reelected if a second term had been allowed.[2]

Between 1974 and 1976 Carter laid the foundation for his bid for the Democratic Party's presidential nomination. He had tried tentatively for the vice presidential nomination in 1972, but decided after talking with other potential Democratic candidates that he was as well qualified as any of them to serve as president. The difficult task ahead was apparent, however, when even his mother responded to his announcement that he was going to run for president by saying, "President of what?"

Carter emerged victorious in the 1976 primaries and at the Democratic National Convention as a candidate who appealed to moderate Democrats and many Christian evangelicals. Fortunately for him, in the early primaries the more liberal candidates divided voter support, and he was able to win in Pennsylvania, which helped to establish his credentials as a national rather than a regional candidate. In the later primaries, however, greater uncertainty about his candidacy began to surface and he won only seven of the final twelve.

Carter faced a weak incumbent in the fall election. President Gerald Ford had barely survived a close primary contest with Ronald Reagan and was hampered by the lingering issue of his pardon of Richard Nixon. Carter released a lengthy list of issue positions during his campaign but did not give a clear sense of where he was heading. He did, however, frequently assert that his administration would be far more open than Nixon's, and he pledged not to lie or deceive the public. These themes drew some support, but they did not clarify his policy goals. By October 1976 the press had begun to decry the lack of substance in the campaign. Thus he lost support in its final days, but Ford was unable to close the gap. Carter was aided in his victory by strong southern support and his ability to hold northern Democratic strongholds such as New York and Massachusetts.

What Manner of Man?

Despite his low-key demeanor, Carter was highly self-confident and ambitious. During his years in the navy, he had openly aspired to become the chief of naval operations. He also was confident enough in alternative career opportunities to return to Plains. In fact, he was so ambitious that he was willing to embark on campaigns when given little chance of victory by the experts.[3]

Highly intelligent, Carter sought vast amounts of information about policy issues. Since he was a "quick read," that information helped him in his campaigning when he often was able to impress observers with his knowledge of national issues. His interest in historical perspectives was limited, however; he preferred gathering technical information on a specific issue. Some analysts believe this trait contributed to his weaknesses as a strategic thinker.

Carter's religious beliefs also were an important defining characteristic. His religious commitment, which intensified with the help of his sister (and evangelist) Ruth Stapleton after he lost his first race for governor in 1966, was one of seeking spiritual growth rather than relying on a certainty that he had the answers. In seeking that growth, he prayed as often as twenty-five times a day while in the White House.

Carter has been described in many different ways by the people who have known him. Staff aide James Fallows, shortly after departing the

White House in 1979, stressed Carter's basic fairness and decency. Carter would be an ideal person to judge one's soul, he noted.[4] Yet he also found that Carter seemed to conduct a passionless presidency. Others have pointed to Carter's honesty and forthrightness, high degree of self-discipline, and tenacious pursuit of personal goals, even in sporting contests. Less-flattering assessments have pointed to his naiveté about the nature of government, limited creativity, and tendencies toward self-righteousness.

Policy Views

President Carter's commitment to government reorganization was unusual; unlike previous presidential candidates, he had made government reorganization a major campaign theme.[5] He also was fond of pointing out existing policies had been influenced too much by special interests. As a result, in some quarters he was perceived as anti-business.[6]

Carter was fiscally conservative but held liberal views on some social and environmental policy issues. Historian Arthur Schlesinger Jr., pointing to Carter's commitment to deficit reduction rather than the traditional programs of the liberal Democratic coalition, called Carter the most conservative Democratic president since Grover Cleveland. Yet on civil rights, Governor Jimmy Carter had surprised Georgians with his declaration that the era of segregation was over and the scope of his efforts. He continued to support civil rights as president.

Challenges and Opportunities

Carter took office at what was "not an opportune time"[7] and in "probably a more restrictive atmosphere than any president [had faced] since World War II."[8] The election results and levels of public support were not overly promising. Carter's margin of victory over Ford in the 1976 election was merely 2.1 percentage points—putting him way down in seventh place in the margins of victory of the post-1932 presidents. In terms of popularity, he began with a respectable 63 percent during his first year, but ultimately ranked as only the eighth most popular president (see Table 1–2). Moreover, Carter was an outsider, with little knowledge of the arcane workings of the Washington community.

The situation in Congress was not promising as well. Party strength looked impressive on the surface, with 292 Democrats in the House and 61 in the Senate (Table 1–3). Their margins were inflated by the large post-Watergate surge of Democrats in the midterm election of 1974, but they gained only one more House seat in 1976. The new Congress also was able to flex its post-Watergate muscle. Reforms aimed at strengthening Congress's role in relation to that of the president had opened the way to hiring more staff to develop congressional proposals and increased the number of subcommittees as ambitious legislators sought to achieve a piece of the action. In fact, many of the newer members had never dealt with a Democratic president and were somewhat reluctant to see a significant transfer of power: "The new president faced a new Congress, one with changed attitudes about itself, fresh faces and new leaders, improved capabilities, and different ways of doing business."[9] In this unpromising legislative setting, the strong supportive role played by Speaker Thomas "Tip" O'Neill, D-Mass.—despite his personal displeasure with Carter's approach to Congress—became one of the few positive influences.

In looking forward to some promising issues, Carter also faced expectations within the Democratic Party coalition that would be difficult to meet. Measures such as health care and welfare reform were popular, but the public was shifting away from support for the other spending measures traditionally promoted by the Democratic Party.[10] Environmental issues were the most promising; Ford had vetoed three environmental bills. Some legislators and citizens also wanted to see the government reduce federal regulation in several areas of the economy.

Unfortunately for Carter, two big problems did not promise easy legislative action.[11] The first was the simultaneous rise in both unemployment and inflation which made it difficult for him to rely on the traditional Keynesian solution of expanded deficit spending. The basic conundrum for policy makers was that an increase in spending or a reduction in taxes aimed at stimulating the economy might worsen levels of inflation. Further complicating the problem, the budget deficit in the preceding year had been 18 percent of total spending (Table 1–3). Economist Anthony Campagne was quite blunt about Carter's predicament when he argued that in this situation the economics profession could not offer clear solutions.[12]

Energy policy presented a second tough problem. A wide variety of proposals had been discussed in the wake of the 1973 energy crisis in which an embargo by the Organization of Petroleum Exporting Countries (OPEC) had contributed to a sharp rise in oil prices. Yet consumers and the producers of various energy sources such as coal and oil disagreed on the appropriate remedial policies. A strong environmental movement presented some opportunities for energy conservation, but that approach sparked controversy among its more conservative, anti-regulatory political and business opponents. According to political scientist Eric Uslaner, this situation was a "zero-sum game" in which bargaining to develop coalitions was difficult because policy choices created both clear losers and clear winners.[13]

But Carter's troubles did not stop there; he encountered further difficulties, especially during his last two years in office. A second OPEC oil embargo forced reconsideration of energy policies in the summer of 1979. Then, on November 4, 1979, 250 Americans were taken hostage at the U.S. embassy in Tehran. Carter's popularity rose somewhat as he undertook an extensive, highly publicized effort to gain their release in the months that followed. Yet when no progress was made and an April 1980 rescue attempt had to be aborted in the Iranian desert because of helicopter failures, his public approval for handling foreign policy fell dramatically. In fact, the hostage crisis was a major liability in his reelection effort. Further complicating Carter's position in 1980 was heightened concern over Soviet intentions after their invasion of Afghanistan in late 1979. Unpopular presidential actions, including a grain embargo against the Soviets that reduced American exports and Carter's refusal to allow the United States to participate in the 1980 Moscow Olympics, soon followed.

Leadership Style

Carter brought a distinct leadership style to the White House. He replaced the "imperial presidency" with an open administration more accessible to the public. And he turned to government reform to improve efficiencies and help to restore confidence in government. In his overall approach to issues, the president considered himself to be a trustee who looked toward long-range concerns rather than simply cutting political deals on Capitol Hill. As such, he developed a personal dislike for many legislators and interest group politics, had confidence in his ability to develop effective policies, and looked for help to government reform, which he had used successfully in Georgia to modernize state government.

The Advisory Process and Approach to Decision Making

Carter recruited many Georgians and campaign aides for his staff and a variety of prominent figures for his cabinet. Of his top aides, six of the nine had worked for him as governor or during his campaign, including key aide Hamilton Jordan, Press Secretary Jody Powell, legislative liaison head Frank Moore, and senior adviser Jack Watson.[14]

Carter sought to increase the legitimacy of his administration and pursue government efficiency by recruiting for his cabinet men and women with extensive Washington experience and strong reputations. Despite the initial "outsider" perspective expressed by Hamilton Jordan that the new administration would not consider Washington establishment figures such as Cyrus Vance, Vance was later asked to serve as secretary of state. Key domestic appointments were former Lyndon Johnson aide Joseph Califano to head the Department of Health, Education, and Welfare (later renamed the Department of Health and Human Services), Michael Blumenthal as secretary of the Treasury, and former Nixon and Ford defense secretary James Schlesinger to head the new Energy Department. For attorney general he turned to another Georgian, Griffin Bell.

The initial organization of Carter's White House stemmed from his confidence in own ability to absorb vast amounts of information and his desire not to replicate Nixon's strong chief of staff model which Carter associated with abuse of power. He envisioned a White House organization in which aides would have equal access to him in a spokes-in-a-wheel operation. His plan proved unworkable, however. He simply did not have time to soak up information about every single policy issue. Nor did he have time to implement properly the managerial demands of such an approach. By mid-1979 Hamilton Jordan had been named chief of staff.

In his decision making, Carter tended to follow up on his intense desire to fulfill his campaign pledges. Jeff Fishel found that Carter basically did just that. Fishel compared ten issues that Carter had stressed during his campaign and the salience of those issues to Carter's agenda during his first two years in office. Fishel found that Carter failed to maintain a high salience for only one issue—tax policy.[15] In some instances, in keeping with the perspective of a trustee president, Carter was primarily motivated by his sense that an important issue was not being addressed by Congress.

The Carter White House tended to look at policy issues from a technical, engineering perspective and pay little attention to the reasons earlier initiatives had failed. For example, administration officials approached welfare reform by collecting a great deal of current data on systemic problems and seeking solutions in a comprehensive manner, but they paid little attention to political feasibility. This tendency to overlook political feasibility was especially evident in James Schlesinger's rushed effort to put together an energy package in the first three months of the Carter presidency. Carter later recognized that the process had been a mistake, but one dictated by the desire for speed.[16] More generally, Carter encouraged his staff to develop good decisions, telling them, "You worry about the policy; I will worry about the politics." He did, though, often consult Hamilton Jordan and First Lady Rosalynn Carter on political feasibility questions. And at points Carter clearly made political decisions, as when he sought to have Joseph Califano cut back on an educational campaign against smoking when the tobacco industry lobbied the White House in opposition to the Califano plan. More often, however, he paid little attention to the political feasibility of an action or decision.

In the same vein, Carter has been widely criticized for how he used his own time in the decision- and policy-making process. His personal involvement on welfare reform in 1977, for example, seemed to put him at the information-gathering level of an assistant secretary for planning. He got too much information and not necessarily the right pieces of information.

The organization and experience of the White House staff also drew criticism, but some observers did note a marked improvement over time. On the minus side, many of Carter's senior staff had no prior Washington experience, and it seemed clear that Carter had not learned good staff work in Georgia. Although the absence of a more hierarchical staff at the outset seemed to prevent timely decisions, some significant improvements were noted. For example, over time fewer special task forces were used and fewer time limits were set on the development of proposals. Along the way, former Georgia lawyer Stuart Eizenstat, chairman of the Domestic Policy Staff (the former Domestic Council), became one of the most powerful men in Washington.[17] In addition, in areas such as hospital cost control, one of the president's early proposals, the initial defeat in 1977 produced a realization that interest group concerns would have to be addressed more extensively. As one strong indication of change, an "almost glitch free" operation was proclaimed in 1980 by political scientist Stephen Hess.[18] In the end, then, Carter seemed to learn from his mistakes, but it was too late to save his reelection chances.

Carter's relationships with his cabinet did not show a comparable improvement over time.[19] His cabinet members were generally quite capable of taking strong roles in developing and promoting policies. Nevertheless, they possessed little personal loyalty to Carter, and, because they often received little direction, they usually just went their own way. Controversies did erupt periodically, however, over specific policies. HEW Secretary Joseph Califano, for example, objected to Carter's cautious approach to several policy issues.[20]

In July 1979 Carter took the unprecedented step of removing no fewer than five of his cabinet officers, including some of the more prominent figures such as Michael Blumenthal, Joseph Califano, and James Schlesinger. He had become increasingly frustrated with press leaks and signs of disloyalty, and some leading Democratic Party officials advised him that to reorient his administration he would have to seek several resignations. The firings, though, produced considerable uncertainty about the stability of the administration and led to a decline in public support.

Administrative Strategies

As noted, Carter was unusually interested in "good government."[21] In keeping with that interest and his desire to streamline White House operations, he successfully sought legislation that would restore the president's reorganization authority, which had expired in 1973. Carter also succeeded in creating two new departments. One was the Department of Energy, an idea that had surfaced in the Ford administration and in Congress. Carter had to compromise significantly on his initial proposal in the face of pressures from various energy interests, but with the aid of several key legislators the measure passed in 1977.[22] Carter also led a fight to establish the Department of Education. Passage of this legislation in 1979 was strongly supported by the National Education Association, which had backed Carter in the 1976 election.

Civil service reform also was high on Carter's agenda as well. His strong efforts to gain legislative support included convening a task force, headed by Les Francis of the legislative liaison staff, to coordinate legislative lobbying; orchestrating calls by cabinet secretaries to key legislators; and making his own phone calls to designated legislators.[23] By pushing an issue that Congress otherwise would not have pursued, Carter was able to see enactment of the most extensive civil service reform since the system was founded in 1883.

Carter's commitment to good government drew mixed assessments. Two public administration specialists found civil service reform "the most impressive achievement of Jimmy Carter's presidency."[24] Yet by 1981 top aide Jack Watson was pondering Carter's efforts: "I think we spent an undue amount of emphasis, time, political capital and energy on governmental reorganization too much as an end in itself rather than as a means to an end." [25]

Carter made a modest effort to shape policies through administrative action. In 1979 he named his most fateful appointment in the midst of considerable concern about the financial markets and inflation. Signaling his desire to fight inflation, Carter nominated Paul Volcker as chairman of the Federal Reserve Board. Volcker, who was actually Carter's second choice, was selected after only a limited staff assessment. In an Oval Office meeting with Carter, Volcker stressed the importance of independence for the Federal Reserve Board and the need to wage a stronger battle against inflation. Carter, convinced that Volcker was the right choice, quickly announced his nomination.[26] The result, as many observers foresaw, was a major effort to reduce the money supply, thereby reducing inflation. Unfortunately for Carter, the negative short-term economic impacts of these actions coincided with his reelection year.

Carter also used administrative roles in addressing social issues. In civil rights he staffed his administration with more African Americans than any president to that time and generally supported existing policies, but he made no concerted new administrative effort. On affirmative action he sought to manage conflicts rather than take strong positions and generally subscribed to a position of defending affirmative action but not quotas.[27] In the abortion arena, he made little effort to support the concerns of religious fundamentalists, at least as many of them saw it, and to either legitimize the ruling in the 1973 *Roe v. Wade* decision or overturn it.[28] That lack of decisive action, according to Barbara Craig and David O'Brien, was reflected in Carter's appointments, which sent mixed signals on various abortion rights matters. Overall, then, Carter's administrative interests were more oriented toward achieving "good government" than toward efforts to use administrative roles in ways that would change substantive policy outcomes and his potential for reelection in 1980.

Public Leadership

Carter was a firm believer in the importance of presidential relationships with the public. In his view, presidents should set a high moral tone while also communicating directly with the public to get around the concerns of special interests.

But the results of Carter's efforts were mixed. His personal popularity fell his first year—a drop surpassed only by Clinton's in 1993, and he periodically received ratings under 30 percent during his last two years in office. His performance looks somewhat better, however, when placed in the context of his circumstances. According to a study by Paul Brace and Barbara Hinckley, he ranks fourth among the modern presidents when popularity levels are viewed in the context of popularity-shaping influences.[29]

Some of Carter's problems stemmed from his poor choice of a persona. He campaigned as an "outsider" and proceeded to dramatically de-emphasize presidential symbols such as the anthem "Hail to the Chief." Yet over time it became apparent that the removal of the trappings of office had gone too far, as the public seemed unmoved by his attempt to present himself as a rather unassuming "nice guy" and an "average American."[30]

Carter also had problems in gaining favorable press coverage. Especially in the beginning he did not go out of his way to court the press. In the aftermath of Watergate when reporters played a key role in the investigation, some journalists seemed anxious to show they could take a critical stance toward a Democratic president. Based on his examination of the content of leading newspapers, Mark Rozell found that views of Carter in these newspapers were more negative than the public's views.[31]

Overall, Carter's public leadership reflected his preferences for less-traditional public relations activities. He held fewer press conferences than most presidents, and he was not particularly skilled at focusing on issues or at presenting his administration in a favorable light. He gave only 1.5 televised voluntary domestic addresses a year—slightly below average. Because Carter preferred to seek direct contact with the electorate, he gravitated toward the use of town meetings, a device he had used successfully in his days as governor and during his election campaign. The town meetings, however, proved to be less effective for a president, as the public seemed more interested in a president who had proposals to present rather than one who simply wanted to listen to the public. Moreover, Carter was unable to get the town meetings on the air, and so in the end they rarely changed anything.[32]

Finally, there was the matter of Carter's speaking style. Because he viewed public addresses as more of a burden than an opportunity, he only achieved mixed results. One problem was his preference for a somber, moralistic tone. As one staffer saw it, "If Carter had delivered FDR's 'nothing to fear' speech, the Depression would still be going on."

Congressional Leadership

Carter's relationships with Congress were marked by considerable tension and widespread criticism. Frank Moore, Carter's one-time liaison with the Georgia state legislature, handled the day-to-day interactions with Congress from the unusually small Office of Legislative Liaison. Especially during 1977, he drew widespread criticism for his lack of experience and Washington savvy. No other top aide had a strong role. Chief of Staff Hamilton Jordan, who enjoyed campaign politics more than legislative tactics, maintained no direct contact with Speaker Tip O'Neill despite his influential White House role.

In general, criticism of Carter and his staff ranged from finger-pointing at poor White House staff work by Washington outsiders ignorant of the ways of Congress, to jibes at the staff's failure to engage in the expected care and feeding of members of Congress, to pundits' observations of Carter's inability to build strong relationships with congressional leaders— and almost everything in between. Carter approached congressional relations as an outsider, failing to move effectively to an insider strategy.

Carter's own relationship with Congress was shaped by his dislike of bargaining and patronage but also by his tenacity in trying to get things done. He continued the traditional morning breakfasts with legislative leaders and maintained a concerted effort to enlist their aid. Frequently, he tried to achieve influence with members of Congress by presenting information rather than direct bargaining; he believed bargaining produced short-term, wasteful policy results, and thus he avoided it.[33] One staff aide was vehement on the subject: "[Carter] doesn't like politicians. . . . He knows there are good ones and bad ones and so on, but he really does not like them. He's anti-politician." [34]

But Carter did change some over time. During his first year he made energy policy a top priority and decided to wait on health care until 1978. Yet he was reluctant to choose among other issues and would even comment that he had "over a hundred priorities." As a result, by March 1977 too many bills were heading for the House Ways and Means Committee, but Carter still did not force himself to pick and choose issues more carefully. As his term progressed, however, he did on occasion work hard on priorities, from civil service reform to hospital cost containment. Efforts to build public support also improved when Anne Wexler took over the public liaison responsibilities and placed greater emphasis on possible interest group coalitions than on the bland "good government" expressions of support the White House had sought for energy legislation in 1977.

Legislative Enactments

No landmark legislation emerged during Carter's four years in office. He attempted a fast-start strategy in 1977 and was able to chalk up several easy victories because of previous Ford vetoes, but he went down to a crashing defeat with his energy proposals. His second year produced several important new enactments, including some in which he played a significant role. During his final two years, Carter clashed even more intensely with liberals in his own party and saw frequent stalemates, but he also hailed some legislative victories. Once again, his levels of influence and success differed among policy areas.

Energy Policies

In 1977 Congress had two topics on the table: energy and everything else. Carter had pushed energy to the top of the agenda. Although there had been some (largely unsuccessful) efforts to decrease America's dependence on foreign oil between 1973 and 1976 and a considerable amount of public discussion, neither the public nor Congress anticipated that President Carter, who had said little on the subject in the 1976 campaign, would present Congress with a major energy initiative.

Carter made his commitment for several reasons. The assessments by the Central Intelligence Agency were sobering, and a record-setting cold wave in January had underscored the nation's energy problems. In addition, the many issues involved in devising an energy policy appealed to Carter's desire to develop a comprehensive policy approach.[35]

The policy proposal submitted to Congress in April was a complex, controversial document containing over one hundred separate initiatives.[36] It emphasized conservation and the development of alternative energy sources more than efforts to expand production. Major initiatives in the proposal called for maintaining price and production controls on natural gas in interstate commerce but at a higher price, taxing foreign crude oil to encourage American production, imposing a "gas guzzler" tax on automobiles, and boosting gasoline taxes dramatically. Conservation measures included mandatory energy efficiency standards for home appliances, reform of electric utility rates, and tax credits for home insulation.

Although Carter tried to rally public support for his proposal, he largely failed. In a period of considerable public skepticism about oil company operations, he was unable to convince a majority of the electorate that the energy crisis was real. The public also could not bring itself to applaud gas taxes and other measures requiring direct consumer outlays. The president was able to generate some public support for the less costly conservation measures, however.

Entries in Carter's own diary describe his coalition-building efforts. He noted he had held meetings several times a week with leaders from "business, agriculture, finance, transportation, the elderly, international trade, local and state government, the news media, consumer affairs, electric utilities, mining, and oil and gas industries for briefings and appeals from me . . . and others." [37] Quite strikingly, this list did not include segments of the liberal Democratic coalition such as labor and representatives of minority groups. In a similar fashion, the Office of Public Liaison sought an educational role and eagerly pursued individual suggestions, but it did little in the way of systematically seeking to organize coalition support.

The defeat of the energy bill can be traced in part to the intense lobbying efforts of the oil and natural gas producers and their allies in Congress. But Carter's efforts also were ineffective. He had taken on a difficult problem and proposed a solution but had paid little attention to its political feasibility. Moreover, his approach to building public support was flawed. He did begin to phone legislators when the energy bill became bogged down in the Senate, but he had little success with key opponents such as arch oil industry supporter Russell Long, D-La. In retrospect, it is not surprising that a flawed leadership effort in behalf of an extremely ambitious and difficult policy proposal would end in defeat.

Carter took a very different and more skillful approach to energy policy in 1978. Most important, he decided to return to the position he had originally taken in the 1976 campaign and support phased decontrol of natural gas prices. That step, plus the elimination of the proposed gasoline tax, substantially improved prospects for passage of the energy bill. Moreover, the Carter administration, which had learned from past mistakes, launched in August and September of 1978 a very impressive executive lobbying effort in behalf of the natural gas compromise. According to Elizabeth Sanders, the White House employed all of the tools of presidential persuasion: "pragmatic bargains involving tangible quid pro quos were struck with individual congressmen; grassroots support was marshaled by lectures to visiting community opinion leaders and high-level conferences with banking and business executives who were subtly reminded of the many ways in which executive prerogatives could be used to help or hurt them."[38] In addition, legislators who supported the measure lobbied those who were undecided.

Despite Carter's distaste for repeatedly dealing with energy policy, a 1979 Iranian boycott of oil sales to the United States forced additional action in 1980. This occurred as motorists were becoming increasingly angry with a new surge in energy prices and long lines at gas stations. Carter's response to the situation came in two different steps. In an attempt to appeal to the more liberal segments of his coalition, he successfully promoted the establishment of a windfall profits tax; in tandem, he used his administrative discretion to deregulate oil prices. Carter sought to have the revenue from the windfall profits tax placed in trust funds for designated programs such as mass transit and assistance for low-income energy consumers. Congress at first resisted the promotion of trust funds but later overcame an intense lobbying effort by the oil industry to establish a modified trust fund approach. Declining oil prices in 1980 and actions by the Reagan administration eliminated that revenue source.

In an attempt to pursue new energy sources, Carter also successfully promoted an initiative seeking to extract oil from shale. In 1979 the House passed a measure calling for creation of a new private industry for oil production from shale, and Carter in turn embraced proposals for synfuel development as part of his July 1979 address that called for both new energy policy initiatives and other steps to overcome a seeming "crisis of confidence."[39] As the battles over the initiatives began in key legislative committees, the Carter administration limited its involvement.[40] The omnibus energy measure finally produced called for $88 billion in new spending. It had a relatively short life, however. A combination of easing energy shortages in the 1980s and the desire for fiscal constraint in the Reagan administration led to a sharp reduction in and ultimately the dismantling of this policy initiative.

Environmental Policies

The struggle over environmental policy began early in Carter's first year as he sought to reduce the number of water projects being built by the U.S.

Army Corps of Engineers. For Carter, unnecessary dams and water projects were the "worst examples" of pork barrel politics.[41] After a veto of some of these projects, Carter agreed to a compromise arranged by House Speaker Tip O'Neill and got a reduction of about half of what he had hoped to achieve.

In 1977 Congress passed three environmental measures that had been vetoed by Gerald Ford or Richard Nixon or both. The Carter administration supported the measures, but interaction with Congress often occurred at the departmental level, and none of these issues achieved the importance the Carter administration attached to energy policy. The most far-reaching bill amended the Clean Air Act by both expanding and reducing the standards being applied. The other two measures established strip mine regulations for surface and underground mining and modified segments of the Clean Water Act.

Other important legislation came at the end of Carter's four years in office. Despite his languishing position in the polls, he was able to help gain passage of two major environmental measures in 1980. A proposal for a "superfund" to address problems such as the dramatic toxic waste episode at Love Canal, New York, in 1977, had been in the works for over two years. Because Carter and the environmentalists had to compromise considerably in 1980, the final measure covered only chemical problems and not oil spills. Nevertheless, a major new effort had been launched.

The environmental measure on which Carter had the strongest impact came a week after his 1980 reelection defeat when Congress passed a measure that more than doubled the size of the country's national parks and almost tripled the area of land designated as wilderness. In the wake of defeats by various energy interests over a two-year period, Carter moved in 1980 to make this his primary legislative initiative. He worked with key legislators such as Democratic House member Morris Udall of Arizona and encouraged the mobilization of interest groups by orchestrating a White House kick-off in July to help build support for the proposed legislation. Carter also watched attentively as on Capitol Hill the inevitable compromises were pursued prior to final passage of the bill.

Taxes, Jobs, and the Minimum Wage

Carter and Congress engaged in repeated conflicts over how to address the problems of a stagnant economy. He had started off badly in 1977. In the wake of his criticism of Ford and 8 percent unemployment, he had proposed a $50 per person tax rebate. He then infuriated supporters a mere two months later when he concluded that signs of an economic upswing made the rebate unnecessary. In the halls of Congress, members and staff bantered about the line that the president had invented a new "Carter bomb" that killed its friends and left its enemies standing. Some tax reform nevertheless did occur.

In 1978 the administration produced another tax reform proposal calling for simplification, greater equity in taxation, and an effort to promote greater incentives for investment. The proposal stalled, however, and for a time was judged to be dead in the House Ways and Means Committee. Earlier, in June 1977, California voters had approved a massive tax reduction initiative (Proposition 13) which served as a catalyst for further action in Congress. But the Carter administration did not join in support until a compromise bill was about to reach the House floor. The measure that finally emerged was significantly different than the original administration proposal. Its major provisions called for reducing the capital gains tax from 30 percent to 28 percent, expanding opportunities for uses of Individual Retirement Accounts (IRAs), and increasing the amount of assistance provided by the earned income tax credit. Ultimately, the tax measures that passed in 1977 and 1978 bore almost no resemblance to the legislation proposed by Jimmy Carter.[42]

The 1977 increase in the minimum wage was achieved through the more typical bargaining between the White House and the other players. The Carter administration bargained with AFL-CIO president George Meany and Democratic members of Congress over the size of the increase. Meany was angered by the administration's initial proposal of a $.20 increase to $2.50 an hour along with future indexing for inflation. They finally agreed on $2.65 an hour, plus indexing. The ultimate legislative compromise produced a bill with no indexing, but a gradual increase to $3.35 an hour.

Carter's proposal to broaden the government's job creation efforts revealed the sharp tensions between Carter and many Democratic liberals. In 1977 the president successfully promoted an expanded jobs program with a multiyear increase of $5.5 billion in funding for the Comprehensive Employment Training Act (CETA).[43] Liberals sought a broader program named after its sponsors, Hubert Humphrey, D-Minn., and Augustus Hawkins, D-Calif. Their bill included broad language calling for a national policy of full employment, increased real income, economic growth, greater productivity, stable prices, and a balanced budget. Carter was at best lukewarm—and many of his aides were opposed—so he gave only reluctant support, bowing to heavy pressure from the Black Caucus and organized labor. Final passage of a bill stripped of its automatic trigger mechanism for new jobs proved to be largely symbolic and did not reduce tensions over economic policy issues.[44]

Economic Deregulation

The period 1977–1980 saw the Carter administration join some liberal and conservative advocates in Congress in promoting deregulation as an anti-inflation strategy. The passage of a bill in 1978 deregulating the airline industry was the first of four important measures. The Carter administration and in particular inflation fighter Alfred Kahn (appointed by Carter in 1979 as head of the Council on Wage and Price Stability) were important players in passage of that legislation, as well as some Senate liberals such as Edward Kennedy, D-Mass. Passage of the bill also was eased by the major divisions within the airline industry itself.[45] With that victory, the government took the relatively rare step of eliminating the Civil Aeronautics Board and its role in regulating the price of airline tickets.

Carter and his administration played an even bigger role in the deregulation of the trucking industry. The initial impetus for reducing the role of the Interstate Commerce Commission came from commission members themselves. Carter then joined that effort and surprised members of Congress by making trucking deregulation a high-priority issue (he even mentioned it in his 1980 State of the Union message). In pushing for a strong measure, he called and met with key legislators. He may have compromised a bit too early, but there was widespread agreement that a far stronger measure emerged because of his strong leadership role. A top staff member, perhaps forgetting the time constraints Carter faced, praised that effort and he suggested that if Carter had made a comparable effort on other legislation he would still be president.[46]

Deregulation of the savings and loan industry also began during the Carter years. Legislators and others, responding to the adverse impact of inflation on this industry together with the technological changes occurring in the nation's financial institutions, had been calling for action to modify regulations.[47] Congress acted in 1978 by lifting the ceilings on the interest rates savings and loan institutions could offer. The industry continued to have difficulties, however, and so Congress took more decisive steps in 1980 by passing the Garn–St. Germain Depository Institutions Act. What turned out later to be the most fateful step came as Rep. Fernand St. Germain, D-R.I., a longtime proponent of the savings and loan industry, successfully pushed for granting its favorite wish—an increase in guaranteed deposits from $40,000 to $100,000. That increase was a big factor in the 1989 federal bailout of the ailing savings and loan associations nationwide.

Health, Social Security, and Welfare

Carter had one success and two losses in his efforts to change health, Social Security, and welfare policies. Social Security provided Carter's success in 1977 as Congress moved to expand the Social Security tax amid projections that a tax increase was needed to maintain the solvency of the Social Security trust fund.[48] This problem arose largely because far higher-than-expected inflation rates had sharply increased benefit levels with the application of the 1972 cost of living adjustment. Carter responded initially to the projected shortfall with a proposal calling for an increase in employer taxes but not taxes on employees. Congress then modified his proposal by increasing the taxes on both employees and employers. Carter thus contributed to this enactment, but the impetus had come from the projections of the Social Security Administration, and Congress significantly modified his initial proposals.

Carter also tackled welfare reform in his first year, in part because of his experiences in dealing with federal–state relations on welfare policy while serving as governor of Georgia. As a first step, he asked Joseph Califano to head a task force charged with developing a comprehensive reform proposal. Apparently, though, the planning process suffered from Carter's lack of a clear direction and difficulties in meeting his desire for a comprehensive policy that included both welfare reform and an overhaul of manpower programs.[49]

Despite indications of public approval of the plan that emerged from the task force, Carter was handicapped by two factors in his dealings with Congress. He had reluctantly agreed to an increase of $2.8 billion in his proposal, but the recently created Congressional Budget Office projected that the actual cost would be $14 billion. These cost concerns increased resistance to the plan. Sen. Russell Long, chairman of the Senate Finance Committee, and Al Ullman, chairman of the House Ways and Means

Committee, already had a plan they regarded as far too ambitious. Thus neither of their committees reported out a bill in 1977, and the administration's later attempts to push smaller bills were unsuccessful.

Carter found health policy issues no easier to tackle.[50] Health care costs were rising rapidly. In fact, once Nixon's cost controls were removed in 1974, hospital costs and health costs generally began to increase at unprecedented, double-digit levels. For labor unions, consumers, and legislative allies such as Sen. Edward Kennedy, the lack of health insurance for the uninsured and the inefficiencies in the present system cried out for a system of national health insurance. During the campaign, then, Carter reluctantly endorsed national health insurance in a speech that had been directly negotiated between Stuart Eizenstat and representatives of the United Auto Workers.

In response to pleas from Senator Kennedy and nudges from HEW Secretary Califano, Carter chose in 1978 to move toward a system of national health insurance while focusing on policies aimed at containing hospital cost increases. Carter submitted a complex cost control proposal to Congress and immediately faced opposition not only from hospitals but also from other groups that feared the precedent of expanded federal regulation. In this instance, Carter fought hard in Congress for his proposal, including direct appeals to key committee members, but he lost by a single vote on a key committee vote and the proposed legislation did not move forward. Carter persisted in 1979 with a less-ambitious proposal that sought to address criticisms made of his previous one. Eventually, however, both Carter and members of Congress began to lose interest in the issue, and the ultimate result was passage of a measure calling only for voluntary efforts at hospital cost containment.

The notion of health insurance for the uninsured produced a stalemate as well. Liberals, led by Senator Kennedy, vehemently criticized Carter's unwillingness to introduce and promote a major federal commitment. After a tense meeting between Kennedy and Carter in mid-1978, the falling-out was complete. Kennedy then proceeded with an unsuccessful initiative of his own and moved toward his decision to challenge Carter for the Democratic presidential nomination in 1980. Subsequent limited efforts by Carter also did not succeed. Health policy specialist Paul Starr attributed the stalemate to the combination of a large deficit, concerns about inflation, and a public that was growing skeptical of new government initiatives. Thus Carter had no realistic opportunity to succeed with a broad system of national health insurance.[51]

Carter and Congress

Carter clearly had difficulty in his relationships with Congress. His effort to undertake a fast start in 1977 was handicapped by his overly large agenda, and he had no clear wins in his efforts to "go public" on major pending legislation. He also probably underachieved in his ability to obtain smaller measures in some controversies and in the extent to which he was able to successfully push his perspectives in legislation that often was developed with little influence from the White House. Yet despite his reputation for disliking legislative affairs, he tenaciously and successfully pursued some measures such as civil service reform and his scaled-back energy package in 1978.

An Assessment

Despite his frequent policy failures, President Jimmy Carter did help to create some domestic policy legacies—notably, energy and environmental policies as well as steps toward deregulation. With help from world market forces, the highly controversial natural gas deregulation had a "soft landing" in the early 1980s without the disruptive higher prices some had feared. The country also made some progress on conservation issues. Tough measures such as a major gasoline tax to reduce consumption had not passed, but steps taken by industry led to considerably more efficient energy use. Although the synfuels program was ultimately abandoned as energy prices dropped in the 1980s, some efforts to develop alternative sources of energy continued. On the environmental front, the government took steps to protect strip mining areas and native lands in Alaska.

Economic deregulation, which the Carter administration had initiated in several areas of the economy, actually picked up speed in the Reagan administration and, along the way, quashed regulatory efforts begun during the Roosevelt administration.[52] The two most prominent acts of deregulation produced different legacies. Airline deregulation, criticized by some for its effects on safety and the possibility it might lead to a cartel, was hailed for its impacts on ticket prices. Conversely, the move to reduce regulations on the nation's savings and loan associations—while also increasing federal insurance coverage of deposits—proved to be a disaster. Final costs to the government by the mid-1990s had reached the stunning figure of $500 billion.

How well then did Carter use his opportunities? Presidential scholar Erwin Hargrove found him to be "a good president who made the most of his opportunities, which however were not great." [53] Granted, the areas in which he failed—such as health and welfare reform—were extremely difficult to address during a time of intense budgetary pressures. Other observers, however, have argued that a president with greater legislative skills would have been able to make at least some progress in these areas. Moreover, Carter could have achieved more goals if he had assigned priorities to his efforts and sought more effectively to build supportive coalitions among key interests and members of Congress.

But Carter's greatest failing was his ineffective public leadership. His first year was especially damaging, as he projected the image of a struggling and not very effective president that was difficult to change. For a "trustee" president seeking to mobilize public support with direct appeals, he also displayed remarkably little interest in improving his modest rhetorical skills. As he followed public opinion away from traditional Democratic Party positions during his final two years in office, he was again quite ineffective in developing support for centrist positions. Ironically, the derisive epithet "Jimmy Hoover" used by some liberal Democrats was, in one sense, apt. Jimmy Carter could be considered an underachiever.

Notes

1. For a discussion of Carter's southern roots, see Betty Glad, *Jimmy Carter: In Search of the Great White House* (New York: Doubleday, 1980).

2. For a discussion of Carter's experiences as governor, see Gary Fink, *Prelude to the Presidency: The Political Character and Leadership Style of Jimmy Carter* (Westport, Conn.: Greenwood Press, 1980).

3. In 1970, for example, Carter vowed that he would openly seek the support of those opposing integration rather than give up that segment of the electorate to his opponent despite the fact that he was not espousing his personal views.

4. James Fallows, "The Passionless President," *Atlantic Monthly,* May 1979, 33–48.

5. Peri E. Arnold, *Making the Managerial Presidency: Comprehensive Reorganization Planning, 1905–1980* (Princeton: Princeton University Press, 1986), 303.

6. Bert Lance, *The Truth of the Matter: My Life In and Out of Politics* (New York: Summit Books, 1991).

7. Anthony S. Campagne, *Economic Policy in the Carter Administration* (Westport, Conn.: Greenwood Press, 1995), xi.

8. Dilys M. Hill and Phil Williams, "Introduction" to *The Carter Years: The President and Policymaking,* ed. M. Glenn Abernathy, Dilys M. Hill, and Phil Williams (New York: St. Martin's Press, 1994).

9. Charles O. Jones, *The Trusteeship Presidency: Jimmy Carter and the United States Congress* (Baton Rouge: Louisiana State University Press, 1988), 67.

10. On this issue it can be argued that some measures of liberalism and conservatism in the electorate did not show a major shift either as of 1976 or as of Reagan's win in 1980. Indications of a "sea change" could be found in various indicators, however. In California the property tax protest culminated in the passage of Proposition 13 in 1978. A perhaps more telling indication of the change: Michael Pertschuk, chairman of the Federal Trade Commission, was astonished to find in March 1978 that his proposed new regulation of advertising that targeted children was being strongly criticized by a most surprising source—the *Washington Post.* See Michael Pertschuk, *Revolt against Regulation: The Rise and Pause of the Consumer Movement* (Berkeley: University of California Press, 1982), 69.

11. Carter's problems nicely fit Skowronek's analysis of the problems a "president of disjunction" faces when his party no longer limits policy ideas that can be used to address changing circumstances. See Stephen Skowronek, *The Politics Presidents Make: Presidential Leadership from John Adams to George Bush* (New Haven: Yale University Press, 1993), chap. 7.

12. Campagne, *Economic Policy in the Carter Administration,* xi.

13. Eric M. Uslaner, *Shale Barrel Politics: Energy and Legislative Leadership* (Stanford: Stanford University Press, 1989).

14. Bert Lance, Carter's original head of the Office of Management and Budget, was a Georgian and a potentially valuable adviser who emphasized political feasibility in many of his assessments. His resignation on September 21, 1977, was a serious loss. The charges leading to resignation stemmed from his practices as head of a small-town Georgia bank. In 1980, however, he was acquitted of those charges. See Lance, *Truth of the Matter,* 16, chap. 8.

15. Jeff Fishel, *Presidents and Promises: From Campaign Pledge to Presidential Performance* (Washington, D.C.: CQ Press, 1985), 91.

16. This emphasis is drawn from Barbara Kellerman, *The Political Presidency: Practice of Leadership* (New York: Oxford University Press, 1984), chap. 10.

17. The growth in Eizenstat's role is emphasized in Walter Williams, *Mismanaging America: The Rise of the Anti-Analytic Presidency* (Lawrence: University Press of Kansas, 1990), 57–60.

18. Stephen Hess, *Organizing the Presidency,* rev. ed. (Washington, D.C.: Brookings, 1988), 147.

19. On staff problems, see ibid., chap. 9; and Colin Campbell, *Managing the Presidency: Carter, Reagan, and the Search for Executive Harmony* (Pittsburgh: University of Pittsburgh Press, 1986).

20. See Joseph A. Califano Jr., *Governing America: An Insider's Report from the White House and the Cabinet* (New York: Simon and Schuster, 1981).

21. Arnold, *Making the Managerial Presidency,* 303.

22. This measure was not included on Mayhew's initial list but nicely reflects Carter's organizational interests. For details, see James E. Katz, *Congress and National Energy Policy* (New Brunswick, N.J.: Transaction Books, 1984), chap. 5.

23. Jones, *Trusteeship Presidency,* 161.

24. P. W. Colby and P. W. Ingraham, "Civil Service Reform: The Views of the Senior Executive Service," *Review of Public Personnel Administration* 1 (1980): 75.

25. Jack Watson interview, April 17, 1981, Miller Center interviews, Jimmy Carter Library, 30.

26. William Grieder, *Secrets of the Temple: How the Federal Reserve Runs the Country* (New York: Simon and Schuster, 1987), 46.

27. Kenneth O'Reilly, *Nixon's Piano: Presidents and Racial Politics from Washington to Clinton* (New York: Free Press, 1995), 344.

28. Barbara H. Craig and David M. O'Brien, *Abortion and American Politics* (Chatham, N.J.: Chatham House, 1993), 162.

29. Paul Brace and Barbara Hinckley, *Follow the Leader: Opinion Polls and the Modern Presidents* (New York: Basic Books, 1992).

30. Mary E. Stuckey, *The President as Interpreter-in-Chief* (Chatham, N.J.: Chatham House, 1991), 102.

31. Mark Rozell, *The Press and the Carter Presidency* (Boulder: Westview Press, 1989), 18, 62–63.

32. Robert S. Littlefield, "Carter and the Media: An Analysis of Selected Strategies Used to Manage the Public Communication of the Administration," in *The Presidency and Domestic Policies of Jimmy Carter,* ed. Herbert D. Rosenbaum and Alexej Ugrinsky (Westport, Conn.: Greenwood Press, 1994), 429.

33. Matthew R. Kerbel, *Beyond Persuasion: Organizational Efficiency and Presidential Power* (Albany: State University of New York Press, 1991), 60.

34. Thomas E. Cronin, *The State of the Presidency* (Boston: Little, Brown, 1980), 216.

35. On Carter's motivations, see Jimmy Carter, *Keeping Faith: Memoirs of a President* (New York: Bantam Books, 1982), 91–93.

36. The story of Carter's failed energy policy initiative has been told in numerous sources. This case study is drawn in particular from Jones, *Trusteeship Presidency,* 135–144; Kerbel, *Beyond Persuasion;* and Kellerman, *Political Presidency,* chap. 10.

37. Carter, *Keeping Faith,* 103.

38. M. Elizabeth Sanders, *The Regulation of Natural Gas: Policy and Politics, 1938–1978* (Philadelphia: Temple University Press, 1981), 187.

39. This speech was originally planned as an energy address, but Carter decided to take a broad approach to what he saw as a national crisis of confidence. The speech was received with moderate favor, but the subsequent firing of five cabinet members raised concerns about the stability of the Carter administration. While Carter does not use the phrase, this address is often known as his "malaise" speech.

40. See Uslaner, *Shale Barrel Politics,* chap. 4.

41. For a review of the water projects fight, see Jones, *Trusteeship Presidency,* 143–149.

42. John F. Witte, *The Politics and Development of the Federal Income Tax* (Madison: University of Wisconsin Press, 1985), 199.

43. For a review of CETA's enactment and economic impact, see Campagne, *Economic Policy in the Carter Administration,* 57–60. In a related measure, Carter resisted pressures from liberals in Congress, the Black Caucus, and organized labor for a sweeping commitment to new federal jobs as a last resort and then acquiesced as Congress passed the Humphrey-Hawkins Act which had symbolic importance but few specific provisions requiring action.

44. Lance T. LeLoup and Steven A. Shull, *Congress and the President: The Policy Connection* (Belmont, Calif.: Wadsworth, 1993), 188.

45. This interpretation draws from Martha Derthick and Paul J. Quirk, *The Politics of Deregulation* (Washington, D.C.: Brookings, 1985).

46. The interpretation of this case study is based on Dorothy Robyn, *Braking the Special Interests: Trucking Deregulation and the Politics of Policy Reform* (Chicago: University of Chicago Press, 1987), chap. 7.

47. For details on this role, see James R. Adams, *The Big Fix: Inside the S and L Scandal: How an Unholy Alliance of Politics and Money Destroyed America's Banking System* (New York: Wiley, 1990).

48. See Edward Berkowitz, *Mr. Social Security: The Life of Wilbur J. Cohen* (Lawrence: University Press of Kansas, 1995); and William W. Lammers, *Public Policy and the Aging* (Washington, D.C.: CQ Press, 1983).

49. For a review of differing views of Carter's failure, see Laurence E. Lynn Jr. and David Whitman, *The President as Policymaker: Jimmy Carter and Welfare Reform* (Philadelphia: Temple University Press, 1981), chaps. 10–11.

50. This account is drawn from William W. Lammers, "Presidential Leadership and Health Policy," in *Health Politics and Policy,* 2d ed., ed. Theodore Litman and Leonard Robbins (Albany: Delmar Publishers, 1991).

51. Paul Starr, *The Social Transformation of American Medicine* (New York: Basic Books, 1982), 405–410.

52. This discussion is drawn from Larry N. Gerston, Cynthia Fraleigh, and Robert Schwab, *The Deregulated Society* (Pacific Grove, Calif.: Brooks/Cole, 1988), chaps. 4–5.

53. Erwin C. Hargrove, *Jimmy Carter as President: Leadership and the Politics of the Public Good* (Baton Rouge: Louisiana State University Press, 1988), 19.

America is never wholly herself unless she is engaged in high moral principle. We as a people have such a purpose today. It is to make kinder the face of the nation and gentler the face of the world.

10

— GEORGE BUSH, INAUGURAL ADDRESS, 1989

George Bush

A Reluctant Guardian

GEORGE BUSH (served 1989–1993) entered the White House in 1989 with a résumé documenting many years of public service. For over two years of his tenure he garnered unusually high public approval ratings, yet when he ran for reelection he suffered a crushing defeat as 62 percent of the electorate, throwing their support toward either Democrat Bill Clinton or independent candidate Ross Perot, concluded that his leadership deficiencies and limited agenda made him poorly equipped to serve a second term. Granted, in 1992 he had been unlucky, stymied, as it were, by a weak economy and a well-run Clinton campaign. Yet critics have wondered whether he, in his leadership endeavors, actually had made the worst of a difficult situation.

Personal Characteristics

Like Presidents Franklin Roosevelt and John Kennedy, George Herbert Walker Bush (1924–) was born to wealth. In fact, he was lampooned at the 1988 Democratic National Convention by Texas state treasurer Ann Richards for having been born with a silver foot in his mouth. Although he was born in Milton, Massachusetts, George grew up in Greenwich, Connecticut. His investment banker father was far less wealthy than Joseph Kennedy and the family ancestry was less distinguished than Roosevelt's, but he enjoyed the upper-class status of elite schools and membership in the Episcopal Church, as well as vacations at the family's spacious summer home on the Maine coast at Kennebunkport. He also was the only president in this century whose father had held national elective office. Prescott Bush manifested some of the sense of service he sought to instill in his sons and daughters when he spent the last ten years of his active career as a moderate Republican senator from Connecticut.[1]

Bush's background also included distinguished military service. He enlisted in the navy in 1942 at only eighteen years of age, and rules were waived to allow him to become the navy's youngest commissioned pilot. In September 1944 one of the fifty-eight missions he flew in the Pacific during World War II produced a life-threatening situation. While he was on a bombing run, a Japanese shell hit his plane. He was able to deliver his bombs on target but soon thereafter had to parachute from his plane. After several hours at sea, he and members of his crew were rescued by a U.S. submarine. His crew praised his leadership, and the navy awarded him with a Distinguished Flying Cross.

Like many veterans after the war, Bush seemed to be a man in a hurry. He entered Yale University in 1945 shortly after marrying his high school sweetheart, Barbara Pierce. At Yale, he majored in economics and earned a Phi Beta Kappa key. A six-foot, two-inch left hander, Bush played first base and served as captain of Yale's baseball team which reached the National Collegiate Athletic Association finals in 1948 before losing to the University of Southern California. After graduation he chose a business career and, making something of a break with his family, he and Barbara moved to Texas. Bush started at the bottom of the Texas oil business with a few sales jobs. Then, with financial assistance from his uncle, Herbert Walker, he established an independent offshore oil drilling firm in 1953. Over the next decade he made a fair amount of money, raised a large family, sold his firm, and began casting his eyes toward a political career.

Career Path

Bush's lengthy political experience began with an unsuccessful effort to win a Houston congressional seat as a highly conservative candidate in 1964. He was successful, though, in the 1966 and 1968 races. In 1970 he responded in part to Richard Nixon's encouragement as he sought election to the Senate. He won the Republican primary but lost to moderate Democrat Lloyd Bentsen in the general election. Later, he served for brief periods in four different roles that included two years as U.S. ambassador to the United Nations, over a year as chairman of the Republican National Committee (where he was a Nixon defender until a few weeks before Nixon's resignation), and two years as U.S. envoy (ambassador) to China. It was with some reluctance that he also served as director of the Central Intelligence Agency for a year (he feared the position would not help his presidential aspirations). When Jimmy Carter assumed the presidency in 1977, he did not accept Bush's offer to remain in office, so George and his family headed back to Texas.

Pursuit of the 1980 Republican nomination began in May 1979 as Bush announced his candidacy with a statement characterized by biographer Fitzhugh Green as "honorable but bland and without . . . originality." [2] He was elated with a surprise victory in the Iowa caucuses, but his defeat by Reagan in New Hampshire and his difficulty in rebounding as Reagan made a strong showing in the South ended his campaign. Bush then eagerly accepted Reagan's offer of the number two spot on the Republican ticket and ended up serving as Reagan's "understudy" for eight years. During that time, he played the role of a loyal vice president who "made few waves." In fact, he referred to his vice presidency as a "wholly owned subsidiary" of the Reagan presidency.

Bush started his own presidential election bid early in 1988 and was able to capture the nomination with relative ease. This time, though, it was Sen. Robert Dole, R-Kans., who stumbled in New Hampshire. He responded on national television to Bush's attacks on his support for tax increases during the Reagan years by sharply admonishing the vice president to "stop lying about my record." Bush's reputation for party loyalty helped him in the South, and throughout the country he often was supported by Republican officeholders who appreciated his extensive speaking and fund-raising support while serving as vice president.

The fall 1988 campaign against Gov. Michael Dukakis of Massachusetts was widely criticized as being highly negative and remarkably lacking in a serious discussion of the issues.[3] Neither Bush nor Dukakis was anxious to talk about the mounting financial costs accruing from federal insurance obligations to cover investor losses in the soaring savings and loan crisis. On the issue of the federal deficit, Bush talked vaguely about savings in spending and "no new taxes." Dukakis, by stressing the monies to be saved by a taxpayer amnesty (allowing those who failed to file tax returns in the past to file without penalty), tried to avoid the problems Democratic nominee Walter Mondale had encountered in 1984 with a commitment to a tax increase.

Undoubtedly, the most widely debated aspect of the 1988 campaign was the emphasis Bush and his campaign staff placed on "wedge" issues. In a successful effort to depict Dukakis as an ultra liberal, Bush attacked the governor for vetoing a Massachusetts law requiring that school classes begin with the recitation of the Pledge of Allegiance (Dukakis's attorney general had advised him the law was unconstitutional). Bush also attacked Dukakis for his state's prison furlough program. In the so-called "Willie Horton" commercial run by an independent Bush support committee, many viewers and analysts felt the Bush campaign was trying to play unfairly on white fears and depict black violence against whites.[4]

Bush was fortunate in his election bid in two respects. First, the strong economy provided an easy basis for promising a continuation of good economic conditions. And, second, Dukakis proved to be a disappointing candidate. He made little attempt early in the race to respond to Bush's television advertisements painting him as a "card carrying member of the American Civil Liberties Union" and an extreme liberal. He also proceeded rather clumsily with his own campaign and never developed an effective electoral college strategy. He thus saw an early seventeen percentage point advantage over Bush and a much more favorable candidate perception turn into an eight percentage point loss. By campaign day, however, both candidates were perceived quite negatively by the voters.

What Manner of Man?

With the exception of his approach to election campaigns, Bush was widely regarded as a thoughtful, kindly person. He was well known for his good manners, which included writing many gracious notes. As president, his thoughtfulness extended to inviting Sen. Edward Kennedy to visit the private quarters of the White House for the first time since the death of his brother John Kennedy. Putting these characteristics in a broader context, *Time* magazine's veteran president watcher Hugh Sidey stated as of 1989 that Bush "may be the mildest, the most unassuming, the least self-centered of the modern presidents."[5]

Yet Bush also was intensely competitive. He pushed hard for any possible advantage in his athletic endeavors, and in his business career he was willing to take risks to succeed. In running for public office he seemed to take the attitude that whatever was needed to win was an acceptable strategy. This mindset was most evident in the presidential campaigns of 1988 and 1992 as he aggressively attacked his opponents' character. In the last days of the 1992 campaign his Democratic opponents Bill Clinton and Al Gore became respectively "Bozo and the Ozone Man."

Intense energy flowed from Bush's competitiveness. During his business career, his hectic schedule and stress had led to sleeplessness and ultimately stomach ulcers. As for his physical activities, he entered the White House at age sixty-four and continued a round of physical activities that included jogging, golf, and tennis. He also undertook foreign travel with a zealousness that both awed and concerned the aides responsible for implementing his schedule. In his first two years, for example, he traveled more abroad than Reagan did his entire eight years in office.

Bush also enjoyed friendships and social activities. He reveled in his large, close-knit family and his many friends. In fact, his wife, Barbara, often had to adjust to a larger or totally unexpected group of dinner guests.

Policy Views

Bush's policy goals often have been characterized as frequently changing and lightly held. For example, he opposed the Civil Rights Act of 1964 but supported housing desegregation legislation in 1968 and then resisted civil rights legislation as president. On abortion, he shifted from pro choice to pro life. In much the same way, he branded Reagan's economic proposals in the 1980 campaign as "voodoo economics" and then loyally supported the same ideas when he served as Reagan's vice president. His most noted reversal occurred in 1990 when he reneged on his 1988 "no new taxes" campaign pledge. In his 1988 nomination acceptance speech he stated energetically, using strong language drafted by Reagan speechwriter Peggy Noonan, that he might be pushed and pushed again by the Democrats to raise taxes but "read my lips; no new taxes." In 1990 he quietly abandoned that pledge.

But even before he entered the White House journalist Gail Sheehy had suggested that Bush held his views lightly and surmised that even his closest associates would be unable to uncover many strongly held views other than general values such as fairness.[6] Similarly, conservative staffer Charles Kolb noted that, in contrast to Reagan, not even Bush's closest advisers knew where he really stood on domestic issues.[7] Bush was certainly not alone among recent presidents in changing positions over the years, but he seemed to stand out for both his casual shifts and his lack of personal intensity about those positions.

Despite the frequent criticism he received for lacking a policy agenda, Bush did formulate and promote some policy goals. His economic Holy Grail was a reduction in the capital gains tax. The 1988 campaign also produced some hints that Bush wanted to differ from Reagan's more strident conservatism and stand at the helm of a "kinder, gentler nation." To that end he promoted passage of the Americans with Disabilities Act, steps toward improving the nation's school system, a greater national concern about some environmental issues, a greater emphasis on voluntarism (labeled "a thousand points of light"), and full funding of Head Start (a preschool education program for disadvantaged children). The 1988 election thus placed in office a president with a limited agenda oriented toward modest changes in the policies Reagan had initiated.[8] George Bush was quite aptly viewed as being more interested in serving his country than in changing or leading it.

Challenges and Opportunities

President Bush faced several challenges during his four years in office. Continued upheavals in the Soviet Union and the collapse of Soviet control of Eastern Europe forced him to manage an end to the cold war. This challenge was addressed cautiously and without loud proclamations of victory which might have made the process more difficult. In August 1990 Bush faced his biggest foreign policy crisis yet. Iraqi military troops, led by Iraqi dictator Saddam Hussein, moved into neighboring Kuwait. The implications of the invasion for oil supplies from the Persian Gulf produced a plight that Bush met with considerable acclaim. Using what some called "Rolodex diplomacy," the president put together an impressive coalition of North American, European, and Middle Eastern countries. Together, these nations launched a successful military operation that forced Iraq's forces out of Kuwait.

Domestically, the savings and loan bailout could no longer be delayed, and few serious students of budgetary politics doubted that the president would have to address serious deficit issues. Thus the domestic scene contained more constraints than opportunities and was "ripe for inaction."[9] Moreover, eight years earlier Reagan had entered the presidency arguing that he had a mandate for change and holding the advantage of confronting a demoralized Democratic Party in Congress; Bush, by contrast, entered after an election that had done little to produce support for new policy initiatives and faced a Democratic Party that had been cheered by its increased strength in Congress. Nevertheless, Republicans were promoting some new initiatives. For example, Rep. Jack Kemp, R-N.Y., was advocating an "empowerment agenda" of nonbureaucratic policy steps such as tenant ownership of public housing. Such ideas faced considerable opposition, however, within both political parties.

The economic conditions in the late 1980s had various impacts on Bush's opportunities. In view of the economic growth and job creation that had begun in 1983, Bush found it hard to argue for a cut in the capital gains tax. Yet when the economy slid into recession in 1991, he was still in a relatively poor position to take strong action. Moreover, this recession differed from the earlier, post–World War II recessions—the downturn was affecting the service sector more than the manufacturing sector. Thus public anxiety (especially among likely middle-class voters) was higher than might be expected from a simple reading of unemployment statistics.

Two other factors offered some possible advantages. To his surprise and delight, Bush was, at least at first, unusually popular. He seemed somewhat skeptical about the value of polling percentages, however, as he liked to point out that the high numbers simply meant that the big story would be his loss of popularity when they inevitably began to fall. Nevertheless, his popularity did seem to create an opportunity for the "domestic Desert Storm" agenda that some aides promoted in the wake of his high support after the Gulf War in 1991. Also on the plus side, there was some indication that Democratic leaders in Congress looked forward to working with Bush after eight years of dealing with Reagan.

Leadership Style

Bush's leadership style has been characterized as that of a "guardian." [10] He professed an admiration for Theodore Roosevelt, but more for his commitment to public service than his activist bully pulpit presidency. Bush was deeply skeptical that government policies could provide positive change and generally saw his role as one of defending the status quo. As a guardian, especially in the foreign policy arena, he preferred to be ready to meet new challenges as they might arise. A desire to subtly differentiate himself from Reagan also was evident as he sought to downplay the rhetorical aspects of the president's role (Reagan's strong suit) while demonstrating that he was a hard worker who was mastering the details of government.

*The Advisory Process and Approach
to Decision Making*

Unlike most presidents, Bush recruited several of his closest friends and campaign aides for his cabinet rather than for top staff positions. He knew ten cabinet members personally.[11] Campaign manager James Baker became secretary of state, and fellow Texans Nicholas Brady and Robert Mosbacher were chosen to head, respectively, the Treasury Department and the Department of Commerce. Other appointees were drawn from Congress, such as Jack Kemp as secretary of housing and urban development, and from prior Republican administrations, such as Elizabeth Dole as secretary of labor. And Bush did not neglect racial minorities. He appointed to his cabinet African American physician Louis Sullivan as secretary of health and human services and two Hispanics—Reagan administration holdover Lauro Cavazos as secretary of education and Manuel Lujan Jr. as secretary of the interior.

The organization of the Bush presidency reflected his preference for dealing with a limited number of top cabinet and staff members and a strong chief of staff. James Baker promoted the use of a troika (as in Reagan's first term), but this suggestion was rejected. Chief of Staff John Sununu played a strong but sometimes negative role in the Bush White House until his forced departure in late 1991. As the former governor of New Hampshire, he had been instrumental in Bush's key primary win in that state the previous year. His selection was seen as a signal to conservative Republicans that "one of them" would have an important voice in the Bush administration. Sununu was quick to display his high intelligence—but equally quick to take exception to views and people he did not like. More than many chiefs of staff, he also sought to promote his own views.[12] With his gruff personal style, Sununu made more enemies than friends. It did not endear him to members of Congress, for example, when the report filtered back to them that he had told a conservative group in late 1990 that Congress could go home until after the 1992 election—nothing else really needed to be done.[13] When Sununu's use of government planes for personal purposes, such as visiting a dentist in Boston, became known in 1991, criticism quickly mounted. Sen. Robert Dole's wry sense of humor came into play as he commented privately that Sununu had "taken so many plane flights he could not start a meeting without being sure that all chairs were in an upright position." By the end of 1991 Bush had concluded that Sununu's effort to defend his use of the taxpayers' planes—Sununu contended he had to be able to be in communication with the Oval Office—was not selling with his numerous critics and had Vice President Dan Quayle deliver the bad news that the president wanted Sununu's resignation. Transportation Secretary Samuel Skinner assumed the chief of staff role for the first half of 1992, followed by James Baker, who reluctantly gave up his position of secretary of state so he could revive Bush's faltering reelection campaign.

The most dominant adviser in shaping Bush's domestic policy was Office of Management and Budget (OMB) Director Richard Darman. An experienced Washingtonian who had served in a low-level position in the Nixon administration and as Chief of Staff James Baker's deputy during the Reagan administration, Darman brought to his role substantial knowledge of domestic policy and a reputation for being a schemer in pursuing elaborate scenarios in the policy-making process. In fact, the term *Darmanesque* was used to refer to his complex schemes. Darman's budget analyses were central to Bush's budgetary strategies. Together with John Sununu, he was the major negotiator in the top-level deficit-reduction negotiations in 1990. In addition, he had a big hand in developing some of Bush's domestic policy speeches.

In his decision making, Bush sought to avoid mistakes and to soften some aspects of Reagan's domestic policy choices in keeping with the theme of a "kinder, gentler" America. Yet conversely he also sought to make decisions that would sustain the support of conservatives who viewed him suspiciously as a "closet moderate." Finally, in part because of budgetary constraints, Bush preferred to take many small steps rather than make a commitment to one or two major initiatives. On pressing decisions he checked political feasibility and used polls to determine the content of his January 1992 State of the Union address as he tried to reassert his domestic agenda.

The process Bush created reflected his own preferences. His cautiousness led to an "in box" approach—he would deal with problems as they arose but would not seek new ideas with his own "out box" requests. His disinterest plainly showed at points, and he became visibly bored in a variety of meetings dealing with domestic policy. Just as with foreign policy, he preferred to deal with a fairly small group of people.

Overall marks for Bush's decision-making process have not been very high. He generally gets credit for operating an orderly process, but some critics believe he relied too heavily on a very few top aides and cabinet members rather than pursuing a more open process. Shirley Warshaw, who looked at Bush's cabinet process, concluded that the White House needed to establish a structure that guided the cabinet's development of domestic policies but in a way that satisfied the campaign agenda without significant increases in funding.[14] This structure was not created, however, until Samuel Skinner took over as chief of staff in 1992.

Administrative Strategies

Administrative strategies were periodically important for Bush. At the outset of his administration he made his belief in government the focal point of an address to top federal officials: "We're all wise in the ways of Washington," he said, "especially you who have served your country with such distinction." [15] Later, however, he showed little interest in reorganization of government to achieve greater efficiency or a sustained interest in implementation issues in specific policy areas. He paid little attention to regulatory policy reform, for example, until late 1991 when a *National Journal* article referred to him as a "re-regulation president" and asserted that he had presided over the greatest expansion in regulatory policies since the early 1970s.

The Bush administration made its most visible effort to leverage policy impact in the area of education. Bush followed up on his campaign promise to be "the education president" with an early initiative, introduced at a well-publicized meeting of the nation's governors in Williamsburg, Virginia, in which Arkansas governor Bill Clinton played a visible role. The actual implementation of the proposed guidelines for the resulting Goals 2000 project did not occur until 1991, however, and the administration made little effort to support the initiative over the long term.

Bush's arsenal of administrative strategies probably came in handiest in his efforts to please segments of the divisive Republican coalition. On abortion, Bush followed Reagan's rhetoric and tactics as he made a modest effort to push new legislation while looking to the courts to provide additional limits.[16] In the wake of criticism of National Endowment for the Arts (NEA) chief John Frohnmayer by Pat Buchanan in his primary challenge, Bush dismissed Frohnmayer from office. On enforcement of civil rights legislation, Bush urged a cautious approach.

Bush took one of his most controversial administrative actions in 1991 when he nominated Clarence Thomas, an African American who was serving as chairman of the Federal Employment Practices Commission (FEPC), to replace retiring Supreme Court justice Thurgood Marshall, the first African American to serve on the Court. With this step, he could continue the tradition of having an African American on the Supreme Court, but also gain a conservative voice since Thomas's skeptical views of many liberal policies were well known. Thomas was confirmed by the Senate, but only narrowly (52–48) and after an exceedingly acrimonious proceeding. Some opponents, including many African Americans, argued that a person with Thomas's views of civil rights was not a worthy successor to Thurgood Marshall. Others pointed to his lack of judicial experience. The conflict intensified with charges of sexual harassment by Anita Hill, a former employee at the FEPC.

Finally, the Bush administration decided to take a closer look at economic and environmental regulations with an eye toward modifying the implementation of recently enacted legislation that had sparked protests from those being affected. The central mechanism was the Council on Competitiveness chaired by Vice President Dan Quayle. This essentially pro-business council met in 1991 and 1992 to secretly review controversial regulatory issues. This strategy had some policy consequences and also produced considerable disagreement. The council decided to recommend about fifty regulatory changes, including a highly controversial one that would have allowed modifications in the implementation decisions for the Clean Air Act without public comment.[17] While some firms were pleased with the council's decisions, others were somewhat reluctant to be involved in a process that was being widely criticized in Congress and in some press commentary as lacking legitimacy. According to political scientists Richard Harris and Sidney Milkis, the process suffered from the limitations of pragmatism without a reasoned defense.[18] In short, the Council's penchant for secrecy and avoidance of public discourse on the administrative role reduced Bush's potential effectiveness.

Public Leadership

Bush's media strategies were designed carefully. He recognized his constraints in his ability to deviate from Reagan's policy positions but felt he could show his independence with a different political style.[19] That style, in turn, reflected Bush's desire to lower the public's expectations, his genuine skepticism about the ability of public addresses to change opinion, his personal dislike of public speaking, and his limited interest in promoting new programs.

Reagan staffer Marlin Fitzwater stayed on as press secretary in the

Bush administration, but, in one of several changes, speechwriters and public liaison officials found themselves reduced in number and status. The administration paid far less attention to the "theme for the day," a device favored by Reaganites, and to efforts to ensure frequent news coverage—and it showed. In his first twenty-two months in office Bush was on the evening news only one-third as often as Reagan in the same time period.[20] The number of press conferences skyrocketed, however, as Bush sought to demonstrate publicly his level of involvement, knowledge of issues, and enjoyment of his job. He did use the presidential bully pulpit from time to time, but in his public speeches Bush's average of one voluntary domestic policy address a year placed him last among presidents serving since 1932 (Table 1–1).

When Bush did try to change the opinion or behavior of others, it often was in conjunction with major policy initiatives. His first specially televised address to the nation dealt with drug use. He continued to pay increased attention to the issue for a time, but it quickly returned to no more than normal levels.

Other speaking opportunities were used sparingly or skipped all together. In 1990, for example, he waited over three months after the decision had been made to explain why he abandoned his pledge not to raise taxes. And after the Gulf War he gave no speech on domestic issues, despite the encouragement of some aides. In April 1992, in a speech made in the wake of the Los Angeles riots, he largely criticized past policies rather than promoting new initiatives or addressing urban issues.

Bush reserved his most extensive use of the bully pulpit for his voluntarism initiative called "a thousand points of light." He devoted many speeches to this initiative and organized a modest-sized staff, directed by fellow Ivy Leaguer Gregg Petersmeyer, to promote and recognize volunteer efforts. Staffers worked to change people's attitudes, discover and encourage leaders, establish supporting institutions, and reduce the vulnerability of volunteers to legal liability.[21] For many reasons, including a fraying of the social net, voluntarism did increase. But it is not possible to determine how much of the credit Bush deserved. For some critics, however, the program characterized as "a thousand points of lite" seemed to focus too much on suburbia and ignore the more difficult problems being confronted in the nation's inner cities.

In implementing his media strategies, Bush was quite successful initially in differentiating himself from Reagan and in creating public perceptions of a "nice, hard working president who was enjoying his job." As a result, he was unusually popular.[22] His problems came with his inability to reassure the public as the economy soured. Some observers wondered, for example, what might have happened if the well-received address he gave on economic issues in September 1992 had been given months earlier.[23] Staffer Charles Kolb also has pointed to Bush's inability to put the actions of his administration together. According to Kolb, Bush and others made virtually no effort to connect legislative priorities, speech writing, and communication outreach through the Office of Public Liaison.[24]

Congressional Leadership

Legislative relationships were defined in the Bush presidency by a moderate use of the traditional legislative liaison role along with a strong role for his first chief of staff, John Sununu. Bush recruited Fred McClure to head his Office of Legislative Liaison. A former staff aide to Sen. John Tower, R-Texas, McClure was the first African American to hold that office.

Bush's preference for dealing with individuals directly was evident in his approach to Congress. He sought to utilize his friendship with House Ways and Means chairman Daniel Rostenkowski, D-Ill., dating back to his own days in Congress, and the associations he had made in more recent years. At the beginning, he sought good relationships with leaders through informal meetings. And periodically he worked the phones for, among other things, the capital gains tax cut in 1989.

Bush took a limited approach to his agenda-setting role in both scope and depth. In 1989 he mentioned some attractive proposals in his initial speeches and messages but left the all-important question of funding mechanisms to Congress. Pundits commented that Bush had "hit the ground strolling" rather than running and called him the president who had created an "Agenda Gap." As one manifestation of that view, Daniel Rostenkowski commented, "People are puzzled, they want to know where he stands."[25] He laid out his most specific agenda in his 1992 State of the Union address.

Bush employed other strategies and tactics more extensively. Until the bitter fight over deficit reduction in 1990 he often was quite conciliatory. And the same pattern of top-level negotiation he favored on foreign policy matters was used on the key issue of deficit reduction. Throughout the four years he also brandished both vetoes and veto threats as an effective source of influence. He was proud of his unbroken record of forty-one successful vetoes, which held until a congressional override of a cable television deregulation bill on October 3, 1992. Bush owed his success rate to his unwillingness, unlike Reagan, to veto a bill when there was a good possibility of a congressional override. Nevertheless, both threats and uses of vetoes were an important part of his legislative strategy as both were often in line with his preferences for preventing domestic policy action.

Legislative Enactments

President Bush had a roller coaster ride in dealing with Congress over his four years in office. The most far-reaching enactment in 1989 addressed the savings and loan crisis. In 1990 Bush had his most significant impact on policy with passage of the Clean Air Act Amendments and the Americans with Disabilities Act. That year also produced landmark deficit-reduction legislation, but within a series of events in which Bush became a virtual bystander in the final deliberations. The next two years witnessed some new legislation but increased animosity between Bush and Congress.

Early Efforts

The combination of overly zealous deregulation in Washington and in some states, the reckless and sometimes corrupt actions by individuals in the savings and loan industry, and the reluctance of Congress to readdress the issue had, by 1989, threatened the solvency of the government programs designed to insure deposits. Just as Franklin Roosevelt had feared when banking insurance was established in 1933, the "heads I win, tails the government loses" aspect of deposit insurance had produced costly results when a far broader program of insurance was instituted. By the mid-nineties that sum had reached $500 billion.

Bush did not have to engage in a significant public role in the savings and loan bailout because Congress was well aware that action could no longer be avoided. The president did, though, have Treasury Secretary Nicholas Brady quickly develop a new proposal. The debate in Congress centered on the levels of contributions to be made by the healthy thrift institutions, the extent to which revenues would be derived from the more costly step of borrowing rather than direct expenditures, and the manner in which costs would be allocated for calculating deficit-reduction targets mandated by legislation known as Gramm-Rudman. The Bush administration entered the fray primarily on the accounting issue—it opposed direct financing—but it apparently did not have a strong bargaining role because the legislation that finally emerged compromised on the accounting issue.

Successful passage of the savings and loan bailout did not carry over to Bush's efforts to achieve his personal favorite—a cut in the capital gains tax. He succeeded in the House but failed in the Senate. At first, Bush and House Ways and Means Committee chairman Rostenkowski pursued a possible compromise. Rostenkowski would seek support of a temporary capital gains tax reduction, and Bush would agree to support, among other things, an expanded earned income tax credit, efforts to block cuts in Medicare payments to inner-city hospitals, and a deficit-reduction package in 1990 that would include a sizable tax hike.[26] This bargain, however, did not materialize. Despite Rostenkowski's shift into opposition, conservative Democrats and many Republicans on the Ways and Means Committee began to see greater legitimacy for a capital gains cut. Thus it passed a measure calling for a temporary reduction and then sent it to the full House for a vote. At this point Speaker Thomas Foley, D-Wash., and Democratic majority leader Richard Gephardt of Missouri sought to marshal their forces for a key vote while Bush began to man the phones in an all-out effort for the capital gains reduction. For some Democrats the issue was increasingly one in which individuals of moderate wealth might be helped rather than simply those with very substantial assets. In the end, then, Bush's strong campaign produced a decisive, 239–190, win in the House for a temporary capital gains tax cut.

Leadership actions in the Senate produced a very different result. Majority leader George Mitchell, D-Maine, who wanted to chalk up some successes in his first year in office, worked very hard to mobilize Democrats around the proposition that it was important for their party leader to win rather than the president. Because of procedural rules associated with Gramm-Rudman provisions, Mitchell also had a major advantage: sixty, not fifty-one votes, would be needed for the capital gains measure to carry. Ultimately, Bush was able to marshal fifty-one votes, but because of the prevailing rule, the measure failed.

Clean Air Act Amendments of 1990

The passage of the first new legislation in the area of air quality control since 1977 was a major policy achievement. Some opportunities existed in this area because of the stalemate that occurred during the Reagan years and growing support within Congress for a variety of proposals seeking to address air pollution problems. Provisions of the sweeping final legislation included: expanded efforts to reduce automobile tailpipe emissions; detailed steps to improve air quality, especially in smog-ridden urban centers like Houston and Los Angeles; the first major restrictions on Midwest industrial pollution from coal-fired burners that had been contributing to the formation of acid rain; a listing of 189 toxic chemicals for which the Environmental Protection Agency must set public health standards; and the first steps to deal with issues such as global warning and the growing hazard of high-altitude ozone depletion—problems that were unknown, even by scientists, when Congress had passed the original Clean Air Act of 1977.

Bush had made air pollution policy a top priority in Congress. In fact, his actions made it virtually certain that some air pollution control legislation would be passed by 1990.[27] Bush had noted the issue during the 1988 campaign, stressed it in his first State of the Union address, and unveiled his proposal with a widely publicized gathering in the East Room of the White House. Although he made no major addresses on the issue while the bill made its way through Congress, he did continue to emphasize the importance of this legislation in a variety of secondary speeches. And Congress recognized the president's significant role. Key legislative promoter Sen. Max Baucus, D-Mont., echoed that recognition when he stated, "The Reagan administration was very much opposed to clean air. The Bush administration is very much in favor of clean air legislation. George Bush deserves major credit."[28]

Americans with Disabilities Act

During the 1988 campaign, Bush had spoken favorably of the Americans with Disabilities Act (ADA), which had been under consideration in Congress for several years. In a speech at the Department of Health and Human Services two days before his inauguration, he also spoke very glowingly in favor of the bill. With the help of the Bush administration and an alliance of supporters that included the disability movement, civil rights groups, and liberals, the legislation passed in the Senate and one of the necessary four House committees in 1989. The bill sought to add the disabled to the groups protected against discrimination by the landmark Civil Rights Act of 1964.

As it did for the Clean Air Act Amendments, the Bush administration articulated the concerns of the business community about specific provisions of ADA. The issue was whether aggrieved parties would be allowed to sue for damages. Attorney General Richard Thornburgh pointed out that legislators had agreed in 1989 to a compromise in which the administration would broaden the public accommodations provision of the act in exchange for language that would indicate an agreement that individuals would not be able to sue for damages. When the language used in the 1964 civil rights legislation was modified in response to a Supreme Court decision, however, Democrats argued that the language used for ADA also should be changed. The Bush administration lost in committee votes on this issue.

The ADA legislation that emerged from Congress in 1990 included major provisions outlining the rights of the disabled vis-à-vis public accommodation and prohibitions against discrimination in employment. Although Bush helped to make this an issue of top legislative concern, he did not engage in any significant personal advocacy once congressional hearings had begun. In shaping the final legislative result, he also failed to reduce the scope of protection being provided in the ADA.

Landmark Deficit Reduction

The Omnibus Budget and Reconciliation Act of 1990 (OBRA 90), the most significant domestic policy of Bush's years in office, was a strong measure that reduced the projected budget deficit by some $482 billion over five years (it cut about two dollars in spending for every dollar in tax increases). It also helped to constrain future spending through its "pay as you go" (PAYGO) provisions; future lawmakers would have to find saving or new revenue for the additional expenditures they imposed. As Congressional Budget Office Director Robert Reischauer saw it, this measure would have a forceful impact on the ability of the federal government to reduce deficits in the 1990s.[29] In the short run, however, its impact was not readily apparent. The federal budget in the next two years reflected the costs of the savings and loan bailout and the reduced revenues and increased spending caused by the recession of 1991–1992. These developments, and the manner in which Bush handled his role, eliminated any possibility that Bush would receive significant credit for the measure in the 1992 election.

The pathway to deficit reduction included top-level negotiation, multiple players, and a series of questionable moves by Bush.[30] In 1989 the Bush administration showed some interest in negotiating a deficit-reduction package, especially OMB Director Richard Darman. But suspicions about the motivations and possible actions of the other side, coupled with the divisive fight over capital gains, produced only a limited effort. As 1990 began, it was increasingly apparent that policy makers faced one of two choices: they had to either negotiate a substantial deficit-reduction package or else see Gramm-Rudman requirements impose deep across-the-board cuts. Bush's initial budget was essentially a bargaining position for his negotiations with Congress. He proposed substantial spending cuts for Medicare and other programs favored by Democrats, small defense cuts, no tax increase, and a new version of the capital gains tax reduction. Again using optimistic economic estimates, the program promised a deficit reduction of $36 billion—a figure well below the Gramm-Rudman required reduction of $64 billion. In part because of the additional spending required for the savings and loan bailout, the mandatory Gramm-Rudman deficit-reduction targets quickly escalated. In that context, some observers in both Congress and the Bush administration grew concerned that an effort to meet the Gramm-Rudman deficit reduction might send the economy into a tailspin. Thus a consensus formed on a revised goal of a long-term measure that would cut the deficit by $50 billion in 1991 and $500 billion over a five-year period.

Politically, Bush was widely viewed as the big loser in the budget battle—and in ways for which he was at least partly to blame. In the final stages his administration had not played the inside bargain game well. More centrally, however, Bush's efforts at public leadership had been remarkably limited. He neglected to explain his reasons for abandoning his "no new taxes" promise. His lack of effectiveness was evident in public opinion polls as his popularity dropped from 74 percent in late August 1990 to 59 percent in early October. According to David Mervin, "The President's conduct during the budget crisis severely damaged his credibility as a leader and eroded respect for his competence in economic policy." [31]

Civil Rights

In 1989 the Supreme Court handed down a decision, *Wards Cove Packing Co. v. Antonio,* that made it more difficult for civil rights claims to be pursued through legal channels.[32] In its ruling the Court rejected the use of affirmative action suits brought on the basis of statistical under-representation of minorities in a specific company. Congress then sought in 1990 to reinterpret congressional intent in ways that would restore the previous understanding and thereby allow the broader use of legal action against claims of civil rights violations. Bush responded with a veto, saying (despite congressional denials) that the new legislation would establish a system of quotas for job hiring. Because Congress was unable to override Bush's veto in 1990, the issue was open to possible action in 1991 when Congress enacted similar legislation. Bush chose to interpret this legislation as enough of a change from the measure he had vetoed in 1990 that he could sign it. Bush's acquiescence was widely attributed to election concerns, the tensions surrounding the rise of overt racists such as former Ku Klux Klan leader David Duke in the Republican Party, and the fallout from his successful elevation of African American Clarence Thomas to the Supreme Court.

Bush and Congress

Bush's limited circumstances were not conducive to a highly productive legislative record. He could rightly take credit for his helpful roles in some major legislation such as the savings and loan bailout, Clean Air Act Amendments, and Americans with Disabilities Act, and his defensive use of vetoes shaped some legislation as well. Yet few observers have given him high marks for legislative leadership. After his most productive first two years, Paul Quirk observed that "it is not difficult to suppose that another president who had set out to attempt cooperative leadership could have accomplished more than Bush did." [33] Looking back after four years, Barbara Sinclair concluded, "He didn't seem to have much he wanted to do. I'm not sure there is much more he could have done. But he didn't really try." [34]

An Assessment

George Bush was ultimately an unlucky president. As the understudy, he faced the difficult task of differentiating himself from his predecessor, Ronald Reagan, while maintaining the appearance of loyalty to Reagan's agenda. After adopting a leadership style that fit his circumstances fairly well, Bush confronted in his reelection year a stubborn recession and broad voter concerns about job security in the face of the new global pressures affecting the nation's economy. The onset of the recession also robbed him of an opportunity to take credit for the lower deficit that was supposed to stem from the deficit-reduction package passed in 1990. In those circumstances, how well did he do?

Bush's policy legacies include most centrally the deficit-reduction measure of 1990, which stands up quite well when compared with some of the more recent deficit-reduction packages. According to Robert Reischauer, onetime director of the Congressional Budget Office, Bush's measure contributed significantly to the movement toward very low deficits by 1997 and the eventual achievement of a balanced budget agreement.[35] Yet while Bush's willingness to accept a tax increase was central to passage of the legislation, his leadership contributions were quite limited. For that reason, the Clean Air Act Amendments, over time, are likely to stand out as the most important legacy in which President Bush fulfilled a variety of leadership roles.

In his overall performance, Bush seemed to have difficulty putting the various pieces of his presidency together. Members of his administration took various actions, but not necessarily with a coordinated sense of purpose or direction. Bush gave some indications of ways in which a president could sustain personal support with a less-glorified public view of the presidency, but even this more modest approach to dealing with the public was never effectively developed. His greatest failing, however, was in his public leadership. His inept handling of the deficit-reduction struggle and the credibility he lost as a domestic policy leader during his last two years in office were arguably the clearest indication that a lack of skill, his difficult circumstances, and his limited personal agenda affected his accomplishments in office—and his reelection prospects.

Bush, then, like Jimmy Carter, proved to be an underachiever. On the domestic front, his decision to be a guardian-type leader may have been a poor one. In the modern era, can a president assume a more diminished role in agenda setting and leadership? The Bush presidency suggests the answer may be no.

Notes

1. Fitzhugh Green, *George Bush: An Intimate Portrait* (New York: Hippocrene Books, 1989), 65.
2. Ibid., 169.
3. Sidney Blumenthal, *Pledging Allegiance: The Last Campaign of the Cold War* (New York: HarperCollins, 1990).

4. Craig Allen Smith and Kathy B. Smith, *The White House Speaks: Presidential Leadership as Persuasion* (Westport, Conn.: Praeger, 1994), 83.

5. Green, *George Bush,* xii.

6. Gail Sheehy, *Character: America's Search for Leadership* (New York: Morrow, 1988), 160.

7. Charles Kolb, *White House Daze: The Unmaking of Domestic Policy in the Bush Years* (New York: Free Press, 1994), 241.

8. On the Tory aspect of Bush's views, see in particular Bert A. Rockman, "The Leadership Style of George Bush," in *The Bush Presidency: First Appraisals,* ed. Colin Campbell and Bert A. Rockman (Chatham, N.J.: Chatham House, 1991), chap. 1.

9. Paul J. Quirk, "Domestic Policy: Divided Government and Cooperative Presidential Leadership," in Campbell and Rockman, *Bush Presidency,* 73.

10. David Mervin, *George Bush and the Guardianship Presidency* (New York: St. Martin's Press, 1996).

11. Shirley A. Warshaw, *Powersharing: White House–Cabinet Relationships in the Modern Presidency* (Albany: State University of New York Press, 1996), chap. 7.

12. Michael Duffy and Dan Goodgame, *Marching in Place: The Status Quo Presidency of George Bush* (New York: Simon and Schuster, 1992), 125.

13. Ibid., 123.

14. Warshaw, *Powersharing.*

15. *Public Papers of the Presidents of the United States: George H. W. Bush, 1989,* vol. 1 (Washington, D.C.: Government Printing Office, 1989).

16. Barbara H. Craig and David M. O'Brien, *Abortion and American Politics* (Chatham, N.J.: Chatham House, 1993), 191.

17. Barry D. Friedman, *Regulation in the Reagan-Bush Era: The Eruption of Presidential Influence* (Pittsburgh: University of Pittsburgh Press, 1995).

18. Richard A. Harris and Sidney M. Milkis, *The Politics of Regulatory Change: A Tale of Two Agencies* (New York: Oxford University Press, 1996).

19. Mary E. Stuckey, *The President as Interpreter-in-Chief* (Chatham, N.J.: Chatham House, 1991), 128.

20. Duffy and Goodgame, *Marching in Place,* 46.

21. Mervin, *George Bush and the Guardianship Presidency,* 106.

22. On the factors producing Bush's early popularity, see in particular George C. Edwards III, "George Bush and the Public Presidency: The Politics of Inclusion," in Campbell and Rockman, *Bush Presidency,* 129–154.

23. Smith and Smith, *White House Speaks,* 82–90.

24. Kolb, *White House Daze,* 41.

25. Edwards, "George Bush and the Public Presidency," 129–154.

26. Quirk, "Domestic Policy," 69–91.

27. *Congressional Quarterly Weekly Report,* June 17, 1989, 1460.

28. Steven V. Roberts and Kenneth T. Walsh, "Is Bush in Nature's Way?" *U.S. News and World Report,* March 19, 1990, 20.

29. Robert D. Reischauer, *Setting National Priorities: Budget Choices for the Next Century* (Washington, D.C.: Brookings, 1996).

30. For helpful case studies of these events, see Richard Darman, *Who's In Control: Polar Politics and the Sensible Center* (New York: Simon and Schuster, 1996); George Hager and Eric Pianin, *Mirage* (New York: Random House, 1997); and Quirk, "Domestic Policy."

31. Mervin, *George Bush and the Guardianship Presidency,*155.

32. *Wards Cove Packing Co. v. Antonio,* 490 U.S. 642 (1989).

33. Quirk, "Domestic Policy," 88.

34. Barbara Sinclair, "How Will George Bush Go Down in History?" *Los Angeles Times,* November 1, 1992, 13.

35. Reischauer, *Setting National Priorities,* 13.

The era of big government is over.

—BILL CLINTON

11

Bill Clinton

*A Perpetual Campaigner
under Siege*

THE PRESIDENCY of Bill Clinton (served 1993–2001) resembled a roller-coaster ride. In his first year he suffered the most rapid three-month loss of popularity for any president on record, and yet the same year he achieved passage of a landmark deficit-reduction package and other new legislation, earning him an 86 percent legislative success score for 1993–1994. His second year saw the resounding defeat of his health care package, damaging charges of a White House cover-up, and a stunning 1994 rebuke for his party as the Republicans gained control of the Senate and House of Representatives for the first time since 1954.

And the shifting fortunes continued. In 1995 Clinton outmaneuvered Republican leaders in Congress on budget politics when they incorrectly assumed he would cave in to their demands. Only a year later, against the predictions of all the pundits, he became the first Democratic president to gain reelection since FDR. Almost immediately, a sex scandal involving a young White House intern dominated the headlines, followed in 1999 by impeachment in the House of Representatives and a trial, but not a conviction, in the Senate. In the aftermath of the 1998 midterm elections—which went surprisingly well for the Democrats—people's views of the president continued to vary. Some were awed by a politically skilled chief executive who, holding office during a transitional period, was remarkably able to land on his feet, and others argued that his personal limitations were producing underachievement. What was the real story of Bill Clinton, the last of the low-opportunity presidents?

Personal Characteristics

William Jefferson Clinton (1946–) brought the baby boom generation and its attitudes to the White House. Virtually all of his predecessors had gained at least some credit for having served in the military. Now the question became: how did he avoid serving in the Vietnam War? And, since he was a student in the 1960s, marijuana use—"I did not inhale," he said—became a campaign issue for a time. Then there was the question of the first lady, who, like many women of the Clintons' generation, had pursued a professional career (lawyer). Just what role should such a first lady play? The young president's usually strong rejection of hierarchical structures in organizing his administration also was viewed as a reflection of the attitudes many baby boomers formed in the 1960s. Clearly, then, the presidency was undergoing a profound generational passage, and this made for some harsh intergenerational criticism of the president and his wife.

Clinton's early family experiences gave little indication he would become the first member of his generation to occupy the presidency.[1] His father died before he was born, and his mother returned to school to train as a nurse anesthetist, leaving Bill living for a time with his grandparents in Hope, Arkansas, before his mother moved the family to Hot Springs. After her remarriage to the alcoholic and sometimes abusive Roger Clinton, young Bill Clinton at times found himself having to aggressively defend his mother. When the family's economic situation improved, Bill was raised as part of the growing southern middle class as he proceeded through his school days in Hot Springs.

Achievement came easily in several areas. His skill with the tenor saxophone led to prominent placement in the all-state band. Following a strong high school performance in which he graduated fourth in a class of 363, he pursued his undergraduate degree, with a major in international relations, at Georgetown University in Washington, D.C. After graduation he left the country for England and two years of study as a Rhodes scholar at Oxford University. He returned to complete his legal studies at Yale Law School.

Career Path

Bill Clinton was involved in more major political campaigns than any of the other post-1932 presidents. In high school and college he ran frequently for office, and, to help pay his college tuition, he worked in the office of Sen. William Fulbright, D-Ark., a highly influential member of Congress and ultimately a strong critic of the Vietnam War. Clinton loved campaigns. He had worked on races in Arkansas, Connecticut, and Texas (as co-chair of the George McGovern presidential campaign in 1972) before his own surprisingly close but unsuccessful bid for a congressional seat in Arkansas in 1974. By the time he ran for the presidency in 1992, he had run in no fewer than eight Arkansas elections.

Clinton's career path to the presidency included ten years as governor of Arkansas. He was elected in 1978, defeated in 1980, and won enough reelection bids to serve until his resignation after winning the presidency in 1992. The early defeat produced a change in his leadership style; he abandoned some of his more ambitious programs, recruited a staff who appeared less Ivy League, and proceeded more cautiously. The one exception to his cautious approach was his strong and largely successful promotion of education reform in 1983. In fact, during his ten years in the governor's office Clinton often showed interest in innovative programs, such as efforts to combat adult illiteracy and different ways of delivering home services to the elderly. He also was highly successful in building support within the state's black community.

Clinton tended to rely on personal persuasiveness in dealing with members of his state legislature. It was nominally controlled by the Democratic Party, but in fact it included diverse factions, some of whom were hesitant about significant political reform. Perhaps it was there that he honed the considerable public relations skill he displayed both in Arkansas and elsewhere as he gained the attention of the national media which pronounced him a rising star among the nation's governors (who designated him one of the "most effective" of their number). But, like all politicians, he also came in for his share of the criticism: his tendency to shift according to changing political winds, the limited attention he paid to the administration of new programs, and his coziness with economic elites which was at variance with his populist political rhetoric.[2]

While serving as governor, Clinton continued to assess possible strategies for achieving his long-standing presidential ambition. In the fall of 1987 he seemed to be planning to run in the 1988 election, but then announced to a very surprised group of reporters and friends that he was not going to enter the race. The official explanation, which appears to have contained some truth, was that he did not want to expose his daughter, Chelsea, to a national campaign. He also was concerned about the manner in which the press had exposed Gary Hart's womanizing, causing the Colorado senator, the early leader in the 1988 race for the Democratic nomination, to abandon his campaign.[3] Clinton won reelection to the governorship in 1990 but in a race that was closely contested as voters wondered whether he had served long enough.

In 1991 Clinton took another look at entering the presidential sweepstakes. Some prominent Democrats—among them, Senators Bill Bradley of New Jersey, Al Gore of Tennessee, and Sam Nunn of Georgia, along with Rep. Richard Gephardt of Missouri and New York governor Mario Cuomo—had decided to pass up a race against the Republican incumbent, George Bush, who was basking in a surge of popularity after the Gulf War. But apparently both Bill and Hillary felt they could win in 1992. For Clinton, a newcomer to the national stage and only forty-five years of age, the prospect of a decent but unsuccessful showing in the Democratic primaries (especially if followed by Bush's reelection) also offered promise as a route to the coveted Democratic nomination in 1996.

Clinton's emergence as the Democratic nominee occurred despite two personal issues that might have torpedoed his candidacy. The first was his explanation of how he avoided serving in the Vietnam War. His initial explanation that he had received a low draft number omitted the fact that he had achieved and later declined an ROTC (Reserve Officers' Training Corps) appointment at the University of Arkansas before receiving the low lottery number. The second issue was Gennifer Flowers, a nightclub singer in Little Rock who claimed she had had a twelve-year affair with Clinton. Clinton helped to defuse this issue when he appeared with Hillary on the television program *Sixty Minutes*. He confessed to having caused "pain in our marriage," and they both spoke of the renewed strength of their relationship.

Clinton displayed considerable energy and political skill as he fought for the nomination, despite the handicap caused by public skepticism about his past behavior. He was helped in the crucial New Hampshire primary by a large network of personal friends who joined his effort. As the campaign progressed, he also realized he had an advantage over most of the other Democratic candidates: his years of work with policy issues in Arkansas had given him a good grasp of policy and an ability to articulate an agenda as a "New Democrat." Then, as he moved down the road toward the nomination, he found that he faced fewer and fewer strong opponents.

As the Democratic nominee, Clinton was both fortunate and effective in the fall campaign. The economy continued to slump, making the reminder "It's the economy, stupid," posted on the wall of his Little Rock campaign office, an apt summary of voter concerns. Clinton also was able to capitalize on and articulate voters' concerns about issues such as health care and the need for fundamental welfare reform, promising to "end welfare as we know it." By comparison, President Bush ran a surprisingly ineffective campaign, poorly organized and lacking focus. In addition, the entry of independent candidate Ross Perot served to divide potential Republican votes in some states. In the end, Clinton was able to put together an electoral college coalition that included some traditionally liberal states, California, some swing states, and four southern states.

What Manner of Man?

Few have doubted Clinton's intelligence, ambition, and high energy level.[4] His ambition for political office was manifested as early as his high school days when he turned from other possible career choices such as music or medicine. A high school trip to Washington as a part of the American Legion's Boys State in 1963 and a handshake from President John Kennedy probably helped to kindle that ambition, along with his mother's continuing encouragement that he aim high. For whatever mix of reasons, he was more clearly a political "young man on the make" than any of the post-1932 presidents except Lyndon Johnson. Hillary Rodham articulated that ambition when she referred as early as 1974 to her friend from Yale who "will be president." Also indicative of his long-standing ambition, after he moved into the Arkansas governor's mansion top staff aide Betsy Wright culled the large network of friends he had cultivated to produce computerized lists of "Friends of Bill."

Clinton's late-night calls to surprised friends and staff both before and after his election were one indication of his high energy level. In fact, his energy was often highest when he was focused on a particular task. During the New Hampshire primary, for example, he ended a day of campaigning by wondering about midnight if there was an all-night bowling alley he could visit. Later, after he moved into the White House, his efforts to overcome early problems produced similar bursts of energy and a White House that was rumored to be suffering from sleep deprivation.

Clinton possessed a high level of self-confidence, but he required validation. Toward that end he sometimes seemed to display his extensive knowledge of issues more to impress listeners than to marshal effective, persuasive arguments. His confidence was shaken at low points during his presidency, such as the first months in office and in the aftermath of the Republican triumph in the 1994 elections. When in one of his low moods, he often blamed others such as staffers or the press for his problems and on occasion would lose his temper in a burst of explosive language.

Although Clinton was highly intelligent and keenly knowledgeable about public policy, he did at times seem to lack conceptual clarity. His intelligence allowed him to do very well in school where he read a great deal, but he often crammed for exams rather than proceeding in a disciplined manner through course materials. In 1972, for example, he campaigned for Sen. George McGovern all fall in Texas and then used borrowed notes to pass his classes at Yale.

As president, he continued to read many books as well as a variety of assessments of policy issues. In this way he developed an understanding of budgetary issues that rivaled the knowledge of longtime committee members in Congress and gave him a major advantage in top-level negotiations with rivals such as Speaker Newt Gingrich, R-Ga. Yet at times Clinton's ability to absorb detail was not an advantage. Like Jimmy Carter, he sometimes spent too much time on unnecessary information.

As for his relationships with friends and constituents, Clinton seemed to have a genuine interest in people and an unusually high degree of empathy. Indeed, from an early age he liked to help others who were in trouble. A friend facing problems could anticipate a long list of suggestions, including people to contact. And Clinton found he could use his empathetic qualities very effectively in town hall-styled meetings, including presidential debates conducted in that manner, and also in some of his presidential roles such as expressing the nation's grief after the terrorist bombing in Oklahoma City in April 1995.

In dealing with others, Clinton often seemed reluctant to openly reveal his opposition to various ideas and suggestions. At times, he even used this trait to see how others would handle an issue, causing confusion among subordinates and other political figures because his noncommittal response was taken inappropriately as an indication of his approval of their ideas. It is not surprising, then, that the epithet "Slick Willie" clung to Clinton from his Arkansas days. It was probably made up by some of those who felt they had been misled by his fence-sitting.

The personal quality that produced the most intense debate about Clinton was his tendency to shade the truth, or dissemble, when it came to personal matters. He faced questions early on in his presidential bid about his draft status during the Vietnam War. Later, when he was in the White House, he drew criticism for his interpretations of suspicious White House operations such as the abrupt dismissal of travel agents, his reasons why FBI files of Republicans came into the hands of White House staffers, and his explanation of the extent to which guest stays in the Lincoln Bedroom were used for fund raising. According to political scientist Stanley Renshon, Clinton tended to dissemble because of a somewhat idealized self-view and thus his difficulty in accurately interpreting his own behavior.[5] Arkansas journalist John Brummett offered this description of Clinton the politician:

> In Arkansas, we knew Clinton as a man who made mistakes and learned from them, who took risks and added drama to legislative sessions with buttonholed legislators. He could be reckless, indiscreet, self-indulgent, dissembling, and disorganized in his personal and professional life and associations, tended to lose interest in programs after he'd managed to get them enacted, and combined seductive personal charm, boundless energy, ego, a burning desire for success and acceptance, and an extraordinary mind into a style of high octane salesmanship and accomplishment that people tended to love or hate, to embrace or resent bitterly.[6]

Historian Arthur Schlesinger Jr. detected multiple qualities as well:

> He is a man of penetrating intelligence. He has impressive technical mastery of complicated issues. He has genuine intellectual curiosity and listens as well as talks. He is a skilled and resilient politician. . . . On the other hand, he lacks self-discipline. His judgment of people is erratic. His political resilience strikes many as flagrant opportunism. . . . He rushes to propitiate the audience before him, often at his own long expense. His scandals and cover-ups are ripe for exploitation by a vindictive opposition.[7]

Policy Views

Like his predecessors, Clinton had policy views that reflected his times and experiences. He came to the presidency from a state lacking a liberal tradition and after having spent more than a decade seeking to develop new policy outlooks that would help the national Democratic Party regain a majority position. From his childhood experiences and years as governor, he brought to the White House his supportive views on civil rights and the death penalty and a moderate orientation on many issues. As a product of one of the nation's poorest states, he wanted to see government help people improve their economic well-being. Thus in his presidential campaign he called for investments in educational training to improve a worker's job prospects. In fact, in the 1992 campaign he touted programs to create new jobs far more than his commitment to cutting the deficit by 50 percent. He also spoke often of the need to help average Americans who were living by the rules and having a hard time. And he spoke of a New Covenant, but with a greater emphasis on individual responsibility than that characterizing the rhetoric of the more traditional liberals.

The need to find a "third way" to address policy issues was central to Clinton's views. As one of the founders of the Democratic Leadership Council—a group supported by the more conservative figures in the Democratic Party—he sought policy approaches that would be more mainstream than the traditional liberal views. In health care, for example, his 1993 proposal ended up being highly regulatory because he wished to avoid a Canadian-style system of direct government financing while also providing universal coverage rather than more limited reforms. More broadly, he wanted to use government to address economic and social problems, yet he wanted to rely largely on market mechanisms and individual initiative. He believed in smaller government but still active government.

Challenges and Opportunities

When Clinton assumed the presidency, he faced the challenge of addressing the concerns of an angry public. It wanted action on health care and the economy but also was skeptical about the effectiveness of many federal policies and uncertain about the intentions of the political parties. Thus an opportunity awaited the new president as well: to build a new coalition. Yet if successful, Clinton would place himself in an unusual position: no president in the twentieth century elected with a divided electorate in a three-party race had been able to build a solid new coalition. Presidents Woodrow Wilson and Richard Nixon could have testified to the difficulties involved.

Several aspects of Clinton's position were not overly promising. In terms of election results, his seven percentage-point winning margin over Bush ranked sixth among the post-1932 presidents, and his 43.0 percent of the total vote put him just behind Nixon (43.4 percent) in ninth place (Table 1–2). As for his personal approval ratings, he started with a respectable 58 percent which dropped to only 38 percent after three months. In addition, Clinton was confronting an increasingly skeptical electorate;

only 22 percent agreed with the proposition that one could trust the government in Washington to do the right thing most of the time.

In Congress, the Democratic majorities in the House and Senate were smaller than those of other newly elected Democratic presidents, but they included fewer conservative southern Democrats. Less promising for Clinton was the growing trend toward partisan voting in Congress and the increased use of filibusters in the Senate to block presidential initiatives.

In view of the economic recession of 1991–1992 and his concentration on creating jobs, Clinton appeared to have a big opportunity to move on his job creation agenda early in his administration. Several factors served to reduce that opportunity, however. Improved economic figures for the fourth quarter of 1992 and improved projections for 1993 lessened the sense of urgency about creating new jobs. At the same time, higher deficit projections reduced support for new spending programs. But therein lay another opportunity for Clinton. The growing demands for deficit reduction may have made it more difficult for him to promote job creation programs with the public and with Congress, but they gave the new president a better opportunity to promote a deficit-reduction plan.

At first, health reform also seemed to be a promising opportunity; opinion polls showed majority support for major changes in the health care system. Yet when the difficulty of obtaining any kind of agreement on a specific policy design was added to the opportunity calculation, the opportunity seemed somewhat less certain. When the public envisioned health care reform, it most often had in mind reducing waste and fraud. But as the intense debate over health policy developed, those responsible for developing specific plans underscored the importance of containing costs and helping those who lacked coverage acquire health insurance. The quest, then, for congressional and public agreement on a specific plan was likely to present major difficulties.

Clinton's opportunities changed dramatically in the wake of the Republican takeover of the House and Senate in the 1994 midterm elections. Agenda control shifted decisively to the Republicans as Clinton struggled, saying, "I'm also relevant here." Fundamentally, however, the Republican move to the right on a variety of issues created a new opportunity for Clinton to establish a centrist position and successfully appeal to voters' apprehensions about the more extremist policy directions of the Republicans in Congress. While Republican newcomers called for a revolution, the voters, on issues from Medicare to environmental protection, seemed more interested in evolution than revolution.

Foreign policy concerns provided some distractions and difficulties but no major disruptions to Clinton's domestic policy roles. In October 1993 the nation was shocked by the slaying of American soldiers stationed in Somalia as part of a humanitarian mission and television pictures of the body of a pilot being dragged through the streets of Mogadishu. In response to the situation, Clinton swung his attention to devising strategies for ending that mission during a time he had hoped to focus on promoting his health policy initiative.[8] White House wavering over U.S. involvement in Haiti also contributed to the public's perception of an indecisive president. And adding to his foreign policy woes, Clinton had to struggle during most of his first term with the civil war in the former Yugoslavia and the level of U.S. participation in resolving that conflict. Ultimately he decided against direct involvement and contributed to the development of plans that, in effect, called for partitioning that war-ravaged land. The lack of more extensive foreign policy debates and actions stemmed from a combination of the president's greater interest n domestic policy and the unfolding of world events.

Clinton's second term began with more limitations than advantages. He was reelected by a far-smaller-than-average margin, and he would have to muster bipartisan support for any new policies since both houses of Congress remained under Republican control. His campaign had featured many minor proposals, but it was primarily a defense of existing programs. Continuing economic growth, however, meant that the opportunities for congressional passage of a multiyear balanced budget agreement had increased dramatically.

Leadership Style

Clinton's early difficulties and the Republican victories in 1994 prompted an extensive presidential search for a better leadership style. At various points during this mission, Clinton expressed admiration for Presidents Franklin Roosevelt, Harry Truman, John Kennedy, and Ronald Reagan (for his effective use of the fast-start strategy). In improving his leadership efforts, the president sought to respond better to drastic changes in his political environment and to incorporate several of his personal characteristics as well as the lessons learned from earlier career experiences. As the president with the most extensive experience in major campaigns prior to his election, he often seemed to be a perpetual campaigner. He studied the public opinion polls incessantly and diligently sought to sell himself and his administration to the public.

The Advisory Process and Approach to Decision Making

As he organized his administration, Clinton tried to keep his campaign commitment to filling his cabinet with Americans from diverse backgrounds—"a Cabinet that looks like America."[9] As a result, the top twenty-three positions included six women, four African Americans, and two Hispanics. It was the most diverse cabinet in American history. Some commentators, though, noted the absence of any Republicans, the law degrees held by two-thirds of his appointees, and the higher-than-average emphasis on university backgrounds. Key domestic policy positions were filled by deficit-reduction "hawks" and former senator Lloyd Bentsen as Treasury secretary. The more liberal voices were those of university president Donna Shalala as secretary of heath and human services and Clinton's fellow Rhodes scholar Robert Reich as secretary of labor.

Personal and policy staffers were chosen far more rapidly than the cabinet and with a lack of attention that Clinton later regretted. The White House staff was a mix of longtime Arkansas associates and campaign aides and Washington veterans and policy experts. Arkansas natives included his first chief of staff, Thomas "Mack" McLarty III and top aide Bruce Lindsey. Director of Communications George Stephanopoulos and Trade Representative Mickey Kantor had been key campaign aides. Leon Panetta, a veteran member of the House of Representatives from California, served first as head of the Office of Management and Budget (OMB) and then as chief of staff. Alice Rivlin, a former director of the Congressional Budget Office, served initially as Panetta's deputy and then as the director of OMB. To head the Council of Economic Advisers, Clinton chose Laura Tyson, an economics professor at the University of California at Berkeley whose research had focused on trade policy issues. Wall Street broker Robert Rubin became a key adviser on economic policy, first as head of the new National Economic Council and later as a highly regarded secretary of the Treasury. Carol Rasco, a veteran of Clinton's governorship, headed his domestic advisers, but she had a less-influential role than in most previous staffs. As his top adviser on health policy, Clinton selected Ira Magaziner, a business consultant and fellow Rhodes scholar.

Also occupying important positions of power in the Clinton White House were Vice President Al Gore and First Lady Hillary Rodham Clinton. Gore, according to some analysts, was the most influential vice president in the nation's history. His standing, however, reflected the trend toward much greater influence for vice presidents. Gore also had a very close relationship with Clinton.[10] The vice president's most public domestic role was undertaken in conjunction with a Clinton administration program aimed at reviewing and then cutting, consolidating, and reshaping the federal government. It was known as the National Performance Review and later renamed the National Partnership for Reinventing Government. More broadly, he had a significant voice in a wide variety of policy deliberations and had at least weekly one-on-one meetings with Clinton.

The significant influence of the first lady on the president was indicated in part by her large staff and prominent West Wing office. During the first two years she led the administration's health care reform effort. And especially in the early days of the administration she was present at a wide variety of meetings and was viewed by staff and cabinet members as an important channel of influence on presidential decisions.

Clinton's decision-making process was characterized by his extensive involvement (perhaps too much) in policy details. And, as noted, he also tended to seek a "third way" in policy disputes. Consultant Dick Morris liked to call this tendency "triangulation," but the president's fondness for hybrid solutions was well established before Morris arrived on the scene in late 1994. Clinton also paid a great deal of attention to opinion polls, often in searching for ways to shape messages such as a slogan to promote the Health Security Act. Political consultants armed with polling data and the results of focus groups had greater access in the Clinton White House than in any previous administration.[11] Political feasibility was tested as well through personal contacts with many members of Congress. Despite criticism from some quarters that he liked to please in making decisions, Clinton did on occasion decide to confront the likely opposition of frequent allies. In the fall of 1993 he made such a choice with his vigorous support of the North American Free Trade Agreement (NAFTA).

Clinton's decision-making process is probably best illustrated by the deficit-reduction package produced by his administration in 1993.[12] The president devoted a great deal of his own time and energy to designing his budget package and seemed interested in even the tiniest details of budgetary operations. The many lengthy meetings seemed to be rather unstructured, both in terms of the deliberations and in terms of exactly who participated. In these meetings, consultants from the campaign, including Paul Begala and Mandy Grunwald, stressed the importance of avoiding any policies that might inflict substantial pain on the middle class. While untidy, the final result of Clinton's decision making in this instance was that he moved away from his middle-class tax cuts and major aspects of his "investments" agenda for job creation toward a policy that enabled him to capitalize on growing public and congressional sentiment for a renewed effort to reduce the deficit.

During his first term, Clinton was hammered by the media and others for his rather chaotic staff processes and inexperienced media relations personnel. Because the president tended to immerse himself in one or a few issues and because he disliked hierarchies, the White House sometimes seemed to resemble a soccer game—lots of people would run to the point of action. As a result, less-salient issues tended to get limited attention. In fact, in the beginning Clinton and his staff seemed to have few plans for how the presidency should actually proceed. According to journalist Elizabeth Drew, plans existed for only the first two weeks.[13]

But things did improve with experience and a few staff changes. In 1994 Chief of Staff Mack McLarty was replaced by Leon Panetta, who imposed greater discipline on staff operations. By 1997 Erskine Bowles was bringing his experience to bear on the White House organization, and cabinet changes were made without any of the gaffes that had occurred in 1993.

Administrative Strategies

Clinton used administrative strategies freely. As noted, in 1993–1994 Vice President Al Gore led an effort to make the federal government leaner and more efficient, and he succeeded in achieving substantial changes. After the Republican victories in the 1994 midterm election, the reform movement took on new urgency as a strategy for avoiding more sweeping Republican-led changes in some agencies.[14] Several observers credited these reform efforts and a tendency toward greater caution in creating new regulations with serving to mute initial Republican efforts to dismantle some agencies and departments.

Clinton's attempts to use administrative strategies to please segments of his electoral coalition produced some modest successes and at least one highly visible failure. Although some supporters felt his quick action on abortion rights conflicted with his image as a "New Democrat," other supporters applauded his actions such as his reversal of the "gag rule" applied during the Bush years, forbidding doctors at federally funded clinics to furnish any information on the option of requesting an abortion. But when Clinton tried to modify the policies on gays in the military, he unleashed a torrent of criticism. During his first week in office, the president sought to make good on a campaign promise to eliminate prohibitions against homosexuals serving in the military. This move, however, triggered an intense protest from Congress, including some leading Democrats such as Sam Nunn, chairman of the Senate Armed Services Committee. The political costs to the president on this issue were immense. By looking weak and indecisive at the outset of his administration, he diminished his "honeymoon" period. Furthermore, in the end he did not achieve a significant change in policy.

Administrative strategies also were in considerable evidence during 1995–1996 when, to keep his presidency in the news, Clinton used a wide variety of executive orders and pursued administrative actions. Consultant Dick Morris played a role in promoting these steps, which included pushing development of the V-chip as an aid for parents trying to select suitable television programming for their children and issuing an executive order requiring teenage mothers on welfare to work or to attend school and live at home.

Public Leadership

Although several of Clinton's early major and secondary speeches were well received—especially his thoughtful and candid remarks on race relations presented to a group of black ministers in October 1993—his first months in office seemed to be something of a "ten-second honeymoon," leading to talk of a failed presidency. Some of his support-building efforts drew skeptical reviews, and he struggled with harsh assessments by the media. In fact, in his first three months only 21 percent of comments by TV reporters were favorable—in stark contrast to Bush's figure of 74 percent. Clinton also found himself receiving four times as many references in the humor segments of late-night TV show hosts as Bush received during his first hundred days in office.[15]

But the poor start could not be traced entirely to questionable staff actions and policy decisions. Clinton also contributed by adopting an unusual media strategy of largely bypassing the Washington media and relying on local news outlets and alternative news sources such as radio and cable television to get his message to the public. The results were mixed;

he was able to go directly to the public, but he also generated resentment (and harsher criticism) from the Beltway pundits. This strategy had, however, met with considerable success during the fall campaign, when during the primaries the national media had been determined to keep aspects of his personal life before the public.

Although some improvements were made, media relationships proved difficult for Clinton. The press resented being bypassed by the White House and greeted a decision to physically limit some of their access to the president with hostility. After three months, David Gergen, a veteran media specialist from the Reagan administration, was recruited (to the dismay of some Clinton staffers) to improve press relations. And he did. He arranged social events such as a barbecue to bring the president and the press together and scheduled an unusually late first formal press conference. The press conference, however, proved to be a brief exception to Clinton's pattern of avoiding such gatherings. Then, unfortunately for Clinton and Gergen, storm clouds appeared on the horizon—a controversial Arkansas real estate venture called "Whitewater"—and media–White House relations became tense once again.

Despite all his problems with the media, Clinton's quest for personal popularity showed some improvement over time. His 34 percent disapproval rating after only a month in office and his June 1993 approval figure of only 37 percent had given way by 1996 to approval ratings of above 50 percent. According to George Edwards, Clinton's figures were particularly low for a president holding office with a strong economy.[16] Contributing to his popularity in 1996 were his January 1996 State of the Union address and his successful resistance to the proposed Republican balanced budget plan. Even during the tense days of impeachment in 1998, Clinton maintained surprisingly high approval ratings.

As for Clinton's major and secondary addresses, communications scholar Craig Allen Smith detected in them a set of rather shrewd strategies. The president did talk a lot about major policy issues, but not often from the Oval Office. He tended to make his secondary appeals to relevant specific groups. The ten occasions on which he promoted NAFTA, for example, were four NAFTA rallies, four national press availabilities, and speeches to the United Nations and the Hispanic Caucus. Clinton was thus able to gain more leverage than any other president who often suffered from low popularity ratings.[17]

In some of his secondary speeches Clinton succeeded in using the bully pulpit quite effectively. His October 1993 speech to black ministers, which asked whether civil rights leader Martin Luther King Jr. would be happy with what he would see today, was a rare opportunity for a president to raise controversial issues with a black audience. During 1995 and 1996 he sought to address a "values agenda" which emphasized family values and the importance of educational achievement in positive ways. As time went on, he found that use of an extemporaneous style allowed him to capitalize on his empathetic qualities and that speeches presented in that style were better received.

But despite his attempts to improve on his public leadership, Clinton was handicapped in several ways. From the start, he was confronted with greater hostility from segments of the media and the electorate than any president since Richard Nixon Conservative talk show hosts such as Rush Limbaugh subjected their audiences to an ongoing barrage of character attacks on Clinton and his family. His critics spent large sums of money as they perpetuated stories about him, often drawn from harsh Clinton critics back in Arkansas. Moreover, the mainstream newspapers, including the *New York Times,* seemed to be slanting their coverage of Whitewater stories beyond the factual merit of the story.[18]

And it did not stop there; Clinton contributed to his own problems. His decision to tell only part of the story on his draft deferment made voters suspicious. Then, once in the White House, he tended to provide information reluctantly when charges were leveled at him and the first lady over the firing of White House Travel Office officials and the manner in which the FBI files of several hundred Republicans came into White House hands. As a result, the public often did not believe a president it was not sure it could trust. Yet a more disciplined approach to his speeches and his move to the center during 1995–1996 contributed to a rise in popularity—in fact, to a level unusually high for a president in his fourth year in office.

Congressional Relations

President Clinton sought to achieve legislative victories through both his own efforts and an effective White House organization. In addition to the traditional legislative liaison structure, Clinton enlisted his chiefs of staff, especially Leon Panetta, in paving the way for congressional passage of favored bills. The administration's most innovative device was the "war room" which coordinated actions between its legislative liaison and public liaison segments. This arrangement was modeled in part on the Clinton campaign's effective swift response mechanism. The war room was used most notably with the deficit-reduction fight and the battle over NAFTA in 1993 and the campaign for health care reform in 1994.

Congressional relations also consumed considerable presidential time and energy. Shortly after his election Clinton initiated a series of meetings with legislators, and, in preparation, learned the names of many of them. In setting up routine leadership meetings, he was surprised to learn how seldom President Jimmy Carter had met with members of Congress; he wanted to meet with them more frequently, he said. He also was a frequent visitor to Capitol Hill, and called individual legislators often—even when he was halfway around the world. Treasury Secretary Lloyd Bentsen judged Clinton to be the most legislatively active of the eight presidents he had observed during his lengthy career in Washington.

Clinton, hoping for a Reagan-like first year, pushed some issues just as his administration was out of the gate. Acting on the assurances of widespread party support he had received from Democratic leaders in early meetings held in Little Rock, the president sought partisan coalitions in 1993. But he faced an uphill struggle. Congress was increasingly partisan, and the Republican minority leader had cautioned him (correctly) that there would be no Republican support for a deficit-reduction package that included a tax increase. Clinton was able, however, to put together a bipartisan coalition—the first of several—to achieve passage of NAFTA.

After the midterm election earthquake Clinton changed his position, moving to the right on several issues while periodically holding firm to shape differences between his positions and those of the Republican-controlled Congress for his reelection effort. But, in contrast to Harry Truman who faced somewhat similar circumstances, he worked hard to help pass new legislation. In his fifth year in office, after surviving reelection, he used top-level negotiations to achieve a five-year agreement for a balanced budget.

Legislative Enactments

Clinton's first term produced surprisingly big, fundamental changes in domestic policy. Despite cries of gridlock and the dramatic three-week government shutdown in late 1995, Congress passed a higher-than-average amount of major legislation, along with landmark deficit reduction in 1993 and welfare reform and telecommunications reform in 1996. According to David Mayhew, 1996 saw the passage of prominent changes in economic regulation policies, including those for agriculture, pesticides, and drinking water.[19] Conspicuously absent, however, was a health reform package bearing any resemblance to Clinton's initial proposal. Once again, the story of these enactments includes congressional as well as presidential strategies and actions.

First-Year Successes and Failures

Of the issues Clinton had promoted strongly during the fall campaign, he enjoyed one partial success and one high-profile failure. The failure came with his inability to achieve passage of an economic stimulus package in March 1993. The measure that Congress did debate was a scaled-back version of his proposed "investments" to put people back to work. It passed in the House but ran into a cohesive Republican filibuster threat in the Senate.

Observers chalked up the defeat to a changing economy, a difficult-to-defend package, and a poor selling job by Clinton, as well as problems with legislative tactics. Economically, the stronger-than-expected performance in the last three months of 1992 weakened the "dire need" argument for the program. The program itself was a catchall of favorite spending ideas rather than a few, more easily defensible commitments.[20] Clinton talked about his program in some settings but made no focused effort to sell it. With the Republicans sensing that they could successfully oppose a president with sagging voter support, the scene was set for an embarrassing presidential defeat. Minority Leader Robert Dole of Kansas mobilized the entire Republican delegation behind a filibuster threat, and Clinton had to retreat.

The first of Clinton's dramatic successes came with the narrow passage of a landmark deficit-reduction package in August. The package was central to Clinton's first-year performance as well as to the economy's subsequent upturn, perhaps explaining why, after a considerable internal struggle, the Clinton administration made deficit reduction its primary domestic policy effort in 1993. As the bill wound its way through the House, it encountered a sometimes tortured process of narrow votes with the Republicans often in unanimous opposition. The bill that finally emerged reduced the deficit by $5 billion over a five-year period through deficit-reduction steps quite similar to the plan a Democratic-controlled Congress had forced on Bush in 1990. Major provisions of the 1993 plan included: tax increases to a top rate of 36 percent for individuals with incomes over

$140,000, a top corporate rate of 35 percent, a $20.8 billion expansion of the earned income tax credit to help the working poor, a $3.5 billion provision for empowerment zones, and $55.8 billion in Medicare cuts.

When the measure reached the Senate, Clinton had to make a series of retreats from his original proposal. The most controversial item was his proposed BTU tax, opposed by senators representing the high energy-producing states. Ultimately, a simpler-to-calculate increase in the gasoline tax was imposed.

The final votes in each house were much closer and more partisan than those normally associated with landmark legislation. In trying to marshal the necessary votes, Clinton tried to increase pressure on Congress through use of a major address. When that approach failed, the politics of deficit reduction became very much an insider's game. In dealing with legislators directly, Clinton spent considerable personal time and mobilized key figures in his administration including Chief of Staff Mack McLarty. In the House, first-year member Marjorie Margolies-Mezvinsky, D-Pa., reluctantly agreed to vote for the plan only if her vote was absolutely necessary to obtain a majority. Republicans greeted her aye with cries of "Bye-bye, Marjorie." In the Senate, Democrat Robert Kerrey of Nebraska balked until the last minute, saying the plan did not go far enough. Ultimately, however, he voted for the bill. Thus Clinton was able to narrowly avoid what many felt would have been a devastating defeat for a first-year president as he succeeded with a major deficit-reduction proposal.[21]

Clinton also enjoyed considerable success with measures long on the congressional agenda. He contributed to their passage to varying degrees, but was aided, no doubt, by the fact that his Republican predecessor had opposed several of the measures, adding to their promise.

Passage of the Family and Medical Leave Act during Clinton's first weeks in office nicely illustrated the advantages of a promising measure.[22] This legislation required employers to provide leave (but not pay) for new mothers and any employees facing demanding family medical matters. Paralleling efforts in California, the first federal legislation was introduced in 1985. After an acrimonious few years, the measure was passed in 1990 but vetoed by Bush. A resounding 390-vote veto override in the House proved the measure's popularity there, but it fell four votes short of the two-thirds override requirement in the Senate. A similar pattern of successful presidential vetoes followed in the next two sessions of Congress.

From the earliest days of his primary campaign Clinton had spoken out forcefully about the family medical leave legislation and had emphasized that he, in contrast to Bush, would be willing to sign the new legislation promptly once in office. This was an easy bill for him to support and helped to strengthen his ties with a supporting coalition that included advocates such as Marian Wright Edelman, the head of the Children's Defense Fund and a longtime political ally of Hillary Rodham Clinton.

The "motor voter" bill, which allowed citizens to register to vote at state motor vehicle departments, proved to be a considerably more difficult measure to push than medical leave legislation. It too had been debated for several years but with considerable Republican resistance. Yet the Clinton administration pushed quite hard for this measure and was instrumental in engineering final compromises that allayed some Republican fears and facilitated passage.

Clinton played his strongest role in successfully promoting legislation providing for a new system of national service known as AmeriCorps.[23] Clinton's emphasis on a service program in his first year paralleled FDR's promotion of the Civilian Conservation Corps and John Kennedy's success in establishing the Peace Corps. Clinton found the concept of a national service program appealing and highly popular on the campaign trail; it could serve as a vehicle for new community activities that crossed racial and class lines. Thus once in office he recruited two legislative staffers to write the legislation and placed veteran staffer Eli Segal in charge of promotion. The president also helped to search for votes when the program ran into resistance in Congress. The program that finally emerged was far smaller than Clinton had originally envisioned but kept its basic philosophy: participants (seventeen years and older with a high school or equivalent degree) would receive education awards for their part-time or full-time work in community programs. The legislation called for an allocation of $300 million in 1994 and $700 million by 1996, with participants receiving awards of slightly under $5,000 a year.

Mounting Difficulties in 1994

Clinton's relationship with Congress soured in 1994 as he suffered from one embarrassing near-defeat and then the total collapse of his health policy initiative. The near-defeat came on a crime bill designed to show he was a "New Democrat" devoted to law enforcement. It called for, among other things, funding to hire 100,000 new police officers. In the House, where there were underlying cleavages on issues such as an assault weapons ban and differing views of prevention programs (typical pork barrel goodies, some thought), coalitions formed on the left and on the right, effectively preventing, through a procedural vote, final consideration of the bill. Chief of Staff Leon Panetta worked virtually around the clock to find solutions that would keep enough factions happy to produce majority support. In the end, the attractiveness of passing a crime bill in an election year prevailed.

The defining event of Clinton's second year in office was the total defeat of his proposed Health Security Act.[24] Public expectations were high at the outset because majorities expected that significant reform would occur. Those expectations were somewhat unrealistic, however, in the face of likely resistance to any specific plan and the difficulties inherent in trying to achieve landmark reform. In retrospect, the one instance in which a president succeeded in dramatically expanding health care coverage was Lyndon Johnson's Medicare proposal in 1965, but Johnson enjoyed a distinctly high opportunity level.

The defeat of Clinton's proposal has been attributed to many different factors.[25] Prior to his election, Clinton had basically committed himself to a new approach to health care reform called "managed competition." He felt that his approach—an effort to control market pressures in the health field—along with employer mandates, would achieve universal coverage while also dealing with the rapidly escalating cost of the nation's health care. Although he was later criticized for a plan to "take over one-seventh of the nation's economy," he was in fact seeking a middle way that avoided the taxation and control mechanisms found in the Canadian health care system, which some were advocating. Unfortunately, this objective ultimately produced an overly elaborate plan that was difficult to explain.

In early 1993 the Task Force on National Health Reform under the leadership of Hillary Rodham Clinton and Ira Magaziner began its work. Its elaborate system of consultation, involving over five hundred experts in various fields, drew criticism, although a smaller group always made the actual decisions. The task group contacted various interest groups and members of Congress, but many of those contacted felt they should be more centrally involved. It also tried to have the outlines of a plan approved in the budget reconciliation process (as Ronald Reagan had done with his economic program in early 1981), but key members of Congress objected. In retrospect, as Jimmy Carter had found in 1977, it was a risky strategy to try to seek a new policy for health care combined with a fast start. The repeated deadlocks in Congress on health issues and the lack of willingness on the part of key committee members to proceed from a skeleton proposal seemed to suggest that the administration needed to develop a new approach. Meanwhile, health policy specialists were pointing out that piecemeal changes in the health care system almost inevitably produced unfortunate adjustments in other aspects of the system. For example, hospitals faced with reduced payments from government programs tend to shift costs to patients covered by private insurance.

Another factor contributing to the defeat of the Health Security Act was its ineffective public promotion by the White House. Clinton was distracted in the fall of 1993, first with NAFTA and then with foreign policy issues. His White House also seemed poorly organized to actually develop the support campaign outlined by the task force. In seeking a message to support the campaign, the White House relied on marketing approaches and simple slogans. Staffers decided from polling results, for example, that "managed competition" sounded too much like the often unpopular "managed care" approach using health maintenance organizations, and the phrase was dropped. Promotions emphasized benefits but did little to explain the mechanisms involved.

With the public unable to understand exactly what changes were being proposed, the Health Security Act became vulnerable to the well-orchestrated opposition campaign that quickly emerged. The Health Insurance Association of America, representing insurance companies that had a large stake in seeing the Health Security Act defeated, began running a series of "Harry and Louise" TV spots showing a middle-aged couple gradually having doubts about the Clinton plan as they discussed it over their dinner table. One dialogue went like this:

> Louise: "This plan forces us to buy our insurance through those new mandatory government health alliances."
> Harry: "Run by tens of thousands of new bureaucrats."
> Louise: "Another billion-dollar bureaucracy."

Republicans also joined the cause through legislative channels. Rep. Dick Armey of Texas displayed a diagram of the Clinton plan that consisted of a large, unintelligible maze of boxes and arrows. By early December Republican strategist William Kristol had begun to urge party members to speak out against a plan that could become a major new entitlement and fundamentally expand support for the Democratic Party.

The uneven public relations battle was won by opponents of the Health Security Act. From strong majority support in the early fall of 1993, support fell to 52 percent by January 1994 and the negatives were up sharply.

Support by seniors seemed to be collapsing. By March, for the first time, more people opposed the plan than supported it. By July only 43 percent supported Clinton's proposal; 47 percent opposed. it Along with his weak public relations effort, Clinton was hurt by his own falling popularity as the controversial Whitewater land deal became a hot political topic.

Had President Clinton started sooner in 1993, submitted a smaller package in a more timely fashion, and enjoyed greater popularity, he might have succeeded in achieving passage of some legislation. He certainly showed no lack of willingness to compromise, however, as difficulties mounted. But the passage of smaller measures was complicated in part by the sobering estimates of the costs of the proposals being considered by conservative Democrats and Republicans. Perhaps more centrally, efforts at compromise proved impossible as Republicans increasingly (and correctly) sensed that a complete rout of Clinton on the health issue would be an advantage rather than a liability in the midterm elections.

Clinton also faced defeats in the areas of campaign finance reform and welfare reform. Campaign finance reform was subjected to the traditional partisan divisions and did not appear to be high on the president's wish list. An interagency task force that included several highly regarded students of welfare policy developed Clinton's welfare reform proposals. The task force struggled, however. While the goal of moving recipients off the welfare rolls and into the ranks of the employed was highly commendable, the associated costs of child support and additional job training could make those efforts more expensive than simply leaving people on welfare. In the face of these underlying conflicts, the task force produced no legislation in 1994.

1995–1996

The 104th Congress began with an unprecedented effort by Republicans and House Speaker Newt Gingrich to control the congressional agenda by pushing a series of measures—the "Contract with America"—popularized during the fall campaign. A majority of the ten Republican measures were passed by the House, but they faced tougher sledding in the Senate. In 1995 major legislation in the form of a Congressional Responsibility Act requiring that laws applying elsewhere also apply to Congress, a curb on unfunded mandates to the states, and restrictions on stockholder lawsuits against securities firms (over Clinton's veto) could be traced to early Republican initiatives.

But the central battle shaping relations between Clinton and the 104th Congress came over Republican plans for a balanced budget to be achieved in seven years.[26] The Republican proposals called for cuts in both taxes and spending, thereby fulfilling Republican desires to reduce the size of the federal government. Because the GOP also wanted to see a moderate increase in defense spending and sought to avoid addressing Social Security issues, the proposed cuts inevitably centered on discretionary programs and two rapidly growing health care entitlement programs—Medicare for the elderly and Medicaid for segments of the poor. Of the proposed cuts of between $900 billion and $1 trillion over seven years, between $250 and $300 billion were to come from reductions in projected Medicare spending. Along with saving money, the proposed reductions in future spending also fulfilled the ideological commitment of many Republicans toward a fundamental redirection of Medicare away from its entitlement basis.

On that note, the game of "chicken" between the two branches of government began. Clinton refused to accept Republican proposals even as the government had to shut down twice for lack of appropriations, including a seventeen-day period from mid-December 1995 to early January 1996. Clinton's standard defense of his opposition to the Republican plan was that the proposed tax cuts rewarded the wealthiest Americans while taking excessive bites out of Medicare, Medicaid, and environmental programs. The similarity between the size of the tax cut and the reductions in future Medicare spending also exposed an obvious vulnerability in the plan: one could argue that Medicare was being cut to give tax breaks to the wealthy. As top-level negotiations proceeded at length, Clinton and his aides continued to resist Republican overtures even as Republican leaders realized that they were losing the battle for public opinion. After negotiations on a seven-year agreement collapsed in January 1996, single-year appropriations to restore government operations were approved. Then, in an effort to strengthen his bargaining position for decisions on the 1997 budget, Clinton put forward his own plan for a balanced budget to be achieved within seven years. This proposal made smaller cuts in Medicare and Medicaid and contained fewer tax cuts. But further action would have to await the outcome of the 1996 elections.

Republican forces in Congress had greater success with the enactment of landmark welfare reform legislation. In 1992, while campaigning, Clinton had articulated widespread public disapproval of the existing Aid to Families with Dependent Children (AFDC) program with a pledge to "end welfare as we know it." The presidential task force that had looked at welfare reform in 1993 had stressed job training and child care along with time limits for receiving AFDC benefits. But it had failed to bring forth any concrete proposals in 1994 as relations between Clinton and Congress deteriorated.

The Republican proposals that emerged in the 104th Congress paid less attention to transitional support and placed a greater emphasis on time limits. One version also eliminated Medicaid in favor of less-comprehensive, state-determined programs. Two Clinton vetoes, however, succeeded in derailing those Republican initiatives.

Republican strategists then designed a welfare reform bill that presented Clinton with a difficult choice. In part because federal AFDC costs were minor, the next welfare reform bill focused substantially on eliminating aid to legal immigrants to achieve the projected savings of $54 billion over five years. (The other major savings was in tighter eligibility requirements for food stamps.) Clinton expressed reservations about these provisions but also indicated his relief that Medicaid would be retained. As for AFDC, it was eliminated, and states were to receive funds to design their own programs for moving people from welfare to the workforce. Other provisions called for penalizing states unable to meet targets and for moving welfare recipients from the welfare rolls within two years.

This bill emerged as Congress was getting ready for its August recess. The Clinton administration was split in its views. Secretary of Labor Robert Reich, Treasury Secretary Robert Rubin, and some aides such as George Stephanopoulos and those who had worked on Clinton's earlier proposals favored a veto. Political adviser Dick Morris and others strongly opposed a veto. In the end, Clinton indicated his displeasure with the bill, especially with the provisions pertaining to legal immigrants, but signaled his willingness to sign the measure. It then passed easily in both houses when Democrats in each body split evenly in their support or opposition. Clinton's campaign rhetoric about ending welfare thus led to welfare reform but in a far different manner than he had initially envisioned.

Other major legislation emerged from a variety of influences. One surprise was the passage of an increase in the minimum wage. Clinton had promoted an adjustment in the minimum wage in his State of the Union address, and Senate Democrats had managed to keep the issue on the front burner. When Mississippi senator Trent Lott replaced Robert Dole as majority leader in 1996, he decided to facilitate passage in return for opportunities to move legislation in several other areas. Republicans in the House were able to add a lower training wage, but many were reluctant to stand against the minimum wage in an election year and passage came with surprising ease.

Clinton also enthusiastically supported efforts to achieve modest health care reform. Senators Edward Kennedy, D-Mass., and Nancy Kassenbaum, R-Kans., successfully eliminated the "job lock" by allowing employees to take their health insurance with them when they moved from one employer to another.

The 1997 Balanced Budget Agreement

In the spring of 1997 top-level negotiators finally met the elusive goal of a five-year balanced budget agreement. White House chief of staff Erskine Bowles led administration negotiators. Several factors figured prominently in this achievement. First, a booming economy had eased budget pressures enormously. Second, each side realized that with the continuation of divided government they could not achieve a more complete victory in the foreseeable future. Third, Republicans were less anxious to pursue fundamental changes in Medicare, and the White House was willing to go along with reductions in expenditures that were focused primarily on providers such as hospitals and physicians. Quite centrally, however, it was the improving economy that made it possible for each side to achieve many of its prized goals. Republicans were delighted with the projected tax cuts, and Clinton was pleased to see opportunities for some new spending.

Clinton and Congress

In his first term Clinton was able to exert some influence in shaping and promoting domestic legislation such as deficit reduction, a national service program, and the Family and Medical Leave Act. With the onset of the 104th Congress, he successfully resisted aspects of the seven-year balanced budget agreement passed by Republican majorities and made some contributions to the productive session in 1996. To some extent, the perceptions of failure in areas such as health care and campaign finance reform were the result of his large agenda.

Perhaps the most surprising aspect of Clinton's first term was the scope of legislation that did emerge despite divided government and complaints of gridlock. Many factors beyond Clinton's agenda-setting contributed to this achievement. Among other things, the Republicans in Congress added salience to a variety of issues, and the dynamics of interest group politics in several areas facilitated significant policy changes.

An Assessment

The first seven years of Clinton's presidency produced most notably the related phenomena of a reduction in federal deficits and a strong economy. Clinton could claim some credit for each. On deficit reduction, he changed course in 1993 and made reducing the deficit his primary emphasis. In fact, because of the impact of the decisions made in 1990 and the five-year package adopted in 1993 he was able to fulfill his campaign commitment of cutting the deficit in half in his first term and actually surpassed his goal as the 1996 figure shrunk to slightly over $100 billion rather than the earlier projection of $300 billion. The agreements reached in 1997 promised a balanced budget by 2002.

The strong economy stemmed in part from Clinton's efforts, using policy tools that differed from those stressed in the 1992 campaign. Deficit reduction was central because lower deficits created greater confidence in the bond markets and lower interest rates. The lower rates, in turn, helped to generate additional demand in the economy without reigniting inflationary pressures. The results were impressive, with unemployment at just under 5 percent (the lowest level in twenty-five years), growth figures consistently in the 3 percent range, and inflation rates also in the 3 percent range.

Federal Reserve Board chairman Alan Greenspan was hailed by many critics for his astute leadership on monetary policy, but some also pointed out that Greenspan's willingness to reduce interest rates was closely related to the fact that deficit reduction was making inflation a less likely problem. The bond market similarly reflected that confidence. Economic forces were at work as well, including the impact of corporate downsizing. While painful to individuals in previous years, those steps nonetheless made American corporations more competitive in the global economy during Clinton's years in the White House.

Of the surprisingly large number of landmark measures enacted on Clinton's watch, arguably the most dramatic was welfare reform, but Clinton could claim some credit for other measures as well. Perhaps the most popular major new legislation was the Family and Medical Leave Act. After 1993, as the political climate changed, Clinton began to pursue small-scale efforts that used federal initiatives in an attempt to leverage efforts by others. In taking these steps he was more active than Bush had been, but eventually, like Bush, he emphasized the pursuit of multiple, smaller programs to a surprising degree. This emphasis was especially evident in his approaches to education policy, where the little chance of new spending led the president to promote standards and other small initiatives.

Overall, President Clinton's performance in relationship to his circumstances warrants both credit and criticism. Given the constraints on domestic initiatives he inherited, he did not miss an opportunity for passing bold new programs, relying on a strong role for the federal government. And, given the Republican surge in 1994, he also can be credited with considerable skill in engineering his own reelection. A less-skilled president or one who refused to modify positions might well have gone down with the ship. He also was able to preserve many service programs that Republicans had hoped to cut or eliminate.

In several other respects, however, Clinton's performance was less impressive. His stormy first two years was one of the factors behind the Republican surge in the midterm elections. In fact, his Health Security Act became an easy target.[27] He also helped to create the forces that produced his marked movement toward a far more conservative interpretation of the political center. Indeed, critics such as former welfare policy analyst Peter Edelman argue that on issues such as welfare reform Clinton undercut progressive policy positions by being too willing to move toward Republican positions. Even worse, on welfare reform Clinton acted despite the availability of opinion polls showing that a decision for or against the proposed revision would have little impact on his support in the fall election.[28] As several of Clinton's predecessors had learned, the task of reorienting a political party during a period of uneasiness in the electorate but after a weak electoral victory is not easy. Yet in some eyes he was overly willing to move toward Republican positions. Clinton also suffered from personal flaws that called his character into question.[29]

As for presidential leadership, Clinton left a mixed legacy. His use of strategies—top-level negotiation, the bully pulpit, and the pursuit of objectives through administrative strategies and the leveraging of small programs—seemed to be modeled on the strategies of other presidents. Indeed, it seems likely that if Bush had used those strategies with comparable skill he might well have gained reelection. (Ironically, in some ways Clinton did a better job with several aspects of the Bush agenda than Bush would have done had he been reelected.)

Clinton's impact on the presidency itself was nevertheless blemished. To some extent, the various "xxxgates" were a function of an adversarial media and an unusually intense group of Clinton-haters. Yet Clinton's tendency to dissemble in the face of accusations also contributed to a climate of distrust. Sadly, the result of that combustible mixture was a decline in the stature of the presidency itself. Clinton demeaned himself and diminished the presidency. In this context his policy successes seem even more surprising.

Notes

1. On Clinton's early life, see David Maraniss, *First in His Class: A Biography of Bill Clinton* (New York: Simon and Schuster, 1995); and Martin Walker, *The President We Deserve: Bill Clinton, His Rise, Falls, and Comebacks* (New York: Crown, 1996).

2. On Clinton as governor, see John Brummett, *Highwire: From the Backroads to the Beltway—The Education of Bill Clinton* (New York: Hyperion, 1994); Diane D. Blair, *Arkansas Government and Politics: Do the People Rule?* (Lincoln: University of Nebraska Press, 1988); and Meredith L. Oakley, *On The Make: The Rise of Bill Clinton* (Washington, D.C.: Regnery Publishing, 1994).

3. Maraniss, *First in His Class*, 442.

4. On psychological characteristics, see Stanley A. Renshon, *High Hopes: The Clinton Presidency and the Politics of Ambition* (New York: New York University Press, 1996); and, by the same author, *The Psychological Assessment of Presidential Candidates* (New York: New York University Press, 1996).

5. Renshon, *Psychological Assessment*, 261–262.

6. Brummett, *Highwire*, 8.

7. Arthur M. Schlesinger Jr., "Rating the President," *American Politics Quarterly* 12 (summer 1997): 188.

8. Theda Skocpol, *Boomerang: Clinton's Health Security Effort and the Turn against Government in U.S. Politics*(New York: Norton, 1996), 78.

9. Shirley Anne Warshaw, *Powersharing: White House–Cabinet Relations in the Modern Presidency* (Albany: State University of New York Press, 1996), 205–206.

10. Thomas E. Cronin and Michael A. Genovese, *The Paradoxes of the American Presidency* (New York: Oxford University Press, 1998), chap. 10; and James W. Davis, *The American Presidency* (Westport, Conn.: Praeger, 1995).

11. George Edwards III, "Frustration and Folly: Bill Clinton and the Public Presidency," in *The Clinton Presidency: First Appraisals,* ed. Colin Campbell and Bert A. Rockman (Chatham, N.J.: Chatham House, 1996), 234.

12. See Elizabeth Drew, *On the Edge: The Clinton Presidency* (New York: Simon and Schuster, 1994); and Bob Woodward, *The Agenda: Inside the Clinton White House* (New York: Simon and Schuster, 1994).

13. Drew, *On the Edge*, 34.

14. Jonathan Weisman, "True Impact of GOP Congress Reaches Well Beyond Bill," *Congressional Quarterly Weekly Report,* September 7, 1996, 2515–2520.

15. Walker, *President We Deserve,* 202.

16. Edwards, "Frustration and Folly," 239.

17. Craig Allen Smith, " 'Rough Stretches and Honest Disagreements': Is Bill Clinton Redefining the Rhetorical Presidency?" in *The Clinton Presidency: Images, Issues, and Communication Strategies,* ed. Robert E. Denton Jr. and Rachel L. Holloway (Westport, Conn.: Praeger, 1996), 239.

18. Gene Lyons, *Fools for Scandal: How the Media Invented Whitewater* (New York: Franklin Square Press, 1996).

19. David Mayhew, "Important Laws, 1995-96," personal communication, January 9, 1997.

20. Robert B. Reich, *Locked in the Cabinet* (New York: Knopf, 1997).

21. Richard Cohen, *Changing Courses in Washington: Clinton and the New Congress* (New York: Macmillan, 1992).

22. The long gestation of this legislation is effectively traced in Ronald D. Elving, *Conflict and Compromise: How Congress Makes the Law* (New York: Simon and Schuster, 1995).

23. Steven Waldman, *The Bill* (New York: Viking, 1996).

24. Useful studies on this legislative failure include Haynes Johnson and David S. Broder, *The System: The American Way of Politics at the Breaking Point* (Boston: Little, Brown, 1996); and Skocpol, *Boomerang.*

25. For a longer review of these issues, see William W. Lammers, "Presidential Leadership and Policy," in *Health Politics and Policy,* 3d ed., ed. Theodore J. Litman and Leonard Robins (Albany, N.Y.: Delmar Publishers, 1997), chap. 5.

26. On this controversy, see Elizabeth Drew, *Showdown: The Struggle between the Gingrich Congress and the Clinton White House* (New York: Simon and Schuster, 1997); and George Hager and Eric Pianin, *Mirage: Why neither Democrats nor Republicans Can Balance the Budget, End the Deficit, and Satisfy the Public* (New York: Random House, 1997).

27. Skocpol, *Boomerang,* xiv.

28. Peter Edelman, "The Worst Thing Bill Clinton Has Done," *Atlantic Monthly,* March 1997, 44.

29. Thomas E. Cronin and Michael A. Genovese, "President Clinton and Character Questions," *Presidential Studies Quarterly* 28 (fall 1998): 892–897.

Conclusion

We give the President more work than a man can do, more responsibility than a man can take, more pressure than a man can bear.

—NOVELIST JOHN STEINBECK

12

Opportunities, Challenges, and Skills
Comparing the Presidents

NOT ALL presidencies are "created equal." And yet the demands and expectations we impose on our presidents set unusually high standards for performance. A review of landmark enactments dramatically underscores the extent to which some presidents have had far greater opportunities than others to contribute to fundamental changes in domestic policy. Moreover, some presidents have used their political opportunities effectively, while others have played their hands rather poorly. A comparison of presidents also reveals that they have varied considerably in their leadership styles, strategies, and skills.

What do these findings say about the future of the presidency? Many historians and political scientists believe presidents who served in the mid-twentieth century generally produced stronger performances than more recent presidents. What does that judgment hold for twenty-first century presidents? This chapter looks at these questions and at what strategies might work most effectively for future presidents and what roles those presidents might best fulfill.

Landmark Enactments

Landmark enactments provide important insights into both presidential leadership and the role of Congress (see Table 12–1). In fact, a look at the distribution of landmark enactments since 1932 demonstrates that the circumstances engulfing any one presidency do indeed have a big impact

TABLE 12-1 Landmark Policy Enactments, 1933-1997

Legislation	Policy-Making Process
ROOSEVELT	
Agricultural Adjustment Act (1933) (modified in 1936)	Presidential coalition building by use of multiple components
Banking Act (1933)	Strong roles by legislative specialists; deposit insurance accepted reluctantly by president
Establishment, Securities and Exchange Commission (1934)	Presidential proposal; shared roles amid strong public support
Establishment, Federal Communications Commission (1934)	Presidential proposal; legislative modification of final provisions
National Housing Act (1934)	Presidential proposal; strong public support; legislative specialist modified some provisions
Social Security Act (1935)	Strong presidential leadership; southern Democrats reduced some provisions
Establishment, National Labor Relations Board. Wagner Act (1935)	No direct presidential role; legislatively driven measure
Fair Labor Standards Act (1938)	Presidential support; considerable legislative leadership
G.I. Bill of Rights (1944)	Presidential promotion; congressional development of specific provisions
TRUMAN	
Employment Act (1946)	Presidential support; extensive interest group and legislative bargaining
Taft-Hartley Act (1947)	Passed over Truman veto
Housing Act (1950)	Presidential initiative; considerable legislative involvement
EISENHOWER	
Civil Rights Act (1957)	Limited presidential leadership; primarily a legislative compromise

TABLE 12–1 *(continued)*

Legislation	Policy-Making Process
JOHNSON	
Civil Rights Act (1964)	Strong presidential support; key roles played by Senate party leaders
Economic Opportunity Act (1964)	Dominant presidential role
Tax cut (1964)	Strong presidential roles in 1963 and 1964; bargaining with revenue committee chairs
Federal Aid to Education (1965)	President-led bargaining with interest groups and a new policy design
Medicare and Medicaid (1965)	Presidential support building, 1962–1965; program expansion by House Ways and Means Committee; presidential intervention in the Senate to avoid derailment
Voting Rights Act (1965)	Strong presidential address; easy passage in response to exposure of continuing violations
Open Housing Act (1968)	Shared presidential and congressional roles
REAGAN	
Economic Recovery Tax Act (1981)	Very effective presidential fast start and "going public" strategies; extensive legislative bargaining
Spending reductions (OBRA 81)	Same as above
Tax Reform Act (1986)	Initial presidential proposal; significant legislative contributions in committee compromises and coalition building
BUSH	
Deficit reduction (1990)	Top-level negotiation; Congress dominant in final stages
CLINTON	
Deficit-reduction package (1993)	Narrow presidential success with a partisan coalition; major legislative modification of final provisions
Welfare reform (1996)	Initial advocacy by president; major congressional initiative during 1995–1996; some modifications after presidential vetoes
Telecommunications reform (1996)	Limited advocacy by president; extensive legislative maneuvering among key interest groups
Balanced budget agreement (1997)	Result of top-level negotiation

on policy outcomes. From 1933 to 1935 the extraordinary circumstances confronting President Franklin Roosevelt (along with his skills) produced seven landmark enactments. Some thirty years later, during the unusual period of John Kennedy's martyrdom in 1964, Lyndon Johnson oversaw passage of three landmark pieces of legislation, and three landmark bills were passed during his peak opportunity in 1965. Two of the three landmark bills passed on Ronald Reagan's watch occurred during his big opportunity in 1981. Thus just over half of the twenty-eight landmark enactments passed after 1932 occurred during the brief periods in which presidents were experiencing distinctly high opportunity levels.

But skills and strategies do matter. Specific strategy choices were evident in several of the high-opportunity situations. They included fast starts in 1933, 1964–1965, and 1981, a third-year shift in 1935, and coalition-building strategies such as the use of broad omnibus bills to maximize support. As the head-to-head comparisons later in this chapter will reveal, the high-opportunity presidents all possessed some impressive political skills that helped them to achieve legislative enactments even though they differed in their range of skills.

This being said, strong presidential leadership and high opportunities are not the only sources of landmark legislation. During periods in which presidents enjoy high opportunities, those same opportunities are likely to be affecting the work of Congress, much like the impact of an activist public mood or a surge in the number of new legislators committed to policy change. For example, as the "First Hundred Days" session was drawing to a close in 1933, FDR would have liked to see the Banking Act delayed until 1934—he personally opposed its provision for deposit insurance. Yet he ultimately accepted the insurance provision, as he agreed to sign the legislation once it passed in 1933. Perhaps more remarkably, in 1935 Congress passed the Wagner Act with its basic guarantees of union organizing rights even as Roosevelt was debating whether he should indicate support for the measure. (For examples of other instances in which members of Congress performed significant policy-making roles, including at several points at which presidents were enjoying high-opportunity levels, see Table 12–1).

A second path to landmark legislation also underscores the importance of Congress. When presidents have not been in influential positions, the primary responsibility for landmark legislation often has shifted to Capitol Hill. This occurred quite notably with the Taft-Hartley Act in 1947, environmental legislation in the 1970s, deficit reduction in 1990, and welfare reform in 1996. Bush contributed to the 1990 legislation by initially agreeing to top-level negotiations and then abandoning his opposition to a tax increase, and Clinton helped to give welfare reform greater prominence with his campaign pledge in 1992 to "end welfare as we know it." Yet in each case the legislative role was predominant in the maneuvering that produced the final legislation.

Within Congress, the size of a president's majority (if there is one) is important to the president's ability to achieve passage of landmark bills. Just how much "skill" did LBJ have to exercise to get his huge majority to support his proposals? Conceivably, Johnson could have lost dozens of votes from his own party and still won passage of legislation.

An electoral mandate (as soft a concept as that may be) also can matter. Ronald Reagan was able to claim a mandate on a few key issues in 1981, which clearly helped him to persuade some members of Congress to support his proposals.

Other conclusions about the president and landmark legislation emerge from the actual patterns of enactments. For example, fundamental changes in policy are somewhat more likely to occur in the first year for a new president and during the first term of two-term presidents. Two landmark enactments were passed during Roosevelt's first year, six during Johnson's (he had two "first years," in 1964 and 1965), two during Reagan's, and one during Bill Clinton's. Depending on whether Johnson experienced the dynamic of a first year in one or both of his years in office, the portion of all first-year enactments is 29 or 39 percent. The first-term tendency is far more pronounced. Presidential tenures extending to second or third terms (FDR) constitute slightly over 60 percent of all the years studied, but only six of the twenty-eight landmark measures listed in Table 12–1—about 20 percent—were enacted after a president's first four years in office.

United rather than divided party control of Congress and the presidency takes on greater importance for landmark legislation than for the broader category of major legislation used in David Mayhew's analysis (see Chapter 1). One of the central reasons why divided government can produce major legislation was evident in 1996, when the Republican-controlled Congress and President Clinton both concluded that compromises to achieve some new policy commitments prior to the fall elections were mutually beneficial. Although landmark welfare legislation also was achieved in 1996, it generally has been more difficult to pass under conditions of divided government. Among the landmark cases, only about a third (nine of twenty-eight) were passed with divided government even though government was divided some 44 percent of the time.

Finally, the frequent observation in this book that both a president's opportunity levels and political skills can make a difference in achieving landmark legislation is just as important in thinking about the moderate- and low-opportunity presidents as in thinking about the high-opportunity presidents whose political skills also varied. Given their more limited opportunity levels, it should not be surprising that the achievements of the moderate- and low-opportunity presidents were fewer than those of the high-opportunity presidents. Where enactments did occur during their time in office, special attention should be paid to the ways they may have played at least significant supporting roles in the legislative dynamics, which sometimes are dominated by congressional leaders.

Comparing Leadership Styles

Presidents' leadership styles stem from their diverse personal characteristics, career paths, perceptions of the failings of their predecessors, and often distinctive views of the president they seek to emulate. Their readings of their level of opportunity also may have an impact, as well as their party affiliation (for a summary of predominant leadership styles and strategies, see Table 12–2).

In fact, leadership orientations show decided party differences. Democratic presidents have tended to be activists. Roosevelt epitomized this role, and both Harry Truman and John Kennedy often sought to emulate FDR's style. Both Jimmy Carter and Bill Clinton showed similar tendencies, at least in the early stages of their administrations, despite the fact that their circumstances made any assertion of FDR-type activism difficult. The Republicans displayed greater variation. Reagan took an activist view of his leadership in his first year, but in some respects he was a "hands off" managerial president who gazed approvingly at the White House portrait of Calvin Coolidge, a president who believed in leaving things alone as much as possible. Richard Nixon too believed in strong presidential leadership and in some ways was more assertive in leadership style than Reagan. Dwight Eisenhower and George Bush had more limited views, and, of the two, Eisenhower was more concerned with the importance of behind-the-scenes leadership.

In decision-making processes, Democratic presidents generally have been more interested in finding new policies to promote; Republican pres-

TABLE 12-2 Presidential Leadership Styles and Strategies, 1933–1997

General Orientation	Approach to Decision Making	Public Leadership	Congressional Leadership	Administrative Strategies
ROOSEVELT				
Pursue a strong role on all leadership dimensions	Undertake an aggressive search for policy ideas from many sources Operate a president-centered process	Develop an optimistic persona Use fireside chats to reassure and build support for a general legislative agenda Use press conferences to shape issues and set agenda	Undertake a strong agenda-setting role Build coalitions with broad proposals Vigorously pursue fast-start and third-year shift strategies	Emphasize experimentation Shape policies extensively
TRUMAN				
Speak for the nation Act decisively	Try to do "the right thing" Pay limited attention to opinion polls	Make periodic use of strong addresses Do not worry about personal image	State a broad agenda Use the veto power aggressively Shape positions to "run against Congress" in 1948	Be willing to take strong action Desegregate armed services by executive order
EISENHOWER				
Defend the dignity of the office Use potential influence cautiously	Develop proposals in a deliberative manner Seek middle-of-the-road positions	Develop a friendly, optimistic persona Use public appeals in a selective, focused manner	Pursue a limited agenda Seek support through conciliation	Prune some New Deal programs

continued

TABLE 12–2 *(continued)*

General Orientation	Approach to Decision Making	Public Leadership	Congressional Leadership	Administrative Strategies
KENNEDY Seek heroic leadership role	Adopt strong staff roles Take pragmatic positions Occasionally take bold action	Develop personal popularity Use policy appeals cautiously Use the bully pulpit to promote individual actions.	Use normal methods but not too forcefully	Periodically take strong action
JOHNSON Be an active leader, like FDR Create a consensus by achieving "something for everyone"	Push very aggressively to develop legislative proposals Test political feasibility carefully	Try to impress the public with facts and bold new plans Manipulate the media	Use legislative knowledge to help steer legislation	Do not worry about implementation while passing legislation
NIXON Be an activist and bold planner, like Wilson	Use staff to shield oneself from conflict Seek some broad proposals Delegate many domestic policy roles Emphasize public relations values and reelection prospects in making decisions	Avoid press conferences and use skills with major addresses Appeal to "Middle America" and isolate opponents	Do the typical things the first two years and then withdraw Seek centrist coalitions	Use administrative role aggressively for reelection purposes Bring surveillance roles into White House operations

CARTER	Avoid a Nixon-like delegation system	Avoid "imperial presidency" symbols	Push a broad initial agenda	Emphasize efforts to promote efficiency and "good government"
Create a presidency that reflects the best aspects of average Americans	Get deeply involved in policy details	Talk simply to and with the American public	Do not spend a lot of time playing to the egos of legislators	
	Seek comprehensive approaches in the public interest	Do not spend a lot of time on public relations efforts and techniques	Gradually develop a more focused approach	
	Pay limited attention to political feasibility			
REAGAN	Delegate extensively and only deal with broad issues	Build a friendly, optimistic persona	Use a fast-start and strong agenda control in 1981; pursue limited involvement after 1981	Push policy change through control of appointments
Adopt early on an assertive role to achieve a longer-run reduction in the role of the federal government	Avoid losing battles	Emphasize speeches and not press conferences		
	Retreat quietly to the center when expedient	Pursue themes for media consumption carefully		
BUSH	Organize a comprehensive process	Seek to show competence and enjoyment of job with frequent press conferences	Propose a limited agenda	Pursue administrative roles for reelection purposes, 1991–1992
Use presidential power only when clearly necessary	Do not push for new initiatives	Take on public addresses very reluctantly	Attempt initial conciliatory role	
	Use only a few advisers on key decisions		Veto extensively	
CLINTON	Explore options in considerable detail	Talk to the American public often, especially 1993–1994	Devote considerable time to legislation	Undertake government reorganization, 1993–1994
Use presidential power to promote a broad range of policy responses	Use fluid decision-making processes	Use major addresses extensively	Pursue partisan support, 1993–1994, then centrist coalitions, 1995–1996	Seek policy influence and visibility, 1995–1996
	Seek distinctive policy proposals			
	Follow polls with great care			

idents have tended to focus on deliberate staff processes. Among the Democrats, Roosevelt and Johnson were especially eager to find new ideas, reflecting in part their desire to maximize high opportunities. Among the Republicans, Nixon put in place energetic operations for analyzing and proposing domestic policies, while Reagan, especially after 1981, was content to conduct only a moderately aggressive search for new ideas. Bush made some efforts to unearth new policy initiatives in 1990, but stood out among presidents of both parties for his distinctively limited pursuit of new policy.

Most presidents of both parties have engaged in extensive assessments of political feasibility in their decision-making processes, even those in strong positions vis-à-vis Congress. Roosevelt, Johnson, and Reagan all consulted extensively with members of Congress. Carter was arguably the least interested in prior assessments of likely congressional reactions, especially in the early stages of his administration. When some presidents paid little attention to Congress, such as Truman on civil rights in 1948, they were primarily posturing with their programs rather than seeking to gain passage of legislation.

Differences in the use of public opinion polls in decision making owe more to the evolution of polling itself as a decision-making tool than to a pattern of party differences.[1] Roosevelt showed an immediate interest when polls emerged in the mid-1930s, yet his successor, Truman, was a reluctant user. Eisenhower showed more interest than Truman. The use of polls really took off with the introduction of new technologies in the 1960s. The White House became a veritable warehouse for stocking the latest public opinion data. President Nixon, according to one aide, studied "all kinds of polls all the time."

Jimmy Carter was not immune to the trend; Pat Caddell was the first pollster to have office space in the White House. Reagan met about once a month with pollster Richard Wirthlin, and Bush's extensive use of polls during the Gulf War was partially mirrored by his attention to factors shaping his own popularity. Clinton gave more access to pollsters in his White House operations than any other president. Moreover, he utilized overnight polling extensively in planning his reelection strategies in 1995–1996.

It is more difficult to determine the degree to which presidents have allowed public opinion data to have a direct influence on their decisions. Clinton and his aides argued that polls are used to help presidents shape their presentation of policies to the voter.[2] For example, Clinton used polls to help him find the right slogans to sell his proposed Health Security Act to the electorate.[3] It is, in fact, difficult to imagine any president being immune to information that suggests what policy choices are likely to be popular with the voters.

Public leadership strategies and levels of success have varied widely among the presidents of each party. Of the Democrats, Roosevelt possessed a remarkable array of skills and displayed an adroit use of strategies. Kennedy adapted very well to the television era, developed a highly effective persona, and delivered some well-received addresses. Truman was something of an anomaly in that he was ineffective in maintaining his popularity and lacked eloquence. But he was able to define his positions forcefully (for example, his ringing denunciation of the Taft-Hartley Act) and in ways that helped to rally his core constituencies. More recently, Carter was probably the least-skilled Democratic president as he seemed uninterested in improving his largely ineffective speaking style. Clinton, like Carter, suffered early in his presidency from a poor portrayal by the press. He did give some strong addresses but sometimes found it difficult to maintain focused themes.

Republican performances were equally varied. Reagan had the best media strategy with his use of the theme for the day and the development of his "nice guy" and "outsider" personas. His domestic selling effort was well orchestrated in 1981, but then it slackened considerably. Eisenhower also was highly successful in developing an attractive persona, in maintaining his popularity, and in his occasional efforts to support his legislative program. Bush stands in interesting contrast to Eisenhower in that they both had a limited agenda. Bush was fairly successful the first two and a half years of his administration in maintaining his popularity, but he could not adapt to changing political circumstances. Perhaps the most telling difference between Bush and Eisenhower is that Ike placed more importance on his public roles and sought professional coaching to improve. Bush, however, was reduced to mocking his own lack of public speaking skills while avoiding obvious possibilities for major addresses. Nixon made some quite successful major addresses—a fact perhaps little recognized—but they often were in the area of foreign policy. His failings were dramatic, such as his relationship with the press during his first term which became increasingly embittered, often at his own instigation.

Party-based differences do emerge when legislative leadership roles are examined more closely. For example, Democrats were more likely to engage in a fast-start strategy, reflecting in part their more robust agendas and their greater opportunities, especially in 1933 (FDR) and 1964–1965 (LBJ). Democrats with less-promising circumstances, such as Carter and Clinton, also tried to exert legislative leadership and each did succeed in achieving some second-tier legislation—for Carter, environmental legislation, and for Clinton, the Family and Medical Leave Act. Each was unsuccessful, however, with larger initiatives such as comprehensive energy legislation and health care reform. Kennedy proceeded somewhat differently. He did make a moderate first-year effort to achieve passage of federal aid to education and Medicare but focused primarily on second-tier issues such as aid to depressed areas. He was criticized for his modest effort, but in light of more recent experiences he may well have been correct in arguing that his own standing and potential for later maneuvers would not be enhanced by resounding public defeats.

With the exception of Reagan, Republican presidents approached their first year differently. Reagan proceeded much like a Democrat as he moved quickly in 1981. Nixon ultimately did produce his Family Assistance Plan (FAP), a proposal with the potential for landmark legislation, but only after he was criticized for his limited agenda. Eisenhower and Bush proceeded with more limited first-year agendas because they preferred to study possible proposals. Each had more success with Congress in their second year than in their first.

In their overall involvement with Congress, Democratic presidents varied considerably and no Republican president stood out for especially high levels of interaction. Democrats Franklin Roosevelt and Lyndon Johnson spent the most time dealing with Congress. Roosevelt often devoted several hours a day to this task, and Johnson was constantly on the telephone and saw many legislators in person. Their time commitments reflected their opportunities, but also their interest in and enjoyment of legislative relations. Efforts by other Democratic presidents were more limited. Truman and Kennedy spent only a moderate amount of time greasing the wheels on Capitol Hill, and Carter was grudging in allocating his time for legislative matters. Clinton, by contrast, spent considerable time talking to legislators in 1993 and in top-level negotiations in 1995–1996.

A look at the use of administrative strategies to pursue "good government" reveals an interesting partisan division. The seemingly plausible expectation that Republican presidents would be more interested in government efficiency is not borne out by their actions. Rather, Democrats have at times been more interested than Republicans in improving government operations, perhaps reflecting Democrats' greater interest in having an efficient bureaucracy in order to enhance programmatic goals. Among the Democrats, Truman took a strong interest in the Hoover Commission reforms, Carter was uniquely interested in efficiency issues, and Clinton promoted his vice president's efforts to streamline federal operations by "reinventing government." Roosevelt's strategies for building government were closely tied to his strategies for control of government, believing that greater White House control meant greater efficiency. Kennedy was quite skeptical of and disinterested in the federal bureaucracy.

Among the Republicans, Nixon developed the most extensive set of proposals seeking to modernize the federal government. In the wake of his reelection victory in 1972, his reorganization strategy became an obvious bid for greater presidential control as he asked for the resignations of cabinet members and envisioned a major cabinet restructuring. Nevertheless, he did display a more general interest in structural issues (such as modernization of the post office) than any of the other Republicans. Eisenhower sought to place a lid on future expansion of government agencies rather than engage in large-scale reform. Despite his extensive involvement in the federal bureaucracy and an early speech to top federal officials stressing their importance, Bush manifested little interest in "good government" issues.

In the use of administrative strategies for policy purposes, a reasonable hypothesis is that presidents who have difficulty achieving policy goals through Congress would be especially active in the administrative arena. For example, Truman circumvented Congress by issuing executive orders to desegregate the military and Nixon took steps in 1971 to establish wage and price controls. Presidents with high opportunities also found administrative strategies extremely important at times. The exception was Johnson, who spent relatively little time worrying about administrative relationships. Roosevelt, by contrast, regarded administrative strategies as an integral part of his effort to implement the New Deal. In other words, the "alphabet soup" of New Deal agencies was cooked up by a president who regarded administrative leadership as crucial to his ability to shape policy development. Reagan stands between Roosevelt and Johnson. He viewed the appointment of men and women who were committed to his desire for less regulation as an important way to change policy. He had, however, far less interest in the specifics of policy than Roosevelt.

In short, presidents have shown marked variation in their views of what the president should do, in the strategies they choose, and in their skills in handling key roles. Those differences are one of the keys to comparative assessments of overall performances.

Comparative Assessments

In the head-to-head comparisons of performance presented in this section, the presidents are grouped into the same three categories used to structure this book: high opportunity, moderate opportunity, and low opportunity. These assessments pay particular attention to the ways in which skills and strategies have helped presidents to meet challenges, use opportunities, and create broad policy legacies.

The High-Opportunity Presidents: Roosevelt, Johnson, and Reagan

Of the high-opportunity presidents, Franklin Roosevelt was the best positioned to chalk up significant achievements, but his challenges also were the most awesome. In dealing with Congress and seeking passage of his preferred legislation, his major challenge was to identify policy solutions that could command legislative support amid the vast array of possibilities being discussed. Lyndon Johnson's opportunity level also was high—in fact, it encompassed an unusually large number of promising issues—but he faced formidable challenges. The first challenge was to achieve passage of significant amounts of domestic legislation that had been stalled or that only recently had begun to move toward passage in Congress. Ronald Reagan's opportunity level was similar to Roosevelt's as it included a repudiation of the opposing party rather than a Johnson-like continuation of the dominant party's position. But his economic challenge—and thus his opportunity—was not as extensive. Reagan's challenge was to address economic problems of stagflation and unemployment while seeking to fulfill his promise to deliver a smaller federal government.

Of these three high-opportunity presidents, Roosevelt's legacy was the largest. He helped to craft a series of regulatory policies and a Social Security system that, a half-century later, remain the mainstay of domestic policy. Johnson's legacy consists of landmark legislation on critical issues such as civil rights, Medicare, and federal aid to education. Reagan's main legacy is in the form of the tax and spending cuts passed in 1981. Unlike FDR and Johnson, Reagan sought primarily to reduce the scope of domestic policy commitments rather than develop new approaches. His actions thus served to prevent the enactment of new programs in the face of mounting deficits rather than to achieve a retrenchment in federal commitments.

Leadership styles contributed to these levels of success. In developing new proposals, both Roosevelt and Johnson employed aggressive strategies that were implemented by energetic aides. Reagan mounted an intensive effort in 1981, but that effort then declined markedly. In public leadership, Roosevelt and Reagan displayed exceptional skills and built effective personas, but Johnson suffered from a public perception that he was a politician who simply could not be trusted. While Roosevelt and Reagan were highly effective in promoting a sense of optimism in difficult times, Johnson, who faced the quite thorny issues of rioting and race relations, was uniquely unsuited for a bully pulpit role as urban problems mounted during his presidency. As for "going public" to build support for new legislation, Reagan made the most sustained effort in 1981. Roosevelt was effective in his ongoing fireside chats, and Johnson correctly concluded that his primary task was to forge legislative coalitions on issues that often already commanded widespread support. Finally, in the ability of these presidents to sustain personal support, Reagan was the most successful with a consistently well-planned media strategy; Johnson was by far the least successful. Although poll findings are not available, Roosevelt in all likelihood would have fared very well in sustaining popular support.

On the legislative front, each of these presidents was successful with a fast-start strategy. Roosevelt and Johnson had broader agendas, but Reagan's performance was at least as well executed. Reagan delegated more of his legislative role than either Roosevelt or Johnson, but he did it effectively. Unlike FDR and Johnson, however, Reagan retreated after his first year, leaving legislative leaders such as Sen. Robert Dole, R-Kans., to bear the fallout from efforts to reduce the soaring deficit. Both Roosevelt and Johnson were far more active than Reagan and used many more strategies. Because Johnson was highly conscious of potential comparisons with Roosevelt's legislative performance, he may have well pushed harder to find all possible areas for enacting new legislation and to achieve greater scope in his proposals. Roosevelt was somewhat more apt than other presidents to seek centrist coalitions and pay greater attention to implementation issues.

In the administrative arena, Roosevelt surpassed both Johnson and Reagan in involvement and effective leadership. He also used the broadest range of strategies as he fostered experimentation and shaped policy without precise legislative specification. Reagan, who had the second highest level of involvement, shaped regulatory policy through control of budgets and personnel selection. But, just as in the legislative arena, his interest waned as his first term progressed. Johnson made the least use of administrative strategies. He chose to focus primarily on the passage of new legislation.

Each president's skills and strategies shaped his ability to confront challenges and utilize opportunities. Roosevelt's activism and pursuit of multiple strategies helped him to promote and facilitate extensive change. Johnson's legislative skills allowed him to effectively promote the Great Society agenda, but he was less successful in adapting to changing political circumstances even though he continued to press for new legislation. Reagan made the most of his opportunities in 1981, and he also could claim credit for effectively creating those opportunities with his election campaign. During his remaining seven years in office, however, he was something of an underachiever. He gave little encouragement to staff aides to develop new proposals that would have tested the level of possible change, and he was rather passive in dealing with Congress.

Overall, of these three presidents Roosevelt was the most skilled and most effective leader. He was at least as skilled as either Johnson or Reagan on each leadership style dimension and used an unusually broad range of strategies and tactics. Both Johnson and Reagan, by contrast, had mixed skills. Johnson was a highly capable legislator, and Reagan was uniquely gifted in the public dimensions of his leadership roles, but Johnson had glaring problems in dealing with the public, and Reagan used a limited range of political strategies and exerted considerably less overall effort than either FDR or Johnson.

The Moderate-Opportunity Presidents: Truman, Eisenhower, and Kennedy

Of the presidents who faced less than high-opportunity levels during their terms in office, Presidents Harry Truman, Dwight Eisenhower, and John Kennedy stand out as relatively strong and successful performers. Thus they surpassed the less-skillful efforts of Jimmy Carter and George Bush and the limitations displayed by Richard Nixon. Truman found himself in the most difficult situation of the three presidents. He faced imposing domestic challenges and the limitations incurred by presidents who succeeded to the office. Truman's legacy lay in his promotion of civil rights and use of administrative strategies to desegregate the armed forces. His greatest legacy, however, was in the area of foreign policy where he stood up to Soviet power in the aftermath of World War II, devised and implemented a "containment" policy to challenge Soviet expansion, developed the Marshall Plan and Truman Doctrine, and established the United States as the leader of the "free world." Truman did not have especially impressive public or legislative leadership skills, but he did have a keen sense of political strategies. He was especially skillful in engineering his election bid in 1948. Given his circumstances, then, Truman performed quite respectably.

Eisenhower had in some respects the most promising opportunities of these three presidents. The military hero, he was twice elected by a wide margin and enjoyed an unusually high level of popularity. Yet he also confronted constraints. In Congress he had to deal with a divided majority Republican coalition during his first two years and thereafter faced Democratic majorities. During his years in the White House, Eisenhower sought to prune aspects of New Deal legislation, strengthen economic capacities, and respond to the urging in many quarters that new problems, including race relations, begin to be addressed. In dealing with the emerging issue of race relations, Ike was limited not only by the strength of the South in Congress but also by his own skepticism about some desegregation efforts.

Eisenhower displayed solid political skills. He worked actively with Congress, kept a close eye on some administrative issues, and demonstrated effective public leadership in not only maintaining his popularity but also using selective, focused public appeals on legislative issues. His legacy has stemmed primarily from his legitimization of aspects of the New Deal such as Social Security and from his successful promotion of infrastructure programs such as the interstate highway program. While a president with stronger policy commitments might have accomplished more, Eisenhower nevertheless produced a solid performance.

Despite his high personal popularity, Kennedy faced definite constraints during his abruptly shortened tenure in office—among them, his narrow election victory in 1960 and a divided Democratic coalition in Congress, accompanied by strong southern conservative strength in key committee positions. Kennedy had many proposals on his agenda but found it difficult to create supportive coalitions. When conditions changed by 1963, creating a greater opportunity for civil rights legislation, he did display forceful presidential leadership.

Kennedy also displayed solid political skills. He was perhaps a bit too cautious with Congress, but he did maintain at least an average level of activity. His public leadership included developing an effective persona and contributing to the emerging era of activism with his use of the bully pulpit. Although Kennedy did not leave a major legacy, he deserves credit for launching a broad set of initiatives in 1963, especially his civil rights measures and an assertive tax-cut plan. He thus joins Truman and Eisenhower in the solid performer category.

The Low-Opportunity Presidents: Nixon, Carter, Bush, and Clinton

Richard Nixon, run out of office by scandal, was ultimately an unsuccessful president on other counts as well. In political skills, he had a clearer sense of potential strategies and their relationship to his reelection needs than either Carter or Bush, and he was more successful than both in his use of public addresses. On domestic issues, his staff system quite effectively generated policy proposals. His leadership of Congress was, at most, average, but his desire for government action in a variety of areas contributed to a climate that fostered big changes in domestic policy. Nixon also used administrative strategies to meet a variety of policy goals such as his new economic policy of August 1971. But only moderate policy legacies could be traced to his actions, such as revenue sharing.

Yet Nixon also had enormous failings. The biggest perhaps was his rhetoric of divisiveness; it contributed to an intensification of political antagonisms. Although second terms are not generally productive, the first year of Nixon's second term, 1973, did hold the promise of action in areas such as health care reform. Hopes were dashed, however, when the nation's capital became preoccupied with the Watergate scandal. Ultimately, Nixon contributed to growing cynicism about national politics and the emergence of congressional measures to contain the presidency, which worked to the disadvantage of his successors. President Bill Clinton was correct in emphasizing at Nixon's funeral in 1994 that evaluations of Nixon must be more than about Watergate. Yet in the end one cannot escape recognizing this flawed president's negative impact on the presidency and the political system.[4]

Of the presidents with limited opportunities, Jimmy Carter and George Bush share several characteristics. In part, they were both unlucky that they had to run for reelection during difficult economic times and face opponents who were highly effective campaigners. Moreover, they did not receive wide recognition for all of their policy achievements, and they possessed distinct limitations in aspects of their leadership skills.

Carter faced greater challenges than the other presidents in this category but had a somewhat greater opportunity. His challenges arose in the areas of energy and fiscal policy during an era of stagflation. His opportunities took the form of some fairly promising issues on the agenda in 1977 and the substantial Democratic majorities in Congress. Yet that coalition was divided, and there were few politically feasible solutions for some of the problems he sought to address.

The president from Georgia contributed to his difficulties with his deficient leadership skills. He did manage to improve his legislative leadership throughout his four years in office, but he was never very effective with his public leadership. Indeed, he was unable to reassure the public that his administration was effectively addressing problems. The unfortunate consequence for Carter was that the public remained largely unaware of his accomplishments, which included several environmental initiatives and a significant start toward deregulation. Greater public leadership could have moved Carter up into the solid performer category.

George Bush faced few challenges until the economic slump of 1991, but he also had quite limited opportunities. An "understudy" of President Reagan, Bush had been elected in a campaign that did little to help develop promising issues. Once in office, he faced Democratic majorities on Capitol Hill and a government saddled with a large deficit. Bush undertook a "reluctant guardian" role with limited skill. He did aid in the passage of important measures such as the Clean Air Act in 1990. But, even though Congress ultimately passed a landmark deficit-reduction package in 1990, Bush was most noted for the extent to which he lost control of the process and thus had little influence on the final outcome. Because of that lack of control, as well as the limited impact the measure had on the deficit in the wake of the 1991–1992 recession, Bush found it difficult to achieve credit for a deficit-reduction package that former Congressional Budget Office director Robert Reichauer found to be a major contribution to the federal government's ability to reduce the deficit in the 1990s. Finally, in his underuse of administrative strategies Bush never fully exploited opportunities for influence.

Bush's difficulties in orchestrating his reelection bid also stemmed from his limited political skills. The contrast with Truman is especially striking. Early on, Truman developed a strategy for dealing with Congress, used his administrative powers aggressively, and campaigned with conviction to rally his coalition. Bush, by contrast, developed his strategies too late, and persistent public doubts about his real convictions on issues contributed to his difficulties.

The lack of more noteworthy legacies for which Bush could claim credit stemmed largely from the absence of formidable domestic challenges and his weak position—not simply his limited political skills. Yet his ineptness was evident at a number of points and underscored the extent to which his lack of political skills also contributed to his difficulties. Bush thus joins Carter as an example of a less-successful president holding office with modest opportunities.

Evaluations of Clinton remain somewhat tentative. In comparative terms, he had a sense of political strategies that rivaled those of all but a few of his predecessors, and he could on occasion engage in effective public leadership roles. His justly criticized early staff processes showed signs of a learning curve because his second term began far more smoothly. More actively involved with Congress than many presidents, Clinton showed considerable skill in outmaneuvering Republicans in 1995–1996 on balanced budget negotiations. More generally, his legacy includes a dramatic reduction in the federal deficit and a strong economy. As for building coalitions, Clinton's effort to steer the Democratic Party in more moderate directions may have longer-term electoral benefits.

Yet despite these achievements, Clinton's performance was in some ways disappointing, in part because of the significant flaws that accompanied his political skills. A Clinton without the disruptive debates over his personal behavior and with a better decision-making process and policy promotion strategy might still not have achieved passage of the landmark health care reform he pushed early in his first term. Yet he probably could have achieved more than the very limited health care legislation that emerged from Congress in 1996. Moreover, without Clinton as an appealing target the Republicans may not have succeeded so overwhelmingly in the 1994 midterm elections and thus may have been less of a force behind the movement to the right during 1995–1996.[5] More fundamentally, Clinton's tendency to shade the truth in defending his actions and those of his administration had an unfortunate impact on the electorate's perceptions of his credibility. Clinton thus achieved marks rivaling those of the more successful presidents who served with only modest opportunities, but he failed to impress the voters with his character.

Conclusion

Who then were the most "effective" or "skilled" of the post-1932 presidents? Given their levels of opportunity, Truman and Nixon, whose level of political opportunity was rather limited, are the overachievers of the group, with FDR, a high-opportunity president, also ranking very high on the list. Underachievers Reagan, Carter, and Bush, presidents who seemed to squander opportunities, were disappointments. (See Table 12–3 for a comparative profile of the modern presidents.)

The stronger evaluations of the mid-century presidents raise a key issue: Are present-day presidents hampered by new forces in demonstrating their skills and taking advantage of opportunities? Presidents serving since 1973 have indeed been affected by a series of limiting influences, including greater public skepticism about government, greater capacities for independent action in Congress, the proliferation of interest groups, economic problems, more fragile electoral coalitions, and a far more adversarial press.[6]

The role of the press is especially important. Had Franklin Roosevelt had to deal with the modern-day press, for example, his confinement to a wheelchair would have complicated his creation of an energetic public persona—the press simply would not have allowed a presidential handicap to go unnoted and unphotographed. Today, in fact, even the smallest details of presidents' physical examinations receive complete coverage and analysis. Likewise, the publication of full-length books by journalists only months after Truman or Eisenhower assumed office would have revealed their problems in trying to get started and reduced their public standing. And Kennedy's womanizing would not have remained a secret but would have been subjected to full coverage (probably complete with tabloid photos), and his serious health problems would have become public knowledge. Thus the solid-performance, mid-century presidents would have found their jobs more difficult in more recent years. Yet it must be noted that Reagan's performance indicates that effective media strategies and public leadership are possible in the contemporary era.

These observations aside, the mid-century presidents were an unusually talented group. Roosevelt would stand out as a remarkable person in any era, Truman possessed uncommon political skills along with a distinctive

Table 12–3 Presidential Rankings on the Skill/Opportunity Scale

High-Opportunity Presidents	Moderate-Opportunity Presidents	Low-Opportunity Presidents
1. Roosevelt	1. Truman	1. Nixon
2. Johnson	2. Eisenhower	2. Clinton
3. Reagan	3. Kennedy	3. Carter, Bush

desire to "do the right thing," and Eisenhower drew on a broader range of experiences than many realized. Kennedy suffered from youthful inexperience, but he did possess a range of political skills.

Although any effort to rate the presidents is fraught with difficulty, Presidents Roosevelt, Truman, and Eisenhower, based on their foreign and domestic policy performances, have consistently ranked above those presidents serving in more recent years. A recent ranking by historian Arthur Schlesinger Jr. based on a survey of presidential scholars categorized Roosevelt as great; Truman as near great; Eisenhower, Kennedy, and Johnson as high average; Clinton, Bush, Reagan, and Carter as average; and Nixon as a failure. Comparable results were achieved in a larger survey.[7] Similarly, in a grouping devised by political scientists Lance LeLoup and Steven Shull, the four presidents who rated high on both their selling skills and their managerial skills were Roosevelt, Kennedy, Truman, and Eisenhower.[8] Thus while the job may have gotten tougher, in some degree the voters also have elevated less-talented individuals to the Oval Office.

Looking Ahead

The future prospects for domestic policy leadership will depend on the roles played by Congress and presidents in that leadership. The landmark legislation passed since 1932 underscores the importance of those roles, and Congress may well become more important in the future. This section draws several lessons from the nation's policy making since 1932 to suggest possible sources of effective leadership and more promising strategies.

The Views from the Opposite Ends of Pennsylvania Avenue

Congress has sometimes shown impressive capacities for shaping domestic policies. On some issues Congress may more accurately reflect public opinion than a president perhaps unduly influenced by ideology or the input of only a few carefully chosen advisers. In fact, Congress should be able to address major policy issues without the president having to act as the dominant player.

A dependence on Congress, however, can create problems. Procedural arrangements and strong committee chairs may thwart or skew action. In the early post–World War II era, for example, the southern Democrats who chaired congressional committees routinely obstructed civil rights and other legislation. More recently, stronger partisanship has reduced opportunities for compromise. In addition, legislators, responding to the nature of their congressional constituencies and reelection concerns, tend to pursue short-run, pork-laden policy outcomes. In short, left to their own instincts legislators may find it hard to take any policy steps that reflect majority views in the electorate and a broad perspective on the country's needs. Effective presidential leadership on domestic policy is, then, still needed.

The Search for Effective Presidents

Effective presidents are not easy to find. For one thing, it is hard to detect the personal characteristics that will influence presidential leadership styles.[9] Thus in looking around for candidates, political parties must search for those ambitious enough to seek the office and shrewd enough to realize the range of strategic choices they are offered, while avoiding office seekers who may possess aspects of those characteristics but also have unhealthy personality traits that could spark unwise and dangerous presidential actions.

Three lessons can be drawn from history about leadership style. First, officeholders must fit the circumstances of their time in office. One can only wonder, for example, how the nation would have fared during the depression if the assassin's bullet that killed the mayor of Chicago and narrowly missed Franklin Roosevelt shortly before his inauguration had placed John Nance Garner, a conservative Texan with legislative bargaining talents but very limited rhetorical skills, in the White House. Conversely, a person with Roosevelt's desire to be "out front" and achieve lots of legislative successes would have been immensely frustrated during the lackadaisical 1950s.

The second lesson is that effective officeholders must possess a wide range of skills. This lesson emerges from a review of the relatively more successful presidents: Roosevelt, Truman, Eisenhower, Kennedy, and, to an extent, Clinton. Eisenhower is perhaps the best example of a president who possessed diverse if not superb skills in several areas—in fact, he was on occasion compared to a decathlon athlete. Johnson and Reagan possessed impressive skills on one or more dimensions that worked to their advantage, but they also possessed limitations; Johnson suffered rhetorical failures and Reagan had difficulty with management and policy evaluations.

The third lesson is that while skills in all leadership areas are essential, those in the area of public leadership are especially important. These skills can contribute to policy development as well as to the ability of a president to sustain the public support necessary to function effectively in general and to shape specific policies. Roosevelt, Eisenhower, Kennedy, Reagan, and Clinton demonstrated the advantages of effective public leadership; Johnson, Carter, and Bush dramatized the problems that can arise from weak skills.

Where should the nation turn to find officeholders with the necessary qualities? Career paths provide some insights but no decisive patterns. The lack of pronounced patterns stems from two factors. First, personal characteristics can make a major difference in the leadership styles of persons who have held similar offices. Key aspects of the leadership exerted by Johnson and Nixon, for example, flowed from distinctive aspects of their personalities and not how many years they occupied various public offices. Second, the various learning experiences gained during a given career reduce potential career path differences. Of those presidents serving in Congress, Lyndon Johnson learned to build coalitions as majority leader. (Ford learned some aspects of coalition building as minority party leader, but he primarily became skilled at building defensive coalitions to prevent legislation from being passed.) Truman, Kennedy, Nixon, and Bush learned committee roles in varying degrees, but they did not gain a broader perspective on legislative leadership. Johnson demonstrated the difficulties a legislator can encounter when having to deal with the national press rather than a friendlier state press, but Kennedy, who also served in Congress, was adroit at media relations.

The four governors who became president underscore the diversity of learning experiences that are gained in that role. Presidents Roosevelt (who served as governor of New York) and Reagan (governor of California) offer some support for Larry Sabato's conclusion that a governorship (although lacking a foreign policy dimension) is preferable to Congress as a training ground for presidents.[10] While they entered their governorships with some skills, both Roosevelt and Reagan learned aspects of public and legislative leadership in settings (large states) similar to that in Washington. Carter and Clinton, who served in much smaller states (Georgia and Arkansas) and dealt with part-time, one-party legislatures, had quite different learning experiences.

Yet there are some relationships between career experiences and leadership style. First, administrative experiences are useful, especially if they have been extensive. Both Roosevelt (as governor) and Eisenhower (as Allied commander) had such experiences, whereas Bush, who had filled many administrative roles during his brief time in various public offices, displayed no more than average administrative interests or skills as president. Second, presidents who once served as legislators, other than Johnson, have not been particularly noted for their legislative leadership skills. Perhaps legislators tend to develop a high degree of respect for congressional independence and thus are reluctant to employ strong-arm tactics. On balance, then, there seems little basis for assuming that a president who emerges from Congress will be above average in legislative leadership. Third, governors often have broader experience with public leadership than legislators and thus may be more likely to be effective presidents. They do need to be quick studies when they arrive in Washington, but their range of experiences in the areas of administrative strategies, personnel selection, and legislative and public leadership—at least for those coming from larger states—more closely resembles presidential responsibilities than the experience gained by members of Congress. This is not to say, however, that knowledge of how Washington works is not important for any presidential contender. Novices, including governors, often make avoidable mistakes because they lack that knowledge.

Strategic Choices

Modern presidents will continue to choose from a variety of strategies and tactics in their domestic policy making. Past performances suggest that it is possible from time to time for a president to use a fast-start strategy. But this strategy is more successful when a candidate is able to develop specific themes in an election campaign and then win by a considerable margin. First-year victories are achieved most easily when they involve policy initiatives carried over from the preceding administration and when at least aspects of existing policy ideas are included in the initial proposals. Both the public and political analysts should not place too much emphasis on the fast-start strategy, however. Successful presidents will perceive new opportunities later in their first or second term.

Top-level negotiation is likely to be another popular strategy. Despite the problems that can arise—such as those Bush encountered in 1990—this is a vehicle for avoiding the difficulties inherent in having to deal with multiple committees in Congress. Interest groups and rank-and-file members of Congress are not fond of this strategy, but it has considerable potential when large, complicated issues such as Social Security and Medicare are on the table. These issues will undoubtedly become more pressing in the future.

Presidents also will continue to adopt public leadership and administrative strategies. For example, they may on occasion "go public" prior to a major vote. Another important public leadership tool is the bully pulpit, whose importance in seeking to shape private behavior rather than simply seeking support for programs is somewhat under-recognized. As the Kennedy performance revealed, the bully pulpit also may help to intensify general levels of public interest in political action.

Finally, presidents will increasingly adopt centrist strategies. Helping the "center to hold" on specific issues is likely to be a key strategy because of the ideological polarization that has emerged in Congress in recent years. More generally, presidents may act to posture themselves in the center, much like President Clinton did in 1995–1996. While seeking to define that center, presidents may, like Franklin Roosevelt in 1935, also try to forge a coalition that will create a different center on major policy issues. Centrist roles will continue to be important vehicles for policy change.

What, then, are the prospects for policy change? Regardless of the strategies they choose, future presidents will face formidable challenges. The job has become tougher, and budgetary pressures may intensify. Yet important strategies will still be available, and a president's strategic choices can make a difference. For those citizens desiring changes in domestic policy, it will be important not only to participate in the selection of presidents, but also to engage in a "bottom-up strategy" of generating pressures that will both help and push presidents toward promoting new policy positions. Often, successes will come only after initial failures and partial responses. Indeed, in the future just as in the past, fundamental policy change will arise from actions already taken by members of Congress, innovative federal officials, state governments, specialists working on new policy approaches, and interest groups. While often messy and uncoordinated, these avenues do give citizens an opportunity to have their voices heard in the policy-making process. Presidents can fulfill crucial roles in this process as they exercise their leadership skills and make their strategic choices, but—like Roosevelt—as facilitators rather than directors of policy change.

Notes

1. John G. Geer, *From Tea Leaves to Public Opinion: A Theory of Democratic Leadership* (New York: Columbia University Press, 1996), 82–86.

2. Dick Morris, *Behind the Oval Office: Winning the Presidency in the Nineties* (New York: Random House, 1997).

3. Theda Skocpol, *Boomerang: Clinton's Health Security Effort and the Turn against Government in U.S. Politics* (New York: Norton, 1996), 116–118.

4. Michael A. Genovese, *The Watergate Crisis* (Westport, Conn.: Greenwood Press, 1999).

5. Ibid.

6. Michael A. Genovese, *The Presidential Dilemma: Leadership in the American System* (New York: HarperCollins, 1995).

7. Arthur M. Schlesinger Jr., "Rating the Presidents," *Political Science Quarterly* 112 (summer 1997): 189; and Robert Murray and Tim Blessing, "The Presidential Performance Study: A Progress Report," *Journal of History* 70 (December 1983): 540–541.

8. Lance T. LeLoup and Steven A. Shull, *Congress and the President: The Policy Connection* (Belmont, Calif.: Wadsworth Publishing, 1993), 78.

9. For a widely read interpretation of these issues, see James David Barber, *Presidential Character: Predicting Performance in the White House*, 4th ed. (Englewood Cliffs, N.J.: Prentice Hall, 1992).

10. For an elaboration of the arguments in favor of recruiting governors rather than legislators, see Larry Sabato, *Goodbye to Good-time Charlie: The American Governorship Transformed* (Washington, D.C.: CQ Press, 1983), chap. 6.

Selected Bibliography

Abbott, Philip. *Strong Presidents: A Theory of Leadership*. Knoxville: University of Tennessee Press, 1996.

Adler, David Gray, and Larry N. George, eds. *The Constitution and the Conduct of Foreign Policy*. Lawrence: University Press of Kansas, 1996.

Arnold, Peri E. *Making the Managerial Presidency: Comprehensive Reorganization Planning, 1905–1980*. Princeton: Princeton University Press, 1986.

Asher, Herbert. *Presidential Elections and American Politics: Voters, Candidates, and Campaigns since 1952*. 5th ed. New York: Harcourt Brace, 1992.

Barber, James David. *Presidential Character: Predicting Performance in the White House*. 4th ed. Englewood Cliffs, N.J.: Prentice Hall, 1992.

Bennett, Anthony. *The American President's Cabinet: From Kennedy to Bush*. New York: St. Martin's Press, 1996.

Blakesley, Lance. *Presidential Leadership: From Eisenhower to Clinton*. Chicago: Nelson-Hall, 1995.

Bond, Jon R., and Richard Fleisher. *The President in the Legislative Arena*. Chicago: University of Chicago Press, 1990.

Brace, Paul, and Barbara Hinckley. *Follow the Leader: Opinion Polls and the Modern Presidents*. New York: Basic Books, 1992.

Brody, Richard A. *Assessing the President: The Media, Elite Opinion, and Public Support*. Stanford: Stanford University Press, 1991.

Burke, John P. *The Institutional Presidency*. Baltimore: Johns Hopkins University Press, 1992.

Burns, James MacGregor. *The Deadlock of Democracy: Two-Party Politics in America*. Englewood Cliffs, N.J.: Prentice Hall, 1963.

———. *Leadership*. New York: Harper and Row, 1978.

———. *The Power to Lead: The Crisis of the American Presidency*. New York: Simon and Schuster, 1984.

———. *Presidential Government: The Crucible of Leadership*. Boston: Houghton Mifflin, 1966.

———. *Roosevelt: The Lion and the Fox*. Norwalk, Conn.: Easton Press, 1989.

————. *Roosevelt: Soldier of Freedom.* New York: Harcourt, Brace, Jovanovich, 1970.

Cannon, Lou. *President Reagan: A Role of a Lifetime.* New York: Simon and Shuster, 1991.

Carter, Jimmy. *Keeping Faith: Memoirs of a President.* New York: Bantam Books, 1982.

Corwin, Edward S. *The President: Office and Powers, 1978–1984.* 5th ed. New York: New York University Press, 1984.

Covington, Cary R., and Lester G. Seligman. *The Coalition Presidency.* Chicago: Dorsey Press, 1989.

Cox, Gary W., and Samuel Kernell, eds. *The Politics of Divided Government.* Boulder, Colo.: Westview Press, 1991.

Crabb, Cecil V., and Pat Holt. *Invitation to Struggle: Congress, the President, and Foreign Policy.* 3d ed. Washington, D.C.: CQ Press, 1989.

Cronin, Thomas E. *The State of the Presidency.* 2d ed. Boston: Little, Brown, 1980.

Cronin, Thomas E., ed. *Rethinking the Presidency.* Boston: Little, Brown, 1982.

Cronin, Thomas E., and Michael A. Genovese. *The Paradoxes of the American Presidency.* New York: Oxford University Press, 1998.

Dallek, Robert. *Hail to the Chief: The Making and Unmaking of American Presidents.* New York: Hyperion Books, 1996.

Darman, Richard. *Who's in Control? Polar Politics and the Sensible Center.* New York: Simon and Schuster, 1996.

Davis, James W. *The American Presidency.* 2d ed. Westport, Conn.: Praeger, 1995.

————. *The President as Party Leader.* New York: Praeger, 1992.

DeGrazia, Alfred. *Congress and the Presidency.* Washington, D.C.: American Enterprise Institute, 1967.

Draper, Theodore. *A Very Thin Line: The Iran-Contra Affair.* New York: Touchstone Books, 1991.

Edwards, George C., III. *At the Margins: Presidential Leadership in Congress.* New Haven: Yale University Press, 1989.

————. *Presidential Influence in Congress.* San Francisco: W. H. Freeman, 1980.

————. *The Public Presidency: The Pursuit of Popular Support.* New York: St. Martin's Press, 1983.

Ellis, Richard, and Aaron Wildavsky. *Dilemmas of Presidential Leadership.* New Brunswick, N.J.: Transaction Publishers, 1989.

Fishel, Jeff. *Presidents and Promises.* Washington, D.C.: CQ Press, 1985.

Fisher, Louis. *The Constitution between Friends.* New York: St. Martin's Press, 1978.

Genovese, Michael A. *The Nixon Presidency: Power and Politics in Turbulent Times.* Westport, Conn.: Greenwood Press, 1990.

————. *Power and the American Presidency, 1789–2000.* New York: Oxford University Press, 2000.

———. *The Presidency in an Age of Limits.* Westport, Conn.: Greenwood Press, 1993.

———. *The Presidential Dilemma: Leadership in the American System.* New York: HarperCollins, 1995.

———. *The Watergate Crisis.* Westport, Conn.: Greenwood Press, 1999.

Greenstein, Fred I. *The Hidden-Hand Presidency: Eisenhower as Leader.* New York: Basic Books, 1982.

Gregg, Gary L. *The Presidential Republic: Executive Representation and Deliberative Democracy.* Lanham, Md.: Rowman and Littlefield, 1997.

Grover, William F. *The President as Prisoner.* New York: State University of New York Press, 1989.

Hargrove, Erwin C. *The Power of the Modern Presidency.* New York: Knopf, 1974.

Hargrove, Erwin C., and Michael Nelson. *Presidents, Politics and Policy.* Baltimore: Johns Hopkins University Press, 1984.

Hess, Stephen. *Organizing the Presidency.* Rev. ed. Washington, D.C.: Brookings, 1984.

Johnson, Haynes, and David Broder. *The System.* Boston: Little, Brown, 1996.

Johnson, Richard T. *Managing the White House.* New York: Harper-Collins, 1974.

Jones, Charles O. *The Presidency in a Separated System.* Washington, D.C.: Brookings, 1994.

Kernell, Samuel. *Going Public: New Strategies of Presidential Leadership.* 3d ed. Washington, D.C.: CQ Press, 1997.

Kernell, Samuel, and Samuel L. Popkin, eds. *Chief of Staff: Twenty-five Years of Managing the Presidency.* Berkeley: University of California Press, 1986.

King, Gary, and Lyn Ragsdale. *The Elusive Executive: Discovering Statistical Patterns in the Presidency.* Washington, D.C.: CQ Press, 1988.

Kingdon, John. *Issues, Agendas, and Alternatives.* 2d ed. Boston: Little, Brown, 1994.

Lammers, William W. *Presidential Politics: Patterns and Prospects.* New York: HarperCollins, 1976.

LeLoup, Lance T., and Steven A. Shull. *Congress and the President: The Policy Connection.* Belmont, Calif.: Wadsworth Publishing, 1993.

Leuchtenberg, William E. *In the Shadow of FDR: From Harry Truman to Ronald Reagan.* Ithaca: Cornell University Press, 1983.

Light, Paul C. *The President's Agenda: Domestic Policy Choice from Kennedy to Carter.* Baltimore: Johns Hopkins University Press, 1982.

Lowi, Theodore J. *The Personal President: Power Invested, Promise Unfulfilled.* Ithaca: Cornell University Press, 1985.

Maltese, John. *Spin Control: The White House Office of Communications and the Management of Presidential News.* Chapel Hill: University of North Carolina Press, 1992.

Maraniss, David. *First In His Class: The Biography of Bill Clinton.* New York: Touchstone Books, 1995.

Mayer, Jane, and Doyle McManus. *Landslide: The Unmaking of a President, 1984–1988.* Boston: Houghton Mifflin, 1988.

Mayhew, David R. *Divided We Govern: Party Control, Lawmaking, and Investigations, 1946–1990.* New Haven: Yale University Press, 1991.

Milkis, Sidney M. *The President and the Parties: The Transformation of the American Political System.* New York: Oxford University Press, 1993.

Miroff, Bruce. *Icons of Democracy: American Leaders as Heroes, Aristocrats, Dissenters, and Democrats.* New York: Basic Books, 1993.

———. *Pragmatic Illusions: The Presidential Politics of John F. Kennedy.* New York: David McKay, 1976.

Murray, Robert K., and Tim H. Blessing. *Greatness in the White House: Rating the Presidents, Washington through Carter.* University Park: Pennsylvania State University Press, 1988.

Nathan, Richard P. *The Administrative Presidency.* New York: Wiley, 1983.

Neustadt, Richard E. *Presidential Power.* New York: Wiley, 1960.

———. *Presidential Power and the Modern Presidents: The Politics of Leadership from Roosevelt to Reagan.* New York: Free Press, 1990.

Patterson, Thomas E. *Out of Order.* New York: Vintage Books, 1994.

Peterson, Mark A. *Legislating Together: The White House and Capitol Hill from Eisenhower to Reagan.* Cambridge: Harvard University Press, 1990.

Pfiffner, James P., ed. *The Managerial Presidency.* College Station: Texas A&M University Press, 1999.

———. *The Strategic Presidency: Hitting the Ground Running.* 2d ed. Lawrence: University Press of Kansas, 1996.

Pious, Richard. *The American Presidency.* New York: Basic Books, 1979.

———. *The Presidency.* Boston: Allyn and Bacon, 1996.

Ragsdale, Lyn. *Presidential Politics.* Boston: Houghton Mifflin, 1993.

———. *Vital Statistics on the Presidency: Washington to Clinton.* Washington, D.C.: CQ Press, 1996.

Reagan, Ronald. *An American Life: The Autobiography.* New York: Simon and Schuster, 1990.

Reich, Robert. *Locked in the Cabinet.* New York: Knopf, 1997.

Rockman, Bert. *The Leadership Question: The Presidency and the American System.* New York: Praeger, 1984.

Rose, Richard. *The Postmodern President: The White House Meets the World.* Chatham, N.J.: Chatham House, 1998.

Rossiter, Clinton. *The American Presidency.* New York: Harcourt, Brace, and World, 1956.

Sabato, Larry. *Feeding Frenzy.* New York: Free Press, 1991.

Schlesinger, Arthur M., Jr. *The Cycles of American History.* Boston: Houghton Mifflin, 1986.

———. *The Imperial Presidency.* Boston: Houghton Mifflin, 1973.

Shull, Steven A., ed. *The Two Presidencies: A Quarter Century Assessment.* Chicago: Nelson-Hall, 1991.

Simonton, Dean Keith. *Why Presidents Succeed.* New Haven: Yale University Press, 1987.

Smith, Hedrick. *The Power Game: How Washington Works.* New York: Ballantine, 1988.

Spitzer, Robert J. *President and Congress: Executive Hegemony at the Crossroads of American Government.* New York: McGraw-Hill, 1993.

Stockman, David A. *The Triumph of Politics: How the Reagan Revolution Failed.* New York: Harper and Row, 1986.

Stuckey, Mary E. *The President as Interpreter-in-Chief.* Chatham, N.J.: Chatham House, 1991.

Sundquist, James L. *Constitutional Reform and Effective Government.* Washington, D.C.: Brookings, 1986.

Tatalovich, Raymond, and Bryon W. Daynes. *Presidential Power in the United States.* Belmont, Calif.: Brooks/Cole, 1984.

Thurber, James A., ed. *Divided Democracy: Cooperation and Conflict between the President and Congress.* Washington, D.C.: CQ Press, 1991.

———. *Rivals for Power: Presidential–Congressional Relations.* Washington, D.C.: CQ Press, 1996.

Walsh, Kenneth T. *Feeding the Beast: The White House vs. the Press.* New York: Random House, 1996.

Walsh, Lawrence E. *Firewall: The Iran-Contra Conspiracy and Cover-up.* New York: Norton, 1997.

Warshaw, Shirley Anne. *The Domestic Presidency: Policy Making in the White House.* Boston: Allyn and Bacon, 1997.

———. *Powersharing: White House–Cabinet Relations in the Modern Presidency.* Albany: State University of New York Press, 1996.

Watson, Richard A. *Presidential Vetoes and Public Policy.* Lawrence: University Press of Kansas, 1993.

Wilson, Robert A., ed. *Character Above All: Ten Presidents from FDR to George Bush.* New York: Simon and Schuster, 1995.

Woodward, Bob. *The Agenda: Inside the Clinton White House.* New York: Simon and Schuster, 1994.

Subject Index

Citations of Authors

Abernathy, M. Glenn, 273n8
Adams, James R., 275n47
Adams, Sherman, 183n8
Allen, Craig, 184n45
Altmeyer, J., 69n54
Ambrose, Stephen E., 183nn4, 18, 184n27, 185n48, 248nn18, 20, 32, 249n45
Anderson, Martin, 129n9, 130n33
Anderson, Patrick, 68n27, 156–157n21
Arnold, Joseph L., 70n57
Arnold, Peri E., 157n22, 184n37, 272n5, 274n21
Asher, Herbert B., 210n4

Barber, James David, 27n39, 95n4, 210n2, 357n9
Bardsley, Lance W., 96n27
Barilleaux, Ryan J., 27n33
Barrett, David M., 96n9
Bauer, Carl M., 212n42
Beam, David R., 130–131n36
Bell, Terrel H., 129n4
Berkowitz, Edward D., 212n36, 275n48
Berman, Larry, 131n43, 183n10, 210n1
Berman, William C., 156n12, 157n34
Bernstein, Barton J., 157n27, 183n11
Bernstein, Carl, 248n6
Bernstein, Irving, 96nn18, 26, 97n30, 212n42
Biggart, Nicole W., 129n2
Birnbaum, Jeffrey H., 130–131n36
Black, Earl, 67n3, 185n62
Black, Merle, 67n3, 185n62
Blair, Diane D., 327n2
Blessing, Tim, 357n7
Blissett, Marlan, 96n17
Blough, Roger, 212n38

Blum, John Morton, 70n59
Blumenthal, Sidney, 296n3
Boettke, Peter J., 130n24
Bond, Jon R., 26n17, 97n31
Boskin, Michael J., 131n47
Bosso, Christopher J., 249n58
Brace, Paul, 12, 26n16, 157n32, 274n29
Branyan, Robert L., 185n53
Broder, David S., 213n49, 328n24
Brodie, Fawn, 248n8
Brody, Richard A., 25n13, 26n15
Brown, Thomas, 213n47
Brownell, Herbert, 183n6, 184n40
Brummett, John, 327nn2, 6
Bumgarner, John R., 95n5, 211n13
Burk, Robert F., 183n5
Burke, John, 183n10
Burns, James MacGregor, 67n2, 68nn12, 13
Bush, George H. W., 297n15

Califano, Joseph A., 96n6, 273n20
Campagne, Anthony S., 272nn7, 12, 275n43
Campbell, Angus, 183n7
Campbell, Colin, 26n30, 130n17, 273n19, 297nn8, 9, 327n11
Cannon, Lou, 129nn1, 7, 13
Carson, Robert B., 68nn20, 22, 24
Carter, Jimmy, 274nn35, 37, 39
Chamberlain, Lawrence H., 69n47
Chambers, Clarke E., 68n19
Childs, Marcus, 184n22
Clifford, Clark, 157n21, 211n23
Cohen, Richard, 328n21
Colby, P. W., 274n24